SURVEYS FROM EXILE

Also available from Verso in Marx's Political Writings series:

Volume 1, *The Revolutions of 1848*
Volume 3, *The First International and After*

SURVEYS FROM EXILE

Political Writings Volume 2

---◆---

KARL MARX

Edited and Introduced by David Fernbach

VERSO

London • New York

This edition published by Verso 2010
Introduction © David Fernbach 1973
Foreword © Tariq Ali 2010
Translations © 1973

The Eighteenth Brumaire of Louis Bonaparte © Ben Fowkes 1973;
The Class Struggles in France, the German-language articles on Britain,
'Articles on the North American Civil War' and the 'Proclamation on Poland by
the German Workers Education Association in London' © Paul Jackson 1973

1 3 5 7 9 10 8 6 4 2

Verso
UK: 6 Meard Street, London W1F 0EG
US: 20 Jay Street, Suite 1010, Brooklyn, NY 11201
www.versobooks.com

Verso is the imprint of New Left Books

ISBN-13: 978-1-84467-608-8 (hbk)
ISBN-13: 978-1-84467-607-1 (pbk)

British Library Cataloguing in Publication Data
A catalogue record for this book is available from the British Library

Library of Congress Cataloging-in-Publication Data
A catalog record for this book is available from the Library of Congress

Typeset in Monotype Times by Hewer Text UK Ltd, Edinburgh
Printed in the US by Maple Vail

Contents

References to Marx and Engels's works in the most frequently quoted
editions have been abbreviated as follows:

MECW 1–5   Marx and Engels, *Collected Works*, Lawrence and
      Wishart, 1975–2005.
MEW 1–39   *Marx-Engels-Werke*, Dietz Verlag, Berlin, 1956–64.

Foreword

The recession caused by the capitalist crisis of 2008 triggered a revival of interest in Marx's *Capital* and his other writings on the specific dynamics of the capitalist mode of production. That this system was the central subject of his work is indisputable, but he never thought of the economy in isolation. Capitalism was, for him and Engels, above all a socio-economic or social formation. 'Politics', as one of Marx's more gifted followers from a subsequent generation wrote, 'is concentrated economics'. What was true, if only partially visible during the first few decades of the twentieth century, can now be seen in full-frontal view. In the traditional capitalist states, democracy is being hollowed out by a process – 'globalization' – that systematically subordinates politics to economics, reducing the basic differences between centre-left and centre-right so that there is virtually no difference between existing mainstream political parties. For all practical purposes, the West is in the grip of a political system that has both the incentive and the means to become increasingly despotic. Whether it does so will depend on the degree and nature of the opposition that it encounters from below.

It is this relegation of politics and its Siamese twins, history and philosophy, which makes the republication of Marx's political and historical writings all the more necessary at this time. We are living in a period of historical transition that began with the overwhelming triumph of capitalism in the last decade of the preceding century. As a result Marx's interventionist essays have suffered in recent years, but not, as is sometimes stated on the right, because their premises have been exploded. Marx's political writings have been a casualty of the downgrading and dumbing-down of politics, sociology and history as scholarly disciplines on both a secondary and tertiary level, especially, but not exclusively in English-speaking cultures.

Many of the new radicals of the present generation find it sexy to read *Capital* while ignoring the politics underlying the project. This would have angered Marx, who regarded his work as a unity, which is how it was read by some of his most astute opponents a century later. Joseph Schumpeter, to take one example, wrote in his classic work *Capitalism, Socialism and Democracy* that:

We have seen how in the Marxian argument sociology and economics pervade each other. In intent and to some degree also in actual practice, they are one. All the major concepts and propositions are hence both economic and sociological and carry the same meaning on both planes.

In other words, it is difficult to grasp the essence of *Capital* without understanding Marx's revolutionary approach to politics and the understanding of history. How could it be otherwise? He belonged to a generation that came of age in the historical period that followed the French Revolution. The cyclical pattern of victory–defeat–restoration–new revolutions–new defeats, and so on, taught him that every historical epoch is a period of transition, of ebb and flow, of crash and renewal, of annihilation and resurgence. The socialism he favoured was based on a society of abundance; its political institutions a reflection of radical, popular sovereignty on every level; its culture transcending the confines of a single nation and creating a world-view. Most importantly, Marx visualized a state that far from becoming huge, unwieldy and authoritarian would be pushed to near oblivion. The contrast between this and what became the reality of 'actually existing socialisms' needs little commentary.

Cosmopolitan by nature, revolutions have no respect for borders and can never remain the exclusive property of the country in which they first occurred. This fact also shapes the counterrevolution. Marx observed that this was certainly the case for Europe and, possibly, North America, where the rise of capitalism, he thought, would produce midwives impatient to drag out new children from the womb of the system. As David Fernbach points out in his introductory text, it didn't quite turn out like that; the 'the rock of Soviet civilization' proved to be hollow. Still, the universality of the revolution, or its originality, was never in doubt. It leapt over the heartlands of capital and moved eastwards: first Russia, then China, later Vietnam and, last of all, the American hemisphere. Ignoring the mainland, it alighted on a small Caribbean island, which, at time of writing, remains the only space where capitalism has not yet been permitted to return.

The collapse of 'communism' resulted in passivity, a loss of hope and a new common sense of the age, according to which no alternatives to the new system were possible. Even the agency that

Marx had hoped would lead to revolutionary change in the West had been dismantled. Fordism lay dead, its founding factory in Detroit covered in cobwebs. Production moved east and China is today the workshop of the world, whose impact it is still far too early to predict.

In times like these, when reaction reigned supreme, Marx and Engels did not attempt to mask reality with false optimism. They had written the *Manifesto* while insurrections and civil war had erupted throughout continental Europe, but the 'spectre of communism' was defeated everywhere. The two authors now argued that the rise of a new revolutionary wave was impossible in the short to medium term and that communists should use the period of defeat to study, educate and work hard to develop theories that explained the mechanics of the world to future generations.

Engels retreated to Manchester to work for the family firm; Marx retired to the British Library to study economics. Their erstwhile comrades in the Communist League resorted to character assassination, denounced Marx and Engels as traitors and referred to them as 'counter-revolutionaries', 'hostile to the proletariat' and isolated 'literati'. Never one to ignore an insult, Marx responded in kind just as he had done earlier to Proudhon's intemperate assaults on Babeuf and his socialists. Like some latter-day unconscious mimics, Proudhon too believed that the world could be changed without taking power, a notion that won him the support of many a charlatan. The violent anti-communist language he used in *System of Economic Contradictions* found few defenders even in his own ranks. Marx responded that 'he (Proudhon) bursts into violent explosions of rage, vociferation and righteous wrath (*irae hominis probi*), foams at the mouth, curses, denounces, cries shame and murder, beats his breast and boasts before man and God that he is not defiled by socialist infamies.' Whatever else it was, the cut and thrust of political debate on the left was never a polite conversation, then or later. Nor were the results of this style of debate always positive.

Some of the writing contained in these volumes is the product of financial necessity. Compelled by poverty and the misery of everyday life in Soho to write regularly for the New York *Tribune*, Marx often cut corners and pronounced on subjects of which he could possess only limited information. This did not apply to his essays on Europe. The brilliant imagery contained in his texts on France remains striking to this day, and *The Eighteenth Brumaire of Louis Bonaparte* still inspires admiration from many non-Marxist writers. Unsurprisingly, he got things wrong, which is why his transformation into a secular icon after 1917 did Marx few favours. It was as if everything he wrote was scripture; memories of communist militants in different parts of the world repeating his phrases parrot-like still make one wince.

The idea of a new Marx Library, which originated on the Editorial Committee of *New Left Review* in 1968, was partly designed to challenge this doctrinal approach. It was a year before the magazine launched New Left Books (NLB), which was, in any case, intended to be a quality hardback publisher producing a limited number of books each year. The NLR was of the opinion that given the political and intellectual turbulence then sweeping the globe, a carefully selected and edited Marx Library with new translations from the German was best suited to a mass paperback imprint. Penguin Books and one of its more gifted publishers, Neil Middleton, appeared to be the perfect match at the time, and so it proved. The general editor of the series was Quintin Hoare, and his choices were happily vindicated by the sales figures. The fact that Penguin keeps most of the Library in print is a unique tribute in these times when commerce dominates all. Ernest Mandel introduced the three volumes of Marx's *Capital*, Lucio Colletti the *Early Writings*, and the *Grundrisse* was translated (for the first time in English) and introduced by the American scholar Martin Nicolaus. The political writings were edited and introduced by David Fernbach, who has helped to update this reissue.

The intellectual and commercial success of New Left Books led to the launch of its paperback imprint, Verso, in 1970. It is therefore only appropriate that as Verso marks its fortieth anniversary (and *New Left Review* its fiftieth), the political writings of the thinker who inspired the founders of both are made available once again. There is, of course, another reason. As the century moves forward it is likely that history will have a few pleasant surprises in store for Europe, Asia and Africa. Few predicted the turn of events in South America, where a combination of mass struggles produced social movements and a new-style social democracy that challenged the neo-liberal form of capitalism and reasserted the social responsibilities of the state. Future generations might thus be grateful to have these political texts available once again.

TARIQ ALI
MAY 2010

Introduction

The Triumph of Reaction

In August 1850 Marx recognized that the revolutionary period of 1848 was at an end. A new revolutionary outbreak was not possible until the next cyclical trade crisis, and if Marx still believed that revolution would surely follow in the wake of this crisis, he no longer believed that a proletarian revolution could succeed in Germany until modern industry had developed more substantially. The development of the revolution, which had earlier seemed a matter of a few years, had now to be counted in decades.[1]

If the 1850s and early 1860s found Marx essentially a spectator of the political scene, this was by force of circumstance, not his own choice. After the split in the Communist League in September 1850, Marx continued to work at rebuilding the League as the nucleus of a proletarian party in Germany and at propagating the ideas of scientific communism on an international scale. But as the reaction consolidated itself throughout Europe, he found himself fighting a losing battle. The Central Committee of the Communist League, which was moved to Cologne following the split, was arrested en bloc in May 1851, and the League's German organization completely destroyed. Marx still attempted to hold together the London district, now once again the League's centre. However, the atmosphere of exile, always demoralizing, was doubly so for the German Communist refugees now that they were cut off from their comrades in Germany. Their community was riven by petty suspicion and intrigue, and many of the best Communists left to start a new life in North America. Marx and Engels themselves suffered the effects of exile. They collaborated with a Hungarian, Bangya, in producing a text attacking their political rivals among the German exiles,[2] and had a nasty shock

---

1. See the Introduction to *The Revolutions of 1848*, pp. 57–60.
2. 'The Great Men of the Exile', in *MECW* 11, pp. 227–326.

when this Bangya turned out to be himself an agent of the Prussian police.

A great deal of Marx's energy was devoted to the defence campaign for the Cologne Communist prisoners, who were only brought to trial in October 1852. After the trial, at which seven of the eleven accused were sentenced to between three and six years' imprisonment for 'attempted high treason', Marx wrote an exposé of the case and of the Prussian political police in general.[3] But the Cologne convictions sealed the fate of the Communist League, and on 17 November the League was formally dissolved, on Marx's proposal.

The dissolution of the Communist League and the virtual disappearance of the German workers' movement for a whole decade indicates the immense gap between the programme Marx and Engels laid down in the *Manifesto of the Communist Party* and the real development of the proletariat at that time. With the collapse of the League Marx was plunged into twelve years of almost complete political isolation. Exiled in London, he had next to no contact with events in Germany, while the greater part of the German Communist workers in London had followed Schapper and Willich.[4] Marx and Engels could have counted scarcely a dozen allies in the 1850s, and only one or two non-Germans. Yet Marx's confidence in the future that his theory predicted for the workers' movement never abated, and in their most extreme isolation he and Engels continued to regard themselves as the true representatives of the workers' party.

His political isolation in the 1850s was compounded by much personal suffering. The first decade of exile was an extremely hard time for Marx and his family. They experienced grinding poverty and had frequently to resort to the pawnshop for loans. Marx was already troubled with the liver disease that was to plague him for the rest of his life, and several of the children that his wife bore died in infancy. In November 1850 Engels moved to Manchester, where he was to work for his family's cotton business for the next twenty years. He was thus able to prevent the Marx household from starving, and consistently sent financial help until Marx's circumstances improved. While Marx and Engels were geographically separated they exchanged letters regularly, sometimes daily. By far the greater

3. 'Revelations Concerning The Communist Trial in Cologne,' in *MECW* 11, pp. 395–456.

4. On Schapper and Willich, see *The Revolutions of 1848*, pp. 58–9, 339–44.

part of the Marx-Engels correspondence dates from the 1850s and 1860s, and it provides a valuable supplement to their other writings, on both general theoretical and political questions.

Classes and the State

Marx and Engels began to analyse the experience of the 1848 revolution in the *Neue Rheinische Zeitung Revue*, five issues of which were produced during 1850. Besides the Reviews of international economic and political developments that they wrote for the *Revue*,[5] this journal also contained Marx's articles later known as *The Class Struggles in France* and Engels's on the Reich Constitution Campaign. After the demise of the *Revue*, Engels wrote the series of articles *Revolution and Counter-Revolution in Germany*[6] and Marx *The Eighteenth Brumaire of Louis Bonaparte*.

Engels called *The Class Struggles in France*, 'Marx's first attempt to explain a section of contemporary history by means of his materialist conception.'[7] Here Marx began, for the first time, to develop a systematic set of concepts for coming to grips with the phenomena of a politics which is certainly that of class struggle – the struggle of groups whose existence and interests are defined by the relations of production – but which is nevertheless politics, practised in the field of ideology and coercion that gives it its specific character. Marx continued his analysis of French developments in *The Eighteenth Brumaire of Louis Bonaparte*. In this work, dealing with the coup d'état of December 1851, he confronts the paradox of a state power that appears not to express the rule of a social class at all, but to dominate civil society completely and to arbitrate class struggles from above.

In the Communist Manifesto, Marx had described the executive of the modern state as simply 'a committee for managing the common affairs of the whole bourgeoisie'.[8] In the rather rarefied presentation of the Manifesto the development of industrial

5. These Reviews are translated in *The Revolutions of 1848*, with the exception of the excerpts that comprise Chapter IV of Engels's 1895 edition of *The Class Struggles in France*, which is followed here. The original *Neue Rheinische Zeitung* was the daily newspaper edited by Marx in Cologne during the German revolution of 1848.

6. These were originally published under Marx's name in the *New York Daily Tribune*; *MECW* 11, pp. 3–96.

7. Introduction to the 1895 edition of *The Class Struggles in France*, in *MECW* 27, p. 506.

8. *The Revolutions of 1848*, p. 69.

capitalism is seen as having simplified class distinctions, to the point that a numerically small bourgeoisie and an 'immense majority' of proletarians confront one another, with intermediate classes rapidly disappearing. Furthermore, the rapid social changes of bourgeois society have swept away all 'ancient and venerable prejudices and opinions',[9] so that the class struggle can be fought out in explicit and demystified terms. The proletariat can unashamedly avow its class interest, and the ideologies that attempt to present the particular interest of the ruling class as the general interest increasingly fail to deceive the masses. To turn from the Manifesto to *The Class Struggles in France* and the *Eighteenth Brumaire* is to turn from a theory that is abstract, although valid at its own level, to a concrete analysis that is correspondingly complex. In the space of less than four years France experienced a whole series of political transformations. The actors that appeared on the political stage were by no means readily identifiable as representatives of social interests, but included such heteroclite and esoteric entities as the Legitimist and Orleanist monarchists, the Montagne and the party of Order, the 'pure' republicans, the Society of 10 December, and the almost comic figure of Louis Napoleon himself. Marx's project in these essays is essentially to decode these and other political forces, to explain why the different classes in French society represented themselves in this way in the political arena, and why their struggles were fought out as struggles between different forms of state.[10]

The starting-point of Marx's explanation is the relatively undeveloped character of French capitalism. 'The struggle against capital in its highly developed modern form – at its crucial point, the struggle of the industrial wage-labourer against the industrial bourgeois – is in France a partial phenomenon.'[11] Industrial capitalism, in other words, was only one of the modes of production found concurrently in France, and the great majority of the French population were still involved either in peasant or petty-bourgeois (i.e., artisan) production. The lower strata of the middle class had not yet sunk into the proletariat, and in place of the industrial bourgeoisie and proletariat, which the Manifesto presents as the only two classes characteristic of developed

9. Ibid., p. 70.

10. The rest of this section draws heavily on Nicos Poulantzas, *Political Power and Social Classes*, London, 1975.

11. *The Class Struggles in France*, below, p. 46.

industrial capitalism, Marx distinguished a much richer variety of classes and fractions of classes, of which *great landowners, financial bourgeoisie, industrial bourgeoisie, petty bourgeoisie* (of various gradations), *industrial proletariat, lumpenproletariat* and *small peasant proprietors* are only the most prominent. (The German '*Fraktion*' has the primary meaning of a parliamentary party, but Marx also uses it for sections of a class that are the basis of different political parties. In order to preserve Marx's concept, we have used the English 'fraction' even in some contexts where it is not in general usage, as indeed Marx himself did when he wrote in English [see below, p. 259].)

Given this plurality of classes, it is not surprising that Marx had to qualify the simple model of *one* ruling class presented in the Manifesto. Marx's analyses of France imply rather the existence, on the one hand, of a *ruling bloc* composed of a plurality of classes or fractions of classes; on the other hand, within this ruling bloc, of a single dominant class or fraction. The Orleanist monarchy of 1830–48 was the rule of the 'financial aristocracy' (i.e., financial bourgeoisie) and the big industrial bourgeoisie, while the Restoration monarchy of 1815–30 had been the rule of the large landowners. In the bourgeois republic of 1848–51 these two wings of the bourgeoisie, still organized under their monarchist banners, 'had found the form of state in which they could rule jointly'.[12] However, within this ruling bloc Marx identifies the financial bourgeoisie as the dominant fraction, under both the Orleanist monarchy and the 1848 republic. 'Our whole account has shown how the republic, from the first day of its existence, did not overthrow the financial aristocracy, but consolidated it.'[13] Although the economic interests of the industrial bourgeoisie were opposed to those of the 'financial aristocracy', and they had even supported the February revolution, they were forced, when the revolution brought with it the threat of the proletariat, to rally round the class that had recently been their adversary.

Since every propertied minority must rely on the exploited masses to fight its battles for it, it can only exert political power by presenting its own particular interest as the interest of society in general. It is thus always necessary for the propertied classes to appear on the political stage in ideological disguise. If 'the

12. *The Eighteenth Brumaire of Louis Bonaparte*, below, p. 165.
13. *The Class Struggles in France*, p. 109.

legitimate monarchy was simply the political expression of the immemorial domination of the lords of the soil' and 'the July monarchy was only the political expression of the usurped rule of the bourgeois parvenus',[14] Marx goes on to stress that this ideological disguise also imprisons those who wear it. Although the 'superstructure of different and specifically formed feelings, illusions, modes of thought and views of life' is created by a class 'out of its material foundations and the corresponding social relations', yet 'the single individual, who derives these feelings, etc., through tradition and upbringing, may well imagine that they form the real determinants and the starting-point of his activity'. The disguise, therefore, has its specific effects on the political struggle. Although as the party of Order, the coalesced bourgeoisie 'ruled over the other classes of society more harshly and with less restriction than ever they could under the Restoration or the July monarchy', at the same time the republic undermined the 'social foundation' of this political rule, since the two fractions of the bourgeoisie 'had now to confront the subjugated classes and contend with them without mediation, without being concealed by the Crown, without the possibility of diverting the national attention by their secondary conflicts among themselves and with the monarchy'.[15]

Moreover, the ideological representation of class interests defines a distinct stratum of ideologists attached to each class. Writing about the Montagne, Marx stresses that what made the democratic ideologists representatives of the petty bourgeoisie was not that they were themselves shopkeepers, but that:

Their minds are restricted by the same barriers which the petty bourgeoisie fails to overcome in real life, and . . . they are therefore driven in theory to the same problems and solutions to which material interest and social situation drive the latter in practice. This is the general relationship between the *political and literary representatives* of a class and the class which they represent.[16]

In certain circumstances the ideological forms in which the class struggle is necessarily fought out can place a party in power that does not represent a well-defined class or fraction at all. After the

14. *The Eighteenth Brumaire of Louis Bonaparte*, p. 173.
15. Ibid., pp. 174–5.
16. Ibid., pp. 176–7.

defeat of the June insurgents, political power was temporarily held by the 'republican fraction of the bourgeoisie', which Marx explicitly notes 'was not a fraction of the bourgeoisie bound together by great common interests and demarcated from the rest by conditions of production peculiar to it', but rather a coterie of 'writers, lawyers, officers and officials'.[17]

What enabled these 'pure republicans' to hold power was the fact that the class bloc that was overthrown by the February revolution had ruled through the political form of the monarchy. The ideologists who stood for republicanism as such, and who did so for specific reasons of French history, thus found themselves in a privileged position in the new order, but, resting on no firm class base, their reign was soon brought to an end with the developing class struggle.

This brings us to the key question of representative democracy. How in Marx's theory can a minoritarian propertied class stably exercise political power through a democratic constitution?

The first point to note is that Marx consistently refuses to idealize the forms of political democracy, to see this particular form of state as privileged in the expression it gives to the forces of civil society. It is not and cannot be in the parliamentary arena that class struggles are resolved. Marx repeats in his more substantial autopsies of the French 1848 revolution what he had stressed as a practical imperative in the *Neue Rheinische Zeitung*: political democracy is brought into being by the struggle of classes and is overthrown by the same struggle. Any illusion to the contrary is *parliamentary cretinism* – 'that peculiar epidemic which has prevailed over the whole continent of Europe since 1848 ... which holds its victims spellbound in an imaginary world and robs them of all sense, all memory, and all understanding of the rough external world'.[18]

Marx by no means dismisses the value of parliamentary democracy for the exploited classes, and indeed he refers to it as 'political emancipation'.[19] He insists only that the social antagonisms that survive political emancipation cannot be resolved by pure reason or the vote of representatives within this particular emancipated sphere.

Rather than defending the results of universal suffrage, Marx directly attacks the 'magical power' which 'republicans of the old

17. Ibid., p. 157.
18. Ibid., pp. 210–11.
19. *The Class Struggles in France*, p. 71.

school' had attributed to it,[20] and brings his bitter irony to bear against the attempt to set abstract standards of justice against the outcome of the class struggle. When the Provisional Government disputed 'the right of the barricade fighters to declare a republic' on the grounds that 'only a majority of the French people had that authority', Marx commented that 'the bourgeoisie allows the proletariat only one form of usurpation – that of fighting'.[21] The possible contradiction between universal suffrage and the class interests of the proletariat was highlighted by the events of May and June 1848. When the Constituent Assembly elected in April proved to have a large reactionary majority, the Paris proletariat attempted to overthrow the Assembly, unleashing against it the desperate insurrection of the June days. Far from condemning the Paris proletariat for attempting to force its will on French society, Marx extolled its 'bold, revolutionary battle-cry . . . *Overthrow of the bourgeoisie! Dictatorship of the working class!*'[22]

That said, Marx does not present in these texts an explanation of how capitalist class rule can be stably maintained through a representative state with universal suffrage. Indeed he was not to be confronted with such a phenomenon until late in his life, precisely because universal suffrage was not conceded in any country (as opposed to being won briefly in periods of revolution) until and unless the threat of working-class revolution had been allayed. In 1850, therefore, universal suffrage appears in Marx's theory of the state as an internally contradictory phenomenon. 'It gives political power to the classes whose social slavery it is intended to perpetuate: proletariat, peasants and petty bourgeoisie. And it deprives the bourgeoisie, the class whose old social power it sanctions, of the political guarantees of this power.'[23] Marx does not just imply that universal suffrage has to be set aside eventually 'by revolution or by reaction',[24] but that it produces of itself an untenable situation, and in fact he goes as far as to assert:

In the older civilized countries, with their highly developed class formation, modern conditions of production, and an intellectual consciousness in which

20. Ibid., p. 56.
21. Ibid., p. 42.
22. Ibid., p. 61.
23. Ibid., p. 71.
24. Ibid., p. 134.

all traditional ideas have been dissolved through the work of centuries, the republic is generally only the political form for the revolutionizing of bourgeois society, and not its conservative form of existence.[25]

In the case of the Second Republic, universal suffrage certainly was an unstable form, even if Marx's generalization from this was to be proved wrong. The disaffection of the proletariat, peasantry and petty bourgeoisie led the bourgeoisie to trust in monarchy as against parliamentary democracy, and the only monarchy that could find a viable popular base was that of Bonaparte.

Bonapartism, at first sight, seems to upset Marx's theory of the state as the organized rule of a class, or even a class bloc. Marx himself wrote, 'France therefore seems to have escaped the despotism of a class only to fall back beneath the despotism of an individual, and indeed beneath the authority of an individual without authority. The struggle seems to have reached the compromise that all classes fall on their knees, equally mute and impotent, before the rifle butt.'[26] However, Marx goes on to resolve this paradox by analysing the Bonapartist regime, if not as the organized rule of a class bloc, nevertheless as the determined product of the class struggle.

There are three basic elements to Marx's analysis of Bonapartism: the opposition *state/society*, the bourgeoisie and the peasantry. Marx's formulations as to the relations between these elements are often rather clumsy, as his concepts are being painfully born out of the analysis of contemporary political phenomena, but the basic relationships are clear enough. Firstly, Marx stresses the continuity of the French state apparatus from its perfection by the first Napoleon through to the 1848 republic. This executive power had been gradually strengthened by the struggle against revolution, until it became a 'frightful parasitic body, which surrounds the body of French society like a caul and stops up all its pores',[27] and indeed strives for power of its own. Under Louis Bonaparte the executive power appeared to have cut quite adrift from any class base, but Marx defines its relationship to two distinct social classes.

On the one hand, Marx introduces the peasantry as the passive class base of Bonapartism: 'Bonaparte represents a class, indeed he represents the most numerous class of French society, the small

25. *The Eighteenth Brumaire*, p. 155.
26. Ibid., p. 236.
27. Ibid., p. 237.

peasant proprietors.'[28] This representation, however, despite the term used, is of a quite distinctive kind. If the peasantry were a necessary precondition of Bonaparte's rule, Marx assuredly does not see the Bonapartist regime as a 'dictatorship of the peasantry' in the way that he speaks of the 'dictatorship of the bourgeoisie' and 'dictatorship of the working class'. In fact, due to their isolation in the productive process, and France's poor means of communication, the peasants were 'incapable of asserting their class interest in their own name', so that 'their representative must appear simultaneously as their master, as an authority over them, an unrestricted governmental power that protects them from the other classes and sends them rain and sunshine from above'. Indeed, Marx goes so far as to say, 'The political influence of the small peasant proprietors is therefore ultimately expressed in the executive subordinating society to itself.'[29]

But this being so, Bonaparte's 'representation' of the peasants complements without the least contradiction his representation, in a quite different sense, of the bourgeoisie itself. Marx not only sees the bourgeois parliamentarians as having paved the way for Bonaparte by their attack on universal suffrage, but more crucially presents the 'extra-parliamentary mass of the bourgeoisie' as having 'invited Bonaparte to suppress and annihilate its speaking and writing part, its politicians and intellectuals . . . [in order] to pursue its private affairs with full confidence under the protection of a strong and unrestricted government'.[30]

How is it that the bourgeoisie can entrust political rule to a power other than itself? How can it be sure that Bonaparte will protect its interests so well, especially given that, once the state machine dominates civil society, depriving all – including the bourgeoisie – of political rights, the class that has voluntarily abandoned political power cannot similarly win it back? Marx does not explicitly answer this question, but the answer in fact lies in the nature of the capitalist mode of production itself. As Marx was to explain in *Capital*, political violence is not continuously needed to extract surplus-value and ensure the expanded reproduction of capitalist relations, which in this respect differ fundamentally from the feudal or slave modes of production. All that is needed is the basic juridical framework that protects the free exchange of commodities, labour-power being

28. Ibid., p. 238.
29. Ibid., p. 239.
30. Ibid., p. 224.

itself an exchangeable commodity. Once pre-capitalist obstacles to capitalist development have been cleared away, the bourgeoisie does not have to direct the state itself, as long as the state power is one that will maintain this juridical framework and repress any revolutionary challenge to it.

In these circumstances, however, the executive power for its part is just as dependent on the capitalist mode of production, for as a 'parasitic body' it itself lives off the surplus-value produced by the workers and is as threatened as the bourgeoisie by proletarian revolution. Bonapartist state and French bourgeoisie thus shared a fundamental unity of interest; while there was certainly room for conflict between them, this could only be secondary in relation to their common antagonism to the proletariat. The peasantry, on the other hand, were only an instrument for Bonaparte's ambition. Unable to organize themselves independently, they needed only the few token gestures in their direction required to avert spontaneous revolt. It is thus not surprising that the Bonapartist regime, besides maintaining the basic functions of the capitalist state, took active measures to further the development of French capitalism, measures probably more far-reaching than a bourgeois-democratic regime would have been able to carry out.

If Marx's mature theory adequately explains the symbiotic relationship between bourgeoisie and Bonapartist state, he was still unwilling, in 1852, to accept this as a viable situation. The early formulations of historical materialism, *The German Ideology* and the Manifesto in particular, assume an identity between what Marx was later to distinguish as the (economically) 'ruling class' and the (politically) 'governing caste'.[31] Only with the further development during the 1850s of Marx's theory of modes of production did economy and polity emerge as fully distinct levels of the social formation.

Marx accordingly underestimated the tenacity of Louis Bonaparte's regime. He optimistically predicted that a rapidly intensifying crisis would arise from the allegedly contradictory demands placed on Bonaparte by his need to appear as the the 'patriarchal benefactor of all classes'[32] – surely a normal functional requisite for any government. Marx's hope that Bonaparte would 'bring the whole bourgeois economy into confusion'[33] was not to be fulfilled, and

31. 'Parties and Cliques', below, p. 279.
32. *The Eighteenth Brumaire*, p. 247.
33. Ibid., p. 248.

indeed Marx offers no satisfactory reason why this should have happened.

Finally, it is clear from Marx's analysis of the French executive that he saw the state as something more than just the instrument of ruling-class power. For Marx, the very existence of a state apparatus separate from civil society – which the bourgeoisie needs in order to maintain its supremacy – involves a specific oppression of civil society by the state, over and above the exploitation of the proletariat by capital which it perpetuates. The task of the proletarian revolution is not merely the abolition of capitalist exploitation, but also the liberation of civil society from domination by its state apparatus. In this context Marx introduces for the first time the concept of the revolution destroying the state apparatus, although still only in an oblique way, and as a task implicitly peculiar to France.[34] Only in 1871 was Marx to spell out, with reference to the Paris Commune, what precisely was involved in 'smashing' the state machine, and what form of organization the proletariat had to put in its place.

England

After completing his book on the Cologne Communist Trial, in December 1852, Marx returned to his economic studies, at least in so far as the needs of earning a living allowed him to do. The results of Marx's theoretical work were slow to appear, and during the 1850s he published only the first two chapters of what was later to be *Capital*.[35] However, in the journalistic work that he undertook, particularly for the *New York Daily Tribune*, Marx was of necessity prolific, and the articles that he and Engels wrote for this paper between 1852 and 1862 fill several volumes of their collected works. Needless to say, there is much in these pieces, which range over a great part of the contemporary economic and political scene, that is not of lasting value, and there are even many issues on which Marx's judgement turned out to be mistaken. Equally, however, there is much in Marx's journalistic work that is of durable importance, and this work is important is a whole, as a moment of Marx's political practice.

When Marx settled permanently in London, in 1849, he was

34. Ibid., p. 237.
35. *A Contribution to the Critique of Political Economy*, in *MECW* 29.

thirty-one years old, and it was in England that he was to spend three-quarters of his adult life. In the 1850s this fact was of course not yet apparent, and Marx's connections with the English working-class movement were not to blossom until the next decade, with the foundation of the International Working Men's Association. Marx's only real comrade in the English workers' movement in the 1850s was Ernest Jones.[36] Marx passed on to Jones's *People's Paper* many of his *Tribune* articles and discussed his political work with him regularly until the Chartist movement finally collapsed in 1858.

It was unfortunate for the development of Marx's politics that he found himself exiled in a country that was, in the third quarter of the nineteenth century, the most stable and crisis-free in the bourgeois world. English Chartism had been mortally wounded in 1848, and it was to be four decades before the period of mid-Victorian prosperity came to an end and a new socialist workers' movement developed. The sluggish English environment undoubtedly acted as a brake on the development of Marx's politics. While the worst years of reaction saw the steady maturation of Marx's general theory and his critique of bourgeois economics, his political theory made little progress compared with the heady developments of the 1848 period. Revolutionary political theory can only develop in response to the new problems and tasks raised by mass struggle, and this was completely lacking in Marx's England.

In England, the relationship between political power and civil society was quite different from that which Marx had studied in France and Germany. In Marx's native land civil society was to a notorious extent dominated by the state, and Marx had attacked Hegel's defence of the state bureaucracy as early as 1843.[37] In his writings on France, also, Marx had isolated the bureaucratic-military apparatus as the key bastion of the rule of capital. The British state of the mid-Victorian period did not possess the immense standing army and bureaucracy of its Continental neighbours, a fact which Marx was to interpret as facilitating the proletarian revolution. Yet the political rule of capital was none the less firmly established in Britain, though the forms it took were subtler and less conspicuous. In the absence of the stormy class struggles that had unveiled to him

36. On Ernest Jones, see the Introduction to *The Revolutions of 1848*, pp. 21–2.

37. In his 'Critique of Hegel's Doctrine of the State'; Karl Marx, *Early Writings*, Harmondsworth, 1975, pp. 57–198.

the nature of bourgeois rule in France, Marx was never able to get to the root of the peculiarities of the British state.

The starting point of Marx's writings on Britain was a review of Guizot's pamphlet on the English revolution of the seventeenth century, which Marx saw as an attempt by Guizot to explain why bourgeois society in England had developed in the form of constitutional monarchy longer than in France. The stable political structure introduced by the English revolution of 1688, which Guizot could only ascribe to the superior intelligence of the English bourgeoisie, Marx attributed to the existence in England of a class of large landowners which had arisen under Henry VIII (from the confiscation and sale of church lands), whose estates were not feudal but bourgeois property, and who could therefore enter into a 'lasting alliance' with the developing commercial and financial bourgeoisie.[38]

In 1852, in his first series of articles for the *New York Daily Tribune*, Marx turned his attention to the two-party system that had dominated British politics since the 1688 revolution. The Tory party was the class party of the large landed proprietors, 'distinguished from the other bourgeois in the same way as rent of land is distinguished from commercial and industrial profit. Rent of land is conservative, profit is progressive.' 'The Tories recruit their army from the farmers ... [and] are followed and supported by the Colonial Interest, the Shipping Interest, the State Church party,' in fact all the sections of the ruling class opposed to the dominance of industrial capital. The Whig party, 'a species which, like all those of the amphibious class, exists very easily, but is difficult to describe', consisted in fact of 'the oldest, richest, and most arrogant portion of English landed property', but were defined politically by serving as 'the *aristocratic representatives* ... of the industrial and commercial middle class'. 'Under the condition that the bourgeoisie should abandon to them, to an oligarchy of aristocratic families, the monopoly of government and the exclusive possession of office, they make to the middle class, and assist it in conquering, all those concessions which in the course of social and political development have shown themselves to have become *unavoidable* and *undelayable*.'[39] Thus a symbiotic relationship is defined between the 'economically ruling class' and

---

38. 'Review of Guizot's Book on the English Revolution', below, p. 254.
39. 'Tories and Whigs', below, pp. 257–9.

the 'politically governing caste' which in some ways parallels that between Bonaparte and the French bourgeoisie.

Thus far, Marx's analysis is indisputable. The problems begin when he comes on to deal with the perspectives for future development. Marx held that constitutional monarchy was not the final political form of bourgeois society in England. Before the English propertied classes were mortally threatened by the proletariat, Marx believed that the industrial bourgeoisie would itself be forced to overthrow the traditional structures of the constitution, because its own 'new requirements' clashed with the interests of the landed proprietors and the old commercial and financial bourgeoisie.

For Marx, the highly mediated political expression of the power of capital provided by the Whig party was an anachronism which corresponded to a more backward state of capitalist development. Marx believed that as industrial capital grew to increasing pre-eminence over other forms of bourgeois property, the industrial bourgeoisie would push aside the old structures of the constitution that represented so many '*faux frais*' (overhead costs) of production – the monarchy, Lords, colonies, standing army and Established Church – and take power directly into its own hands in the form of a democratic republic. The Free Traders were therefore 'the party of the self-conscious bourgeoisie' (in this sense, industrial bourgeoisie), which would necessarily strive 'to make available its social power as a political power as well, and to eradicate the last arrogant remnants of feudal society'.[40] The economic strength of the Tories had been broken by the repeal of the Corn Laws in 1846, but Marx held that the Tories still attempted 'to maintain a political power, the social foundation of which has ceased to exist' by means of 'a *counter-revolution*, that is to say, by a reaction of the state against society', an attempt which Marx believed 'must bring on a crisis'.[41]

Even though the manufacturers, faced as they were with the working class as their own 'arising enemy', might 'strive to avoid every forcible collision with the aristocracy', yet 'historical necessity and the Tories press them onwards. They cannot avoid fulfilling their mission, battering to pieces Old England.' 'When they will have conquered exclusive political dominion . . . the struggle against

40. 'The Chartists', below, p. 262.
41. 'Tories and Whigs', p. 258.

capital will no longer be distinct from the struggle against the existing government.'[42]

As for the English working class, Marx believed that the Chartist programme of universal suffrage was the direct road to its supremacy. Universal suffrage was 'the equivalent for political power for the working class of England, where the proletariat forms the large majority of the population, where, in a long, though underground civil war, it has gained a clear consciousness of its position as a class'.[43] Marx was of course wrong in his predictions. The industrial bourgeoisie managed to integrate itself politically and culturally into the old ruling bloc, and the aristocratic 'mask'[44] was to remain for at least a further half-century to camouflage and mystify the rule of capital. The Chartists' six points were one by one conceded by the ruling classes, but they did not lead, as Marx had hoped, to working-class political power.

The root of Marx's error was his application to England of a political model worked out on the basis of Continental experience.[45] On the Continent, particularly in France, which Marx saw as the paradigm of bourgeois political development, the industrial bourgeoisie had joined more than once in revolution against the old ruling classes, and the Communist Manifesto indeed presents the 'battering to pieces' of the old regime by the industrial bourgeoisie as part of a historically necessary process. Marx had already had to recognize, with respect to Germany, that the general schema of the Manifesto could be distorted by relative backwardness;[46] he did not yet understand that it could be equally distorted, in a different direction, by England's relative precocity.

The constitutional settlement of 1688 had a firmer basis than Marx ascribed to it. As the first capitalist nation, England acquired in the eighteenth century the unrivalled mastery of the world market that stimulated the industrial revolution. Under the constitutional monarchy, and with its market secured by the sea power already developed by the commercial bourgeoisie, the industrial capitalist class that began to form in the late eighteenth

42. 'The Chartists', p. 264.

43. Ibid.

44. 'The British Constitution', below, p. 284.

45. The critique of Marx's analysis of English politics presented here is indebted to arguments developed by Tom Nairn, particularly in 'The Fateful Meridian', *New Left Review* I/60.

46. See the Introduction to *The Revolutions of 1848*, pp. 35, 46.

century had no fundamental quarrel with the traditional ruling classes. Significantly, it remained untouched by the rationalist ideology of the Enlightenment, which logically 'should' have expressed its interests, as, despite the *'faux frais'* represented by the trappings of state, it did not face the obstacle to its development represented by the absolutist state that its counterparts on the Continent had to overcome. The industrialists rallied behind their elders and betters in the Napoleonic wars, which, for the English ruling classes, were less motivated by counter-revolutionary zeal than a continuation of the trade wars against the French monarchy. Jacobinism did evoke a certain response among the English artisans and petty bourgeoisie, but it was crushed by a united front of all the exploiting classes. The contradiction between the industrialists and the old ruling classes was already a secondary one, and the campaigns over the Reform Bill and the Corn Laws in no way ruptured the underlying alliance. Indeed, the repeal of the Corn Laws weakened the landlords' economic strength only marginally (grain prices were only to fall substantially with the opening-up of the American prairies in the 1870s) and was a price that the Tories were prepared to pay. Further, the absence of a bureaucratic-military state apparatus in England made Marx's expectations of a Tory counter-revolution, a 'reaction of the state against society', rather far-fetched. In April 1848, after all, the government could only resist the threat of Chartist insurrection by enrolling the bourgeois citizens of London en masse as a special constabulary.

The English working class were held in check by mechanisms just as effective as the Continental forces of repression. The industrial workers of the nineteenth century had no revolutionary tradition within historic memory to draw on, and the half-hearted reluctance of the Chartists to employ 'physical force' witnesses to the hold that the ideology of the 'British Constitution', Anglo-Saxon liberty and the rule of law had for them. Furthermore, the Chartist party consistently represented the 'aristocracy of labour', the 10–15 per cent of skilled craftsmen who, in the heyday of English capitalism's world monopoly, enjoyed a highly privileged position over the unorganized mass of the working class. After the moral defeat of 1848 most former Chartists turned their energies away from politics and into building the 'new model unions' whose very existence depended on this division among the working class and ultimately on British imperialism. Two decades later, when it became clear to the ruling class that working-class suffrage was not a threat but that the great majority of workers would vote for the ruling-class parties, the Second Reform Bill enfranchised the bulk of the male working class. The Chartist demands, revolutionary had they been won by force, proved recuperative when they were given by grace of the ruling classes who allowed the workers into the hallowed pale of the British Constitution.

India, China and Imperialism

In his articles on India and China, written between 1853 and 1858, Marx confronted for the first time the relationship between the capitalist metropolises and their colonies and satellites. In the Manifesto, Marx and Engels had portrayed bourgeois society as spreading homogeneously out from its original base and held that national differences were being abolished as the bourgeoisie of the most advanced nations forced other nations 'to become bourgeois themselves'.[47] This analysis had obvious implications for the proletarian movement. If the lands that European capitalism drew into its world market were destined to run through the same development as the capitalist heartlands, then the proletariat could only wish to speed the process of colonization, as a necessary condition for the transition to communism on a world scale. It was on these grounds that Engels could write in 1848, for example: 'The conquest of Algeria is an important and fortunate fact for the progress of civilization.'[48]

In the early 1850s, Marx and Engels had still not freed themselves from the Eurocentric view of human development that imperialism itself had engendered. It was not that they had any illusions about the bourgeoisie's 'civilizing' mission. When Marx first turned his attention to India, he wrote, 'The profound hypocrisy and inherent barbarism of bourgeois civilization lies unveiled before our eyes, turning from its home, where it assumes respectable forms, to the colonies, where it goes naked.'[49] But quite ignorant of Asian social history, Marx could describe Hindu society as 'undignified, stagnatory and vegetative', as a 'passive sort of existence'[50] that

47. *The Revolutions of 1848*, p. 71.

48. 'Extraordinary Revelations.–Abd-El-Kader.–Guizot's Foreign Policy', *Northern Star*, 22 January 1848; *MECW* 6, p. 471.

49. 'The Future Results of the British Rule in India', below, p. 324.

50. 'The British Rule in India', below, p. 306.

had 'no history at all' and was 'the predestined prey of conquest'.[51]
It was only European capitalism, he believed, that had drawn Asia
into world history. Marx did not realize that capitalist exploitation
in India was not simply more barbaric than its domestic form, but
essentially different in nature. Thus, analysing the benefits that
Britain derived from the Indian empire, Marx distinguished between
the interests of the traditional ruling class – the 'moneyocracy' and
'oligarchy' that had 'directly exploited' India – and the interest
of the industrial bourgeoisie. He argued that although it was the
cheap cotton textiles of Lancashire that had been responsible for
the ruin of native Indian industry, the British industrial bourgeoisie
had itself eventually lost by this, and stood to gain by the creation
of 'fresh productive powers'[52] in India as the basis of extended
trade. Although capitalism, in its most vicious form, was imposed
on colonized territories such as India from without, Marx still
predicted for these countries the same historical trajectory as that
of the capitalist metropolises themselves; the only possible course
of development for backward Asia was to follow in the wake of
the advanced Europe that exploited it. Industrialization within
capitalist relations was the precondition for Indian liberation, and
Marx believed that the British were laying the basis for all-round
industrialization with the building of railways.[53] British capital,
which by its initial impact had ruined India, would in the long run
rebuild the Indian economy, as part of the global 'material basis
of the new world' that it was the bourgeoisie's historical mission
to create. The social revolution that was to 'master the results of
the bourgeois epoch' for human needs was still in the hands of the
'most advanced peoples' of western Europe.[54]

On this premise, Marx could only see in the revolt that broke out in
1857 a blind reaction to the misery inflicted by the British. Although
he denounced the oppression that had provoked the uprising, and the
atrocities that accompanied its suppression, Marx did not acclaim
the 'Indian mutiny' as a revolutionary struggle, as he did not accept
that an independent India could have a viable path of national
development ahead of it.[55]

An exchange of letters between Marx and Engels in October

51. 'The Future Results of the British Rule in India', pp. 319–20.
52. 'The East India Company – Its History and Results', below, p. 315.
53. 'The Future Results of the British Rule in India', pp. 321–3.
54. Ibid., p. 325.
55. Marx's articles on the Indian revolt are printed in *MECW* 15.

1858 shows their momentary awareness that international capitalist relations posed a problem for their theory of the proletarian revolution which they had not yet solved. Writing to Marx on 7 October, Engels explained Ernest Jones's concessions to the bourgeois Reform movement in the following terms:

It seems to me that Jones's new move, taken in conjunction with the former more or less successful attempts at such an alliance, is really bound up with the fact that the English proletariat is actually becoming more and more bourgeois, so that this most bourgeois of all nations is apparently aiming ultimately at the possession of a bourgeois aristocracy and a bourgeois proletariat alongside the bourgeoisie. For a nation that exploits the whole world this is of course to a certain extent justifiable.[56]

The next day Marx wrote to Engels: 'The difficult question for us is this: on the Continent the revolution is imminent and will immediately assume a socialist character. Is it not bound to be crushed in this little corner, considering that in a far greater territory the movement of bourgeois society is still in the ascendant?'[57] The problem that Marx posed here and the implications of Engels's remarks on the 'bourgeoisification' of the English proletariat are both momentous for the theory of scientific communism. Indeed, Engels's thesis runs quite counter to the Communist Manifesto. It is very strange, then, that neither Marx nor Engels seriously attempted to solve this complex of problems. This gap in their theory was later to have dire consequences for the Marxist movement, as the European workers' parties came to value their imperialist privilege so highly that they blindly followed their respective ruling classes into inter-imperialist war.

In his later years Marx was to revise considerably his views on the stagnant character of Indian society, and also to deny that the west European path of historical development was a necessary model for all societies.[58] But if in this respect he overcame his

56. *MECW* 40, p. 343.

57. Ibid., p. 346.

58. On the latter point see Marx's letter to the editorial board of *Otechestvenniye Zapiski*, November 1877; *MECW* 24, pp. 196–201. Although Marx did not deal explicitly with India in his later writings, Kovalevsky's theory of the rural commune, which Marx accepted, showed Indian society in a quite different perspective. For an account of the development of Marx and Engels's theories of Asiatic and pre-class societies, see Maurice Godelier's Preface to *Sur les sociétés pré-capitalistes*, Éditions sociales, Paris, 1970.

initial Eurocentrism, Marx still did not develop a theory of the way in which metropolis and colony are linked by capitalism in a relationship which substantially modifies the course of development of both.

From today's vantage point, and with the development of the Marxist theory of imperialism from Lenin onwards, we can see the answer to Marx's 'difficult question'. The specific exploitation of what are now the 'third world' countries by the imperialist metropolises is not necessarily dependent on direct political occupation, but is effected quite adequately through market relationships and the movements of trade and capital. Capitalist relations of production force the underdeveloped countries into a vicious specialization in primary products, often turning over entire countries to a single crop. Industrial development in these countries is generally impossible without a strong protectionist policy, even a state monopoly of foreign trade, and comprehensive economic planning. The local bourgeoisie, however, typically remains weak and tied to imperialism, and is unable to overcome the imperialist division of labour. At the same time imperialism fosters in the metropolis a working-class interest in colonial exploitation, whether part of the proceeds is passed to a privileged 'labour aristocracy', as Lenin held, or whether, as seems more probable today, it enables the metropolitan working class as a whole to enjoy a more tolerable standard of living. On top of this economic base an ideology is built up that ties the working class disastrously to its own exploiters. Imperialism determines the historical trajectories of both metropolis and colony, in opposed directions. Those countries oppressed by imperialism cannot simply share in the 'ascendant movement of bourgeois society', but can only develop by throwing off imperialist domination. After the socialist revolution in Russia it became possible for countries that made anti-imperialist revolutions to escape from the tyranny of the world market and industrialize within socialist relations of production. There is thus no problem of the proletarian revolution in the capitalist metropolises being 'crushed in this little corner'. The problem is rather that as long as these countries dominate a great part of the world, the overthrow of capitalism in its heartlands is much more difficult, and indeed has nowhere yet taken place.[59] While Marx equated

59. Czechoslovakia and the German Democratic Republic, where socialist trans-

'civilization' with Europe and expected the socialist revolution to spread across the world in the same direction as capitalism, the course of the revolution has been the exact opposite: not from West to East, but from East to West.

Marx paid less attention to China than to India, partly no doubt because of its less direct relationship with Britain. His articles on China deal mainly with the immediate political events of the Taiping rebellion and the Second Opium War of 1856–8, and their repercussions in the British political arena. Occasionally, however, there are some comments that are of general interest for Marx's politics. In the Review from the *Neue Rheinische Zeitung Revue* for January–February 1850 Marx noted the reported existence of a 'Chinese socialism', which he maintained 'may bear the same relation to European socialism as Chinese to Hegelian philosophy'.[60] It was 'the cotton bales of the English bourgeoisie' that had brought 'the oldest and most unshakeable empire on earth ... to the brink of a social revolution', and 'such a revolution cannot help but have the most important consequences for the civilized world'. Despite the 'socialist' ideology, Marx seems to ascribe to the impending Chinese revolution a bourgeois character of the classical European kind, imagining written on the Great Wall of China 'the legend: *République chinoise; Liberté, Égalité, Fraternité*'. In 'Revolution in China and in Europe', written in 1853, Marx again posits a dialectical relationship between Chinese and European developments.[61] Yet while at an abstract level he makes great play with this theme, the only concrete mediation that he cites is that the loss of the Chinese market through political chaos would precipitate the next trade crisis in Europe. China did indeed turn out to have a distinctive socialist revolution, though its ultimate impact on Europe is still uncertain.

Russia, Europe and America

Between 1853 and 1856, Marx and Engels's contributions to the *New York Daily Tribune* were dominated by the 'Eastern question' – the conflict between Russia and Turkey, and the ensuing Crimean War. They insisted that the defeat of Turkey by Russia would lead to a

---

formation was conducted in the 1940s under the protection of the Soviet defence 'umbrella', are exceptions that prove the rule.

60. *The Revolutions of 1848*, p. 277.

61. Below, pp. 325–33.

great expansion of Russian power in Europe, and would therefore be 'an unspeakable calamity for the revolutionary cause'. 'In this instance the interests of the revolutionary democracy and of England go hand in hand.'[62]

Marx and Engels undoubtedly made a great error of judgement here. If Russia was the main enemy of the revolution in Europe, it was not the only one, and its ability to intervene in Europe was not unlimited. There is at least a trace of paranoia in Marx and Engels's vigorous support for the anti-Russian alliance of three other empires – Britain, France and Turkey. Marx systematically condemned the British government for failing to prosecute the Crimean War with sufficient vigour, and attempted to show that Palmerston, Foreign Minister and later Prime Minister, was in fact in the pay of the Russian cabinet. Marx's diatribes against Palmerston, quite inadequately founded, were eagerly seized upon by the demagogic anti-Russian faction of the Tory party and reprinted as fly-posters in large editions. Marx also wrote for the *Free Press*, a paper belonging to the prominent Tory Turkophile David Urquhart, a series of articles titled 'Revelations of the Diplomatic History of the Eighteenth Century', in which he sought to demonstrate the peculiarly and permanently expansionist character of tsarist foreign policy and the continuous connivance of the English governing caste with it.[63]

It is particularly sad that Marx's contributions to Ernest Jones's *People's Paper*, the one revolutionary organ of the British working class in this period, should have consisted to a large extent of articles encouraging British workers to support the victory of their government in what was essentially an inter-imperialist war.

Throughout Europe the 1850s were a period of reaction, though also one of rapid economic development. All through this decade the workers' and democratic movements were almost completely silenced by the counter-revolution. But the tasks that the defeated bourgeois revolutions had failed to carry out were not simply ignored. They were instead carried out by a 'revolution from above', to the extent essential for capitalist development, but in a distorted and anti-popular way. Under the shock of 1848, and in

62. 'The Real Issue in Turkey', in *MECW* 12, pp. 13–17.
63. Marx's 'The Story of the Life of Lord Palmerston' is printed in *MECW* 12, and 'Revelations of the Diplomatic History of the Eighteenth Century' in *MECW* 15.

response to the pressure of the bourgeoisie, the forces of reaction undertook extensive modernization in the 1850s. The Prussian state actively promoted industrial development through its direction of the banking system; the Austrian empire destroyed remaining local privileges and built up a highly efficient bureaucracy; Bonaparte used his 'unrestricted government' to foster the development of commerce and industry.

The economic crisis that broke out in 1857 did not have the revolutionary results Marx anticipated. Instead of detonating popular uprising throughout Europe, it led, in the first instance, to international war, when Louis Bonaparte sought to allay the threat of popular discontent by attacking Austria in the name of Italian unification. After the defeat of the 1848 revolutionary movement in Italy the kingdom of Piedmont-Sardinia, comparatively advanced economically, set out to unify Italy under its hegemony, with Cavour setting the model that Bismarck was to follow in Germany a decade later. Under the guise of the 'principle of nationalities' Bonaparte allied with Cavour to drive Austria out of Venice and Lombardy, for which France was rewarded with two Piedmontese provinces with a mixed Franco-Italian population: Savoy and Nice. After the Austrian defeat, Bonaparte, under pressure from the other powers, reneged on his bargain with Cavour and agreed to leave Venice in Austrian possession. A popular movement now broke out in central and southern Italy, inspired by Garibaldi's landing in Sicily, which brought the whole country except Venice and Rome into the new kingdom of Italy.

The international political crisis of 1859 led Marx and Engels to intervene with a pamphlet, written by Engels and published anonymously in Germany,[64] which betrays some basic misconceptions about the nature of European politics in this transitional period. In his pamphlet Engels countered the specious argument of the pro-Austrian 'great Germans' that, for military reasons, Germany must be defended on the Po. But although he declared that a united Germany would not need an inch of Italian soil for its defence, he accepted the Habsburg argument that Bonaparte aimed to annex the left bank of the Rhine and that Germany (which at this moment meant Austria) should not concede its positions in Italy while the Bonapartist threat still obtained. Engels not only made German national unification

---

64. 'Po and Rhine', in *MECW* 16, pp. 211–54.

the only touchstone of the international conflict; he grossly overestimated France's military potential as against Austria and Prussia, and exaggerated the counter-revolutionary character of the Bonapartist regime. He also failed to understand the importance of the Italian Risorgimento. Besides accomplishing the important result of Italian unity, this had, in fact, a far more popular character than did the German unification movement of the 1860s.

Although Marx recognized that 'the reaction carries out the programme of the revolution',[65] he and Engels did not appreciate the extent to which the revolutionary programme of 1848 had been overtaken by history. Their judgement on the crisis of 1859 would no doubt have been different had they seen that the revolutionary-democratic road to national unity in Germany had been closed, instead of expecting a rebirth of the movement of 1848. Distanced from events in Germany, they failed to realize how far the national movement of the bourgeoisie had been co-opted by the Prussian state. But elsewhere, as in Italy, where there were still weak absolutist regimes which did not enjoy bourgeois support, a revolutionary-democratic nationalism of the 1848 type was still possible. Although Marx and Engels had little chance of influencing events in Italy at this period, it would surely have been more consistent of them to have supported Mazzini and Garibaldi, despite their limitations and the bombastic rhetoric that Marx justifiably detested.[66]

Marx's last journalistic articles, written mainly for the Viennese *Die Presse*, cover the civil war in the United States. Marx's position on the American Civil War is notable for his unconditional support of the Northern side. Marx saw the war as 'nothing less than a struggle between two social systems: the system of slavery and the system of free labour. The struggle has broken out because the two systems can no longer peacefully co-exist on the North American continent. It can only be ended by the victory of the one system or the other.'[67]

65. '"Erfurtery" in the Year 1859', in *MECW* 16, pp. 404–6.

66. Ferdinand Lassalle, who was soon to found the German social-democratic movement and was at this time in frequent correspondence with Marx, had a more realistic judgement of the state of affairs in Germany and refused to support Austria in any way in its defence of German territory and power. (See the Introduction to *The First International and After*, pp. 20–22.)

67. 'The Civil War in the United States', below, p. 351.

Marx's analysis of the conflict, as far as it goes, is accurate, and his support for the North basically justified from the standpoint of the working class. Nevertheless, matters were not as simple as Marx portrayed them. From today's perspective it is impossible to ignore both the popular character of the resistance of the Southern smallholders and the imperialist dimension of the war aims of the North, of which the devastation and exploitation of the Southern territories were an inevitable by-product. Further, Marx was highly susceptible to Lincoln's demagogy, and even though Lincoln was only forced by the logic of the war to proclaim the abolition of slavery, Marx referred to him as a 'single-minded son of the working class'.[68]

Marx's enthusiasm for Lincoln and the Northern cause was excessive, and rested on an inadequate understanding of the nature of the American social formation and the federal state. It is easy to see how in the 1860s Marx could enthusiastically compare the achieved bourgeois democracy of the USA with the bureaucratic states of Continental Europe and even aristocratic England. In the circumstances where the English ruling classes were firmly united in support of the Southern slave-owners and it was necessary to struggle to win the English workers away from ruling-class ideology, it is understandable that Marx bent the stick a little too far in the opposite direction. But the populist rhetoric of American capitalism veiled a reality which was predatory and imperialist even in the 1860s, and the war against the South was undoubtedly part of its imperial expansion.

During the 1850s and early 1860s Marx was faced with several political phenomena of a new kind, and extended his horizon from a European to a global one. Yet he made several errors of judgement. He did not understand the peculiarities of the British social and political system. He did not understand the general character of European development after the defeat of the 1848 revolution. He exaggerated the negative role of tsarist Russia and the positive role of federal America. Most seriously, he did not develop a theory of imperialism.

By contrast to the brilliance of Marx's analyses of the class struggles in France, his other surveys from exile provide us with some particular important insights, but no major development

68. 'Address of the International Working Men's Association to Abraham Lincoln, President of the United States', in *MECW* 20, pp. 19–21.

of political theory. In the last instance, the relative weakness of Marx's political writings from 1852 to 1863 must be ascribed to his isolation from political activity, itself due to the absence of open class struggle. With the resurgence of the workers' movement in the 1860s and 1870s, Marx's political theory was also to advance to new ground.

If it had not been for his need to earn a living by journalistic work, Marx would in fact have written very little on politics during this decade, as he concentrated his creative energies in a different direction: the development of his theory of historical materialism and of his critique of bourgeois economics. The *Grundrisse* was written in 1857–8, *A Contribution to the Critique of Political Economy* published in 1859, and in 1861 Marx began work on *Capital* itself. These are his real achievements during the years of reaction.

The Italian Risorgimento, which meant so little to Marx, in fact marked the beginning of the revival of the democratic and workers' movements. This was given a strong stimulus by the Polish insurrection of 1863, which evoked a long-unprecedented gesture from Marx in the form of a 'Proclamation' which he drew up on behalf of the German Workers Educational Association.[69] In 1864, the new tide was to bring Marx back into organized political activity. Marx's exile was to be ended, not by his return to Germany, but by the foundation, in England itself, of a new centre of the proletarian movement: the International Working Men's Association.

*

All texts written by Marx in German have been newly translated for this volume. Historical annotation for *The Class Struggles in France* and *The Eighteenth Brumaire of Louis Bonaparte* was provided by Ben Fowkes.

DAVID FERNBACH
1973 AND 2010

---

69. Marx's position on the Polish question is discussed in the Introductions to *The Revolutions of 1848* (pp. 49–52) and *The First International and After* (pp. 63–6). On the German Workers Educational Association, see below, p. 354, n. 1.

The Class Struggles in France: 1848 to 1850[1]

With the exception of only a few chapters, every important section in the annals of the revolution from 1848 to 1849 carries the heading: *Defeat of the Revolution!*

What was overcome in these defeats was not the revolution. It was the pre-revolutionary, traditional appendages, the products of social relationships which had not yet developed to the point of sharp class antagonisms – persons, illusions, ideas and projects from which the revolutionary party was not free before the February revolution, from which it could be freed not by the *February victory*, but only by a series of *defeats*.

In a word: revolutionary progress cleared a path for itself not by its immediate, tragi-comic achievements, but, on the contrary, by creating a powerful and united counter-revolution; only in combat with this opponent did the insurrectionary party mature into a real party of revolution.

To demonstrate this is the task of the following pages.

I. THE DEFEAT OF JUNE 1848

From February to June 1848

After the July revolution,[2] as the liberal banker Laffitte[3] was

1. The first three chapters of *The Class Struggles in France* were originally published in numbers 1, 2 and 3 of the *Neue Rheinische Zeitung. Politisch-ökonomische Revue*, Hamburg, 1850. The fourth chapter consists of two excerpts from the 'Review: May–October 1850' in the final double number 5/6 of the *Revue*, added by Engels when *The Class Struggles in France* was first published as a separate pamphlet in 1895 (see p. 128). *The Class Struggles in France* is translated here from the text of the 1895 pamphlet, as printed in *MEW* 7.

2. The revolution of July 1830 overthrew the legitimate Bourbon monarchy restored in 1815 and replaced it with the constitutional Orleanist or July monarchy, with Louis Philippe as its king (1830–48).

3. Jacques Laffitte became Louis Philippe's first Prime Minister (August 1830– March 1831).

escorting his *compère*,[4] the Duke of Orleans,[5] in triumph to the Hôtel de Ville,[6] he dropped the remark: 'From now on the bankers will rule.' Laffitte had betrayed the secret of the revolution.

Under Louis Philippe it was not the French bourgeoisie as a whole which ruled but only one fraction of it – bankers, stock-market barons, railway barons, owners of coal and iron mines and forests, a section of landed proprietors who had joined their ranks – the so-called *financial aristocracy*. It sat on the throne, it dictated laws in parliament and made official appointments from the ministries to the tobacco bureaux.

The actual *industrial bourgeoisie* formed part of the official opposition; that is, it was represented in parliament only as a minority. Its opposition became increasingly determined as the autocracy of the financial aristocracy became more absolute and as the latter grew more secure in its domination of the working class after the revolts of 1832, 1834 and 1839 had been choked in blood.[7] Grandin,[8] the factory-owner from Rouen, the fanatical mouthpiece of bourgeois reaction both in the Constituent and Legislative National Assemblies, was Guizot's[9] sharpest opponent in the Chamber of Deputies. In the last days of Louis Philippe Léon Faucher,[10] later known for his impotent efforts to make a name for himself as the Guizot of the French counter-revolution, conducted a journalistic campaign in the name of industry against the speculators and their train-bearer, the government.

4. Accomplice.

5. Louis Philippe's previous title.

6. The town hall of Paris.

7. The Paris rising of June 1832 was an attempted republican insurrection by the secret societies; the Lyons workers' rising of April 1834 was led by the Société des Droits de l'Homme (Society of the Rights of Man), a republican secret society, but supported by the workers' mutual aid associations; the Paris rising of May 1839 was an attempted revolutionary putsch led by Blanqui and Barbès, and animated by republican and semi-socialist ideas (such as the introduction of a system of progressive taxation and a declaration of state bankruptcy).

8. Victor Grandin was a leading member of the 'dynastic', i.e., loyal, opposition under Louis Philippe.

9. François Guizot was an historian, and *de facto* Prime Minister from 1840 to 1848.

10. Léon Faucher, a journalist and economist, was originally an Orleanist, but later went over to Bonaparte. He was a member of both the Constituent and Legislative National Assemblies, and Minister of the Interior from December 1848 to May 1849.

Bastiat[11] agitated in the name of Bordeaux and the whole of wine-producing France against the ruling system.

The *petty bourgeoisie* in all its social gradations, just like the *peasant class*, was completely excluded from political power. Finally, in the official opposition, or completely outside the *pays légal*,[12] were the *ideological* representatives and spokesmen of the classes mentioned, their scholars, lawyers, doctors, etc., in a word, their so-called *authorities*.

As a result of its financial difficulties the July monarchy was from the very beginning dependent upon the big bourgeoisie,[13] and this dependence became the inexhaustible source of increasing financial difficulties. It was impossible to subordinate the state administration to the interests of national production without balancing the budget, without balancing state expenditure and state revenue. And how was it to establish this balance without damaging interests which were, every one of them, pillars of the ruling system, and without organizing the redistribution of taxes, which meant shifting a considerable part of the tax burden on to the shoulders of the big bourgeoisie?

The indebtedness of the state was, on the contrary, in the *direct interest* of that fraction of the bourgeoisie which ruled and legislated in parliament. The *state deficit* was, in fact, the actual object of its speculation and its main source of enrichment. At the end of each year a new deficit. After four or five years a new loan. And every new loan gave the financial aristocracy a fresh opportunity to swindle the state, which was artificially kept hovering on the brink of bankruptcy and was forced to do business with the bankers on the most unfavourable terms. Every new loan provided yet another opportunity to plunder that section of the public which invested its money in government securities by means of manoeuvres on the Bourse, into the secrets of which the government and the parliamentary majority were initiated. In general, the uncertain position of government bonds and the bankers' possession of state secrets put them and their associates in parliament and on the throne in a position to create sudden,

11. Frédéric Bastiat was a leading *laissez-faire* economist, active in the free-trade agitation of the late 1840s.

12. Literally 'legal country', i.e., the political nation, those who enjoyed the right to vote under the narrow franchise of the Restoration and the July monarchy.

13. I.e., the financial bourgeoisie or 'financial aristocracy'.

unusual fluctuations in the price of government securities, which invariably resulted in the ruin of a mass of smaller capitalists and in the fabulously speedy enrichment of the big gamblers. The fact that the state deficit served the direct interests of the ruling fraction of the bourgeoisie explains why the *extraordinary* state expenditure in the last years of Louis Philippe's reign was more than double the extraordinary state expenditure under Napoleon, indeed almost reaching the annual sum of 400 million francs, while France's total average exports rarely reached 750 million francs. The enormous sums of money which thus flowed through the hands of the state gave rise, moreover, to crooked delivery contracts, bribery, embezzlement and roguery of all kinds. The wholesale swindling of the state through loans was repeated on a retail basis in public works. The relationship between parliament and government was reproduced in the relationship between individual administrative departments and individual entrepreneurs.

In the same way that it exploited government spending in general and government loans in particular, the ruling class exploited the *construction of railways*. Parliament heaped the main burdens on the state and secured the golden fruit for the speculating financial aristocracy. We recall the scandals in the Chamber of Deputies when by chance it came to light that all members of the majority, including a number of ministers, were stockholders in the same railway projects which, as legislators, they subsequently had carried out at state expense.

On the other hand, the smallest financial reforms came to grief as a result of the bankers' influence. Thus, for instance, Rothschild[14] protested, over the question of *postal reform*, whether the state was to be allowed to reduce the sources of revenue with which to pay interest on its ever-increasing debt.

The July monarchy was nothing more than a joint-stock company for the exploitation of France's national wealth, whose dividends were divided among ministers, parliament, 240,000 voters and their adherents. Louis Philippe was the director of this company – a Robert Macaire[15] of the throne. Commerce, industry, agriculture, shipping – the interests of the industrial

14. James, baron de Rothschild, head of the Paris banking house, possessed great political influence under the July monarchy.

15. Robert Macaire was the character created by the contemporary actor Frédérick Lemaître as a satire on the clever swindlers who flourished in this epoch.

bourgeoisie were inevitably in permanent peril and at a permanent disadvantage under this system. Cheap government, *gouvernement à bon marché*, is what it had written on its banner in the July days.

While the financial aristocracy made the laws, controlled the state administration, exercised authority in all public institutions, and controlled public opinion by actual events and through the press, the same prostitution, the same blatant swindling, the same mania for self-enrichment – not from production but by sleight-of-hand with other people's wealth – was to be found in all spheres of society, from the Court to the Café Borgne.[16] The same unbridled assertion of unhealthy and vicious appetites broke forth, appetites which were in permanent conflict with the bourgeois law itself, and which were to be found particularly in the upper reaches of society, appetites in which the wealth created by financial gambles seeks its natural fulfilment, in which pleasure becomes *crapuleux*,[17] in which money, filth and blood commingle. In the way it acquires wealth and enjoys it the financial aristocracy is nothing but the *lumpenproletariat reborn at the pinnacle of bourgeois society*.

And the non-ruling fractions of the French bourgeoisie cried, 'Corruption!' The people cried, '*À bas les grands voleurs! À bas les assassins!*'[18] when in 1847, on the most honoured stages of French society, the same scenes were publicly enacted which regularly lead the lumpenproletariat into brothels, workhouses, lunatic asylums, before the courts, into the dungeons and onto the scaffold.[19] The industrial bourgeoisie saw its interests endangered, the petty bourgeoisie was incensed, the popular imagination was outraged, Paris was inundated with pamphlets – *La dynastie Rothschild, Les juifs – rois de l'époque*, etc. – in which the rule of the financial aristocracy was denounced and castigated with varying degrees of wit.

Rien pour la gloire! Glory doesn't bring any profit. *La paix partout et toujours!*[20]

War lowers the prices of the 3 and 4 per cent bonds! This is what

16. This term was applied in Paris to disreputable bars and cafés.

17. Debauched.

18. 'Down with the great thieves! Down with the murderers!'

19. A number of high-level scandals occurred in France in 1847, including the suicide of the duc de Choiseul-Praslin, and the condemnation of Teste, former Minister of Public Works, for embezzlement.

20. 'Peace everywhere and always.'

the France of the stock-exchange sharks had inscribed on its banner. Its foreign policy thus dissolved in a series of insults to French national pride, and this national pride responded all the more vigorously as the rape of Poland ended with the annexation of Cracow by Austria and as Guizot became actively involved in the Swiss Sonderbund war on the side of the Holy Alliance. The victory of the Swiss liberals in this sham war strengthened the self-respect of the bourgeois opposition in France; the bloody revolt of the people in Palermo affected the paralysed mass of the people like an electric shock and reawakened their great revolutionary memories and passions.[21]

The outbreak of general discontent was finally accelerated and brought to the pitch of revolt by two economic events of world importance.

The *potato blight* and the *crop failures* of 1845 and 1846 aggravated the general ferment among the people. In France, as on the rest of the Continent, the rising prices of 1848 provoked bloody conflicts. While the people struggled for basic necessities, the financial aristocracy indulged in shameless orgies. In Buzançais starving rebels were executed,[22] in Paris surfeited *escrocs*[23] were snatched out of the hands of the courts by the royal family!

The second great economic event to accelerate the outbreak of the revolution was a *general commercial and industrial crisis* in England. Heralded as early as autumn 1845 by the wholesale ruin of speculators in railway shares, delayed during 1846 by a series of circumstantial factors such as the imminent abolition of the corn duties, this crisis finally broke out in autumn 1847 with the bankruptcies of the great London wholesale grocers. They were rapidly followed by the insolvencies of the land banks and the closure of factories in the English industrial districts. The after-effects of this crisis on the Continent were not yet at an end when the February revolution broke out.

21. Annexation of Cracow by Austria in agreement with Russia and Prussia on 11 November 1846; Swiss Sonderbund [separatist] war from 4 to 28 November 1847; rising in Palermo on 12 January 1848; at the end of January, a nine-day bombardment of the town by the Neapolitan regime. [*Note by Engels to the 1895 edition.*]

22. In January 1847, at Buzançais in central France, the starving local inhabitants attacked a consignment of corn supplies. This resulted in a battle with the troops, for which in March 1847 a number of rioters were condemned to death, and others to forced labour.

23. Swindlers.

The devastation of commerce and industry resulting from the economic epidemic made the rule of the financial aristocracy even more intolerable. Throughout France the bourgeois opposition campaigned for *electoral reform* with a series of banquets, aiming to win a parliamentary majority and overthrow the ministry of the Bourse. In Paris the industrial crisis had the particular effect of forcing a huge number of manufacturers and wholesale merchants, who could not conduct business with foreign markets under the existing circumstances, onto the domestic market. They set up large establishments, whose competition ruined masses of *épiciers* and *boutiquiers*.[24] Hence the innumerable bankruptcies among this section of the Paris bourgeoisie; hence their revolutionary behaviour in February. It is well known how Guizot and the Chambers replied to the proposed reforms with an unmistakable challenge, how Louis Philippe decided too late to form a government under Barrot,[25] how it came to hand-to-hand fighting between the people and the army, how the army was disarmed by the passive behaviour of the National Guard,[26] and how the July monarchy was forced to make way for a provisional government.

In its composition the Provisional Government which arose from the February barricades inevitably reflected the different parties who shared the victory. It could be nothing other than a *compromise between the various classes* who together overthrew the July monarchy, but whose interests were mutually hostile. In its *great majority* it consisted of representatives of the bourgeoisie: the republican petty bourgeoisie was represented by Ledru-Rollin and Flocon,[27] the republican bourgeoisie by the people

24. Grocers and small shopkeepers.

25. Odilon Barrot led the 'dynastic' opposition under the July monarchy, and was Prime Minister from December 1848 to October 1849.

26. The National Guard had existed since 1789, with some interruptions. As reorganized by Louis Philippe in 1831 it was limited to property-owning citizens. In 1848, however, it abandoned the July monarchy and joined the republican forces. It was democratized in February 1848 by the admission of all (male) citizens between the ages of 20 and 60.

27. Alexandre Ledru-Rollin was the editor of the newspaper *La Réforme* and the leader of the radical-democratic party. In 1848 he was Minister of the Interior in the Provisional Government, a member of the Executive Commission and a deputy in the Constituent Assembly. After 13 June 1849 he went into exile in England. Ferdinand Flocon was a journalist and politician, associated with the *Réforme*.

from the *National*,[28] the dynastic opposition by Crémieux, Dupont de l'Eure,[29] etc. The working class had only two representatives, Louis Blanc and Albert.[30] Finally, Lamartine's[31] presence in the Provisional Government did not really represent any actual interests, any particular class; he represented the February revolution itself, the common uprising with its illusions, its poetry, its imaginary content, and its phrases. But this spokesman of the February revolution also belonged to the *bourgeoisie* – both in his social position and in his views.

If Paris, as a result of political centralization, rules France, in moments of revolutionary upheaval the workers rule Paris. The Provisional Government's first act was to attempt to free itself from this overpowering influence by sending out an appeal from drunken Paris to sober France. Lamartine disputed the right of the barricade fighters to declare a republic: only a majority of the French people had that authority; their vote must be awaited, the Paris proletariat must not tarnish its victory by an attempt at usurpation. The bourgeoisie allows the proletariat only *one* form of usurpation – that of fighting.

At midday on 25 February the republic had still not been declared; however, the ministries had already been divided up among the bourgeois elements of the Provisional Government and among the generals, bankers and lawyers of the *National*. But this time the workers were determined not to tolerate any trickery like that of July 1830.[32] They were ready to take up the

28. See p. 63.

29. Adolphe Crémieux was a liberal lawyer who had gained a reputation in the 1840s for defending republicans; he was Minister of Justice from February to May 1848, and a member of both Assemblies from 1848 to 1851. Jacques Dupont de l'Eure, a veteran of the 1789 and 1830 revolutions, was the head of the Provisional Government.

30. Louis Blanc pioneered modern 'democratic socialism' with his scheme for self-governing 'National Workshops' set up by government action, which were gradually to supersede the capitalist economy. In August 1848 he went into exile in England. Albert was the pseudonym of Alexandre Martin, a metal worker and a member of republican secret societies under the July monarchy.

31. Alphonse de Lamartine, the poet and author of a history of the Girondins (1847), was a moderate republican with radical leanings. He was made Foreign Minister in the Provisional Government of February 1848 and appointed in May to the National Assembly's Executive Commission.

32. In July 1830 the Paris workers were the main force in the revolution that overthrew the Bourbon dynasty, but their aspirations for a republic were thwarted by the big bourgeoisie.

struggle again and to gain a republic by force of arms. Raspail[33] went to the Hôtel de Ville with this message. In the name of the Paris proletariat he *ordered* the Provisional Government to declare the republic; if this order from the people was not carried out within two hours he would return at the head of 200,000 men. The corpses of the fallen were scarcely cold, the barricades had not been cleared away, the workers had not been disarmed, and the only force with which they could be met was the National Guard. Under these circumstances the Provisional Government's reservations, arising from diplomatic considerations and its legal scruples, disappeared. The time limit of two hours had not passed and on all the walls of Paris the gigantic, historic words shone forth:

République française! Liberté, Égalité, Fraternité!

With the proclamation of the republic based on universal suffrage even the memory of the limited aims and motives which had driven the bourgeoisie into the February revolution was forgotten. Not just a few fractions of the bourgeoisie but all classes of French society were suddenly propelled into the arena of political power; they were forced to quit the boxes, the pit, the gallery and to act for themselves on the revolutionary stage! The illusion of an arbitrary state power confronting bourgeois society had disappeared with the constitutional monarchy, as had the whole series of subordinate struggles provoked by this illusory power!

By dictating the republic to the Provisional Government, and through the Provisional Government to the whole of France, the proletariat immediately came into the foreground as an independent party; but at the same time it challenged the whole of bourgeois France to enter the lists against it. What it conquered was the ground on which to struggle for its revolutionary emancipation, by no means this emancipation itself.

The first task of the February republic was rather to *complete the rule of the bourgeoisie,* by allowing *all the property-owning classes* to enter the political arena along with the financial aristocracy. The majority of the great landowners, the Legiti-

33. François-Vincent Raspail was a natural scientist and a democratic journalist with Blanquist leanings; he took part in both 1830 and 1848. He was elected a member of the Constituent Assembly in 1848, and in 1849 condemned to five years' imprisonment for his role in the June days of 1848 – a sentence later commuted to exile.

mists, were freed from the political impotence to which they had been condemned by the July monarchy. The *Gazette de France*[34] had not campaigned with the opposition papers in vain; neither had La Rochejacquelein[35] sided in vain with the revolution during the 24 February sitting of the Chamber of Deputies. As a result of universal suffrage the nominal property-owners, the peasants, who form the vast majority of the French people, had been made arbiters of the fate of France. The February republic finally allowed the unadulterated power of the bourgeoisie to emerge by knocking aside the crown behind which capital had concealed itself.

Just as the workers, in the July days, had fought for and won the *bourgeois monarchy*, so in the February days they fought for and won the *bourgeois republic*. Just as the July monarchy was forced to proclaim itself a *monarchy surrounded by republican institutions*, so the February republic was forced to proclaim itself a *republic surrounded by social institutions*. The proletariat *forced* this concession to be made, too.

Marche, a worker, dictated the decree in which the newly formed Provisional Government pledged itself to guarantee the workers a livelihood by means of labour, to provide all citizens with employment, etc. A few days later, when it had forgotten its promises and seemed to have lost sight of the proletariat, a mass of 20,000 workers marched on the Hôtel de Ville, with the demand, '*Organize labour! Let us form our own Ministry of Labour!*' Reluctantly, and after long debate, the Provisional Government appointed a permanent special commission charged with *finding* means of improving the situation of the working classes! This commission was composed of delegates from the Paris trade corporations and was presided over by Louis Blanc and Albert. The Luxembourg Palace was assigned to it as a meeting place. In this way the representatives of the working class were banished from the seat of the Provisional Government, the bourgeois part of which retained the real government power and the administrative reins exclusively in its own hands. *Alongside* the Ministries of Finance, Trade and Public Works, alongside the Bank and the Bourse a *socialist synagogue* arose, whose high priests, Louis Blanc and Albert, had the task of discovering the promised land,

34. The press organ of the Legitimist (i.e., pro-Bourbon) party.
35. Henri, marquis de La Rochejacquelein was a Legitimist politician, a member of both Assemblies and later a Senator under Napoleon III.

proclaiming the new gospel and giving work to the Paris proletariat. Unlike any profane state power they had no budget or
executive power at their disposal. They were supposed to dash the
supporting pillars of bourgeois society to the ground by running
their heads against them. While those in the Luxembourg sought
the philosophers' stone, in the Hôtel de Ville they minted the
coinage for circulation.

And yet it was impossible for the claims of the Paris proletariat – so far as they went beyond the bourgeois republic – to
assume any form other than the nebulous one provided by the
Luxembourg.

The workers had carried out the February revolution together
with the bourgeoisie, and they tried to secure their interests *alongside* the bourgeoisie, just as in the Provisional Government itself
they had installed a worker alongside the bourgeois majority.
Organize labour! But the bourgeois form of organized labour is
wage labour. Without it there would be no capital, no bourgeoisie,
no bourgeois society. The workers' *own Ministry of Labour*! But
the Ministries of Finance, Trade, Public Works – are these not
the *bourgeois* ministries of labour? *Alongside* them a *proletarian*
Ministry of Labour was bound to be a ministry of impotence, a
ministry of pious wishes, a Luxembourg Commission. Just as the
workers believed that they could emancipate themselves alongside the bourgeoisie, so they believed that they could accomplish
a proletarian revolution within the national walls of France
alongside the remaining bourgeois nations. But French relations
of production are determined by France's foreign trade, by its
position on the world market and by the laws of this market; how
was France to break these laws without a European revolutionary
war, which would have repercussions on the despot of the world
market, England?

As soon as it has risen up, a class in which the revolutionary
interests of society are concentrated finds the substance and material
of its revolutionary activity in its own immediate situation: enemies
to be struck down; measures to be taken, dictated by the needs of the
struggle – the consequences of its own actions drive it on. It does not
conduct theoretical investigations into its task. The French working
class was not in a position to do this; it was still incapable of carrying
out its own revolution.

In general, the development of the industrial proletariat is
conditioned by the development of the industrial bourgeoisie.

Only under the rule of the bourgeoisie does it begin to exist on a broad national basis, which elevates its revolution to a national one; only under the rule of the bourgeoisie does it create the modern means of production, which also become the means of its revolutionary liberation. It is only the rule of the bourgeoisie which serves to tear up the material roots of feudal society and level the ground, thus creating the only possible conditions for a proletarian revolution. French industry is more highly developed and the French bourgeoisie more revolutionary than that of the rest of the Continent. But was not the February revolution aimed directly against the financial aristocracy? This fact proves that the industrial bourgeoisie did not rule France. The industrial bourgeoisie can only rule when modern industry adapts all property relations to suit its own requirements, and industry can only achieve this power when it has conquered the world market, for national boundaries do not suffice for its development. By and large, however, French industry is only able to retain its control even of the domestic market by a more or less modified system of protective duties. Thus, although in Paris the French proletariat possesses enough real power and influence at the moment of revolution to spur it to efforts beyond its means, in the rest of France it is crowded together in separate and dispersed industrial centres, and is almost submerged by the predominance of peasant farmers and petty bourgeois. The struggle against capital in its highly developed modern form – at its crucial point, the struggle of the industrial wage-labourer against the industrial bourgeois – is in France a partial phenomenon, which, after the days of February, was not able to provide the national substance of a revolution. All the less so, as the struggle against secondary forms of capitalist exploitation – the struggle of the peasant against usury and mortgages, of the petty bourgeois against the wholesale merchant, banker and manufacturer, in a word, against bankruptcy – was still hidden in the general uprising against the financial aristocracy. Nothing is more easily explained, then, than the fact that the Paris proletariat attempted to secure its interests *alongside* those of the bourgeoisie, instead of asserting them as the revolutionary interests of society itself, and that it lowered the *red* flag before the tricolour. The French workers could not move a step forward, nor cause the slightest disruption in the bourgeois order, until the course of the revolution had aroused the mass of the nation, the peasants and the petty bourgeoisie, located between the proletariat and the bourgeoisie, against this order, against the rule of capital, and until it had forced them to join forces with their protagonists, the proletarians. The workers were only able to gain this victory at the price of the terrible defeat of June.

It remains to the credit of the Luxembourg Commission, this creation of the Paris workers, that it disclosed the secret of the revolution of the nineteenth century from a European platform: *the emancipation of the proletariat*. The *Moniteur*[36] could not help blushing when it had officially to propagate the 'wild ravings' which hitherto had lain buried in the apocryphal writings of the socialists and had only reached the ears of the bourgeoisie from time to time as remote legends, half-terrifying, half-ludicrous. Europe started up in surprise from its bourgeois doze. Thus, in the ideas of the proletarians, who confused the financial aristocracy with the bourgeoisie in general, in the imagination of republican worthies, who even denied the existence of classes or who at most admitted them to be the result of the constitutional monarchy, in the hypocritical phrases of those bourgeois fractions which had been excluded from power up to now, the *rule of the bourgeoisie* was abolished with the establishment of the republic. At that time all the royalists turned into republicans and all the millionaires of Paris turned into workers. The phrase which corresponded to this imaginary abolition of class relations was *fraternité*, general fraternization and brotherhood. This pleasant abstraction from class antagonisms, this sentimental reconciliation of contradictory class interests, this fantastic transcendence of the class struggle, this *fraternité* was the actual slogan of the February revolution. The classes had been divided by a mere *misunderstanding*, and Lamartine christened the Provisional Government of 24 February '*un gouvernement qui suspend* ce malentendu terrible qui existe entre les différentes classes'.[37] The Paris proletariat revelled in this magnanimous intoxication of brotherhood.

Having been forced to proclaim the republic, the Provisional Government, for its part, did everything to make it acceptable to

36. *Le Moniteur universel*, the official newspaper of successive French regimes from 1799 to 1869.

37. 'A government which removes *this terrible misunderstanding which exists between the different classes*'; speech in the Chamber of Deputies, 24 February 1848.

the bourgeoisie and to the provinces. The bloody terror of the first French republic was disavowed with the abolition of the death penalty for political crimes; the press was opened to all opinions; the army, the courts and administration remained, with few exceptions, in the hands of the old dignitaries; none of the great culprits of the July monarchy was called to account. The bourgeois republicans of the *National* enjoyed themselves exchanging monarchist names and customs for those of the First Republic. As far as they were concerned the republic was only a new evening dress for the old bourgeois society. The young republic sought its chief virtue not in frightening others but rather in constantly taking fright itself, and in disarming resistance and ensuring its further existence by its own soft compliance and lack of resistance. It was loudly announced to the privileged classes at home and the despotic powers abroad that the republic was of a peaceable nature. Its motto was: Live and let live. In addition, shortly after the February revolution the Germans, Poles, Austrians, Hungarians, Italians – all peoples revolted in a manner corresponding to their own situations. Russia and England – the former intimidated, the latter itself agitated – were unprepared. The republic, therefore, was not confronted by a *national* enemy. Consequently there were no great foreign complications to kindle energy, to accelerate the revolutionary process, to drive forward or throw overboard the Provisional Government.

The Paris proletariat, which saw in the republic its own creation, naturally acclaimed every act of the Provisional Government, making it easier for the latter to establish itself in bourgeois society. It willingly allowed itself to be used by Caussidière[38] for police services, to protect property in Paris, just as it allowed Louis Blanc to arbitrate in wage disputes between workers and masters. It was a *point d'honneur* to keep the bourgeois honour of the republic unsullied in the eyes of Europe.

The republic encountered no resistance either at home or abroad. As a result it was disarmed. Its task was no longer to transform the world by revolution but only to adapt itself to the conditions of bourgeois society. The fanaticism with which the

38. Marc Caussidière, a socialist-inclined revolutionary democrat who had taken part in conspiratorial activity under the July monarchy, was appointed Prefect of Police in Paris by the Provisional Government, and also elected to the Constituent National Assembly. After the defeat of the June insurrection he emigrated to England.

Provisional Government undertook this task is testified to most eloquently of all by its *financial measures*.

Both *public credit* and *private credit* were, of course, shaken. *Public credit* is based on the confidence that the state will allow itself to be exploited by the financial sharks. But the old state had disappeared and the revolution was primarily directed against the financial aristocracy. The vibrations from the last European commercial crisis had not yet died away. Bankruptcy still followed on bankruptcy.

Private credit was therefore paralysed, circulation restricted, production at a standstill before the February revolution broke out. The revolutionary crisis intensified the commercial crisis. And if private credit is based on the confidence that bourgeois production – the full range of relations of production – and bourgeois order are inviolable and will remain unviolated, what sort of effect must a revolution have which calls into question the basis of bourgeois production, the economic slavery of the proletariat, and which sets up in opposition to the Bourse the sphinx of the Luxembourg Commission? The revolt of the proletariat is the abolition of bourgeois credit, for it signifies the abolition of bourgeois production and its social order. Public and private credit are the thermometers by which the intensity of a revolution can be measured. *They fall, the more the passion and potency of the revolution rises.*

The Provisional Government wanted to strip the republic of its anti-bourgeois appearance. It had to attempt, therefore, to peg the *exchange value* of this new form of state and its *quotation* on the Bourse. Private credit inevitably rose together with the daily quotation of the republic on the Bourse.

In order to remove even the *suspicion* that it would not or could not honour the obligations accepted by the monarchy, in order to encourage confidence in the bourgeois morality and solvency of the republic, the Provisional Government resorted to a form of boasting as undignified as it was childish. It paid out the interest on the 5, 4½ and 4 per cent bonds *before* the legal date of payment. The bourgeois aplomb and self-confidence of the capitalists suddenly awoke when they saw the anxious haste with which the Provisional Government sought to buy their confidence.

The financial embarrassment of the Provisional Government was, of course, not diminished by a theatrical stroke which robbed it of its stocks of ready cash. The financial predicament could no longer be concealed and the *petty bourgeoisie, domestic servants* and *workers* had to pay for the pleasant surprise which had been prepared for the state creditors.

It was declared that amounts exceeding one hundred francs could no longer be drawn on savings bank books. The sums of money deposited in the savings banks were confiscated and transformed by decree into an irredeemable national debt. In this way the *petty bourgeois*, who was already hard pressed, was embittered against the republic. As he received state debt certificates in place of his savings bank books he was forced to go to the Bourse to sell them, and thus to deliver himself up to the hands of the financial sharks against whom he had conducted the February revolution.

The financial aristocracy, which ruled under the July monarchy, had its high church in the Bank. Just as the Bourse controls state credit, the Bank controls commercial credit.

As it was directly threatened by the February revolution, not merely in its rule but in its very existence, the Bank tried from the outset to discredit the republic by fostering a general lack of credit. It suddenly terminated the credit of bankers, manufacturers and merchants. As this manoeuvre did not immediately provoke a counter-revolution it inevitably reacted on the Bank itself. The capitalists withdrew the money which they had deposited in the vaults of the Bank. The holders of banknotes rushed to its counter in order to change them for gold and silver.

The Provisional Government could have legally forced the Bank into bankruptcy without violently interfering in its dealings; it only needed to remain passive and to leave the Bank to its fate. The *bankruptcy of the Bank* would have been the deluge which in a trice would have swept from the soil of France the financial aristocracy, the mightiest and most dangerous enemy of the republic, the golden pedestal of the July monarchy. And once the Bank was bankrupt the bourgeoisie itself would have been forced to regard it as a last desperate chance of salvation if the government had formed a national bank and had placed national credit under the supervision of the nation.

But, on the contrary, the Provisional Government established a *compulsory rate* for the Bank's notes. It did more; it transformed all provincial banks into branches of the Banque de France and allowed it to cast its net over the whole of France. Later it pledged the *state forests* to the Bank as a guarantee for a loan which it contracted from it. Thus, the February revolution directly consolidated and extended the bankocracy which it was supposed to overthrow.

Meanwhile the Provisional Government was writhing under the incubus of a growing deficit. It begged in vain for patriotic sacrifices. Only the workers threw it alms. A new heroic step had to be taken: the imposition of a *new tax*. But who was to be taxed? The stock-exchange sharks, the Bank kings, the state creditors, the *rentiers*, the industrialists? That was not the way for the republic to curry favour with the bourgeoisie. It would have meant on the one hand endangering state and commercial credit, on the other hand, trying to purchase them with such great sacrifices and humiliations. But somebody had to cough up. Who was sacrificed to bourgeois credit? *Jacques le bonhomme*, the peasant.

The Provisional Government imposed a surcharge of 45 centimes in the franc on the four direct taxes. The government press tried to make the Paris proletariat believe that the new tax would primarily hit the big landed proprietors, the recipients of the milliard francs compensation paid by fiat of the Restoration.[39] But in reality it hit the *peasant class* above all, that is, the great majority of the French people. *It was they who had to pay the costs of the February revolution*, and among them the counter-revolution found its main material. The 45-centimes tax was a question of life and death for the French peasant; he made it a question of life and death for the republic. For the French peasant the republic represented, from this moment on, the 45-centimes tax, and in the Paris proletariat he saw the wastrel who was making himself comfortable at *his* expense.

While the revolution of 1789 began by relieving the peasant of his feudal burdens, the revolution of 1848 introduced itself to the rural population by levying a new tax, in order not to endanger capital and in order to keep the machinery of state running.

There was only *one* way for the Provisional Government to remove all these difficulties and force the state to change course – *declaring state bankruptcy*. The reader will remember how in the National Assembly Ledru-Rollin subsequently told of the virtuous indignation with which he had rejected this presumptuous

39. In 1825 the Restoration regime decreed this sum in compensation to the aristocratic landowners whose property had been confiscated during the first French revolution.

suggestion from the stock-exchange shark Fould,[40] the present French Minister of Finance. Fould had handed him the apple from the tree of knowledge.

The Provisional Government had succumbed to the old bourgeois society by honouring the bills which it had drawn on the state. It had become the harassed debtor of this bourgeois society instead of facing it as a threatening creditor, who had to collect the revolutionary debts of many years' standing. It had to strengthen the shaky structure of bourgeois relationships, in order to fulfil obligations which need only be fulfilled in the context of these relationships. Credit became a condition of its existence, and the concessions and promises made to the proletariat became just so many *fetters* which it *had to* break free of. The emancipation of the workers – even as a *phrase* – became intolerably dangerous for the republic, for it represented a permanent protest against the restoration of credit, which is based on the untroubled and unqualified acceptance of the existing economic class relationships. It was necessary, therefore, *to have done with the workers*.

The February revolution had thrown the army out of Paris. The National Guard, that is, the bourgeoisie in its various social gradations, was the only power. However, alone it did not feel itself a match for the proletariat. Moreover, gradually and piecemeal it was obliged to open its ranks and allow armed proletarians to join, albeit after the fiercest resistance and after creating a hundred different obstacles. Consequently there remained only one way out: *to set one section of the proletariat against the other*.

For this purpose the Provisional Government formed twenty-four battalions of Mobile Guards, each composed of a thousand young men between fifteen and twenty. For the most part they belonged to the lumpenproletariat, which, in all towns, forms a mass quite distinct from the industrial proletariat. It is a recruiting ground for thieves and criminals of all sorts, living off the garbage of society, people without a definite trace, vagabonds, *gens sans feu et sans aveu*,[41] varying according to the cultural level of their particular nation, never able to repudiate their *lazzaroni* character; during their youthful years – the age at which the Provisional Government recruited them – they are thoroughly tractable,

40. Achille Fould was a banker and Orleanist politician who switched his allegiance to Bonaparte in 1849. He sat in the Constitutional Assembly, and was Minister of Finance 1849–60 and 1861–7.

41. People without hearth or home.

capable of the greatest acts of heroism and the most exalted self-sacrifice as well as the lowest forms of banditry and the foulest corruption. The Provisional Government paid them 1 franc 50 centimes a day; that is, it bought them. It gave them their own uniform, thereby distinguishing them outwardly from the blouses of the workers. In part it assigned officers from the standing army to lead them and in part they themselves elected young sons of the bourgeoisie, who entranced them with rodomontades about dying for the fatherland and devotion to the republic.

Thus the Paris proletariat was confronted by an army of 24,000 youthful, strong, foolhardy men, drawn from its own midst. The workers *cheered* the Mobile Guard as it marched through Paris! They recognized in it their protagonists on the barricades. They regarded it as the *proletarian* guard in contrast to the bourgeois National Guard. Their error was pardonable.

Besides the Mobile Guard the government decided to rally around itself an army of industrial workers. Minister Marie[42] enrolled hundreds of thousands of workers thrown on the streets by the crisis and the revolution into so-called National Workshops. Hidden behind this grandiose name was nothing other than the use of workers for tedious, monotonous, unproductive *earthworks* for a daily wage of 23 sous. *English workhouses in the open* – this is all these National Workshops were. In them the Provisional Government thought it had formed *a second proletarian army against the workers*. However, the bourgeoisie was mistaken in the National Workshops, just as the workers were mistaken in the Mobile Guard. It had created an *army for mutiny*.

But *one* object was achieved.

National Workshops was also the term used for the people's workshops which Louis Blanc preached about in the Luxembourg Palace. By virtue of their common designation the Marie workshops, which were planned in direct *opposition* to the Luxembourg proposals, presented the occasion for a plot of errors worthy of a Spanish servants' comedy.[43] The Provisional Government itself

42. Alexandre Marie de Saint-Georges, a lawyer and bourgeois republican politician, was Minister of Public Works in the Provisional Government of 1848, Chairman of the Constituent National Assembly, and Minister of Justice in Cavaignac's government (October–December 1848).

43. In the seventeenth-century comedies of Lope de Vega and Calderón, a humorous effect was often obtained by masters' masquerading as their servants and *vice versa*.

surreptitiously spread the rumour that these National Workshops were the invention of Louis Blanc, and this seemed all the more plausible as Louis Blanc, the prophet of national workshops, was a member of the Provisional Government. And in the half-naïve, half-deliberate confusion of the Paris bourgeoisie, in the artificially moulded public opinion of France and Europe, these *workhouses*[44] were seen as the first realization of socialism, which was pilloried together with the National Workshops.

It was not in what they were but in their name that the National Workshops embodied the protest of the proletariat against bourgeois industry, bourgeois credit and the bourgeois republic. As a result the whole hatred of the bourgeoisie descended upon them. In the National Workshops it had also found the target against which it could direct its attack as soon as it had gathered its strength sufficiently to break openly with the February illusions. All dissatisfaction, all resentment on the part of the *petty bourgeois* was also directed against these National Workshops, which became the common target. With veritable fury they reckoned up the money which the proletarian idlers were consuming while their own situation was becoming more intolerable day by day. 'A state income for sham work – so that's socialism!' they grumbled to themselves. They sought the reason for their predicament in the National Workshops, the declamations of the Luxembourg Commission, the processions of workers marching through Paris. And nobody was more fanatical about the alleged machinations of the communists than the petty bourgeois, who tottered helplessly on the brink of bankruptcy.

Thus, in the approaching fray between bourgeoisie and proletariat all the advantages, all decisive positions, all the middle strata of society were in the hands of the bourgeoisie, at the same time as the waves of the February revolution broke high over the whole Continent and every postal delivery brought a fresh report of revolution, now from Italy, now from Germany, now from the remotest south-east of Europe, and sustained the general intoxication of the people by delivering continual testimony of a victory which it had already forfeited.

17 March and *16 April* saw the first skirmishes in the great class struggle which the bourgeois republic hid beneath its wing.

17 March revealed the ambiguous situation of the proletariat, which prevented it from taking any decisive action. Its demonstra-

44. In English in the original.

tion was originally intended to drive the Provisional Government back onto a revolutionary course, if possible, to bring about the exclusion of its bourgeois members and to force the postponement of the election dates for the National Assembly and the general staff of the National Guard.[45] But on 16 March the bourgeoisie represented in the National Guard organized a hostile demonstration directed against the Provisional Government. Shouting '*À bas Ledru-Rollin!*' it forced its way to the Hôtel de Ville. And on 17 March the people were forced to shout, 'Long live Ledru-Rollin! Long live the Provisional Government!' They were forced to take sides with the bourgeois republic, which seemed to be in danger, *against* the bourgeoisie. The people strengthened the position of the Provisional Government instead of seizing control of it. 17 March fizzled out in a melodramatic scene, and although the Paris proletariat once again displayed its giant body on this day, the bourgeoisie both inside and outside the Provincial Government was all the more determined to break it.

16 April was a *misunderstanding* engineered by the Provisional Government with the help of the bourgeoisie. The workers had gathered in large numbers on the Champ de Mars and in the Hippodrome in order to prepare for the elections for the general staff of the National Guard. Suddenly the rumour spread from one end of Paris to the other, with lightning speed, that the workers had armed themselves and gathered on the Champ de Mars, led by Louis Blanc, Blanqui,[46] Cabet[47] and Raspail, with the intention of marching from there to the Hôtel de Ville to overthrow the Provisional Government and to proclaim a communist government. The general alarm was sounded – later Ledru-Rollin, Marrast[48] and Lamartine all fought for the honour of having taken this initiative – and within one hour 100,000 men

45. This demonstration was organized by Blanqui and his party, who hoped to delay the elections, due on 9 April and 18 April respectively, until they had won over a greater section of the plebeian classes.

46. Auguste Blanqui was the outstanding French workers' leader of the nineteenth century, but still believed that the overthrow of the bourgeois state could be accomplished by conspiratorial means. See the Introduction to *The Revolutions of 1848*, pp. 24–5.

47. Étienne Cabet was the author of the communist utopia *Voyage en Icarie*.

48. Armand Marrast, a journalist and bourgeois republican, was editor-in-chief of *Le National* (see below, p. 63). After the February revolution he became a member of the Provisional Government and Mayor of Paris, and later chairman of the Constituent National Assembly.

were under arms, the Hôtel de Ville was occupied at all points by the National Guard, the cry, 'Down with the Communists! Down with Louis Blanc, Blanqui, Raspail, Cabet!' thundered through Paris and innumerable deputations paid homage to the Provisional Government, all of them ready to save the fatherland and society. When the workers finally appeared in front of the Hôtel de Ville to hand the Provisional Government a patriotic collection, taken at the Champ de Mars, they learnt to their amazement that bourgeois Paris had defeated their shadow in a carefully conducted mock battle. The terrible attempt of 16 April furnished the pretext *for the recall of the army to Paris* – the actual purpose of this clumsily arranged farce – and for reactionary federalist demonstrations in the provinces.

The National Assembly, elected by *direct, universal suffrage*, was convened on 4 May. Universal suffrage did not possess the magical power attributed to it by republicans of the old school. They saw throughout France, at least among the majority of Frenchmen, *citoyens* with the same interests, views, etc. This was their *cult of the people*. Instead of their *imaginary* people the electors revealed the *real* people, that is, the representatives of the different classes which comprised the people. We have seen why the peasants and petty bourgeois had to vote under the leadership of bourgeois spoiling for a fight and big landowners thirsty for restoration. But although universal suffrage was not the miracle-working magic wand which the republican worthies had assumed, it possessed the incomparably greater merit of unleashing the class struggle, of allowing the various middle strata of bourgeois society to get over their illusions and disappointments, of propelling all fractions of the exploiting class at one go to the heights of state power and thus tearing off their deceitful masks, while the monarchy, with its electoral system based on property qualifications, only allowed particular fractions of the bourgeoisie to compromise themselves, while it kept the others concealed backstage and adorned them with the halo of a common opposition.

In the Constituent National Assembly which met on 4 May the *bourgeois republicans*, the republicans of the *National*, had the upper hand. Even Legitimists and Orleanists at first only dared show themselves under the mask of bourgeois republicanism. The battle against the proletariat could only be joined in the name of the republic.

The republic dates from 4 May, not from 25 February – that is, the republic recognized by the French people; this is not the republic which the Paris proletariat thrust upon the Provisional Government, not the republic with social institutions, not the vision which hovered before the fighters on the barricades. The republic proclaimed by the National Assembly, the only legitimate republic, is not a revolutionary weapon against the bourgeois order but rather its political reconstitution, the political reconsolidation of bourgeois society – in a word, *the bourgeois republic*. This assertion rang out from the rostrum of the National Assembly and was re-echoed in the whole republican and anti-republican bourgeois press.

As we have seen, the February republic was in reality – and could be nothing else but – a *bourgeois* republic, but the Provisional Government was forced by direct pressure of the proletariat to proclaim it a *republic with social institutions*. The Paris proletariat was still incapable, except in its *imagination*, in its *fantasy*, of moving beyond the bourgeois republic; when it came to action it invariably acted in the service of the republic. The promises made to the proletariat came to represent an intolerable danger for the new republic, and the Provisional Government's entire existence took the form of a struggle against the demands of the proletariat.

In the National Assembly all France sat in judgement upon the Paris proletariat. The Assembly immediately broke with the social illusions of the February revolution; without beating about the bush it proclaimed the *bourgeois republic*, nothing but the bourgeois republic. It immediately excluded Louis Blanc and Albert, the representatives of the proletariat, from the Executive Commission which it appointed; it rejected the suggestion of a special Ministry of Labour; it received with stormy acclamation the statement by Minister Trélat:[49] 'It is now merely a question of *re-establishing labour on its old basis.*'

But all this was not enough. The February republic had been fought for and won by the workers with the passive assistance of the bourgeoisie. The proletarians rightly regarded themselves as the victors of February, and they made the arrogant claims of victors. They had to be defeated on the streets, they had to be shown that they would be defeated as soon as they fought not

49. Ulysse Trélat, a doctor and bourgeois republican, was deputy chairman of the Constituent National Assembly in 1848 and Minister of Public Works from May to June.

with but *against* the bourgeoisie. Just as the February republic with its socialist concessions had needed a battle conducted by the proletariat united with the bourgeoisie against the monarchy, a second battle was necessary in order to sever the republic from these socialist concessions, to assert the official dominance of the *bourgeois republic*. The bourgeoisie had to reject the demands of the proletariat arms in hand. The real birthplace of the bourgeois republic was not the *February victory* but the *June defeat*.

The proletariat accelerated the decision when it forced its way into the National Assembly on 15 May, seeking in vain to recapture its revolutionary influence, and only succeeded in handing over its energetic leaders to the jailors of the bourgeoisie.[50] *Il faut en finir!* This situation must end! With this cry the National Assembly gave vent to its determination to force the proletariat to the decisive battle. The Executive Commission issued a series of provocative decrees, such as the prohibition of public meetings, etc. From the rostrum of the Constituent National Assembly the workers were directly provoked, insulted and derided. But, as we have seen, the National Workshops represented the actual point of attack. Imperiously, the Constituent National Assembly brought them to the attention of the Executive Commission, which was only waiting to hear its own plan announced as the decree of the National Assembly.

The Executive Commission began by making entry into the National Workshops more difficult, by replacing the day wage by piece-work, by banishing workers not born in Paris to the Sologne, ostensibly for the construction of earthworks. These earthworks were only a rhetorical formula with which to disguise their expulsion, as the workers announced to their comrades when they returned, disillusioned. Finally, on 21 June a decree appeared in the *Moniteur* which ordered the forcible expulsion of all unmarried workers from the National Workshops, or their enrolment in the army.

The workers were left with no choice; they had either to starve or to strike out. They answered on 22 June with the gigantic insurrection, in which the first great battle was fought between the two great classes which divide modern society. It was a fight for

50. On 15 May Blanqui and the proletarian party led a mass assault on the newly elected National Assembly, aiming to overthrow it and set up a new Provisional Government. After the assault was repulsed by the National Guard, Blanqui, Barbès, Albert and Raspail were all arrested.

the preservation or destruction of the *bourgeois* order. The veil which shrouded the republic was torn asunder.

It is well known how the workers, with unheard-of bravery and ingenuity, without leaders, without a common plan, without supplies, and for the most part lacking weapons, held in check the army, the Mobile Guard, the Paris National Guard and the National Guard which streamed in from the provinces, for five days. It is well known how the bourgeoisie sought compensation for the mortal terror it had suffered in outrageous brutality, massacring over 3,000 prisoners.

The official representatives of French democracy were so immersed in republican ideology that the meaning of the June battle only began to dawn on them after a few weeks. It was as though they were stupefied by the powder and smoke in which their fantastic republic dissolved.

The immediate impression which the news of the June defeat made on us, the reader will allow us to describe in the words of the *Neue Rheinische Zeitung*.[51]

The last official remnant of the February revolution, the Executive Commission,[52] has melted away like an apparition before the seriousness of events. Lamartine's fireworks[53] have turned into Cavaignac's[54] incendiary rockets. '*Fraternité*', the brotherhood of opposing classes, one of which exploits the other, this '*fraternité*' was proclaimed in February and written in capital letters on the brow of Paris, on every prison and every barracks. But its true, genuine, prosaic expression is *civil war* in its most terrible form, the war between labour and capital. This fraternity flamed up in front of all the windows of Paris on the evening of 25 June. The Paris of the bourgeoisie was illuminated, while the Paris of the proletariat burned, bled and moaned in its death agony.

Fraternity lasted only as long as there was a fraternity of interests between bourgeoisie and proletariat. Pedants of the old revolutionary traditions of 1793; constructors of socialist systems, who went begging to the bourgeoisie on behalf of the people, and who were allowed to

51. The following passage is quoted from 'The June Revolution', *The Revolutions of 1848*, pp. 130–31. It was first published in the *Neue Rheinische Zeitung* of 29 June 1848.

52. The Executive Commission set up by the Constituent Assembly replaced the Provisional Government on 10 May 1848 and lasted until 24 June.

53. An allusion to Lamartine's fiery declarations to the European governments.

54. Louis-Eugène Cavaignac, a general and moderate republican, was made Minister of War in May 1848, and in June was given dictatorial powers to suppress the Paris insurrection.

preach long sermons and to compromise themselves as long as the proletarian lion had to be lulled to sleep[55]; republicans, who wanted to keep the whole of the old bourgeois order, but remove the crowned head; supporters of the dynastic opposition, upon whom chance had foisted the fall of a dynasty instead of a change of ministers; Legitimists, who wanted not to cast aside the livery but to change its cut: all these were the allies with whom the people made its February. . . .

The February revolution was the *beautiful* revolution, the revolution of universal sympathy, because the conflicts which erupted in the revolution against the monarchy slumbered harmoniously side by side, as yet *undeveloped*, because the social struggle which formed its background had only assumed an airy existence – it existed only as a phrase, only in words. The June revolution is the *ugly* revolution, the repulsive revolution, because realities have taken the place of words, because the republic has uncovered the head of the monster itself by striking aside the protective, concealing crown.

Order! was Guizot's battle-cry. *Order!* screamed Sébastiani,[56] Guizot's follower, when Warsaw became Russian. *Order!* screamed Cavaignac, the brutal echo of the French National Assembly and the republican bourgeoisie. *Order!* thundered his grapeshot, as it lacerated the body of the proletariat.

None of the innumerable revolutions of the French bourgeoisie since 1789 was an attack on *order*; for they perpetuated class rule, the slavery of the workers, *bourgeois* order, no matter how frequent the changes in the political form of this rule and this slavery. June has violated this order. Woe unto June!

'Woe unto June!' the echo resounds from Europe.

The Paris proletariat was *forced* into the June insurrection by the bourgeoisie. This in itself sealed its fate. It was neither impelled by its immediate, avowed needs to fight for the overthrow of the bourgeoisie by force, nor was it equal to this task. It had to be officially informed by the *Moniteur* that the time was past when the republic found itself obliged to show deference to its illusions; only its defeat convinced it of the truth that the smallest improvement in its position remains a *utopia* within the bourgeois republic, a utopia which becomes a crime as soon as it aspires to become

55. See *Manifesto of the Communist Party*, section III, 3; *The Revolutions of 1848*, pp. 94–7.

56. Horace, comte Sébastiani, was the French Minister of Foreign Affairs from 1830 to 1832. In 1831 he refused to protest against the tsar's suppression of the Polish revolution and called for a return by both parties to the treaty settlement of 1815. By this the greater part of Poland formed part of the Russian empire, with the tsar as its king.

reality. In place of demands which were exuberant in form but petty and even bourgeois in content, which it had hoped to wring from the February republic, the bold, revolutionary battle-cry appeared: *Overthrow of the bourgeoisie! Dictatorship of the working class!*

By making its burial place the birthplace of the *bourgeois republic*, the proletariat forced this republic to appear in its pure form, as the state whose avowed purpose it is to perpetuate the rule of capital and the slavery of labour. Permanently aware of its scarred, irreconcilable and invincible enemy – invincible because its existence is a precondition of its own life – bourgeois rule, freed from all fetters, was inevitably transformed, all at once, into bourgeois terrorism. Now that the proletariat was temporarily removed from the stage and the dictatorship of the bourgeoisie officially recognized, the middle strata of bourgeois society, the petty bourgeoisie and the peasant class, were obliged to ally themselves with the proletariat, as their own situation became more intolerable and their antagonism to the bourgeoisie sharper. As they had earlier sought the cause of their misfortune in the rise of the working class, they were now compelled to find it in its defeat.

If the June insurrection increased the self-confidence of the bourgeoisie all over the Continent and led it into an open alliance with the feudal monarchy against the people, who was the first victim of this alliance? The continental bourgeoisie itself. The June defeat prevented it from consolidating its rule and from bringing the people, half-satisfied, half-discontented, to a standstill at the lowest stage of the bourgeois revolution.

The June defeat finally betrayed to the despotic powers of Europe the secret that France must, at all costs, maintain peace abroad in order to be able to conduct civil war at home. Thus the peoples who had begun their struggle for national independence were abandoned to the superior power of Russia, Austria and Prussia, but at the same time the fate of these national revolutions was made subject to the fate of the proletarian revolution and they were robbed of their apparent autonomy, their independence of the great social upheaval. The Hungarian, the Pole, the Italian shall not be free as long as the worker remains a slave!

Finally, with the victories of the Holy Alliance, Europe has assumed a form in which any new proletarian uprising in France will immediately coincide with a *world war*. The new French revolution will be forced to leave its natural soil immediately and to *conquer the European* terrain, on which alone the social revolution of the nineteenth century can be carried out.

It is only as a result of the June defeat, therefore, that all the conditions have been created under which France can seize the *initiative* of the European revolution. Only since it has been dipped in the blood of the *June insurgents* has the tricolour become the flag of the European revolution – *the red flag*!

And we cry, *The revolution is dead! – Long live the revolution!*

II. 13 JUNE 1849

From June 1848 to 13 June 1849

25 February 1848 had brought France the *republic*; 25 June thrust *revolution* upon her. And whereas before February revolution had meant *the overthrow of the form of government*, after June it meant *the overthrow of bourgeois society*.

The June struggle had been led by the *republican* fraction of the bourgeoisie; as a result of its victory political power inevitably fell into its hands. The state of siege laid Paris at its feet, gagged and unable to resist; a moral state of siege prevailed in the provinces, which were ruled by the threatening, brutal arrogance of the victorious bourgeoisie and the unbounded property fanaticism of the peasants. There was no danger, therefore, from *below*!

Together with the revolutionary power of the workers the political influence of the *democratic republicans* was also broken – the republicans, that is, in the sense of the *petty bourgeoisie*, which was represented in the Executive Committee by Ledru-Rollin, in the Constituent National Assembly by the party of the Montagne[57] and in the press by the *Réforme*. On 16 April they had conspired together with the bourgeois republicans against the proletariat; in the June days they had jointly waged war against it. As a result, they themselves demolished the very basis on which their party existed as a power, for the petty bourgeoisie can only maintain a revolutionary attitude towards the bourgeoisie as long as the proletariat stands behind it. They were dismissed. The sham alliance which the bourgeois republicans had reluctantly and perfidiously made with them during the period of the Provisional

57. The radical-democratic party in the Second Republic (1848–51) was known as the Montagne (Mountain), after the name given to the Jacobin party in the First Republic.

Government and the Executive Commission was openly broken. Scorned and rejected as allies, they were reduced to the level of satellites to the men of the tricolour, from whom they could wring no concessions but whose rule they had to support whenever this rule, and with it the republic, seemed to be threatened by the anti-republican fractions of the bourgeoisie. Lastly, these fractions, the Orleanists and the Legitimists, were from the outset in the minority in the Constituent National Assembly. Before the June days they themselves only dared react beneath the mask of bourgeois republicanism; the June victory led the whole of bourgeois France for the moment to hail its saviour in the person of Cavaignac, and when, shortly after the June days, the anti-republican party re-established its independence, the military dictatorship and the state of siege in Paris only allowed it to stretch out its feelers very timidly and cautiously.

Since 1830 the *bourgeois republican* fraction, its writers, its spokesmen, its authorities, its men of ambition, its deputies, generals, bankers and lawyers, had gathered around a Paris journal, *Le National*. It had its subsidiary newspapers in the provinces. The coterie around the *National* represented the *dynasty of the tricolour republic*. It immediately took possession of all state dignities, the ministries, the prefecture of police, the post office directorship, the positions of prefect, the senior officers' posts now vacant in the army. At the head of the executive power stood its general, Cavaignac; its editor-in-chief, Marrast, became the permanent chairman of the Constituent National Assembly. As master of ceremonies he also did the honours of the worthy republic in his salons.

Even revolutionary French writers, awed, as it were, by the republican tradition, have reinforced the erroneous belief that in the Constituent National Assembly the royalists held sway. On the contrary, after the June days the Constituent Assembly remained the *exclusive representative of bourgeois republicanism*, and this aspect was all the more accentuated as the influence of the tricolour republicans outside the Assembly collapsed. In so far as it was a question of maintaining the *form* of the bourgeois republic the Assembly had the votes of the democratic republicans at its disposal; in so far as it was a question of maintaining the *substance*, then not even its manner of speech distinguished it any longer from the royalist fractions of the bourgeoisie, for it is precisely the interests of the bourgeoisie, the material conditions of its class rule and class exploitation, which form the substance of the bourgeois republic.

It was not royalism, therefore, but bourgeois republicanism which found expression in the life and activities of this Constituent Assembly, which, in the end, did not die and was not killed off, but simply decayed.

Throughout the duration of its rule, as long as it occupied the centre of the stage with its grand state drama, an uninterrupted sacrificial ceremony was being performed in the background – the June insurgents who had been taken prisoner were continually being sentenced by court martial or deported without trial. The Constituent National Assembly had the tact to admit that in the case of the June insurgents it was not trying criminals but crushing enemies.

The first act of the Constituent National Assembly was the appointment of a commission of inquiry into the events of June and 15 May and into the part played by the socialist and democratic party leaders during these days. The inquiry was aimed directly at Louis Blanc, Ledru-Rollin and Caussidière. The bourgeois republicans were burning with impatience to get rid of these rivals. They could not have entrusted the execution of their vengeance to any more suitable individual than M. Odilon Barrot, the former leader of the dynastic opposition, the embodiment of liberalism, the *nullité grave*,[58] the thorough nonentity, who had not only to revenge a dynasty but also to settle with the revolution for thwarting his period of office as premier. This was a sure guarantee of the inexorability of his vengeance. This same Barrot, then, was appointed chairman of the commission of inquiry and he instituted regular legal proceedings against the February revolution, which may be summarized as follows: 17 March, *demonstration*, 16 April, *conspiracy*, 15 May, *attempt*, 23 June, *civil war*! Why did he not extend his learned judicial investigations as far back as 24 February? The *Journal des Débats* answered that 24 February was the *founding of Rome*.[59] The origin of states becomes lost in a myth which must be believed and not discussed. Louis Blanc and Caussidière were handed over to the courts. The National Assembly completed the task of purging itself which it had begun on 15 May.

58. Pompous nobody.

59. A reference to the leader of 28 August; the *Journal des Débats* was the leading Orleanist paper.

The Provisional Government's plan of taxing capital by means of a mortgage tax – taken up again by Goudchaux[60] – was rejected by the Constituent Assembly; the law limiting the working day to ten hours was repealed; imprisonment for debt was reintroduced; the large majority of the French population, which can neither read nor write, was excluded from jury service. Why not from the franchise also? The deposit of caution money by journals was reintroduced; restrictions were imposed on the right of association.

But in their haste to provide the old bourgeois order with its old guarantees, and to erase every trace left behind by the revolutionary tide, the bourgeois republicans encountered a resistance which provided an unexpected threat.

No one had fought with more fanaticism in the June days for the salvation of property and the restoration of credit than the Parisian petty bourgeoisie – café and restaurant proprietors, *marchands de vins*, small traders, shopkeepers, craftsmen, etc. The shopkeeper had gathered his strength and had marched on the barricade in order to restore the flow of business from the street into the shop. But behind the barricade stood the customers and the debtors; in front of it the creditors. And when the barricades had been pulled down, the workers crushed, and the shop-keepers rushed back to their shops, drunk with victory, they found their entrances barricaded by one of the saviours of property, an official agent from the powers of credit, who handed them threatening notices: Overdue promissory notes! Overdue rents! Overdue bonds! Indeed, time had also run out for both shop and shopkeeper!

Salvation of property! But the houses in which they lived were not their property; the shops which they kept were not their property; the goods in which they dealt were not their property. Neither their business, nor the plate from which they ate, nor the bed in which they slept belonged to them any longer. They were the ones from whom *this property had to be saved* – in the interests of the house-owner who had let the house, the banker who had discounted the promissory notes, the capitalist who had advanced the cash, the manufacturer who had entrusted the goods to these shopkeepers for sale, the wholesale dealer who had sold the raw materials to the craftsmen on credit. *Restoration of credit!* But,

60. Michel Goudchaux, a banker and bourgeois republican, had been Minister of Finance in the Provisional Government.

having gathered its strength, credit proved to be a vigorous and jealous god, driving the insolvent debtor out of his four walls with wife and child, handing his supposed property over to capital and throwing the man himself into the debtors' prison, which had once more cast its threatening shadow over the corpses of the June insurgents.

The petty bourgeoisie realized with horror that by crushing the workers they had delivered themselves unresisting into the hands of their creditors. Since February their creeping bankruptcy, which they had apparently ignored, had become chronic, and after June it was declared openly.

Their *nominal property* had been left unchallenged as long as it had been a question of driving them to the battlefield *in the name of property*. Now that the great issue with the proletariat had been settled, the small business with the shopkeepers could be settled in turn. In Paris the mass of paper in default amounted to over 21 million francs, in the provinces to over 11 million. The proprietors of more than 7,000 Paris firms had not paid their rent since February.

While the National Assembly had set up an inquiry into the *political guilt*, which went back as far as the end of February, the petty bourgeoisie, for its part, now demanded an inquiry into the *civil debts* up to 24 February. They assembled *en masse* in the vestibule of the Bourse, and for every merchant who could prove that his insolvency was due solely to the commercial stagnation caused by the revolution and that his business had been on a sound footing on 24 February, they demanded with threats an extension of the period of payment by decree of the commercial court and an order compelling creditors to liquidate their claims in return for a moderate percentage payment. This question was debated as a legislative proposal in the National Assembly in the form of the '*concordats à l'amiable*'. The Assembly vacillated; then it suddenly learnt that at that moment at the Porte St Denis thousands of wives and children of the June insurgents had prepared a petition requesting an amnesty.

In the presence of the resurrected spectre of June the petty bourgeoisie trembled; the National Assembly recovered its implacable spirit. The main points of the *concordats à l'amiable*, the 'amicable agreements' between creditor and debtor, were rejected.

Thus, long after the democratic representatives of the petty bourgeoisie had been repulsed by the republican representatives of the bourgeoisie in the National Assembly, the actual economic significance of this parliamentary split became manifest in the sacrifice of the petty-bourgeois debtors to the bourgeois creditors. A large section of the petty bourgeoisie was completely ruined, and the rest were only allowed to continue their business on conditions which made them the absolute serfs of capital. On 22 August 1848 the National Assembly rejected the *concordats à l'amiable*; on 19 September 1848, in the middle of a state of siege, the prince, Louis Bonaparte,[61] and the prisoner of Vincennes, the communist Raspail, were elected representatives of Paris. But the bourgeoisie elected the usurious money-changer and Orleanist Fould. So from all sides at once there came an open declaration of war against the Constituent National Assembly, against bourgeois republicanism, against Cavaignac.

There is no need to elaborate on how the mass bankruptcy of the Paris petty bourgeoisie had inevitable repercussions far beyond those immediately hit, nor on how bourgeois commerce was inevitably shaken once again, while the state deficit was swollen further by the costs of the June insurrection, nor on how government revenues constantly declined as a result of the interruption in production, restricted consumption and decreasing imports. Cavaignac and the National Assembly could not resort to any other measure than a new loan, which forced them even further under the yoke of the financial aristocracy.

While the petty bourgeoisie reaped bankruptcy and liquidation by court order as the fruit of the June victory, Cavaignac's janissaries, the Mobile Guard, found their reward in the soft arms of the courtesans and, as 'the youthful saviours of society', they received homage of all kinds in the salons of Marrast, the *gentilhomme*[62] of the tricolour, who simultaneously played Amphitryon[63] and the troubadour of the worthy republic. The preferential social treatment and disproportionately higher pay given to the Mobile Guard embittered the *army* while, at the same time, all the national illusions disappeared with which bourgeois republicanism – by way of its paper, the *National* – had been able

61. Louis Bonaparte, nephew of the emperor Napoleon, was elected President of France in December 1848 for a four-year term; on 2 December 1851 he overthrew the republican constitution and ruled as emperor until 1870 under the title Napoleon III.

62. Knight.

63. Lavish host, after the son of Alkaios, king of Tyre, in the Greek legend.

to win the allegiance of a part of the army and the peasant class under Louis Philippe. The role of mediation which Cavaignac and the National Assembly played in *northern Italy* in order, together with England, to betray it to Austria – this one day of rule destroyed eighteen years of opposition for the *National*. No government was less national than that of the *National* and none was more dependent upon England, while under Louis Philippe it had lived according to a daily paraphrase of Cato's dictum: '*Delenda est Carthago*';[64] none was more servile towards the Holy Alliance, while from a Guizot it had demanded the tearing-up of the Treaty of Vienna.[65] An irony of history made Bastide, the former foreign affairs editor of the *National*, French Minister of Foreign Affairs, so that he could refute his articles, one by one, with each of his dispatches.

For a moment both the army and the peasant class had believed that with military dictatorship, foreign war and '*gloire*' were now the order of the day in France. But Cavaignac did not represent the dictatorship of the sabre over the bourgeoisie but the dictatorship of the bourgeoisie by the sabre, and they now required the soldier only as gendarme. Beneath the stern features of his anti-republican resignation Cavaignac concealed insipid submissiveness to the humiliating conditions of his bourgeois office. *L'argent n'a pas de maître!* Money has no master! He idealized this old election slogan of the *tiers-état*,[66] as did the Constituent Assembly in general, by translating it into political language: The bourgeoisie has no king; the true form of bourgeois rule is the republic.

And the development of this *form*, the preparation of a republican *constitution*, was the 'great organic task' of the Constituent National Assembly. The re-christening of the Christian calendar as a republican one, or of St Bartholomew as St Robespierre, no more changed wind and weather than this constitution changed, or was intended to change, bourgeois society. Where it went beyond a *change of costume*, it documented the *existing* facts. Thus it solemnly registered as fact the existence of the republic, the existence of universal suffrage, the existence of a

64. Carthage must be destroyed.

65. The Treaty of Vienna of June 1815, together with the Treaties of Paris (May 1814 and November 1815), confined France to its frontiers of 1790 and erected safeguards against French expansionism.

66. Third estate.

single sovereign National Assembly in place of two constitutionally limited Chambers. It registered and regulated the fact of Cavaignac's dictatorship by replacing the stationary, irresponsible, hereditary monarchy with an ambulatory, responsible, elective monarchy, with a quadrennial presidency. To the same degree, therefore, it elevated to the status of a constitutional law the extraordinary power which the National Assembly had providently invested in its chairman in the interests of its own safety after the terror of 15 May and 25 June. The rest of the Constitution was a work of terminology. The royalist labels were torn off the machinery of the old monarchy and republican labels were stuck on. Marrast, the former editor-in-chief of the *National*, now editor-in-chief of the Constitution, acquitted himself of this academic task not without talent.

The Constituent Assembly resembled that Chilean official who wanted to regulate property relations on the land more exactly by means of a cadastral survey at the very moment when subterranean rumblings had already heralded the volcanic eruption which was to rend asunder the ground beneath his very feet. While in theory it measured out the forms which gave republican expression to bourgeois rule, in reality it only retained its power by the suspension of all formulas, by force *sans phrase*,[67] by the *state of siege*. Two days before it began its work on the Constitution it proclaimed a prolongation of the state of siege. Earlier constitutions had been made and accepted as soon as the process of social upheaval had come to rest, as soon as the newly formed class relationships had become established, and at the same time as the warring fractions of the ruling class had resorted to a compromise which allowed them to continue the struggle among themselves and at the same time to exclude the exhausted masses from the struggle. This Constitution, on the other hand, did not sanction any social revolution; it sanctioned the momentary victory of the old society over the revolution.

In the first draft of the Constitution, composed before the June days, the *droit au travail*, the right to work, was contained as a preliminary, clumsy formula, summarizing the revolutionary claims of the proletariat. It was changed into the *droit à l'assistance*, the right to public assistance. And which modern state does not feed its paupers in one form or another? The right to work is, in the bourgeois sense, nonsense, a wretched, pious wish. But behind

67. Pure and simple.

the right to work stands power over capital, behind power over capital the appropriation of the means of production, their subjection to the associated working class, that is, the abolition of wage labour, capital and their mutual relationship. Behind the 'right to work' was the June insurrection. The Constituent Assembly, which placed the revolutionary proletariat *hors la loi*, outside the law, in reality, had to exclude its formula from the Constitution, the law of laws, as a matter of principle; it had to pronounce its anathema upon the 'right to work'. But it did not stop here. As Plato banished the poets from his republic, from its republic it banished for all time *progressive taxation*. And progressive taxation is not only a bourgeois measure, which can be applied on a large or small scale within the existing relations of production, it was the only means of tying the middle strata of bourgeois society to the 'respectable' republic, the only means of reducing the national debt and of holding the anti-republican majority of the bourgeoisie in check.

On the question of the *concordats à l'amiable* the tricolour republicans had indeed sacrificed the petty bourgeoisie to the big bourgeoisie. They raised this deed to the level of a principle with the legal prohibition of progressive taxation. They put bourgeois reform on a par with proletarian revolution. But which class, then, remained as the mainstay of their republic? The big bourgeoisie. And the mass of this class was anti-republican. While it exploited the republicans of the *National* with a view to consolidating the old economic order, it intended, on the other hand, to exploit the re-established social relations in order to restore the corresponding political forms. At the beginning of October Cavaignac already felt obliged to make Dufaure and Vivien,[68] former ministers under Louis Philippe, ministers of the republic, no matter how much the brainless puritans of his own party grumbled and raged.

While the tricolour Constitution rejected any compromise with the petty bourgeoisie and was unable to win the allegiance of any new social group to the new form of government, it hurried, on

68. Jules-Armand Dufaure, a lawyer and originally an Orleanist politician, sat in both Assemblies as a republican and was Minister of the Interior in Cavaignac's government (October–December 1848), and again under Louis Bonaparte's presidency (June–October 1849). Alexandre Vivien, also a lawyer and originally an Orleanist politician, became Minister of Public Works in Cavaignac's government.

the other hand, to restore to its traditional inviolability a body which represented the grimmest and most fanatical defender of the old state. It elevated the *irremovability of judges*, which had been called into question by the Provisional Government, to a constitutional law. Having removed *one* king, scores of kings arose again in the shape of irremovable inquisitors of legality.

The French press has dealt with the contradictions of Monsieur Marrast's Constitution from many points of view; for example, the coexistence of two sovereign powers, the National Assembly and the President, and so on.

But the most comprehensive contradiction in the Constitution consists in the fact that it gives political power to the classes whose social slavery it is intended to perpetuate: proletariat, peasants and petty bourgeoisie. And it deprives the bourgeoisie, the class whose old social power it sanctions, of the political guarantees of this power. It imposes on the political rule of the bourgeoisie democratic conditions which constantly help its enemies towards victory and endanger the very basis of bourgeois society. It demands from the one that it should not proceed from political emancipation to social emancipation and from the other that it should not regress from social restoration to political restoration.

The bourgeois republicans were bothered little by these contradictions. The less *indispensable* they became – and they were only indispensable as the protagonists of the old society against the revolutionary proletariat – the more they sank, a few weeks after their victory, from the position of a *party* to that of a *coterie*. And they treated the Constitution as a huge *intrigue*. What was to be constituted in it was above all the rule of the coterie. The President was to be a protracted Cavaignac and the Legislative Assembly a protracted Constituent Assembly. They hoped to be able to reduce the political power of the masses to a sham power and to manipulate the sham power sufficiently themselves to confront the majority of the bourgeoisie with the permanent dilemma of the June days: *the rule of the* National *or the rule of anarchy.*

Work on the Constitution began on 4 September and was finished on 23 October. On 2 September the Constituent Assembly had resolved not to dissolve itself until the organic laws which supplemented the Constitution had been enacted. None the less, it now decided to bring its very own creation, the President, to life as early as 10 December, long before the course of its own activity

had come to a close. So confident was it of hailing in the constitutional *homunculus* the son of his mother. As a precaution the
provision was made that should none of the candidates receive
two million votes, the election would pass from the nation to the
Constituent Assembly.

These precautions were in vain! The first day on which the
Constitution came into force was the last day of the Constituent
Assembly's rule. Its death sentence lay in the depths of the ballot
box. It sought the 'son of his mother' and found the 'nephew
of his uncle'. Saul Cavaignac slew one million votes but David
Napoleon slew six million. Saul Cavaignac was beaten six times
over.

10 December 1848 was the day of the *peasant insurrection*. The
symbol that expressed their entry into the revolutionary movement, clumsy but cunning, rascally but naïve, oafish but sublime, a
calculated superstition, a pathetic burlesque, an inspired but stupid
anachronism, a momentous, historic piece of buffoonery, an unde-
cipherable hieroglyph for the understanding of the civilized – this
symbol bore unmistakably the physiognomy of the class which
represents barbarism within civilization. The republic had announced
itself to the peasants with the *tax collector*; they announced themselves to the republic with the *emperor*. Napoleon was the only man
who had exhaustively represented the interests and the imagination
of the peasant class, newly created in 1789. By inscribing his name
on the frontispiece of the republic this class declared war abroad
and the enforcement of its class interests at home. For the peasants
Napoleon was not a person but a programme. They marched on the
polling stations with banners flying, drums beating and trumpets
sounding, shouting, '*Plus d'impôts, à bas les riches, à bas la république, vive l'empereur.*' No more taxes, down with the rich, down
with the republic, long live the emperor! Behind the emperor lurked
the peasant war. The republic which they voted down was the *republic of the rich*.

10 December was the coup d'état of the peasants, who overthrew
the existing government. And from this day forth, having taken a
government from France and given her a new one, their eyes were
immediately fixed on Paris. Having once been the active heroes of
the revolutionary drama they could no longer be thrust back into the
inactive, acquiescent role of the chorus.

The other classes contributed to the completion of the peasants' electoral victory. For the *proletariat* the election of Napoleon meant the removal of Cavaignac from office, the overthrow of the Constituent Assembly, the dismissal of bourgeois republicanism, the annulment of the June victory. For the *petty bourgeoisie* Napoleon represented the rule of the debtor over the creditor. For the majority of the *big bourgeoisie* Napoleon's election represented an open breach with the party which it had temporarily had to make use of against the revolution but which became intolerable to it as soon as this class tried to consolidate the temporary situation as the constitutional position. Napoleon in place of Cavaignac represented for them the monarchy in place of the republic, the beginning of the royalist restoration, a tentative hint given to Orleans, the Bourbon *fleur-de-lis* concealed beneath the Bonapartist violets. Finally, the *army*, in voting for Napoleon, voted against the Mobile Guard, against the idyll of peace and in favour of war.

Thus it happened, as the *Neue Rheinische Zeitung* put it,[69] that the simplest man in France acquired a significance of the most multifarious kind. Precisely because he was nothing he was able to signify everything, except what he in fact was. Meanwhile, no matter how different the meaning of the name Napoleon on the lips of the various classes, each of them used it to write on its ballot paper: Down with the party of the *National*, down with Cavaignac, down with the Constituent Assembly, down with the bourgeois republic. Minister Dufaure declared publicly in the Constituent Assembly that 10 December was a second 24 February.

The petty bourgeoisie and proletariat had voted *en bloc for* Napoleon in order to vote *against* Cavaignac and, by combining their votes, to rob the Constituent Assembly of the final decision. The most progressive sections of each class, however, put forward their own candidates. Napoleon was the *common name* for all the parties in coalition against the bourgeois republic; Ledru-Rollin and Raspail were the *proper names*, the former of the democratic petty bourgeoisie, the latter of the revolutionary proletariat. The votes for Raspail – as the proletarians and their socialist spokesmen declared aloud – were intended as a mere demonstration: each vote a protest against the presidency as such, that is, against the Constitution itself, each vote a vote against

69. Marx is referring to an article by Ferdinand Wolff in the *Neue Rheinische Zeitung* of 21 December 1848.

Ledru-Rollin, the first act by which the proletariat declared itself to be an independent political party distinct from the democratic party. This party, however – the democratic petty bourgeoisie and its parliamentary representative, the Montagne – treated the candidature of Ledru-Rollin with the seriousness which it habitually uses to solemnly dupe itself. This, it may be added, was its last attempt to set itself up against the proletariat as an independent party. The democratic petty bourgeoisie and its Montagne, as well as the republican bourgeois party, were beaten on 10 December.

Besides a Montagne France now possessed a Napoleon, a proof that both were only the lifeless caricatures of the great realities whose name they bore. Louis Napoleon, with the emperor's hat and the eagle, parodied the old Napoleon no more wretchedly than the Montagne, with its phrases borrowed from 1793 and its demagogic poses, parodied the old Montagne. The traditional superstitious belief in 1793 was thus shed with the traditional belief in Napoleon. The revolution could only come into its own when it had won its *own, original* name, and it could only do this when the modern revolutionary class, the industrial proletariat, came to the fore as a dominant force. It may be said that 10 December took the Montagne by surprise and sowed confusion in its mind precisely because on this day the classical analogy with the old revolution was interrupted, with a laugh, by a derisive peasant joke.

On 20 December Cavaignac laid down his office and the Constituent Assembly proclaimed Louis Napoleon President of the Republic. On 19 December, the last day of its exclusive rule, it rejected a proposal of amnesty for the June insurgents. Would not the revocation of the decree of 27 June, by which it had condemned 15,000 insurgents to deportation, having dispensed with legal sentences, mean the revocation of the June battle itself?

Odilon Barrot, Louis Philippe's last Prime Minister, became Louis Napoleon's first Prime Minister. Just as Louis Napoleon did not date his rule from 10 December, but from a decree of the Senate of 1804, he found a Prime Minister who did not date his ministry from 20 December but from a royal decree of 24 February. Like a legitimate heir of Louis Philippe, Louis Napoleon smoothed over the change of regime by retaining the old ministry, which, moreover, had not had time to wear itself out because it had not had time to embark on life.

The leaders of the royalist fractions of the bourgeoisie advised him to make this choice. The head of the old dynastic opposition, which had unconsciously been the stepping-stone to the republicans of the *National*, was even more suited to function fully consciously as the stepping-stone from the bourgeois republic to the monarchy.

Odilon Barrot led the only old opposition party which had not exhausted its strength in the unceasing but fruitless struggle for ministerial portfolios. In rapid succession the revolution propelled all the old opposition parties to the heights of state power so that they were obliged to deny and repudiate their old phrases not only in what they did but even in what they said, and so that finally, united in a repulsive conglomeration, they might be hurled by the people into the carrion-pit of history. And no apostasy was spared this Barrot, this embodiment of bourgeois liberalism, who for eighteen years had concealed the base hollowness of his mind beneath a studied solemnity of bearing.[70] When, at certain moments, the all too striking contrast between the thistles of the present and the laurels of the past startled even Barrot himself, a glance in the mirror restored his ministerial composure and his human self-admiration. What he saw reflected in the mirror was Guizot, whom he had always envied, who had always been his master, Guizot himself, but Guizot with the Olympian brow of Odilon. What he overlooked were the Midas' ears.

The Barrot of 24 February first became manifest in the Barrot of 20 December. Barrot, the Orleanist and Voltairean, was joined by the Legitimist and Jesuit Falloux – as Minister of Education.

A few days later the Ministry of the Interior was given to Léon Faucher, the Malthusian. Law, religion and political economy! The Barrot ministry contained all this and in addition a combination of Legitimists and Orleanists. Only the Bonapartist was missing. Bonaparte still concealed his desire to play Napoleon, for Soulouque did not yet play Toussaint-Louverture.[71]

The party of the *National* was immediately ejected from all the high posts in which it had made itself at home. The posts of Prefect

70. Marx is here paraphrasing a passage from Lawrence Sterne's novel *Tristram Shandy*, chapter 11.

71. Toussaint-Louverture led the black revolution in Haiti that secured independence from Spanish and English colonialism. Faustin Soulouque, President of the Haitian republic, foreshadowed Louis Bonaparte by proclaiming himself emperor on 26 August 1849, while distinguished only for his ignorance, cruelty and vanity.

of Police, Post Office Director, Public Prosecutor, Mayor of Paris, were all occupied by the old creatures of the monarchy. Changarnier,[72] the Legitimist, was given the joint supreme command of the National Guard of the department of Seine, the Mobile Guard and the regular troops of the First Army Division;[73] Bugeaud,[74] the Orleanist, was appointed commander-in-chief of the Army of the Alps. This change of officials continued without interruption under Barrot's government. The first action of his ministry was the restoration of the old royalist administration. In a trice the official scene changed – scenery, costumes, language, actors, supernumeraries, extras, prompters, the position of the parties, the dramatic motifs, the nature of the conflict, the total situation. Only the antediluvian Constituent Assembly still occupied its old position. But, from the moment the Assembly had installed Bonaparte, Bonaparte Barrot and Barrot Changarnier, France emerged from the period of republican constitution and entered the period of the constituted republic. And what was the point of a Constituent Assembly in a constituted republic? Once the earth had been created there remained nothing else for its Creator but to flee to heaven. The Constituent Assembly was determined not to follow His example; the Assembly was the last refuge of the bourgeois republican party. All control over the executive had been wrested from it, but did it not still possess constituent omnipotence? Its first thought was at all costs to secure the position of sovereignty which it occupied, and starting from here to reconquer the ground which it had lost. If the Barrot ministry could be displaced by a ministry of the *National*, the royal personnel would have to vacate the administrative palaces forthwith and the tricolour personnel would move in again in triumph. The Assembly decided on the overthrow of the ministry, and the ministry offered it an opportunity for attack which could not have been more suitable had the Constituent Assembly invented it itself.

It will be remembered what Louis Bonaparte signified for the peasants: no more taxes! He sat in the President's chair for six days and on the seventh, 27 December, he proposed to his ministry the *retention of the salt tax*, abolished by decree of the Provisional

72. Nicolas Changarnier, a general and a deputy in both Assemblies, was rewarded with this post for his part in the suppression of the June insurrection.

73. The First Army Division comprised the Paris garrison.

74. Thomas Bugeaud de la Piconerrie was a marshal of France and a deputy to the Legislative National Assembly.

Government. The salt tax shares with the wine tax the privilege of being the scapegoat of the old French financial system, particularly in the eyes of the rural population. The Barrot ministry could not have put into the mouth of the man chosen by the peasants a more biting epigram dedicated to his electors than the words: *Restoration of the salt tax!* With the salt tax Bonaparte lost his revolutionary salt – the Napoleon of the peasant insurrection dissolved like an apparition, and nothing remained but the great unknown of royalist, bourgeois intrigues. And it was not unintentional that the Barrot ministry made this act of tactlessly rough disillusionment the first administrative act of the President.

The Constituent Assembly, for its part, eagerly seized the double opportunity of overthrowing the ministry and setting itself up as the representative of the peasants' interests in opposition to the man elected by the peasantry. It rejected the proposal of the Minister of Finance, reduced the salt tax to a third of its earlier amount, thus increasing a national deficit of 560 million francs by 60 million francs, and after this *vote of no confidence* calmly awaited the resignation of the ministry. So little did it understand the new world around it and its own changed position. Behind the ministry stood the President and behind the President stood six million voters, each of whom had cast in the ballot box a vote of no confidence in the Constituent Assembly. The Constituent Assembly gave the nation its vote of no confidence back. What a ridiculous exchange! It forgot that its votes were no longer legal tender. The rejection of the salt tax only brought to maturity the decision of Bonaparte and his ministry '*to have done*' with the Constituent Assembly. The long duel now began which occupied the entire latter half of the Constituent Assembly's existence. 29 January, 21 March, 8 May are the *journées*, the great days of this crisis, each day a forerunner of 13 June.

The French, Louis Blanc for example, have seen in 29 January the day on which a constitutional contradiction emerged, the contradiction between a sovereign, indissoluble National Assembly created by universal suffrage, and a President who according to the letter of the Constitution was answerable to the Assembly, but who was in reality not only likewise sanctioned by universal suffrage – unifying in his person, furthermore, all those votes which were divided and split up a hundredfold among the individual members of the National Assembly – but who was also in full possession of the whole executive power over which the National Assembly hovered as a mere moral power. This interpretation of 29 January confuses the language of the struggle on the platform, in the press and in the clubs, with its real content. The confrontation between Louis Bonaparte and the Constituent National Assembly was not a confrontation between one one-sided constitutional power and another, it was not a confrontation between the executive and the legislature. It was a confrontation between the constituted bourgeois republic itself and the instruments of its constitution, the ambitions, intrigues and ideological demands of the revolutionary fraction of the bourgeoisie, which had founded it and now discovered to its amazement that its constituted republic looked like a restored monarchy. This revolutionary fraction of the bourgeoisie now found that it wanted to hold on by force to the constituent period with its conditions and illusions, its language and its personalities, and to prevent the mature bourgeois republic from assuming its complete and natural form. Just as the Constituent National Assembly was represented by Cavaignac who after his fall had rejoined its ranks, so Bonaparte represented the Legislative National Assembly, which had not yet parted company with him; that is, the National Assembly of the constituted bourgeois republic.

The significance of Bonaparte's election could only become clear when, in the repeat performance represented by the elections to the new National Assembly, the multifarious meanings of his name were substituted for the one word Bonaparte. The mandate of the old Assembly was annulled as a result of 10 December. Thus on 29 January it was not the President and the National Assembly of the *same* republic which faced each other; it was the National Assembly of the nascent republic and the President of the fully fledged republic: two powers which embodied two completely different periods in the life process of the republic. There was, on the one hand, the small republican fraction of the bourgeoisie which alone could proclaim the republic, wrest it from the revolutionary proletariat by street fighting and a reign of terror, and could draft in the Constitution its ideal fundamental features; and there was, on the other, the whole royalist mass of the bourgeoisie, which alone could rule in this constituted bourgeois republic, strip the Constitution of its ideological trimmings and bring about by its legislation and administration the indispensable conditions for the subjugation of the proletariat.

The storm which broke on 29 January had been gathering throughout the month. With its vote of no confidence the Constituent Assembly wanted to force the Barrot ministry to resign. The Barrot ministry, on the other hand, proposed to the Constituent Assembly that it pass a definitive vote of no confidence in itself, that it decide on suicide and decree its *own dissolution*. At the behest of the ministry Rateau,[75] one of the most obscure deputies, laid this motion before the Assembly on 6 January – before the same Constituent Assembly which had already resolved in August not to dissolve itself until it had issued a whole series of organic laws which would supplement the Constitution. The government supporter Fould declared outright before the Assembly that its dissolution was necessary '*to restore the stability of credit*'. And did it not impair the stability of credit by prolonging provisional rule and by calling Barrot – and with him Bonaparte and the constituted republic – into question? The Olympian Barrot became a raging Roland[76] at the prospect of having the premiership, which he had finally laid his hands on, torn from his grasp after enjoying the office for scarcely two weeks, the office which the republicans had already robbed him of for a decennium – that is, for ten months. Before this wretched Assembly he out-tyrannized the tyrant. The mildest of his words were: 'No future is possible with it.' It did indeed now only represent the past. 'It is incapable', he added ironically, 'of providing the republic with the institutions necessary for its consolidation.' Indeed, its categorical opposition to the proletariat was accompanied by a breakdown in its bourgeois energy, and in its opposition to the royalists its republican exuberance revived anew. Thus, it was doubly incapable of consolidating the bourgeois republic, which it no longer comprehended, with the necessary institutions.

Together with Rateau's proposal the ministry organized a *storm of petitions* throughout the country and daily, from all corners of France, bundles of *billets-doux* landed on the doorstep of the Constituent Assembly, more or less categorically requesting it to *dissolve* itself and make its will. The Assembly, for its part, organized counter-petitions, in which the petitioners requested its continuing existence. The electoral struggle between Bonaparte

75. Jean-Pierre Rateau was a lawyer and a deputy in both the Constituent and Legislative Assemblies. He was a Bonapartist.
76. After Charlemagne's nephew, famed for his audacious exploits.

and Cavaignac was renewed as a struggle of petitions for and against the dissolution of the National Assembly. The petitions were to be belated commentaries on 10 December. This agitation continued throughout January.

In its conflict with the President the Constituent Assembly could not refer back to the general election as its origin, for appeal was made to universal suffrage. It could not base itself on any regularly constituted power as it was a question of a struggle against legal power. It was not in a position to overthrow the ministry by a vote of no confidence, as it had attempted on 6 and 26 January, as the ministry did not ask for its confidence. Only *one* possibility was left to it, that of *insurrection*. The armed forces of insurrection were *the republican part of the National Guard*, the Mobile Guard and the centres of the revolutionary proletariat, the *clubs*. In December the Mobile Guard, heroes from the days of June, formed the organized armed forces of the republican bourgeois fraction, just as before June the National Workshops had formed the organized armed forces of the revolutionary proletariat. Just as the Executive Commission of the Constituent Assembly directed its brutal attack against the National Workshops when it felt compelled to put an end to the intolerable demands of the proletariat, so Bonaparte's ministry directed its attack against the Mobile Guard when it felt obliged to put an end to the intolerable demands of the republican bourgeois fraction. It ordered the *disbandment of the Mobile Guard*. One half was dismissed and thrown onto the streets; the other half was organized on monarchist instead of democratic lines, and its pay was reduced to the usual pay of the regular troops. The Mobile Guard found itself in the same situation as the June insurgents, and every day the press printed *public confessions*, in which it acknowledged its blame for June and implored the proletariat for forgiveness.

And the *clubs*? The moment the Constituent Assembly had called the President into question in the person of Barrot, and hence the constituted bourgeois republic and the bourgeois republic in general, all the constituent elements of the February republic ranged themselves around it – all the parties which wanted the overthrow of the existing republic and a process of violent retrogression in order to transform it into the republic of their class interests and principles. What had been done was undone; the crystallizations of the revolutionary period became fluid again;

the republic over which they were fighting was once more the unde-
fined republic of the February days: and each party reserved for
itself the right to provide the definition. For a moment the parties
took up their old positions of February. The tricolour republicans
of the *National* leant once more on the democratic republicans of
the *Réforme* and pushed them as their protagonist into the forefront
of the parliamentary struggle. The democratic republicans leant
again on the socialist republicans – they announced their reconciliation and unity in a public manifesto on 27 January – and prepared
the background for insurrection in the clubs. The ministerial press
rightly treated the tricolour republicans of the *National* as the resurrected insurgents of June. In order to secure their position at the
head of the bourgeois republic they called the bourgeois republic
itself into question. On 26 January Minister Faucher proposed a
law on the right of association; the first paragraph ran: '*Clubs are
prohibited.*' He proposed that this bill be discussed immediately as
a matter of urgency. The Constituent Assembly rejected the motion
of urgency and on 27 January it put forward a resolution with 230
signatures proposing that the ministry be impeached for violating
the Constitution. *Impeachment* of the ministry at a moment when
such an act tactlessly exposed the impotence of the judge, namely
the majority in the Chamber, or served as an impotent protest by the
accuser against this majority itself – this was the great revolutionary trump card which the latter-day Montagne played from now on
whenever the crisis reached a peak. Poor Montagne, crushed by the
weight of its own name!

On 15 May Blanqui, Barbès, Raspail, etc., had tried to break up
the Constituent Assembly by forcing their way into the chamber
at the head of the Paris proletariat. Barrot intended to inflict a
moral 15 May on the Assembly with his plan to dictate its self-
dissolution and to close its meeting place. This same Assembly
had appointed Barrot to conduct an inquiry against the accused of
May, and now, at the moment that he confronted it like a royalist
Blanqui, as it sought allies against him in the clubs, among the
revolutionary proletariat and in Blanqui's party, at this moment
the implacable Barrot tormented it with the proposal to withdraw
the May prisoners from the jurisdiction of the Court of Assizes
and to transfer them to the High Court, the *haute cour* devised by
the party of the *National*. It was remarkable how his panic over
a ministerial portfolio could produce from the head of a Barrot

pearls worthy of a Beaumarchais! After long vacillation the National Assembly accepted his proposal. In its treatment of the May assailants it reverted to its normal character.

While the Constituent Assembly was forced into *insurrection* against the President and the ministers, President and ministers were forced into a coup against the Constituent Assembly, for they possessed no legal means of dissolving it. But the Constituent Assembly was the mother of the Constitution and the Constitution was the mother of the President. With a coup d'état the President would tear up the Constitution and invalidate his republican claim. He would then be forced to produce his imperial claim; but the imperial claim would call forth the Orleanist claim, and both paled before the claim of the Legitimists. The fall of the legal republic could only result in the rise of its extreme antipode, the Legitimist monarchy, at a moment when the Orleanists were still nothing more than the defeated party of February and Bonaparte the victor of 10 December, when both could only oppose the republican usurpation with their own equally usurped monarchist claims. The Legitimists were aware of the advantage of the hour; they conspired openly. In General Changarnier they hoped to find their General Monk.[77] The approach of the *white monarchy* was proclaimed as openly in their clubs as was that of the *red republic* in the proletarian clubs.

The ministry would have rid itself of all problems by means of a happily suppressed uprising. 'Legality is the death of us,' cried Odilon Barrot. An uprising would have allowed it to dissolve the Constituent Assembly under the pretext of the *salut public*[78] and to violate the Constitution itself in the interests of the Constitution. Odilon Barrot's brutal behaviour in the National Assembly, the motion to dissolve the clubs, the unceremonious removal of fifty tricolour prefects and their replacement by royalists, the disbandment of the Mobile Guard, the maltreatment of its leaders by Changarnier, the reinstatement of Professor Lerminier,[79] who had been intolerable even under Guizot, the toleration of Legitimist boasting – each of these was a provocation for an uprising. But the uprising did not take place. It awaited its

77. The English general who in 1660 used the troops under his command to secure the restoration of the Stuarts.

78. Public safety.

79. Jean Lerminier was an ultra-reactionary jurist who had resigned from the Collège de France in 1839 after protests from his students.

signal from the Constituent Assembly and not from the ministry.

Finally came 29 January, the day on which the motion of Mathieu de la Drôme,[80] proposing the categorical rejection of Rateau's motion, was to be put to the vote. Legitimists, Orleanists, Bonapartists, Mobile Guard, Montagne, clubs, all conspired on this day, each as much against its supposed ally as against its supposed enemy. Bonaparte, mounted on horseback, reviewed a section of the troops on the Place de la Concorde; Changarnier play-acted with a display of strategic manoeuvres; the Constituent Assembly found its building occupied by the military. This Assembly, the focal point of all conflicting hopes, fears, expectations, ferments, tensions, conspiracies, this lion-hearted Assembly did not hesitate for a moment when it came nearer than ever before to the *Weltgeist*.[81] It resembled the warrior who not only feared to use his own weapons, but also felt obliged to keep his opponent's intact. Scorning death it signed its own death warrant and rejected the categorical rejection of Rateau's motion. Even though itself in a state of siege, it imposed limits on a constituent activity whose necessary context had been the state of siege in Paris. It revenged itself in a worthy manner the next day by conducting an inquiry into the fright which the ministry had given it on 29 January. The Montagne demonstrated its lack of revolutionary energy and political intelligence by allowing itself to be used by the party of the *National* as the crier in this great comedy of intrigue. The party of the *National* had made its last attempt to maintain in the constituted republic the monopoly rule which it has possessed in the formative stage of the bourgeois republic. It had failed.

Whereas in the January crisis the existence of the Constitutional Assembly was at stake, in the crisis of 21 March the existence of the Constitution was at stake; in January it was a matter of the *National* party's personnel, in March it was a matter of its ideals. It goes without saying that the honourable republicans surrendered the noble sentiments of their ideology more cheaply than the worldly pleasures of governmental power.

On 21 March Faucher's bill against the right of association – *the suppression of the clubs* – was on the agenda of the National

80. Philippe Mathieu de la Drôme was a Montagne deputy in both Assemblies.

81. In Hegel's philosophy of history, the transpersonal force of historical reason.

Assembly. Article 8 of the Constitution guarantees all Frenchmen the right of association. This prohibition of the clubs, therefore, represented an unequivocal violation of the Constitution, and the Constituent Assembly itself was to canonize the profanation of its saints. But the clubs were the meeting points, the conspiratorial haunts of the revolutionary proletariat. The National Assembly itself had forbidden the union of the workers against the bourgeoisie. And what were these clubs other than a union of the whole working class against the whole bourgeois class – the formation of a workers' state against the bourgeois state? Were they not, every one of them, constituent assemblies of the proletariat and hard-hitting army divisions for revolt? What the Constitution had to constitute above all, was the rule of the bourgeoisie. Therefore the constitutional right of association could clearly refer only to those associations which were compatible with the rule of the bourgeoisie, that is, with bourgeois order. If, for the sake of theoretical propriety, the Constitution was expressed in general terms, were not the government and the National Assembly there to interpret and apply it in the specific case? And if in the primeval epoch of the republic the clubs were in fact prohibited by the state of siege, had they not, in an ordered, constituted republic, to be prohibited by law? The tricolour republicans had nothing with which to counter this prosaic interpretation of the Constitution except its own high-flown phrases. A section of them, Pagnerre, Duclerc,[82] etc., voted for the ministry and thus presented it with a majority. The other section, with the archangel Cavaignac and church father Marrast at their head, withdrew to a special room once the article prohibiting the clubs had been passed – and there they 'took counsel'. The National Assembly was paralysed; it no longer had a quorum. At the right moment Mr Crémieux reminded those gathered in the room that the way out led directly on to the street and that it was no longer February 1848 but March 1849. Suddenly enlightened, the party of the *National* returned to the chamber followed by the Montagne, who had been duped again. Constantly tormented by revolutionary desires, the Montagne no less constantly grasped at constitutional possibilities and still felt more at home behind the bourgeois republicans

82. Laurent Pagnerre, a publisher and bourgeois republican politician, was General Secretary of the Provisional Government in 1848. Charles Duclerc, a lawyer and former Orleanist politician who turned republican in 1848, was Minister of the Interior in Cavaignac's government.

than in front of the revolutionary proletariat. Thus the comedy was played out. And the Constituent Assembly itself had decreed that violation of the letter of the Constitution was the only appropriate way to realize its spirit.

Only one point remained to be settled: the relationship of the constituted republic to the European revolution – its *foreign policy*. On 8 May 1849 there was an unusually excited mood in the Constituent Assembly, whose term of life was due to come to an end in a few days. The attack by the French army on Rome, its repulse by the Romans, its political infamy and military disgrace, the assassination of the Roman republic by the French republic, the first Italian campaign of the second Bonaparte[83] was on the agenda once again. The Montagne had once more played its trump card; Ledru-Rollin had laid on the President's desk the inevitable bill of impeachment against the ministry, and this time against Bonaparte, too, for violation of the Constitution.

The motive of 8 May was repeated later as the motive of 13 June. Let us discuss the military expedition to Rome.

In the middle of November 1848 Cavaignac had dispatched a battle-fleet to Civitavecchia to protect the Pope, to take him on board and transport him to France. The Pope was to consecrate the worthy republic and to secure Cavaignac's election as President. With the Pope Cavaignac wanted to hook the priests, with the priests the peasants and with the peasants the presidency. Although it was in the first instance election propaganda, Cavaignac's expedition was also a protest and a threat issued against the Roman revolution. It contained in embryo the intervention of France on the side of the Pope.

This intervention, in company with Austria and Naples, on behalf of the Pope and against the Roman republic, was resolved upon in the first meeting of Bonaparte's ministerial council on 23 December. Falloux in the ministry meant the Pope in Rome – and in the Rome of the Pope. Bonaparte no longer needed the Pope to become the peasants' President, but he needed the conservation of the Pope in order to conserve the President's peasants. Their gullibility had made him President. With the loss of their faith they would lose their gullibility and with the loss of the Pope they would lose their faith. And the coalition of Orleanists and

83. An ironic allusion to Napoleon Bonaparte's first Italian campaign of 1796, in which the people of northern Italy welcomed him as their liberator from the Austrian yoke.

Legitimists who ruled in Bonaparte's name! Before the king was restored the power had to be restored which consecrates kings. Apart from their royalism, without the old Rome under his secular rule there would be no Pope; without the Pope there would be no Catholicism; without Catholicism there would be no French religion; and without religion what would become of traditional French society? The mortgage which the peasant has on heavenly possessions guarantees the mortgage which the bourgeois has on the peasant's possessions. The Roman revolution, therefore, was an attack on property and bourgeois order as dreadful as the June revolution. The re-establishment of bourgeois rule in France required the restoration of papal rule in Rome. Lastly, a blow struck against the Roman revolutionaries was a blow struck against the allies of the French revolutionaries; the alliance of the counter-revolutionary classes in the constituted French republic was inevitably continued in the alliance of the French republic with the Holy Alliance, with Naples and Austria. The decision of the ministerial council of 23 December was no secret to the Constituent Assembly. On 8 January Ledru-Rollin had already interpellated the ministry on the matter; the ministry had issued a denial and the National Assembly had proceeded with the agenda. Did it trust the ministry's word? We know that it spent the whole of January passing votes of no confidence in the government. But if it was part of the ministry's role to lie it was part of the National Assembly's role to feign belief in these lies and thereby to save the republican *dehors*.[84]

In the meantime Piedmont had been beaten, Charles Albert had abdicated, and the Austrian army was knocking at the gates of France.[85] Ledru-Rollin interpellated vehemently. The ministry proved that it had only continued Cavaignac's policy in northern Italy, just as Cavaignac had only continued the policy of the Provisional Government, that is, of Ledru-Rollin. This time it actually reaped a vote of confidence from the National Assembly and it was authorized to occupy temporarily a convenient point in northern Italy in order to give support to the peaceful negotiations with Austria over the integrity of Sardinian territory[86] and

84. Appearances.
85. By the end of August 1848 the Austrian army under Radetsky had defeated Charles Albert at Custozza and retaken Milan and all Lombardy.
86. I.e., the territory of the Sardinian monarchy, which, besides the island of Sardinia, comprised Piedmont, Savoy and Nice.

the Roman question. As is well known, the fate of Italy is decided on the battlefields of northern Italy. Thus either Rome would fall with Piedmont and Lombardy, or France would have to declare war on Austria and thus on the European counter-revolution. Did the National Assembly suddenly take the Barrot ministry for the old Committee of Public Safety, or itself for the Convention?[87] Why, then, the military occupation of a point in northern Italy? The expedition against Rome was concealed beneath this transparent veil.

On 14 April a force of 14,000 men under Oudinot sailed for Civitavecchia. On 16 April the National Assembly voted the ministry a credit of 1,200,000 francs in order to maintain a fleet of intervention in the Mediterranean for three months. It thus gave the ministry all the means it needed to intervene against Rome while pretending to allow it to intervene against Austria. It did not see what the ministry was doing; it only heard what it said. Such faith as this was not to be found in Israel; the Constituent Assembly was in the position of not daring to know what the constituted republic had to do.

Finally, on 8 May, the last scene in the comedy was played. The Constituent Assembly requested the ministry to take rapid measures to direct the Italian expedition back to the goal which had been planned for it. That same evening Bonaparte inserted a letter in the *Moniteur* in which he paid the highest tribute to Oudinot. On 11 May the National Assembly rejected the bill of impeachment against Bonaparte and his ministry. As for the Montagne, which, instead of rending this tissue of deceit, took the parliamentary comedy tragically in order to take part itself in the role of Fouquier-Tinville,[88] did it not reveal its natural petty-bourgeois calf's hide beneath the borrowed lion's skin of the Convention?

The latter half of the life of the Constituent Assembly can be resumed as follows: on 29 January it conceded that the royalist fractions of the bourgeoisie were the natural leaders of the republic which it had constituted; on 21 March that the violation of the Constitution was in fact its implementation; and on 11 May that the bombastically announced passive alliance of the French republic with the struggling peoples signified its active alliance with the European counter-revolution.

87. I.e., of 1792–4.
88. Antoine Fouquier-Tinville was the Public Prosecutor at the revolutionary tribunal under the rule of the Convention.

This wretched Assembly quit the stage after giving itself the satisfaction – two days before the anniversary of its establishment on 4 May – of rejecting the motion of amnesty for the June insurgents. With its power destroyed, mortally hated by the people, rejected, abused, contemptuously cast aside by the bourgeoisie whose tool it was, forced in the second half of its life to disavow the first half, robbed of its republican illusions, without any great achievements to its credit in the past, without hope in the future, its living body dying bit by bit, it was able to galvanize its own corpse back into life only by continually recalling and reliving the victory of June. Like a vampire living off the blood of the June insurgents it was only able to retain its self-confidence by constantly and repeatedly damning those who had already been damned!

It bequeathed a state deficit, increased by the costs of the June insurrection, by the loss of the salt tax, by compensation paid out to the plantation owners for the abolition of Negro slavery, by the costs of the Rome expedition, by the loss of the wine tax, which it repealed at its last gasp like a malicious old man who takes pleasure in burdening his laughing heir with a compromising debt of honour.

At the beginning of March the election campaign had begun for the Legislative National Assembly. Two main groups confronted each other: the *party of Order* and the *democratic socialist* or *Red party*. Between the two stood the *Friends of the Constitution*, the name under which the tricolour republicans of the *National* tried to present a party. The *party of Order* was formed immediately following the days of June; only after 10 December had allowed it to get rid of the *National* coterie, the bourgeois republicans, was the secret of its existence revealed: the *coalition of the Orleanists* and *Legitimists* in *one party*. The bourgeois class was divided into two great fractions which had alternately maintained a monopoly of power – *big landed property* under the *Restoration*, the *financial aristocracy* and the *industrial bourgeoisie* under the *July monarchy*. Bourbon was the royal name for the dominance of the interests of one fraction; Orleans was the royal name for the dominance of the interests of the other. The *nameless realm of the republic* was the only form of rule under which both fractions were able to maintain their common class interest with equal power and without giving up their mutual rivalry. Since the bourgeois republic could be nothing other than the perfected and most purely developed rule of the whole bourgeois class, could it be anything else but the rule of the Orleanists supplemented by the Legitimists, the rule of the Legitimists supplemented by the Orleanists, the *synthesis of the Restoration and the July monarchy*? The bourgeois republicans of the *National* did not represent any large economically based fraction of their class. As opposed to the two bourgeois fractions, which only understood their *particular* rule, their only significance and historical claim lay in having asserted, under the monarchy, the *general* rule of the bourgeois class, in having asserted the *nameless realm of the republic*, which they idealized and embellished with antique arabesques but in which they hailed above all the rule of their coterie. Although the party of the *National* could hardly believe its own eyes when it caught sight of the royalist coalition at the head of the republic which it had founded, the royalists deceived themselves no less as far as their joint rule was concerned. They did not realize that although each of their fractions, taken in isolation, was royalist, the product of their chemical fusion was inevitably *republican*, that the white and the blue monarchies could not help but neutralize each other in the tricolour republic. Although their opposition to the revolutionary proletariat and to the intermediate classes, which increasingly grouped themselves around the proletarian centre, forced them to summon their united strength and to conserve this strength in its organized form, each fraction of the party of Order had to oppose the restorationist and usurpatory desires of the other by asserting their joint rule – the *republican form* of bourgeois rule. Thus, we find the royalists initially believing in an imminent restoration, later conserving the republican form, while foaming with rage and uttering deadly invective against it, and finally confessing that they can only tolerate each other in the republic and postponing the restoration indefinitely. Their enjoyment of united rule itself strengthened the two fractions and made each of them even more unable and unwilling to subordinate itself to the other, unable and unwilling, that is, to restore the monarchy.

In its election programme the party of Order proclaimed outright the rule of the bourgeois class, the preservation, that is, of the vital conditions of its rule: *property, family, religion, order!* It naturally represented its class rule and the conditions of this class rule as the rule of civilization, as providing the necessary conditions for material production and for the social relationships which result from material production. The party of Order had enormous financial resources at its disposal; it had organized branches throughout France; it had all the ideologists of the old society in its pay; it had the influence of the existing government power at its disposal; it possessed an army of unpaid vassals in the mass of the petty bourgeoisie and peasants, who, still separated from the revolutionary movement, found in the high dignitaries of property the natural representatives of their petty property and their petty prejudices. Represented throughout the country by innumerable petty monarchs, the party of Order could punish the rejection of its candidates as insurrection and could dismiss rebellious workers, recalcitrant farm labourers, servants, clerks, railway officials, registrars and all the functionaries who are its social subordinates. Finally, here and there, it was able to maintain the myth that the republican Constituent Assembly had prevented the Bonaparte of 10 December from revealing his miraculous powers.

We have not considered the Bonapartists in connection with the party of Order. They were not a serious fraction of the bourgeois class but a collection of old, superstitious invalids and young, incredulous adventurers. The party of Order was victorious at the elections, and it sent a great majority into the Legislative Assembly.

Faced with the coalition of the counter-revolutionary bourgeoisie those sections of the petty bourgeoisie and peasantry which were already revolutionized naturally had to ally themselves with the high dignitaries of the revolutionary interests, the revolutionary proletariat. We have seen how the democratic spokesmen of the petty bourgeoisie in parliament, the Montagne, were driven, as a result of parliamentary defeats, to join the socialist spokesmen of the proletariat and how the petty bourgeoisie itself outside parliament was driven, as a result of the brutal assertion of bourgeois interests and by bankruptcy, to join the proletariat proper. On 27 January the Montagne and the socialists had celebrated their reconciliation; they repeated their act of union in the great February banquet of 1849. The socialist and the democratic parties, the party of the workers and the party of the petty bourgeoisie, united to form the *social-democratic party* – the *Red* party.

Although the French republic had been paralysed for a moment by the agony that followed the June days, since the raising of the state of siege on 19 October it had experienced an uninterrupted series of feverish excitements. First the struggle for the presidency; then the struggle between the President and the Constituent Assembly; the struggle over the clubs; the trial in Bourges,[89] which – by comparison with the petty figures of the President, the royalist coalition, the worthy republicans, the democratic Montagne and the socialist doctrinaires of the proletariat – made the real proletarian revolutionaries look like primordial monsters such as only a deluge could leave behind on the surface of society, or such as could only precede a social deluge; the election campaign; the execution of Bréa's murderers;[90] the continual prosecution of the press; the violent state interference with the banquets carried out by the police; the insolent royalist provocations; the exhibition of the portraits of Louis Blanc and Caussidière on the pillory; the uninterrupted struggle between the constituted republic and the Constituent Assembly, which continually brought the revolution back to where it had started, made the victors into vanquished, the vanquished into victors, and in a trice reversed the position of the parties and classes, their political disagreements and alliances; the rapid course of the European counter-revolution; the glorious Hungarian struggle; the armed uprisings in Germany; the Rome expedition; the ignominious defeat of the French army before Rome[91] – in this vortex of events, in this torment of historical unrest, in this dramatic ebb and flow of revolutionary passions, hopes and disappointments, the different classes in French society had to count the epochs of their development in weeks as they had previously counted them in half-centuries. A considerable section of the peasantry and the provinces had been revolutionized. They had become disappointed in Napoleon, and they were offered by the Red party the substance in place of the name, and in place of illusory freedom from taxation the repayment of the milliard

89. The High Court at Bourges sat from 7 March to 3 April to try the leaders of the 15 May attempt. Blanqui was condemned to ten years' imprisonment, Barbès and Albert to deportation for life, and others to long terms of imprisonment.

90. General Jean-Baptiste Bréa was killed while commanding a unit against the June insurgents; two men were convicted of his murder.

91. The Hungarian revolution was defeated in summer 1849 by Russian intervention; the German Reich Constitution Campaign was in May and June; and it was May 1849 when Oudinot first advanced on Rome, was soundly beaten by Garibaldi and retreated to Civitavecchia.

francs paid to the Legitimists, the settlement of mortgages and the abolition of usury.

The army itself was infected with revolutionary fever. In supporting Bonaparte it had voted for victory and he gave it defeat. In him it had voted for the Little Corporal[92] who concealed the great revolutionary commander, and he gave it back the great generals behind whom the pipe-clay corporal takes refuge. There was no doubt that the Red party, the democratic coalition, would inevitably celebrate, if not victory, at least great triumphs, that Paris, the army and a large part of the provinces were bound to vote for it. Ledru-Rollin, the leader of the Montagne, was elected in five departments; no leader of the party of Order, and no candidate of the actual proletarian party, achieved such a victory. This election reveals to us the secret of the democratic socialist party. On the one hand, the Montagne, the parliamentary protagonist of the democratic petty bourgeoisie, was forced to unite with the socialist doctrinaires of the proletariat. (The proletariat, forced by the terrible material defeat of June to recover its strength in intellectual victories and, as yet unable to seize the revolutionary dictatorship, had to embrace the doctrinaires of proletarian emancipation, the socialist sectarians.)[93] On the other hand, the revolutionary peasants, the army and the provinces ranged themselves behind the Montagne. Thus, the Montagne became lord and master in the revolutionary camp, and by coming to an understanding with the socialists it set aside all differences within the revolutionary party. In the latter half of the Constituent Assembly's existence it represented the republican pathos of this body and made people forget its sins in the Provisional Government, the Executive Commission and the June days. Just as the party of the *National*, true to its half-and-half nature, had allowed itself to be oppressed by the royalist ministry, the party of the Mountain, which had been pushed aside during the period of the *National* party's omnipotence, rose up and made its strength felt as the parliamentary representative of the revolution. In fact, the party of the *National* had nothing to oppose the royalist fractions with,

92. This was the pet name given to Napoleon I by his army.

93. By 'socialist sectarians' Marx refers to the Fourierists and Proudhonists who preached abstention from political struggle and sought to emancipate the proletariat by various utopian remedies; see the Introduction to *The Revolutions of 1848*, pp. 22–5, and section III of the Communist Manifesto, ibid., pp. 23–7.

except ambitious personalities and idealistic humbug. The party of the Mountain, on the other hand, represented a mass hovering between the bourgeoisie and the proletariat, whose material interests demanded democratic institutions. By comparison with the Cavaignacs and the Marrasts, therefore, Ledru-Rollin and the Montagne took up a position more truly within the revolutionary movement; from a consciousness of this momentous situation they drew all the greater courage, the more the expression of revolutionary energy was limited to parliamentary attacks, the tabling of bills of impeachment, threats, the raising of voices, thundering speeches and extremes which never went beyond phrases. The peasants were more or less in the same position as the petty bourgeoisie; they had more or less the same demands to make. All the middle strata of society, so far as they were driven to join the revolutionary movement, were bound to find their hero in Ledru-Rollin. Ledru-Rollin was the leading personage of the democratic petty bourgeoisie. To oppose the party of Order the half-conservative, half-revolutionary, and wholly utopian reformers of this social order had first to be pushed to the fore.

The party of the *National*, the 'Friends of the Constitution *quand même*',[94] the *républicains purs et simples*, were completely beaten in the elections. A tiny minority from this party was elected to the legislature; their most notorious leaders disappeared from the stage, even Marrast, editor-in-chief and Orpheus of the worthy republic.

On 28 May the Legislative Assembly gathered; 11 June brought a repetition of the collision of 8 May; in the name of the Montagne Ledru-Rollin tabled a bill of impeachment against the President and the ministry for violation of the Constitution, for the bombardment of Rome. On 12 June the Legislative Assembly rejected the bill of impeachment, just as the Constituent Assembly had rejected it on 11 May, but this time the proletariat drove the Montagne onto the streets, not, however, for a street battle but for a street procession. It should suffice to say that the Montagne was at the head of this movement to know that the movement was defeated and that June 1849 was a caricature, as ludicrous as it was contemptible, of June 1848. The great retreat of 13 June was eclipsed only by the even greater battle report of Changarnier, the great man improvised by the party of Order. Every social

94. Regardless.

epoch needs its great men, and if it does not find them it invents them, as Helvétius said.

On 20 December only one half of the constituted republic was in existence, the President; on 28 May it was completed by the other half, the Legislative Assembly. In June 1848 the constituent bourgeois republic had engraved its name in the birth register of history by an unspeakable battle against the proletariat; in June 1849 the constituted bourgeois republic had done the same by an ineffable comedy with the petty bourgeoisie. June 1849 was the Nemesis of June 1848. In June 1849 it was not the workers who were defeated; it was the petty bourgeois who stood between them and the revolution who were felled. June 1849 was not a bloody tragedy between wage labour and capital, but a lamentable prison-filling drama acted out between debtor and creditor. The party of Order had won; it was all-powerful. It now had to show what it was.

III.   THE CONSEQUENCES OF 13 JUNE 1849

From 13 June 1849 to 10 March 1850

On 20 December [1848] the Janus head of the *constitutional republic* had shown only *one* face: the executive face with the indistinct, shallow features of Louis Bonaparte. On 28 May 1849 it showed its second face: the *legislative* face, pitted with scars left behind from the orgies of the Restoration and the July monarchy. With the Legislative National Assembly the phenomenon of the *constitutional republic* was completed, the republican form of government, that is, in which the rule of the bourgeois class is constituted – in other words, the joint rule of the two great royalist fractions which form the French bourgeoisie, the coalition of the Legitimists and the Orleanists, the *party of Order*. At the same time as the French republic thus became the property of the royalist coalition, the European coalition of counter-revolutionary forces embarked on a general crusade against the last sanctuaries of the March revolutions. Russia invaded Hungary; Prussia marched against the army upholding the Reich constitution, and Oudinot bombarded Rome. The European crisis was obviously approaching a decisive turning point; the eyes of all Europe were directed at Paris, and the eyes of Paris at the Legislative Assembly.

On 11 June Ledru-Rollin mounted the rostrum. He did not

make a speech; he formulated a requisitory against the ministers, naked, unadorned, factual, concentrated, forceful.

The attack on Rome is an attack on the Constitution; the attack on the Roman republic is an attack on the French republic. Paragraph V[95] of the Constitution reads, 'The French Republic will never employ its armed forces against the freedom of any people whatsoever' – and the President is using the French army against the freedom of Rome. Paragraph 54 of the Constitution forbids the executive to declare any war whatsoever without the consent of the National Assembly. The resolution of the Constituent Assembly of 8 May expressly orders the ministers to redirect the Roman expedition to its original purpose with all speed; it forbids them, therefore, no less expressly to wage war against Rome – and Oudinot is bombarding Rome. Ledru-Rollin thus called the Constitution itself as a witness for the prosecution against Bonaparte and his ministers. As the tribune of the Constitution he hurled a threat in the direction of the royalist majority of the National Assembly: 'The republicans will ensure that respect is paid to the Constitution – by every means possible, even by force of arms!' '*By force of arms!*' the Montagne re-echoed a hundred times over. The majority answered with a frightful tumult; the chairman of the National Assembly called Ledru-Rollin to order; Ledru-Rollin repeated his challenging declaration, and finally he laid on the chairman's desk a motion proposing the impeachment of Bonaparte and his ministers. By 361 votes to 203 the National Assembly resolved to move on from the bombardment of Rome to the regular agenda.

Did Ledru-Rollin believe he could defeat the National Assembly with the Constitution and the President with the National Assembly?

The Constitution, it is true, forbade any attack on the freedom of foreign peoples, but according to the ministry what the French army was attacking in Rome was not 'freedom' but the 'despotism of anarchy'. Despite all its experiences in the Constituent Assembly had the Montagne still not understood that the interpretation of the Constitution did not belong to those who had made it but only to those who had accepted it? That its wording was bound to be interpreted in accordance with its viable sense, and that the bourgeois sense was the only viable one? That Bonaparte and the royalist majority in the National Assembly were the authentic

95. The paragraphs of the French Constitution with roman numerals are from the introductory section.

interpreters of the Constitution, just as the priest is the authentic interpreter of the Bible and the judge the authentic interpreter of the law? Was the National Assembly, which had been given life by the general election, to feel bound by the testamentary provision of the dead Constituent Assembly, whose vital will had been broken by the likes of Odilon Barrot? By appealing to the resolution passed by the Constituent Assembly on 8 May, had Ledru-Rollin forgotten that on 11 May the same Constituent Assembly had rejected his first motion proposing the impeachment of Bonaparte and his ministers; that it had acquitted them; that it had thus sanctioned the attack on Rome as 'constitutional'; that he was only lodging an appeal against a judgement which had already been delivered; and that, lastly, he was appealing from the republican Constituent Assembly to the royalist Legislative Assembly? The Constitution itself calls insurrection to its assistance in a special paragraph, in which it summons every citizen to protect it. Ledru-Rollin based his position on this paragraph. But, at the same time, are the public powers not organized to protect the Constitution and is not the Constitution only violated the moment one of the public constitutional powers rebels against the others? And the President of the republic, the ministers of the republic, the National Assembly of the republic were all in the most harmonious agreement.

What the Montagne attempted on 11 June was '*an insurrection within the limits of pure reason*', that is, a purely *parliamentary insurrection*. The majority of the Assembly, intimidated by the prospect of an armed uprising by the popular masses, was supposed to destroy its own power and the significance of its own election in the persons of Bonaparte and his ministers. Had the Constituent Assembly not made a similar attempt to annul the election of Bonaparte by insisting so obstinately on the dismissal of the Barrot-Falloux ministry?

There was no lack of models from the time of the Convention for parliamentary insurrections which had suddenly and radically transformed the relation of majority and minority – and was the new Montagne to fail where the old Montagne had succeeded? – nor did the present circumstances seem unfavourable for such an undertaking. Popular unrest in Paris had reached an alarming pitch; the army did not seem favourably disposed towards the government, judging by its vote at the elections; the legislative majority itself was still too young to have consolidated its position, and, in addition, it consisted of old gentlemen. If the Montagne succeeded in bringing about a parliamentary insurrection, the helm of state would immediately fall into its hands. The democratic petty bourgeoisie, for its part, wished, as always, for nothing more fervently than to see the battle fought out above its head, in the clouds, between the departed spirits of parliament. Finally, both the democratic petty bourgeoisie and its representatives, the Montagne, would, by means of a parliamentary insurrection, fulfil their great ambition, that of breaking the power of the bourgeoisie without unleashing the proletariat or letting it appear other than in a reduced perspective; the proletariat would have been used without becoming dangerous.

After the vote of the National Assembly on 11 June a meeting took place between several members of the Montagne and delegates from the secret workers' societies. The latter urged that an attack be made that very evening. The Montagne decisively rejected this plan. On no account did it want to let the leadership slip out of its grasp; it suspected its allies as much as it suspected its opponents, and rightly so. The memory of June 1848 surged through the ranks of the Paris proletariat more vigorously than ever. Nevertheless, it was chained to the alliance with the Montagne. The latter represented the greater part of the departments; it exaggerated its influence in the army; it had the democratic section of the National Guard at its disposal; it had the moral strength of the shopkeepers behind it. To begin the insurrection at this moment against the will of the Montagne would have meant for the proletariat – decimated, moreover, by cholera and driven out of Paris in considerable numbers by unemployment – a useless repetition of the June days of 1848, without the situation which had forced that desperate struggle. The proletarian delegates did the only rational thing. They committed the Montagne to *compromise* itself, that is, to overstep the limits of the parliamentary struggle should its bill of impeachment be rejected. Throughout 13 June the proletariat maintained the same sceptically watchful position and waited for a serious, irrevocable clash between the democratic National Guard and the army in order to rush into the battle and to propel the revolution forward beyond the petty-bourgeois aim set for it. The proletarian commune which was to take its place beside the official government in the event of victory was already formed. The Paris workers had learnt their lesson in the bloody school of June 1848.

On 12 June Minister Lacrosse[96] himself proposed to the Legislative Assembly that they proceed at once to the discussion of the bill of impeachment. During the night the government had made every provision for defensive and offensive measures; the majority of the National Assembly was resolved to drive the rebellious minority out onto the street; the minority itself could no longer retreat; the die was cast. The bill of impeachment was rejected by 377 votes to eight. The Montagne, which had abstained, rushed furiously into the propaganda halls of 'peaceful democracy', into the newspaper offices of the *Démocratie pacifique*.[97]

This withdrawal from the parliament building robbed it of its strength, just as withdrawal from Earth robbed Antaeus, her giant son, of his strength. Though they were Samsons in the precincts of the Legislative Assembly, in the precincts of 'peaceful democracy' they were only Philistines. A long, noisy, aimless debate developed. The Montagne was determined to compel the observance of the Constitution by any means possible, '*except by force of arms*'. It was supported in this decision by a manifesto and by a deputation of the 'Friends of the Constitution', which was the name assumed by the wreckage left over from the coterie of the *National*, the bourgeois republican party. While six of its remaining parliamentary representatives had voted *against* and the others all *for* the rejection of the bill of impeachment, while Cavaignac placed his sabre at the disposal of the party of Order, the larger extra-parliamentary section of the coterie greedily seized the opportunity to emerge from its position as a political pariah and to push its way into the ranks of the democratic party. Did they not appear as the natural shield-bearers of this party, which concealed itself behind their shield, behind their *principle*, behind the *Constitution*?

The 'Mountain' laboured till daybreak. It gave birth to a '*Proclamation to the people*', which on the morning of 13 June occupied a more or less shamefaced place in two socialist journals.[98] It declared that the President, the ministers and the majority of

96. Bertrand, baron de Lacrosse, an Orleanist and later a Bonapartist, was Minister of Public Works in 1848–9 and 1851, and deputy chairman of the Constituent and Legislative National Assemblies.

97. *La Démocratie pacifique* was a Fourierist daily paper edited by Considérant. At a meeting in its offices, the Montagne deputies rejected armed struggle and decided to confine themselves to peaceful demonstration.

98. Marx is alluding to the poem (quoted by Athenaeus in the *Deipnosophistai*) in which a mountain gives birth to a mouse.

the Legislative Assembly were 'outside the Constitution' (*hors la constitution*) and summoned the National Guard, the army and finally the people to 'rise up'. '*Long live the Constitution!*' was the slogan which it issued, a slogan which meant nothing other than '*Down with the revolution!*'

In response to the Montagne's proclamation the petty bourgeoisie held a so-called *peaceful demonstration* on 13 June; that is, a street procession moved along from the Château d'Eau through the boulevards, 30,000 strong, mostly members of the National Guard, unarmed, interspersed with members of the secret workers' sections, shouting '*Long live the Constitution!*', a slogan which was uttered mechanically, ice-cold, and with a bad conscience by the demonstrators themselves, and which, instead of swelling up like thunder, was ironically tossed back by the echo of the people who milled about on the pavements. Deep-chested notes were missing from the many-voiced chorus. And as the procession turned by the meeting place of the 'Friends of the Constitution' and a hired herald of the Constitution appeared on the roof of the building violently cleaving the air with his *claqueur* hat, letting the slogan '*Long live the Constitution!*' fall like hail from his monstrous lungs onto the heads of the pilgrims, even they seemed to be overcome by the comedy of the situation. It is well known how, when the procession arrived at the corner of the rue de la Paix, it was met in the boulevards in a thoroughly unparliamentary manner by the dragoons and chasseurs of Changarnier, how, in an instant, it scattered in all directions, casting over its shoulder the occasional cry 'to arms' so that the parliamentary call to arms of 11 June might be fulfilled.

The majority of the Montagne, assembled in the rue du Hasard, scattered as the violent dispersion of the peaceful procession, the vague rumours of the murder of unarmed citizens on the boulevards, and the growing tumult on the streets seemed to herald the approach of an uprising. Ledru-Rollin, at the head of a small band of deputies, saved the honour of the Montagne. Under the protection of the Paris artillery, which had assembled in the Palais National, they betook themselves to the Conservatoire des Arts et Métiers[99] where the 5th and 6th legions of the National Guard were due to arrive. But the Montagnards waited for the 5th and 6th legions in vain. These cautious National Guards left

99. Museum of Arts and Trades.

their representatives in the lurch; the Paris artillery itself prevented the people from erecting barricades; chaotic disorder made any decision impossible, and the regular troops advanced with fixed bayonets. Some of the representatives were taken prisoner; others escaped. Thus ended 13 June.

If 23 June 1848 was the insurrection of the revolutionary proletariat, 13 June 1849 was the insurrection of the democratic petty bourgeoisie, each of these two insurrections the *classical* and *pure* expression of the class which had carried it out.

Only in Lyons did it come to an obstinate, bloody conflict. Here, where the industrial bourgeoisie and the industrial proletariat confront each other directly, where the workers' movement, unlike that in Paris, is not incorporated in, and determined by, the general movement, 13 June, in its repercussions, lost its original character. Wherever else it struck in the provinces it did not ignite – *a cold flash of lightning*.

13 June closes the first *period in the life of the constitutional republic*, which had begun its normal existence with the meeting of the Legislative Assembly on 28 May 1849. The whole course of this prologue was filled by the noisy struggle between bourgeoisie and petty bourgeoisie, as the latter resisted in vain the consolidation of the bourgeois republic, for which it had itself continuously conspired in the Provisional Government and the Executive Commission, for which it had fought desperately against the proletariat during the June days. 13 June broke its resistance and made the *legislative dictatorship* of the united royalists a *fait accompli*. From this moment on the National Assembly was only *the party of Order's Committee of Public Safety*.

Paris had put the President, the ministers and the majority of the National Assembly in a '*state of impeachment*'; they put Paris in a '*state of siege*'. The Montagne had declared the majority of the Legislative Assembly '*outside the Constitution*'; for violating the Constitution the majority handed the Montagne over to the High Court[1] and proscribed everything that still possessed any vitality. It was decimated to a rump without head or heart. The minority had gone so far as to attempt a *parliamentary insurrection*; the majority elevated its *parliamentary despotism* to a law. It

---

1. In a decree of 10 August 1849 the National Assembly decided to bring 'the accomplices and abettors of the conspiracy and attempt of 13 June' to the High Court.

decreed new *standing orders*, which abolished the freedom of the rostrum and empowered the chairman of the National Assembly to punish representatives who violated these standing orders with censorship, fines, confiscation of salaries, temporary expulsion or prison. Over the rump of the Montagne was hung the rod in place of the sword. The rest of the Montagne deputies owed it to their honour to quit the Assembly *en masse*. Such an act would have hastened the dissolution of the party of Order. It was bound to disintegrate into its original component parts the moment not even the semblance of an opposition existed to hold these together any longer.

At the same time as they lost their *parliamentary* power the democratic petty bourgeois were robbed of their *armed* power by the dissolution of the Paris Artillery and of the 8th, 9th and 12th legions of the National Guard. On the other hand, encouraging tribute was paid from the rostrum of the National Assembly to the legion of high finance, which, on 13 June, had raided the printing houses of Boulé and Roux, had smashed the presses, laid waste to the offices of the republican journals, and arbitrarily arrested editors, compositors, printers, forwarding clerks and errand boys. The disbandment of sections of the National Guard suspected of republicanism was repeated throughout the length and breadth of France.

A new *press law*, a new *law of association*, a new *law on the state of siege*, the Paris prisons overcrowded, political refugees driven out,[2] all journals which went beyond the limits of the *National* suspended, Lyons and the five surrounding departments delivered up to the brutal chicanery of military despotism, the ubiquitous courts, the often purged army of civil servants purged once again – these were the inevitable, the constantly recurring *commonplaces* of the victorious forces of reaction; they are only worth mentioning after the massacre and deportations of June, because this time they were directed not only against Paris but also against the departments, not only against the proletariat but, above all, against the middle classes.

The repressive laws, which left the declaration of a state of siege to the discretion of the government, which gagged the press more firmly and abolished the right of association, absorbed all

2. Marx had arrived in Paris on 3 June 1849 as a political refugee from Germany. On 19 July he was ordered to leave Paris, and after obtaining a stay of execution, he left Paris on 24 August for London.

the legislative activity of the National Assembly throughout June, July and August.

However, this period is characterized by the exploitation of victory, not *in fact* but *in principle*; not by resolutions passed by the National Assembly, but by the motivation of these resolutions; not by the matter itself, but by the phrase; not by the phrase, but by the accent and gesture which give life to the phrase. The ruthless and unashamed expression of *royalist sentiments*, the contemptuously superior insults aimed at the republic, the coquettishly frivolous divulging of restorationist aims, in a word, the boastful violation of *republican propriety* give this period its particular tone and colour. '*Long live the Constitution!*' was the battle-cry of the *vanquished* of 13 June. The *victors*, therefore, were absolved from the hypocrisy of constitutional, that is, republican, talk. The counter-revolution subjugated Hungary, Italy and Germany, and they believed that the restoration was already before the gates of France. Among the masters of ceremonies in the party of Order a veritable competition developed to document their royalism in the *Moniteur* and to confess, repent and ask the forgiveness of God and man for any liberal sins they might by chance have committed under the monarchy. No day went by without the February revolution being declared a public calamity from the rostrum of the National Assembly, without some Legitimist provincial squire solemnly maintaining that he had never recognized the republic, without one of the craven deserters of and traitors to the July monarchy relating the belated acts of heroism which he would have performed but for the philanthropy of Louis Philippe or for other misunderstandings. What was to be admired in the days of February was not the magnanimity of the victorious people but the self-sacrifice and moderation of the royalists, which had allowed the people to achieve their victory. One representative proposed donating part of the relief money intended for those wounded in February to the Municipal Guard,[3] which was alone in having earned the gratitude of the fatherland at that time. Another wanted a decree for the erection of an equestrian statue

3. Under the July monarchy the Municipal Guard put down a number of insurrections with ferocity, and was particularly hated by the people in February 1848. The Provisional Government at first intended to dissolve it, but a para-military force of this nature soon turned out to be necessary to suppress opposition from the left. It was therefore kept in being, from May 1848 under the name of Republican Guard.

of the Duke of Orleans in the Place du Carrousel. Thiers[4] called the Constitution a dirty piece of paper. One after the other they appeared at the rostrum: Orleanists who repented their conspiracy against the legitimate monarchy; Legitimists who accused themselves of having hastened the overthrow of monarchy in general by opposing the illegitimate monarchy; Thiers, who regretted having intrigued against Molé;[5] Molé, who regretted having intrigued against Guizot; Barrot, who regretted having intrigued against all three. The slogan, 'Long live the social-democratic republic!' was declared unconstitutional; the slogan, 'Long live the republic!' was prosecuted as social-democratic. On the anniversary of the Battle of Waterloo a representative declared, 'I fear the invasion of the Prussians less than the entry of revolutionary refugees into France.' To the complaints about the terrorism organized in Lyons and the neighbouring departments, Baraguey-d'Hilliers[6] answered, 'I prefer the white terror to the red terror.' (*J'aime mieux la terreur blanche que la terreur rouge.*) And the Assembly applauded wildly every time an epigram directed against the republic, against the revolution, against the Constitution, in favour of the monarchy, in favour of the Holy Alliance, fell from the lips of their speakers. Every slightest infringement of republican formalities, for example, that of addressing the representatives as '*citoyens*', aroused the enthusiasm of the knights of Order.

The Paris by-elections of 8 July, held under the influence of the state of siege and the abstention of a large section of the proletariat from the ballot box, the taking of Rome by the French army, the entry into Rome of the red eminences, with the inquisition and monkish terrorism in their train;[7] all these added new victories to the victory of June and heightened the intoxication of the party of Order.

Finally, in the middle of August, half with the intention of attending the Departmental Councils which had just assembled, half because of exhaustion from the orgy of tendentiousness,

4. Louis-Adolphe Thiers was an historian and politician. Twice Prime Minister under Louis Philippe, he was a leading Orleanist under the Second Republic and, after supervising the suppression of the Paris Commune of 1871, became the first President of the Third Republic (1871–3).

5. Louis, comte Molé was an Orleanist politician, Prime Minister from 1836 to 1839, and a deputy in both Assemblies.

6. Achille, comte Baraguey-d'Hilliers was a Bonapartist general, and a deputy in both Assemblies. In 1851 he commanded the Paris garrison.

7. This refers to the commission of three cardinals who entered Rome with the French army to restore the reactionary papal regime.

which had lasted for many months, the royalists decreed a two-month prorogation of the National Assembly. With transparent irony they left behind a Commission of twenty-five representatives,[8] the cream of the Legitimists and Orleanists, a Molé and a Changarnier, to represent the National Assembly and to serve as *guardians of the republic*. The irony was more profound than they suspected. Condemned by history to help in the overthrow of the monarchy which they loved, they were destined by history to conserve the republic which they hated.

The prorogation of the Legislative Assembly *closes the second period in the life of the constitutional republic, the period in which it sowed its royalist wild oats*.

The state of siege in Paris had been raised again, the press had resumed its activities once more. During the suspension of the social-democratic press, during the period of repressive legislation and royalist blustering, *Le Siècle*, the old literary representative of the *constitutional-monarchist petty bourgeoisie, became republicanized*; *La Presse*, the old literary advocate of the *bourgeois reformers, became democratized*; *Le National*, the old classical organ of the *bourgeois republicans*, became socialized.

The *secret societies* grew in extent and intensity the more the *public clubs* became impossible. Each of the workers' *industrial cooperatives*, tolerated as purely commercial societies, although economically of no significance, became politically a means of cementing the proletariat. 13 June had chopped off the official heads of the various semi-revolutionary parties; the masses that remained found their own head. The knights of Order had intimidated the country with prophesies of the terror of the red republic; the base excesses, the hyperborean barbarity of the victorious counter-revolution in Hungary, in Baden[9] and in Rome washed the '*red republic*' white. The discontented intermediate classes of French society began to prefer the promises of the 'red republic' with its problematic terrors to the terrors of the red monarchy with its actual hopelessness. No socialist spread more propaganda in France than Haynau.[10] *À chaque capacité selon ses œuvres*.[11]

8. The Standing Commission of the Assembly was provided for in the Constitution, to safeguard the latter during the Assembly's recess.

9. Baden was the chief stronghold of the German Reich Constitution Campaign.

10. Julius Jakob, Freiherr von Haynau was an Austrian field-marshal notorious for his cruel reprisals against the Hungarian nationalists in 1849.

11. To each according to his works.

Meanwhile Louis Napoleon exploited the National Assembly's recess to make princely tours in the provinces; the most hot-blooded Legitimists made pilgrimages to the descendant of St Louis[12] at Ems, and the mass of the party of Order's deputies intrigued in the Departmental Councils, which had just met. It was a matter of making them put forward what the majority of the National Assembly did not yet dare, a *motion of urgency for the immediate revision of the Constitution*. According to itself, the Constitution could not be revised until 1852, and then only by a National Assembly summoned for this specific purpose. But if the majority of the Departmental Councils expressed themselves in favour of revision, would the National Assembly not have to sacrifice the virginity of the Constitution to the voice of France? The National Assembly entertained the same hopes with regard to the provincial assemblies as the nuns in Voltaire's *La Henriade* with regard to the pandours. But the Potiphars of the National Assembly, with a few exceptions, found they were dealing with just so many provincial Josephs. The vast majority did not want to understand the importunate insinuation. The revision of the Constitution was thwarted by the very instruments with which it was to have been called into existence, by the votes of the Departmental Councils. The voice of France, namely the voice of bourgeois France, had spoken, and it had spoken against revision.

At the beginning of October the Legislative National Assembly assembled again – *tantum mutatus ab illo*.[13] Its physiognomy was completely changed. The unexpected rejection of revision by the Departmental Councils had placed it back within the limits of the Constitution and had indicated the limits of its term of life. The Orleanists had become suspicious as a result of the pilgrimages of the Legitimists to Ems; the Legitimists had become mistrustful as a result of the negotiations of the Orleanists with London;[14] the journals of both fractions had fanned the flames and weighed the rival claims of their pretenders. Orleanists and Legitimists grumbled in unison at the machinations of the Bonapartists, which became evident on the princely tours, in the more or less transparent emancipatory endeavours of the President, in the

12. This was Henri-Charles d'Artois, comte de Chambord, grandson of Charles X and pretender to the French throne under the title of Henri V. He lived at Ems near Wiesbaden.

13. How great a change since then.

14. The deposed Louis Philippe lived at Claremont near London.

presumptuous language of the Bonapartist newspapers; Louis Bonaparte grumbled at a National Assembly which found only the Legitimist and Orleanist conspiracies legitimate, and at a ministry which permanently betrayed him to this National Assembly. Finally, the ministry itself was split on the Rome policy and the *income tax*, which had been proposed by Minister Passy[15] and decried as socialist by the conservatives.

One of the first bills that the Barrot ministry presented to the re-assembled Legislative Assembly was a credit demand of 300,000 francs for a widow's pension for the Duchess of Orleans.[16] The National Assembly approved it and added to the French nation's list of debts a sum of 7 million francs. While Louis Philippe thus continued successfully to play the role of the *pauvre honteux*, the shamefaced beggar, the ministry neither dared move a salary increase for Bonaparte nor did the Assembly seem inclined to give it. And Louis Bonaparte, as ever, vacillated before the dilemma: *aut Caesar aut Clichy!*[17]

The second credit demand made by the ministry, for nine million francs to cover *the costs of the Rome expedition*, increased the tension between Bonaparte on the one hand and the ministers and the National Assembly on the other. Louis Bonaparte had inserted in the *Moniteur* a letter to his military aide, Edgar Ney, in which he tied the papal government to constitutional guarantees. The Pope, for his part, had issued an address, *motu proprio*,[18] in which he rejected any limits on his restored rule. Bonaparte's letter, a deliberate indiscretion, lifted the veil of his cabinet in order to reveal himself to the glances of the gallery as a benevolent genius, misunderstood and fettered in his own house. He flirted, not for the first time, with the 'furtively beating wings of a free soul'.[19] Thiers, the commission's *rapporteur*, completely ignored Bonaparte's beating wings and contented himself with translating

15. Hippolyte Passy, an economist and Orleanist politician, was Minister of Finance from 1849 to 1850.

16. Helène, duchesse d'Orléans was the widow of Ferdinand, Louis Philippe's eldest son.

17. Either Caesar or Clichy. Clichy was the Paris debtors' prison during the mid-nineteenth century.

18. 'Of his own accord', the general name for a papal message sent without the collaboration of the cardinals and generally dealing with internal administrative arrangements of the papal state. This particular *motu proprio* was published on 12 September 1849.

19. A phrase from Georg Herwegh's poem 'From the Mountain'.

the papal allocution into French. It was not the ministry but Victor Hugo[20] who tried to save the President with an agenda in which the National Assembly was to express its agreement with Napoleon's letter.

Allons donc! Allons donc![21] With this disrespectful, flippant interjection the majority buried Hugo's motion. The President's policy? The President's letter? The President himself? *Allons donc! Allons donc!* Who the devil takes Monsieur Bonaparte *au sérieux*? Do you believe, Monsieur Victor Hugo, that we believe that you believe in the President? *Allons donc! Allons donc!*

The breach between Bonaparte and the National Assembly was finally accelerated by the discussion on the *recall of the Orleans and Bourbons*. In default of the ministry the President's cousin, the son of the ex-king of Westphalia,[22] had proposed this motion, which had no other function than that of reducing the Legitimist and Orleanist pretenders to the same level as, or even a *lower* one than, the Bonapartist pretender, who at least was already at the pinnacle of state power.

Napoleon Bonaparte was disrespectful enough to make the *recall of the banished royal families* and the *amnesty for the June insurgents* parts of one and the same motion. The indignation of the majority forced him immediately to apologize for this sacriligious juxtaposition of the holy and the impious, the royal races and the proletarian brood, the fixed stars of society and its swamp lights, and to assign to each of these its proper rank. The majority energetically rejected the recall of the royal family, and Berryer,[23] the Demosthenes of the Legitimists, left no doubt as to the significance of their vote. The public degradation of the pretenders, that is what they intend! They want to rob them of their halo, of the last trace of majesty which is left to them, the *majesty of exile*! What, declared Berryer, would the people think of the pretender who, forgetting his illustrious origins, came here to live as a simple private citizen! Louis Bonaparte could not be told more clearly that his presence in France did not mean that he had won, that while the royalist coalition needed him here in France on the President's chair as a *neutral man*, the serious pretenders to the

20. Victor Hugo, the novelist, was a deputy in both Assemblies. He originally supported the party of Order, but broke with it over the Rome expedition.

21. Come off it!

22. Jérôme Bonaparte was a deputy in both Assemblies.

23. Pierre-Antoine Berryer was a lawyer and a deputy in both Assemblies.

throne had to remain withdrawn from profane sight by the mists of exile.

On 1 November Louis Bonaparte answered the Legislative Assembly with a message which announced, in rather blunt terms, the dismissal of Barrot's ministry and the formation of a new one. The Barrot-Falloux ministry was the ministry of the royalist coalition: the Hautpoul[24] ministry was Bonaparte's own ministry, the organ of the President in his confrontation with the Legislative Assembly, the *ministry of clerks*.

Bonaparte was no longer merely the *neutral man* of 10 December 1848. His possession of executive power had caused a number of interests to group around him; the struggle against 'anarchy' forced the party of Order itself to increase his influence, and even if he was *no longer* popular, the party of Order was *unpopular*. Could he not hope to force the Orleanists and the Legitimists, as a result of their rivalry and the necessity of some sort of monarchist restoration, to a recognition of the *neutral pretender*?

The third period in the life of the constitutional republic dates from 1 November 1849 and ends with 10 March 1850. It did not only see the beginning of the regular play of constitutional institutions so admired by Guizot – the squabble between executive and legislature. In the face of the restorationist desires of the united Orleanists and Legitimists it saw Bonaparte defend his actual power: the republic. In the face of Bonaparte's restorationist desires the fractions of the party of Order defended their joint power: the republic. The Orleanists confronted the Legitimists, and the Legitimists the Orleanists, as the representatives of the status quo: the republic. All these fractions of the party of Order, each of which had its own king and restoration *in petto*, in turn enforced the joint rule of the bourgeoisie in opposition to the usurpatory and mutinous desires of the rival pretenders: they enforced that form of society in which particular claims of the various parties were held in check and neutralized – *the republic*.

The royalists made of *the monarchy* what Kant makes of the republic – the only rational form of state: a postulate of practical reason, which can never be realized but whose achievement must always be the goal striven for and adhered to in one's beliefs.

24. Alphonse, marquis d'Hautpoul was a Legitimist general, later a Bonapartist. He sat in the Legislative National Assembly and was Minister of War from 1849 to 1850.

Thus, the constitutional republic, which had been produced by the bourgeois republicans as a hollow ideological formula, became in the hands of the royalist coalition a form filled with substance and life. And Thiers spoke truer than he knew when he said, 'We, the royalists, are the true pillars of the constitutional republic.'

The overthrow of the coalition ministry and the appearance of the ministry of the clerks have a second significance. Its Minister of Finance was Fould. Fould's appointment to the Ministry of Finance represented the official surrender of French national wealth to the Bourse, the administration of public property by the Bourse and in the interests of the Bourse. With Fould's appointment the financial aristocracy announced its own restoration in the *Moniteur*. This restoration necessarily supplemented the other restorations, each forming a link in the chain of the constitutional republic.

Louis Philippe had never dared make a real *loup-cervier* (stock-exchange shark) Minister of Finance. Since his monarchy was the ideal name that covered the rule of the big bourgeoisie, the privileged interests had to bear ideologically disinterested names in his ministries. But the bourgeois republic, on all fronts, pushed into the foreground what the different monarchies, the Legitimist no less than the Orleanist, had kept concealed in the background. It brought back to earth what they had transferred to the heavens. It replaced the names of the saints with the bourgeois proper names of the dominant class interests.

Our whole account has shown how the republic, from the first day of its existence, did not overthrow the financial aristocracy but consolidated it. The concessions which were made to it were a fate passively submitted to rather than actively striven for. With Fould, however, governmental initiative fell back into the hands of the financial aristocracy.

It might be asked how the bourgeois coalition was able to bear and tolerate the rule of finance, which under Louis Philippe had been based on the exclusion or subordination of the other fractions of the bourgeoisie.

The answer is simple.

First of all, the financial aristocracy itself forms a decisive and substantial part of the royalist coalition, whose common governmental power is called a republic. Are not the spokesmen and authoritative figures of the Orleanists the old allies and accomplices of the financial aristocracy? Does it not itself represent the golden phalanx of Orleanism? As far as the Legitimists are concerned, even at the time of Louis Philippe they had taken a practical part in all the speculative orgies on the Bourse, in mines and in railways. The combination of large landed property and high finance is in general a *normal fact*, as evidenced by England, and even Austria.

In a country such as France, where the volume of national production is disproportionately smaller than the size of the national debt, where government bonds form the most important object of speculation and the Bourse forms the chief market for the investment of capital which is intended to be turned to account unproductively, in such a country a countless mass of people from all bourgeois or semi-bourgeois classes inevitably have an interest in the national debt, stock-market gambles and finance. Do not all these subaltern interested parties find their natural supporters and commanders in the fraction which represents these interests on the broadest basis?

How does public property come to fall into the hands of high finance? Due to the growing indebtedness of the state. And what causes the indebtedness of the state? The constant excess of its expenditure compared with its revenue, a disproportion which is both the cause and the effect of the system of state loans.

One way for the state to free itself from this indebtedness would be to curb its expenditure, that is, simplify and reduce the size of the government organism, govern as little as possible, employ as small a personnel as possible and have as few dealings with bourgeois society as possible. This course was impossible for the party of Order, whose means of repression, official interference in the name of the state and omnipresence through the organs of state, were bound to increase the more the rule of its class and its conditions of life were threatened from an increasing number of quarters. The *gendarmerie* cannot be reduced in size while attacks on persons and property increase.

Alternatively, the state would have to try to avoid debt and produce an immediate but temporary balance in the budget by placing *extraordinary taxes* on the shoulders of the richest classes. But was the party of Order to sacrifice its own wealth on the altar of the fatherland in order to withdraw the national wealth from exploitation by the Bourse? *Pas si bête!*[25]

25. It is not so stupid.

Thus, without a total revolution in the French state there can be no revolution in the French state budget. This state budget inevitably led to state indebtedness and this inevitably led to the dominance of the trade in state securities, the rule of the state creditors, bankers, money-dealers and sharks of the Bourse. Only one fraction of the party of Order directly participated in the overthrow of the financial aristocracy – the *manufacturers*. We are not speaking of the medium-sized or smaller people engaged in industry, but rather the rulers of the manufacturing interests, who had formed the broad basis of the dynastic opposition under Louis Philippe. Their interests indubitably lie in a reduction of production costs, hence a reduction of taxation, which is a factor in production costs, hence a reduction of the state debt, the interest on which increases taxation, and hence in the overthrow of the financial aristocracy.

In England – and the largest French manufacturers are petty bourgeois compared with their English rivals – we really find the manufacturers, a Cobden, a Bright,[26] at the head of the crusade against the Bank and the stock-exchange aristocracy. Why not in France? In England industry predominates; in France, agriculture. In England industry requires *free trade*; in France, protective tariffs, a national monopoly alongside the other monopolies. French industry does not dominate French production; French industrialists, therefore, do not dominate the French bourgeoisie. In order to assert their interest against the other fractions of the bourgeoisie they cannot, as can the English, take the lead in a movement and at the same time pursue their own class interests to the extreme; they must follow in the train of the revolution and serve interests which are opposed to the overall interests of their class. In February they had misunderstood their position; February sharpened their wits. And who is more directly threatened by the workers than the employer, the industrial capitalist? In France, therefore, the manufacturer inevitably became the most fanatical member of the party of Order. What is the reduction of his *profit* by finance *compared with the abolition of profit by the proletariat*?

In France the petty bourgeois does what the industrial bourgeois would normally have to do; the worker does what would normally be the task of the petty bourgeois. Who then does the task of the worker? Nobody. It is not accomplished in France; it is only

26. Richard Cobden and John Bright were the leaders of the English 'Free Trade' party (see 'The Chartists', below, pp. 262–3).

proclaimed. And it will not be accomplished within any national walls. The class war within French society will be transformed into a world war in which nation confronts nation. The worker's task will begin to be accomplished only when the world war carries the proletariat to the fore in the nation that dominates the world market, i.e., England. The revolution which here finds not its end but its organizational beginning is no short-winded revolution. The present generation is like the Jews, whom Moses led through the wilderness. They not only have a new world to conquer; they must perish in order to make room for the men who are equal to a new world.

Let us return to Fould.

On 14 November Fould came to the rostrum of the National Assembly and explained his financial system: an apology for the old system of taxation! Retention of the wine tax! Withdrawal of Passy's income tax!

Passy, too, was no revolutionary; he was an old minister of Louis Philippe's. He was a puritan of the Dufaure school and one of the most intimate confidants of Teste, the scapegoat of the July monarchy.[27] Passy, too, had praised the old system of taxation and had recommended the retention of the wine tax; but he had also torn aside the veil from the state deficit. He declared a new tax, the income tax, to be necessary if state bankruptcy was to be avoided. Fould, who had recommended state bankruptcy to Ledru-Rollin, recommended to the Legislative Assembly a state deficit. He promised economies, the nature of which was later revealed as, for example, reducing expenditure by 60 million francs and increasing the floating debt by 200 million francs – conjuring tricks in the arrangement of figures, in the drawing up of accounts, which all finally added up to new loans.

Alongside the other jealous fractions of the bourgeoisie, the financial aristocracy under Fould did not behave in such a shamelessly corrupt manner as under Louis Philippe. But the system remained the same, with a steady increase in debts and the dis-

27. On 8 July 1847, before the Chamber of Peers in Paris, began the trial of Parmentier and General Cubières, charged with bribing civil servants with a view to obtaining a concession for a salt works, and of the then Minister of Public Works, Teste, for accepting such financial bribes. During the trial Teste attempted to commit suicide. All were sentenced to pay heavy fines and Teste, in addition, to three years imprisonment. [*Note by Engels to the 1895 edition.*]

guising of the deficit. And gradually the old Bourse swindling emerged more and more into the open, as evidenced by the law on the Avignon railway, by the mysterious fluctuations in government securities, for a moment the talk of all Paris, finally by Fould's and Bonaparte's abortive speculations on the elections of 10 March.

With the official restoration of the financial aristocracy the French people soon had to face a 24 February once again.

In an attack of misanthropy directed against its heir the Constituent Assembly had abolished the wine tax for the year of our Lord 1850. With the abolition of old taxes, new debts could not be paid. Creton,[28] a cretin of the party of Order, had already moved the retention of the wine tax before the prorogation of the Legislative Assembly. Fould took up this motion in the name of the Bonapartist ministry, and on 20 December 1849, on the anniversary of Bonaparte's proclamation as President, the National Assembly decreed the *restoration of the wine tax*.

The proposer of this resolution was not a financier but the Jesuit leader Montalembert.[29] His deduction was strikingly simple: taxes are the maternal breast at which the government is suckled. The government is represented by the instruments of repression, the organs of authority, the army, the police, the officials, the judges, the ministers, the *priests*. The attack on taxation is an attack by the anarchists on the sentinels of order, who protect the material and spiritual production of bourgeois society from the incursions of the proletarian vandals. Taxation is the fifth god beside property, family, order and religion. And the wine tax is indisputably a tax – furthermore, no ordinary one, but a traditional, a respectable tax, a tax with monarchist loyalties. *Vive l'impôt des boissons!*[30] *Three cheers and one cheer more!*[31]

When the French farmer talks of the devil, he pictures him in the guise of a tax collector. From the moment that Montalembert deified taxes the peasant became godless, an atheist, and threw himself into the arms of the devil, *socialism*. The religion of order had forfeited the allegiance of the peasant; the Jesuits had forfeited it; Bonaparte had forfeited it. 20 December 1849 had irrevocably

28. Nicolas Creton was a lawyer and Orleanist, and a deputy in both Assemblies.

29. Charles, comte de Montalembert was a member of both Assemblies and the leader of the clerical party. Originally an Orleanist, he went over to Bonaparte in 1861.

30. Long live the tax on drinks!

31. In English in the original.

compromised 20 December 1848. The 'nephew of his uncle' was not the first in his family to be defeated by this wine tax, which, in Montalembert's expression, smelt the revolutionary storm in the air. The true Napoleon, Napoleon the great, had declared on St Helena that the reintroduction of the wine tax had contributed more to his overthrow than anything else, as it had alienated the peasants of southern France from him. Already the favourite object of popular hatred under Louis XIV (see the writings of Boisguillebert and Vauban),[32] it had been abolished by the first revolution; Napoleon had reintroduced it in 1808 in a modified form. When the Restoration entered France it was not only the cossacks that trotted before it but also promises of the abolition of the wine tax. The *gentilhommerie* naturally did not need to keep its word to the *gent taillable à merci et miséricorde.*[33]

1830 had promised the abolition of the wine tax. It was not its nature to do what it said or to say what it would do. 1848 promised the abolition of the wine tax just as it promised everything. Finally, the Constituent Assembly, which promised nothing, made, as already mentioned, a testamentary provision according to which the wine tax was to disappear on 1 January 1850, and just ten days before 1 January 1850 the Legislative Assembly reintroduced it. The French people were thus in its perpetual pursuit. When they had thrown it out of the door, they saw it come in again through the window.

The popular hatred of the wine tax can be explained by the fact that it unites all that is odious about the French taxation system. The way it is levied is odious; the way it is distributed is aristocratic, for the rates of taxation remain the same for the most common and for the most expensive wines. It increases in geometric progression as the consumer's wealth decreases, an inverted progressive tax, and so directly provokes the poisoning of the working class as a premium on adulterated and imitation wines. It reduces consumption by establishing customs offices at the gates of all towns over 4,000 inhabitants and by transforming every town into a foreign country with protective tariffs against French wine. The great wine merchants, but even more so the small ones, the *marchands de vins*, the small wine-shop keepers

32. Pierre le Pesant, sieur de Boisguillebert, was the founder of classical political economy in France; Sebastien le Prêtre, marquis de Vauban, was a marshal, military engineer and economist.

33. People taxable at their pleasure and at their mercy.

whose livelihood is directly dependent upon the consumption of wine are, every one of them, avowed enemies of the wine tax. And lastly, by reducing consumption, the wine tax reduces the producers' market. While it prevents the workers in the towns from paying for the wine, it prevents the wine growers from selling it. And France numbers a wine-growing population of about twelve million. The hatred of the people in general for the wine tax, and the particular fanaticism of the peasants, is then understandable. And, furthermore, they saw in its restoration not a particular or more or less chance event. The peasants have a kind of historical tradition, which is handed down from father to son, and in this tradition the saying goes that whenever it wants to deceive the peasants every government promises the abolition of the wine tax, and that as soon as it had deceived the peasants it retains or reimposes the wine tax. On the question of the wine tax the peasants test the bouquet, the inclination, of the government. The restoration of the wine tax on 20 December meant: *Louis Bonaparte is like the others*. However, he was not like the others, he was an *invention of the peasants*, and by petitioning in millions against the wine tax they took back the votes which, a year before, they had given to the 'nephew of his uncle'.

The rural population of France – over two thirds of the total – consists for the most part of so-called free *landowners*. The first generation, which was freed gratuitously from feudal burdens by the revolution of 1789, did not have to pay for the soil. But the following generations paid, in the form of the *price of the land*, what their forefathers, as semi-serfs, had paid in the form of rent, tithes, socage, etc. The more the population grew, the more the land was partitioned. The plots of land became dearer, for the smaller they became the more the demand for them increased. But as the price which the peasant paid for the land rose, whether he bought it directly or had it accounted as capital by his coparceners, so in the same measure the *indebtedness of the peasant*, that is, his *mortgage*, inevitably grew also. The debt claim with which land is encumbered is called the *mortgage*, a pawn-ticket for the land. Just as *privileges* accumulated on medieval estates, so *mortgages* accumulate on modern plots of land. On the other hand, under the parcelling system the land is purely an *instrument of production* for its owners. Now, the more the land is divided, the more its fertility diminishes. The use of machinery on the land, division of labour, and great soil enrichment measures such as the digging of canals for drainage and irrigation and the like, become more and more impossible, while the *overhead costs* of cultivation grow proportionally, the more the instrument of production is itself divided up. All this happens regardless of whether the owner of the land possesses capital or not. But the more the land is partitioned, the more the plot of land with its utterly miserable inventory forms the total capital of the peasant farmer, the more capital investment in the land is reduced and the more the cottager lacks the land, money and education necessary to apply the advances in agronomy, so much the more the cultivation of the land retrogresses. Finally, the *net profit* decreases in the same proportion as the *gross consumption* increases, as the whole family of the peasant is held back by its holding from pursuing other occupations and yet is not placed in a position to live by it.

To the same degree, therefore, that the population, and with it the partitioning of the land, increases, the *instrument of production*, the soil, *becomes more expensive*, its *fertility* decreases, *agriculture declines and the peasant falls into debt*. What was an effect becomes in turn a cause. Each generation leaves the next even more indebted; each new generation begins under more unfavourable and more burdensome conditions; mortgages beget mortgages, and if it becomes impossible for the peasant to offer his smallholding as a security for *new debts*, that is, to encumber it with new mortgages, he falls a direct victim to *usury* and the *usurious interest rates* become all the more exorbitant.

And thus it has come about that the peasant cedes to the capitalist – in the form of *interest* on *mortgages* encumbering the soil, in the form of interest on *non-mortgaged usurious advances* – not only a ground rent, not only the industrial profit, in a word, not only the *whole net profit*, but even *a part of his wages*, so that he has sunk to the level of an *Irish tenant farmer* – and all under the pretext of being a *private proprietor*.

This process was accelerated in France by the ever-increasing *tax burden* and by *legal costs*, partly caused by the formalities with which French legislation surrounds landed property, partly by the innumerable conflicts between the smallholdings, which bound and cross each other on all sides, partly by the litigiousness of the peasants, whose enjoyment of property is limited to the fanatical defence of their imaginary property, their *property rights*.

According to a statistical tabulation for 1840, French agricultural production amounted to a gross value of 5,237,178,000 francs. Of this, 3,552,000,000 francs went on the costs of cultivation, including consumption by the labour force. There remains a net product of 1,685,178,000 francs, of which 550 million must be deducted for interest on mortgages, 100 million for legal officials, 350 million for taxes and 107 million for registration money, stamp duty, mortgage fees, etc. One third of the net product remains, 598 million francs;[34] when spread over the population this is not even 25 francs *per capita* net product. These calculations naturally include neither usury outside the field of mortgage nor the costs of lawyers, etc.

The position of the French peasants, after the republic had added new burdens to their old ones, is understandable. It is evident that their exploitation differs only in *form* from that of the industrial proletariat. The exploiter is the same: *capital*. The individual capitalists exploit the individual peasants by means of *mortgage* and *usury*; the capitalist class exploits the peasant class by means of *state taxes*. The peasant's claim to property is the talisman with which capital has hitherto held him under its spell, the pretext on which it set him against the industrial proletariat. Only the fall of capital can raise the peasant, only an anticapitalist, proletarian government can break his economic poverty and his social degradation. The *constitutional republic* is the dictatorship of his united exploiters; the *social-democratic* or *red* republic is the dictatorship of his allies. And the scales rise or fall according to the votes which the peasant casts into the ballot box. He himself has to decide his fate. This is the way the socialists spoke in pamphlets, almanacs, calendars and leaflets of all kinds. This language became more comprehensible to the peasant as a result of the counter-publications of the party of Order, which also addressed him and, striking the true peasant tone with their crude exaggeration and brutal interpretation and representation of the intentions and ideas of the socialists, over-stimulated his lust for forbidden fruit. But most comprehensible of all was the language of the actual experience which the peasant had gained from the use of the franchise and the disappointments which had overwhelmed him, blow upon blow, with revolutionary speed. *Revolutions are the locomotives of history.*

34. Either Marx or his source for these figures has made a mistake; the exact figure here would be 578,178,000. However, the *per capita* net product would then be even less.

There were various symptoms of the gradual revolutionizing of the peasants. It was already evident in the elections to the Legislative Assembly; it was evident in the state of siege in the five departments bordering Lyons; it was evident several months after 13 June in the election of a Montagnard in place of the former chairman of the Chambre introuvable[35] in the department of Gironde. It was evident on 20 December 1849 in the election of a red deputy in place of a deceased Legitimist deputy in the department of Gard,[36] the promised land of the Legitimists, scene of the most terrible atrocities against republicans in 1794 and 1795, and centre of the *terreur blanche* of 1815, when liberals and Protestants were murdered in public. This revolutionizing of the most stationary class has become most obvious since the reintroduction of the wine tax. The government measures and laws of January and February 1850 were directed almost exclusively against the departments and the *peasants*. This is the most striking proof of their progress.

Hautpoul's circular, in which the gendarme was appointed inquisitor of the prefect, of the sub-prefect and, above all, of the mayor, in which espionage was organized even into the hiding places of the remotest village community; *the law against schoolteachers*, in which the authorities, the spokesmen, the educators and the interpreters of the peasant class were subjected to the arbitrary power of the prefect and were hounded like beasts, these proletarians of the educated class, from one community to another; *the bill against the mayors*, in which the Damocles sword of dismissal hung over their heads and they, the presidents of the peasant communities, were permanently confronted by the President of the republic and the party of Order; the *ordinance* which transformed the seventeen military divisions of France into four pashalics[37] and imposed the barracks and the bivouac of the French as their national salon; the *education law*, whereby the party of Order proclaimed the unconsciousness and forcible

35. This is the name given by history to the fanatically ultra-royalist, reactionary Chamber of Deputies elected immediately after the second overthrow of Napoleon in 1815. [*Note by Engels to the 1895 edition.*]

36. Favaune, the Montagne's candidate, was elected deputy for Beaune with an absolute majority.

37. By a decree of 10 March 1850 the government redivided France into five large military divisions, putting the most reactionary generals at the head of the Paris region. The republican press nicknamed these divisions pashalics, after the despotic power of the Turkish pasha.

stupefaction of France as conditions vital for its own existence under the rule of universal suffrage – what were all these laws and measures? Desperate attempts to reconquer the departments and their peasantry for the party of Order.

Regarded as *repression*, they were wretched measures which wrung the neck of their own intentions. The major measures, such as the retention of the wine tax, the 45-centime tax, the disdainful rejection of the peasants' petitions for the repayment of the thousand million francs,[38] etc., all these legislative thunderbolts struck the peasant class only once, wholesale, from the centre of government; the laws and measures quoted here made the attack and resistance *general*, the talking-point in every cottage; they inoculated every village with the revolution; *they made the revolution a local matter and a matter for the peasants*.

On the other hand, did these proposals of Bonaparte's and their acceptance by the National Assembly not demonstrate that the two powers of the constitutional republic were united as long as the problem was of repressing 'anarchy' – all classes, that is, that rose up against the bourgeois dictatorship? Had not Soulouque, directly after his harsh message, assured the Legislative Assembly of his *dévouements*[39] to order in the announcement which followed immediately from Carlier, a dirty, mean caricature of Fouché, like Bonaparte's shallow caricature of Napoleon?[40]

The *education law* shows us the alliance of the young Catholics and old Voltaireans. Could the rule of the united bourgeoisie be anything else but the despotic coalition of the pro-Jesuit Restoration and the July monarchy with its free-thinking pretensions? Had not the weapons which the one bourgeois fraction had distributed among the people for use against the other in their struggle for supremacy to be torn from the people again now that it confronted their united dictatorship? Nothing outraged the

38. See above, p. 51.
39. Devotion.
40. Bonaparte's message to the Legislative Assembly of 31 October 1849 announced the dismissal of the Barrot ministry and the formation of a new one. Pierre Carlier, the Bonapartist Prefect of Police in Paris, called on 10 November for the formation of a 'social league against socialism', in order to support 'religion, work, family, property and fidelity to the government'; this was to take living form as the Society of 10 December (see below, pp. 197–8). Joseph Fouché, a former Jacobin who ended up working for Louis XVIII, had been Police Minister under Napoleon and was distinguished by his lack of principles.

Paris shopkeepers more than the coquettish display of Jesuitism, not even the rejection of the *concordats à l'aimable*.

Meanwhile, the clashes between the various fractions of the party of Order, and between the National Assembly and Bonaparte, continued. The National Assembly was far from pleased when Bonaparte, immediately after his coup d'état, after securing his own, Bonapartist, ministry, summoned before him the invalids of the monarchy who had been newly appointed prefects and made their unconstitutional agitation for his re-election as President a condition of their office. It was far from pleased when Carlier celebrated his inauguration by banning a Legitimist club; when Bonaparte founded his own journal, *Le Napoléon*, which betrayed the secret desires of the President to the public, while his ministers had to deny them from the rostrum of the Legislative Assembly. It was far from pleased by the defiant retention of the ministry despite the various votes of no confidence; by the attempt to win the goodwill of NCOs by a daily increment of four sous, and the goodwill of the proletariat by a plagiarism of Eugène Sue's *Mystères*,[41] an honour loan bank. It was far from pleased, finally, by the effrontery with which the ministers were made to propose the deportation of the remaining June insurgents to Algiers in order to heap the unpopularity *en gros*[42] on the Legislative Assembly, while the President reserved popularity for himself *en détail*[43] by individual acts of clemency. Thiers dropped threatening references to 'coups d'état' and '*coups de tête*',[44] and the Legislative Assembly revenged itself on Bonaparte by rejecting every legislative proposal which he put forward on his own behalf, by investigating with a noisy display of mistrust every proposal he made in the public interest in order to see whether he was not aspiring to increase Bonaparte's personal power by increasing the executive power. In a word, it *revenged itself by a conspiracy of contempt*.

For its part, the Legitimist party was vexed to see the more talented Orleanists take control of almost all posts and to see *centralization* grow while it sought its salvation in the principle of *decentralization*. And this was what was happening. The counter-

41. The sentimental social-reformist novelist Eugène Sue, and his book *The Mysteries of Paris*, had been criticized by Marx in *The Holy Family*.

42. Wholesale.

43. Retail.

44. Rash acts.

revolution *centralized by force*; that is, it prepared the mechanism of revolution. It even *centralized* the gold and silver of France in the Paris Bank through the compulsory quotation of banknotes, and so created the *ready war chest* of the revolution.

Lastly, the Orleanists were vexed to see the principle of legitimacy emerge in opposition to their own bastard principle and to find themselves permanently snubbed and maltreated as the bourgeois *mésalliance* of a noble spouse.

Gradually we have seen peasants, petty bourgeois, the middle classes in general siding with the proletariat, driven into open conflict with the official republic and treated by it as antagonists. *Resistance to bourgeois dictatorship, need for a change in society, retention of democratic republican institutions as the means to this end, regrouping around the proletariat as the decisive revolutionary force* – these are the common characteristics of the *so-called party of social democracy, the party of the red republic*. This party of Anarchy, as its opponents christened it, is no less a coalition of various interests than the party of Order. From the smallest reform of the old social disorder to the overthrow of the old social order, from bourgeois liberalism to revolutionary terrorism – this is the distance between the extremes which form the starting point and the finishing point of the 'party of Anarchy'.

Abolition of the protective tariffs – socialism! For it strikes at the monopoly of the *industrial* fraction of the party of Order. Regulation of the state budget – socialism! For it strikes at the monopoly of the *financial* fraction of the party of Order. Free admission for foreign meat and corn – socialism! For it strikes at the monopoly of the third fraction of the party of Order, *large landed property*. In France the demands of the free-trade party, that is, of the most advanced English bourgeois party, appear as so many socialist demands. Voltaireanism – socialism! For it strikes at a fourth fraction of the party of Order – the Catholic fraction. Freedom of the press, freedom of association, universal public education – socialism, socialism! They strike at the general monopoly of the party of Order.

So rapidly had the course of the revolution ripened conditions that reformists of all shades, even the most moderate claimants of the middle classes, were forced to group themselves around the banner of the most extreme party of revolution, around the *red flag*.

Yet however manifold the *socialism* of the various major

sections of the party of Anarchy, according to the economic conditions and the consequent overall revolutionary demands of their class or class fraction, in *one* point it is in harmony: in proclaiming itself the *means of emancipating the proletariat*, and proclaiming the emancipation of the latter as its *aim*. Deliberate deception by some, self-deception by others, who give out the world transformed in accordance with their own needs as the best world for all, as the realization of all revolutionary claims and the removal of all revolutionary conflicts.

And concealed beneath the *general* socialist phrases of the 'party of Anarchy', all more or less identical, there is the socialism of the *National*, of the *Presse* and of the *Siècle*, which is more or less consistent in its desire to overthrow the rule of the financial aristocracy and to liberate industry and commerce from the forces which have fettered them hitherto. This is the socialism of industry, trade and agriculture, whose rulers in the party of Order deny these interests in so far as they no longer accord with their private monopolies. There is a distinction between this *bourgeois socialism*, to which, as to every variety of socialism, a section of the workers and the petty bourgeoisie rallies, and socialism proper, *petty-bourgeois socialism*, socialism *par excellence*. Capital hounds the members of this class mainly as a creditor, so they demand *credit institutions*; it crushes them by *competition*, so they demand *producers' cooperatives* supported by the state; it overwhelms them by *concentration*, so they demand *progressive taxation*, limitations on inheritance, the taking over of large construction projects by the state, and other measures that will *forcibly check the growth of capital*. Since they dream of the peaceful implementation of their socialism – allowing possibly for a second, brief February revolution – the coming historical process appears to them as an *application* of systems, which the thinkers of society, either in company with others, or as single inventors, devise or have devised. In this way they become the eclectics or adepts of existing socialist *systems*, of *doctrinaire socialism*, which was the theoretical expression of the proletariat only as long as it had not yet developed further and become a free, autonomous, historical movement.[45]

The *utopia*, *doctrinaire socialism*, subordinates the total movement to one of its elements, substitutes for common social pro-

---

45. See the Introduction to *The Revolutions of 1848*, pp. 22–5, and section III of the *Manifesto of the Communist Party*, ibid., pp. 93–7.

duction the brainwork of individual pedants and, above all, in its fantasy dispenses with the revolutionary struggle of classes and its requirements by means of small conjuring tricks or great sentimentalities; fundamentally it only idealizes the existing society, takes a picture of it free of shadows and aspires to assert its ideal picture against the reality of this society. While this socialism is thus left by the proletariat to the petty bourgeoisie, while the struggle of the various socialist leaders among themselves holds up each of the so-called systems in contrast to the others as a solemn adherence to one of the intermediate points along the path of social revolution – the proletariat rallies ever more around *revolutionary socialism*, around *communism*, for which the bourgeoisie itself has invented the name of Blanqui. This socialism is the *declaration of the permanence of the revolution*, the *class dictatorship* of the proletariat as a necessary intermediate point on the path towards the *abolition of class differences in general*, the abolition of all relations of production on which they are based, the abolition of all social relations which correspond to these relations of production, and the revolutionizing of all ideas which stem from these social relations.

The scope of this account does not allow further discussion of this subject.

We have seen: just as in the party of Order the *financial aristocracy* inevitably took the lead, so, too, in the 'party of Anarchy' did the *proletariat*. While the various classes which united in a revolutionary league rallied around the proletariat, while the departments became more and more unsafe and the Legislative Assembly itself became even more sullen towards the pretensions of the French Soulouque, the long-deferred and delayed by-elections approached which were to replace the Montagnards proscribed after 13 June.

The government, despised by its enemies, abused and humiliated daily by its supposed friends, saw only *one* means of escaping from the repugnant and untenable situation – a *revolt*. A revolt in Paris would have permitted it to proclaim a state of siege in Paris and the departments and thus to control the elections. On the other hand, the friends of order were obliged to make concessions to a government which had achieved a victory over anarchy, if they did not want to appear as anarchists themselves.

The government set to work. At the beginning of February 1850, provocation of the people by chopping down the liberty trees.[46] In vain. If the liberty trees lost their place the government itself lost its head and recoiled, frightened by its own provocation. The National Assembly, however, received this clumsy attempt at emancipation by Bonaparte with ice-cold mistrust. The removal of the wreaths of immortelles from the July Column[47] was no more successful. It gave a part of the army the opportunity for revolutionary demonstrations and the National Assembly cause for a more or less veiled vote of no confidence in the ministry. The government press threatened in vain the abolition of universal suffrage and the invasion of the cossacks. Hautpoul's direct challenge to the Left, issued in the middle of the Legislative Assembly, to betake itself onto the streets, and his declaration that the government was ready to receive it, was also in vain. Hautpoul received only a call to order from the chairman, and the party of Order, with silent, malicious pleasure, allowed a deputy of the Left to mock Bonaparte's usurpatory desires.[48] Finally, the prophesy of a revolution on 24 February was also in vain. The result of the government's prophesy was that the people ignored 24 February.

The proletariat did not allow itself to be provoked into a *revolt*, because it was about to carry out a *revolution*.

Unhindered by the provocations of the government, which only increased the general irritation at the existing situation, the election committee, completely under the influence of the workers, nominated three candidates for Paris: de Flotte, Vidal and Carnot. De Flotte was a June deportee, who had been amnestied as a result of one of Bonaparte's popularity-seeking schemes; he was a friend of Blanqui's and had taken part in the attempt of 15 May. Vidal, known as a communist writer by his book *On the Distribution of Wealth*, was a former secretary to Louis Blanc in the Luxembourg Commission. Carnot, the son of the Convention's organizer of victory, was the least compromised member of the *National* party, Minister of Education in the Provisional Government and the Executive Commission, with his democratic public

46. The tradition of planting liberty trees, generally oaks or poplars, dated back to the revolution of 1789; the trees in question here had been planted after February 1848.

47. The July Column, erected to celebrate the 1830 revolution, had been decked with immortelles after the February revolution.

48. When deputy Pascal Duprat stated on 16 February that Louis Bonaparte would have to choose between the role of his uncle or that of Washington, a Left deputy interrupted, 'Or Soulouque.'

education bill a living protest against the education law of the Jesuits. The three candidates represented the three allied classes. At the head, the June insurgent, the representative of the revolutionary proletariat; next to him, the doctrinaire socialist, the representative of the socialist petty bourgeoisie; finally, the third, the representative of the republican bourgeois party, whose democratic formulas had gained a socialist significance in the struggle with the party of Order and had long since lost their own significance. It was a *general coalition against the bourgeoisie and the government, as in February*. But this time the *proletariat was the head of the revolutionary league*.

In spite of all endeavours the socialist candidates won. The army itself voted for the June insurgent against its own War Minister, La Hitte.[49] The party of Order was thunderstruck. The departmental elections brought them no solace; they produced a majority for the Montagnards.

The election of 10 March 1850 was the revocation of June 1848! The butchers and deporters of the June insurgents returned to the National Assembly, but bowed down, in the wake of the deportees, with their principles on their lips. *It was the revocation of 13 June 1849*: the Montagne, proscribed by the National Assembly, returned to the National Assembly, but as the advanced trumpeters of the revolution, no longer as its commander. *It was the revocation of 10 December*: Napoleon had failed with his minister, La Hitte. There is only one analogy in the parliamentary history of France: the rejection of d'Haussez, a minister of Charles X, in 1830. Finally, the election of 10 March 1850 was the annulment of the election of 13 May [1849], which had given the party of Order a majority. The election of 10 March was a protest against the majority of 13 May. 10 March was a revolution. Behind the ballot slips lay the paving stones.

'The vote of 10 March means war,' cried Ségur d'Aguesseau,[50] one of the most advanced members of the party of Order.

With 10 March 1850 the constitutional republic entered a new phase, *the phase of its dissolution*. The different fractions of the majority are again at one with each other and with Bonaparte; they are again the saviours of order; he is again their *neutral man*.

---

49. Jean-Ernest Ducos, vicomte de La Hitte was a general and Bonapartist, Foreign Minister and Minister of War, 1849–51.

50. Raymond, comte de Ségur d'Aguesseau was a lawyer and an opportunist politician.

If they remember that they are royalists this only happens out of despair at the possibility of the bourgeois republic; if he remembers that he is a pretender, this only happens because he despairs of remaining President.

At the command of the party of Order Bonaparte answers the election of de Flotte, the June insurgent, with the appointment of Baroche[51] as Minister of the Interior – Baroche, the prosecutor of Blanqui and Barbès, Ledru-Rollin and Guinard.[52] The Legislative Assembly answers the election of Carnot with the adoption of the education law and the election of Vidal with the suppression of the socialist press. The party of Order seeks to dispel its own fear with trumpet blasts from its press. 'The sword is holy,' cries one of its organs. 'The defenders of order must take the offensive against the Red party,' declares another. 'Between socialism and society there is a duel to the death, an unceasing, relentless war; in this duel of desperation one or the other must perish; if society does not destroy socialism, socialism will destroy society,' crows another cock of order. Erect the barricades of order, the barricades of religion, the barricades of the family. An end must be made of the 127,000 voters of Paris![53] A Bartholomew's night for the socialists! And for a moment the party of Order believes its own confidence in its victory.

Their organs hold forth most fanatically against the '*shopkeepers of Paris*'. The June insurgent elected as a representative by the shopkeepers of Paris! This means a second June 1848 is impossible; it means a second 13 June [1849] is impossible; it means the moral influence of capital is broken; it means that the bourgeois Assembly now represents only the bourgeoisie, that big property is lost because its vassal, small property, seeks its salvation in the camp of the propertyless.

The party of Order, of course, returns to its inevitable *commonplace*: *More repression!* it calls, *Tenfold repression!* But its powers of repression have been reduced tenfold while resistance has increased a hundredfold. Must not the main instrument of repression itself, the army, be repressed? And the party of Order

51. Pierre-Jules Baroche, a lawyer and a deputy in both Assemblies, was originally an Orleanist, but had become a Bonapartist by 1850.

52. Auguste-Joseph Guinard was a Montagne deputy in the Constituent National Assembly, condemned to exile for life for his part in the demonstration of 13 June 1849.

53. De Flotte had gained 126,643 votes in the election of 15 March.

speaks its last word: 'The iron ring of stifling legality must be broken. The *constitutional republic is impossible*. We must fight with our true weapons; since February 1848 we have fought the revolution with *its* weapons on *its* terrain; we have accepted *its* institutions; the Constitution is a fortress which only protects the besiegers and not the besieged! By smuggling ourselves into holy Ilion in the belly of the Trojan horse we have, unlike our fore-fathers, the *Grecs*,[54] not conquered the hostile city but made prisoners of ourselves.'

However, the basis of the Constitution is *universal suffrage*. *The destruction of universal suffrage* – this is the last word of the party of Order, of the bourgeois dictatorship.

On 4 May 1848, 20 December 1848, 13 May 1849 and 8 July 1849, universal suffrage declared them right. On 10 March 1850 universal suffrage declared that it had itself been wrong. Bourgeois rule as the product and result of universal suffrage, as the express act of sovereign will of the people – this is what the bourgeois Constitution means.

But does the Constitution still have any meaning the moment that the content of this suffrage, this sovereign will, is no longer bourgeois rule? Is it not the duty of the bourgeoisie to regulate the franchise so that it demands what is reasonable, *its* rule? By repeatedly terminating the existing state power and by creating it anew from itself does not universal suffrage destroy all stability; does it not perpetually call all existing powers into question; does it not destroy authority; does it not threaten to elevate anarchy itself to the level of authority? Who could still doubt this after 10 March 1850?

By repudiating universal suffrage, with which it had draped itself hitherto and from which it drew its omnipotence, the bourgeoisie openly confesses: *Our dictatorship has existed hitherto by the will of the people; it must now be consolidated against the will of the people.* And, with all consistency, it no longer seeks its supports in France, but outside, abroad, in *invasion*.

With the invasion, like a second Coblenz,[55] with its seat established in France itself, it arouses all the national passions against itself. With this attack on universal suffrage it gives the new

54. Grecs – A play on words: Greeks, but also professional cheats. [*Note by Engels to the 1895 edition.*]

55. Coblenz had been the centre of the counter-revolutionary emigration during the first French revolution.

revolution a *general pretext*, and the revolution needs such a pretext. Every *particular* pretext would divide the fractions of the revolutionary league and expose their differences. The *general* pretext dulls the perceptions of the half-revolutionary classes; it enables them to deceive themselves as to the *specific character* of the coming revolution, as to the consequences of its own deeds. Every revolution needs a banquet question. Universal suffrage is the banquet question of the new revolution.

The bourgeois fractions in their coalition are already condemned, in so far as they take flight from the only possible form of their *joint* power, from the mightiest and most complete form of their *class rule*, the *constitutional republic*, by returning to the subordinate, incomplete, weaker form of the *monarchy*. They resemble that old man who, in order to regain his youthful strength, fetched out his boyhood clothes and tormented his withered limbs by trying to get them on. Their republic had only *one* merit; *it was the forcing house of the revolution*.

10 March 1850 bears the inscription: *Après moi le déluge!* After me the deluge!

IV. THE ABOLITION OF UNIVERSAL SUFFRAGE IN 1850

(The continuation of the three preceding chapters is to be found in the 'Review' in the double number 5/6 of the *Neue Rheinische Zeitung* [*Revue*], which was the last to appear. After a description of the great commercial crisis which broke out in England in 1847 and an explanation of how political complications came to a head in the revolutions of February and March 1848 as a result of its repercussions on the European continent, it is then shown how the commercial and industrial prosperity which set in again in the course of 1848 and increased still further in 1849 paralysed the revolutionary upsurge and made possible the simultaneous victories of the forces of reaction. Then, with particular reference to France, it is said:)[56]

The same symptoms have been evident in France since 1850. Parisian industry is working at full capacity, and even the cotton factories of Rouen and Mulhouse are in quite a good state, although here, as in England, high prices have had a dampening

56. Foreword written by Engels for the 1895 edition. This chapter is composed of two separate excerpts from the 'Review: May–October 1850', as indicated here by the asterisk on p. 131. The remainder of this 'Review' is printed in *The Revolutions of 1848*.

effect. The development of prosperity in France has been further encouraged, in particular, by comprehensive tariff reform in Spain and by reduction of duties on various luxury goods in Mexico. Exports of French goods to both markets have increased significantly. The accumulation of capital in France has led to a series of speculative ventures conducted on the pretext of the large-scale exploitation of the Californian gold-mines. A large number of companies have emerged whose low stock prices and prospectuses with socialist overtones have made a direct appeal to the purses of the petty bourgeoisie and workers, but which jointly and severally add up to that pure form of fraud which is peculiar to the French and Chinese. One of these companies is even under the patronage of the government. The French import duties brought in some 63 million francs in the first nine months of 1848, 95 million in the corresponding period of 1849 and 93 million in 1850. Moreover, in September 1850 this revenue rose again by more than a million francs over the same month in 1849. Exports have also risen in 1849 and even more so in 1850.

The most striking proof of the restored prosperity is the reintroduction of cash payments by the Bank following the law of 6 August 1850. On 15 March 1848 the Bank had been empowered to suspend its cash payments. At that time its notes in circulation, together with those of the provincial banks, amounted to 373 million francs (£14,920,000). On 2 November 1849 the circulation stood at 482 million francs, or £19,280,000, an increase of £4,360,000, and on 2 September 1850, 496 million francs, or £19,840,000, an increase of about £5 million. During this time no depreciation of the notes occurred; on the contrary, the increased note circulation was accompanied by a constant accumulation of gold and silver in the Bank's vaults, so that in summer 1850 its cash reserves ran to about £14 million, an incredible amount for France. The fact that the Bank was thereby in a position to increase its note issue, and thus its active capital, by 123 million francs, or £5 million, proves conclusively how correct was our assertion in an earlier number that the financial aristocracy was not only not overthrown by the February revolution but in fact actually strengthened by it.[57] This becomes even more evident from a survey of French bank legislation of the last few years. On 10 June 1847 the Bank was empowered to issue 200-franc notes; the lowest note until then had been 500 francs. A decree of 15

57. Above, p. 109.

March 1848 declared the notes of the Bank of France to be legal tender and relieved the Bank of the obligation to exchange them for cash. Its note issue was limited to 350 million francs, and it was now empowered to issue 100-franc notes. A decree of 27 April ordered the merger of the departmental banks with the Bank of France; another decree of 2 May 1848 raised the total note issue to 452 million francs, and a decree of 22 December 1849 further raised the maximum issue to 525 million francs. Finally the law of 6 August 1850 reintroduced the convertibility of notes into coin. These facts, the continuous increase in circulation and the concentration of all French gold and silver in the Bank vaults, led Monsieur Proudhon to the conclusion that the Bank would have to cast off its old skin and metamorphose itself into a Proudhon-type people's bank.[58] He did not even need to know the history of the English Bank restrictions of 1797–1819,[59] he needed only direct his attention across the Channel to see that this situation, unknown to him in the history of bourgeois society, was no more than an eminently normal bourgeois event, which was only now taking place in France for the first time. It is clear that the supposedly revolutionary theoreticians who talked so big, in the manner of the Provisional Government in Paris, were just as ignorant of the nature and outcome of the measures which had been taken as were the gentlemen of the Provisional Government themselves.

In spite of the industrial and commercial prosperity which France is enjoying at the moment, the mass of the population, the 25 million peasants, are in the throes of a great depression. The good harvests of the past few years have forced down corn prices in France even lower than in England, and the position of the debt-ridden peasants, sucked dry by usury and burdened by taxes, is by no means splendid! But the history of the last three years has sufficiently proved that this class is absolutely incapable of any revolutionary initiative.

Just as the period of crisis occurred later on the Continent than in England, so did the period of prosperity. The original process always takes place in England; it is the demiurge of the bourgeois cosmos. The different phases of the cyclical motion of bourgeois

58. Proudhon had currently put forward this position in a pamphlet directed against the bourgeois economist Frédéric Bastiat, entitled *Gratuité de crédit*. Marx had criticized Proudhon's doctrines in *The Poverty of Philosophy*.

59. Between 1797 and 1821, under the Bank Restriction Act of 1797, the British banks were absolved from the requirement of exchanging notes for specie.

society occur on the Continent in a secondary and tertiary form. On the one hand, the Continent exports far more to England than to any other country, and these exports depend on conditions in England, particularly with regard to the overseas market. England exports far more to countries overseas than does the whole Continent, so that the quantity of continental exports to these countries always depends on England's exports at the time. So, although the crises produce revolution on the Continent first, they nevertheless have their roots in England. These violent convulsions must necessarily occur at the extremities of the bourgeois organism rather than at its heart, where the possibility of restoring the balance is greater. On the other hand, the degree to which the continental revolutions have repercussions on England is also the thermometer by which one can measure how far they really challenge bourgeois conditions of life, rather than affecting only its political formations.

While this general prosperity lasts, enabling the productive forces of bourgeois society to develop to the full extent possible within the bourgeois system, there can be no question of a real revolution. Such a revolution is only possible at a time when *two factors* come into *conflict*: the *modern productive forces* and the *bourgeois forms of production*. Far from giving rise to new revolutions, the various squabbles in which the individual fractions of the continental party of Order now indulge and compromise themselves are, on the contrary, only possible because the basic situation at the moment is so secure and – what the forces of reaction do not know – so *bourgeois*. All reactionary attempts to hold up bourgeois development will rebound in the face of this basic situation, as will all the moral outrage and enthusiastic proclamations of the democrats. *A new revolution is only possible as a result of a new crisis; but it will come, just as surely as the crisis itself.*

*

Let us now return to France.

The victory which the people had won in alliance with the petty bourgeoisie in the election of 10 March was annulled by the people themselves when they provoked the new election of 28 April. Vidal was elected in the department of Bas-Rhin as well as in Paris.[60] The Paris committee, on which the Montagne and the

60. Bas-Rhin was one of the departments of Alsace, with Strasbourg as its capital.

petty bourgeoisie were strongly represented, induced him to accept for Bas-Rhin. The victory of 10 March ceased to be decisive. The date for a decision was postponed yet again, the people's resilient mood weakened, and they became used to legal triumphs instead of revolutionary ones. The revolutionary significance of 10 March, the rehabilitation of the June insurrection, was finally completely destroyed by the candidature of Eugène Sue, the sentimental petty-bourgeois social dreamer, whom the proletariat could at best accept as a joke, as a favour to the *grisettes*.[61] To oppose this well-intentioned candidature, the party of Order, which had become bolder as a result of its opponents' vacillating policy, put forward a candidate who was to represent their June *victory*. This strange candidate was the Spartan *paterfamilias* Leclerc,[62] whose heroic armour, however, was stripped from his body piece by piece by the press, and who was spectacularly defeated in the election. The new electoral victory of 28 April made the Montagne and the petty bourgeoisie over-confident. They were already rejoicing at the thought of being able to achieve their aims by purely legal means, without pushing the proletariat into the foreground again with a new revolution. They fully counted on bringing Monsieur Ledru-Rollin into the presidential chair and a majority of Montagnards into the Assembly by means of universal suffrage in the new elections of 1852. The party of Order, completely reassured by the forthcoming election, by Sue's candidature and by the mood of the Montagne and petty bourgeoisie that the latter were determined to remain peaceful whatever happened, answered both election victories with an *electoral law* which abolished universal suffrage.

The government took great care not to take responsibility for the presentation of this bill. It made an apparent concession to the majority by delegating the preparation of the bill to the high dignitaries of this majority, the seventeen burgraves.[63] Thus the

61. Working girls.

62. Alexandre Leclerc was a Paris merchant.

63. The Commission of Seventeen was set up by the Minister of the Interior on 1 May 1850 to draft a new electoral law. 'Burgraves' was the nickname given to the committee of the leading Orleanist and Legitimist parliamentarians which formulated the policy of the party of Order in the National Assembly. In fact the Commission of Seventeen included not only the five most important burgraves, Molé, Berryer, de Broglie, Montalembert and Thiers, but also a number of people chosen by the government from outside the Assembly.

abolition of universal suffrage was not proposed to the Assembly by the government; the majority of the Assembly itself made the proposal.

On 8 May the project was brought before the Chamber. The whole social-democratic press rose to a man to preach to the people dignified behaviour, *calme majestueux*, passivity, and trust in its elected representatives. Every article in these papers was an admission that a revolution would inevitably lead to the destruction of, above all, the so-called revolutionary press and that it was therefore now a question of self-preservation. The supposedly revolutionary press betrayed its whole secret. It signed its own death warrant.

On 21 May the Montagne opened the debate by moving the rejection of the entire proposal on the grounds that it violated the Constitution. The party of Order answered that the Constitution would be infringed if necessary, but that this was not necessary because the Constitution was capable of any interpretation and the majority alone had the authority to decide on the correct interpretation. The Montagne countered the uncontrolled and wild attacks of Thiers and Montalembert with a decent and educated humanism. They presented arguments based upon a legal foundation; the party of Order referred them to the foundations upon which the law stands – bourgeois property. The Montagne whimpered: *Did they really want to do their best to bring about a revolution?* The party of Order replied that they would wait and see.

On 22 May the preliminary question was settled by a vote of 462 to 227. The same men who had demonstrated so solemnly and thoroughly that the National Assembly and every single deputy would be abandoning their responsibility if they abandoned the people, their mandator, remained in their seats and sought to make the country act in their stead with petitions. They still remained seated and unmoved when the law was passed in spectacular fashion on 31 May. They tried to revenge themselves with a protest, in which they put on record their innocence of this gross violation of the Constitution, a protest which they did not even submit openly but smuggled into the chairman's pocket behind his back.

An army of 150,000 men in Paris, the long postponement of the decision, the calls for restraint from the press, the pusillanimity of the Montagne and the newly elected representatives, the majestic calm of the petty bourgeoisie and, above all, the commercial and industrial prosperity: all these prevented any attempt at revolution on the part of the proletariat.

Universal suffrage had fulfilled its mission, the only function which it can have in a revolutionary period. The majority of the people had passed through the school of development it provided. It had to be abolished – by revolution or by reaction.

On a subsequent occasion the Montagne soon expended even more energy. From the rostrum, War Minister Hautpoul had called the February revolution a dire catastrophe. The spokesmen of the Montagne, who distinguished themselves, as usual, by their noisy moral indignation, were prevented from speaking by the chairman, Dupin.[64] Girardin[65] proposed to the Montagne that they immediately leave *en masse*. Result: the Montagne remained seated, but Girardin was cast out from their midst as unworthy.

The electoral law required its completion by a new press law. This was not long in coming. A bill proposed by the government, considerably sharpened by the amendments of the party of Order, raised caution money, imposed an extra stamp duty on novels in magazine form (in answer to the election of Eugène Sue), taxed all publications up to a certain number of pages appearing in weekly or monthly editions and, in conclusion, decreed that every article in a journal had to bear the signature of its author. The regulations concerning caution money killed the so-called revolutionary press; the people regarded its demise as retribution for the abolition of universal suffrage. However, neither the purpose nor the effect of the new law was limited to this section of the press. So long as the press was anonymous it appeared as the organ of a public opinion without number or name; it was the third power in the state. With the signature of each article a newspaper became merely a collection of journalistic contributions by more or less well-known individuals. Every article sank to the level of an advertisement. Hitherto the newspapers had circulated as the paper money of public opinion; now they were reduced to more or less worthless promissory notes, whose value

64. André-Marie Dupin was a lawyer and an Orleanist politician, chairman of the Chamber of Deputies from 1832 to 1839 and of the Legislative Assembly from 1849 to 1851; subsequently a Bonapartist.

65. Émile de Girardin was a journalist and politician of varying political views. Before 1848 he opposed Guizot, during the revolution he was a 'pure republican', and later he became a Bonapartist. He sat in the Legislative Assembly from 1850 to 1851.

and circulation depended on the credit, not only of the issuer, but also of the endorser. The press of the party of Order, which had provoked the abolition of universal suffrage, had also urged the most extreme measures against the bad press. However, the good press itself, in its sinister anonymity, had become uncomfortable for the party of Order and even more so for its individual provincial representatives. The party of Order demanded to be confronted only by paid writers, with names, addresses and further personal particulars. The good press bewailed in vain the ingratitude with which their services were rewarded. The law was passed; the regulation concerning the inclusion of names hit them most of all. The names of the Republican daily columnists were fairly well known, but the respectable firms of the *Journal des Débats*, the *Assemblée nationale*, the *Constitutionnel*,[66] etc., with their loftily proclaimed political wisdom, cut wretched figures when the mysterious company suddenly turned out to be corrupt *penny-a-liners*[67] of long practice who defended all possible causes for ready cash, like Granier de Cassagnac, or spineless old scribblers who call themselves statesmen, like Capefigue, or coquettish fops, like Monsieur Lemoinne[68] of the *Débats*.

In the debate on the press law the Montagne had already sunk to such a level of moral degradation that it was obliged to limit itself to applauding the splendid tirades of an old notable from the days of Louis Philippe, Monsieur Victor Hugo.

With the election law and the press law the revolutionary and democratic party quits the official stage. Before its departure home, shortly after the end of the session, both fractions of the Montagne – the social democrats and the democratic socialists – issued manifestos, two declarations of incompetence, in which they proved that although force and success had never been on their side, they had nevertheless always been on the side of eternal justice and all the other eternal truths.

Let us now examine the party of Order. As the *Neue Rheinische Zeitung* said in its last issue:[69]

66. These were all daily papers which supported the party of Order.

67. English in the original.

68. Bernard-Adolphe Granier de Cassagnac was an Orleanist before the 1848 revolution, later a Bonapartist and a member of the Legislative Body under the Second Empire. Jean-Baptiste Capefigue was a novelist and historian, and an ultra-royalist. John-Emile Lemoinne was the English correspondent of the *Journal des Débats*.

69. See above, pp. 108–9.

In the face of the restorationist desires of the united Orleanists and Legitimists ... Bonaparte defend[ed] his actual power: the republic. In the face of Bonaparte's restorationist desires the fractions of the party of Order defended their joint power: the republic. The Orleanists confronted the Legitimists, and the Legitimists the Orleanists, as the representatives of the status quo: the republic. All these fractions of the party of Order, each of which had its own king and restoration *in petto*, in turn enforced the joint rule of the bourgeoisie in opposition to the usurpatory and mutinous desires of the rival pretenders: they enforced that form of society in which particular claim of the various parties were held in check and neutralized – the republic ... And Thiers spoke truer than he knew, when he said, 'We the royalists, are the true pillars of the constitutional republic.'

This comedy of these *republicains malgré eux* – the aversion to the status quo and the constant attempts to consolidate it; the incessant conflicts between Bonaparte and the National Assembly; the ever-renewed threat that the party of Order would split up into its component parts, and the ever repeated reunification of its fractions; the attempt made by each fraction to transform every victory against the common enemy into a defeat for its temporary allies; the petty jealousy on both sides, the vindictiveness, the harassment, the tireless drawing of swords, which always ends with the farcical *baiser Lamourette*[70] – this unedifying comedy of errors has never developed in a more classical fashion than in the last six months.

The party of Order also regards the electoral law as a victory against Bonaparte. Had the government not abdicated power by leaving the formulation and responsibility for its own proposal to the Commission of Seventeen? And was not Bonaparte's main strength against the Assembly based on the fact that he was the choice of six million voters? Bonaparte, for his part, treated the electoral law as a concession to the Assembly, with which he claimed to have bought harmony between the legislative and executive powers. By way of payment the base adventurer demanded an increase in his civil list of three million francs. Could the National Assembly enter into a conflict with the executive at a moment when it had divested the great majority of the French people of its rights? It rose up in anger, and it seemed prepared to

70. 'Lamourette's kiss': on 7 July 1792 Lamourette, a deputy, prevailed on his warring colleagues in the Constitutional Assembly to forget their differences and embrace one another; needless to say, this reconciliation was specious and transient.

bring matters to a head. Its Commission rejected the motion and the Bonapartist press issued warnings and pointed to the disinherited, disenfranchised people. After a large number of noisy transactions the Assembly finally gave way on the particular issue, but at the same time it gained its revenge on the question of principle. Instead of granting him the annual increase in the civil list of three million francs demanded on principle, it made him an accommodation of 2,160,000 francs. Not satisfied with this, it made this concession only after it had been supported by Changarnier, the general of the party of Order and the protector with whom they had saddled Bonaparte. So it actually approved the two million francs not for Bonaparte but for Changarnier.

This gift, flung at his feet *de mauvaise grâce*,[71] was picked up by Bonaparte in quite the same spirit as it was given. Again the Bonapartist press raged against the National Assembly. When the amendment on journalists' signatures – which was particularly aimed at the less important papers which represented Bonaparte's private interests – was first introduced during the debate on the press law, the main Bonapartist paper, *Le Pouvoir*, published an open and virulent attack on the National Assembly. The ministers had to disassociate themselves from the paper before the Assembly; the publisher of the *Pouvoir* was summoned before the bar of the Assembly and the highest possible fine, 5,000 francs, was imposed upon him. The next day the *Pouvoir* published an even more insolent article against the Assembly, and by way of governmental revenge the Public Prosecutor brought actions against several Legitimist papers for violating the Constitution.

Finally the question arose of the prorogation of parliament. Bonaparte wanted this in order to be able to operate unhindered by the Assembly. The party of Order wanted it, partly in order to complete its fractional intrigues and partly so that the individual deputies could pursue their private interests. Both needed it in order to consolidate and increase the victories of the forces of reaction in the provinces. The Assembly thus adjourned from 11 August until 11 November. However, as Bonaparte made absolutely no secret of the fact that his sole concern was to rid himself of the burdensome supervision of the National Assembly, it added to the vote of confidence a stamp of no confidence in the President. All Bonapartists were excluded from the Standing

71. In a bad spirit.

Commission of twenty-eight members who stayed on during the recess to act as the moral guardians of the republic. In place of the Bonapartists even a few republicans from the *Siècle* and the *National* were voted in, in order to demonstrate to the President the allegiance of the majority to the constitutional republic.

Shortly before and especially shortly after the parliamentary adjournment the two great fractions of the party of Order, Orleanists and Legitimists, showed signs of wanting reconciliation through an alliance of the two royal houses under whose banner they fought. The papers were full of suggestions for such a reconciliation, which had supposedly been discussed at Louis Philippe's sick bed at St Leonards, when Louis Philippe's death suddenly simplified the situation. Louis Philippe was the usurper, Henri V the usurped; the comte de Paris,[72] on the other hand, was the rightful heir to Henri V's throne, as the latter had no children. Now every pretext for opposition to the fusion of the dynastic interests was removed. But at precisely this moment the two fractions of the bourgeoisie discovered that it was not devotion to a particular royal house which divided them, but that it was rather their separate class interests which divided the two dynasties. The Legitimists, who had undertaken the pilgrimage to Henri V's royal camp at Wiesbaden, just as their rivals had gone to St Leonards, received the news there of Louis Philippe's death.[73] They immediately formed a ministry *in partibus infidelium*,[74] which consisted mostly of members of the commission of moral guardians of the republic and which, on the occasion of a domestic squabble in the bosom of the party, stepped forward with the most unequivocal proclamation of divine right.[75] The Orleanists rejoiced over the compromising scandal which this manifesto provoked in the press and did not disguise for one second their open enmity towards the Legitimists.

During the adjournment of the National Assembly the Departmental Councils met. The majority of them declared in favour of a revision of the Constitution hedged to a greater or lesser degree

72. Louis-Philippe-Albert, grandson of Louis Philippe.

73. On 26 August 1850.

74. 'In the lands of the infidels': a favoured expression of Marx's, taken from the title of Catholic bishops appointed to non-Christian territories where they could not reside.

75. Marx refers to the Wiesbaden manifesto of August 1850, in which the comte de Chambord rejected the idea of an appeal to the people as the basis of monarchist restoration.

by clauses and safeguards; that is, they declared themselves in favour of a 'solution' in the form of a monarchist restoration, which was not more closely defined. At the same time they admitted that they were not authorized and, in fact, too cowardly to find such a solution. The Bonapartist fraction immediately interpreted this wish for revision as meaning an extension of Bonaparte's presidency.

The constitutional solution – Bonaparte's retirement in May 1852, the simultaneous election of a new President by the whole electorate, the revision of the Constitution by a revisionary chamber in the first four months of the new presidency – is completely intolerable for the ruling class. The day of the new presidential election would be the day of decision for all the opposing parties: Legitimists, Orleanists, bourgeois republicans and revolutionaries. A decision between the different parties would have to be reached by force. If the party of Order succeeded in joining forces through the candidature of a neutral man outside the dynastic families, he would still be faced with Bonaparte. In its struggle with the people the party of Order is continually obliged to increase the power of the executive. Every increase in the power of the executive office increases the power of its bearer, Bonaparte. To the same degree, therefore, that the fractions of the party of Order strengthen their joint power, they increase the strength behind Bonaparte's dynastic pretensions and increase his chances of frustrating the constitutional solution by force on the day of decision. Despite the party of Order he will no more bother about the one supporting pillar of the Constitution than they – despite the people – bothered about the other supporting pillar on the question of the electoral law. Bonaparte would apparently appeal to universal suffrage against the National Assembly. In a word, the constitutional solution puts the whole status quo in question, and behind this danger to the status quo the bourgeois sees chaos, anarchy and civil war. He sees his purchases, his sales, his bills, his marriage, his notarial contracts and agreements, his mortgages, his ground rents, his house rents, his profits and all his sources of income endangered in May 1852, and he cannot expose himself to this risk. Behind the threat to the political status quo there lies the hidden danger that the whole of bourgeois society will collapse. The only possible solution for the bourgeoisie is the postponement of a solution. It can only save the constitutional republic by a violation of the Constitution, by a prolongation of the powers of the President. This is also the last word of the press of the party of Order after the long-drawn-out and profound debates about 'solutions' which they involved themselves in after the session of the Departmental Councils. Thus to its shame the mighty party of Order finds itself obliged to take seriously the ludicrous, vulgar and hated person of the pseudo-Bonaparte.

This sordid figure has also deceived himself as to why he has increasingly assumed the character of the man of destiny. While his party had enough insight to ascribe his growing importance to circumstances, he believed it to be due solely to the magic power of his name and his unceasing caricature of Napoleon. He became more enterprising day by day. He countered the pilgrimages to St Leonards and Wiesbaden with his tours of France. The Bonapartists had so little trust in the magic effect of his personality that everywhere they sent along crowds of people from the Society of 10 December[76] – that organization of the Paris lumpenproletariat – packed into railway trains and post-chaises, to function as hired applauders. They fed this marionette with speeches which, according to the reception in the various towns, proclaimed republican resignation or unflagging resilience as the electoral slogan of presidential policy. In spite of all these manoeuvres these journeys were anything but triumphal processions.

Believing he had inspired the people with enthusiasm, Bonaparte set about winning the army. He had great reviews held on the plain of Satory near Versailles, in which he sought to buy the soldiers with garlic sausage, champagne and cigars. If the genuine Napoleon was able to raise the spirits of his soldiers, flagging from the hardships of his conquering campaigns, by the occasional show of patriarchal familiarity, the pseudo-Napoleon thought that the grateful troops would shout: '*Vive Napoleon, vive le saucisson!*' that is, hurrah for the sausage [*Wurst*], hurrah for the clown [*Hanswurst*]!

These reviews brought to a head the long-restrained conflict between Bonaparte and his War Minister, Hautpoul, on the one hand, and Changarnier on the other. In Changarnier the party of Order had found its really neutral man, of whom there could be no question of his having his own dynastic claims. They had chosen him as Napoleon's successor. Furthermore, with his conduct on 29 January and 13 June 1849 Changarnier had become the party of Order's great general – a modern Alexander,

---

76. See *The Eighteenth Brumaire*, below, p. 197.

whose brutal intervention had in the eyes of the timid bourgeoisie severed the Gordian knot of the revolution. Basically just as ludicrous as Bonaparte, he had thus come to power in the cheapest possible way, and he was used by the National Assembly to supervise the President. He himself made a great show of the patronage which he gave Napoleon, for example in the matter of the civil list, and he behaved in an ever more domineering fashion towards the President and his ministers. When, during the discussion of the electoral law, an insurrection was expected, he forbade his officers to take any orders at all from the War Minister or from the President. The press also helped to magnify the figure of Changarnier. In view of its complete lack of great personalities the party of Order naturally felt urged to ascribe all the strength which its class lacked to one single individual and to build him up to a monstrous size. Thus the myth of Changarnier '*the bulwark of society*' was created. The presumptuous charlatanry and the mystique of self-importance with which Changarnier condescended to bear the world on his shoulders form a laughable contrast to the events during and after the review at Satory, which irrefutably proved that it required only a stroke of the pen from the infinitely small person of Bonaparte to reduce the colossus Changarnier, this fantastic offspring of bourgeois fear, to the dimensions of mediocrity and to transform him from the heroic saviour of society into a pensioned general.

Bonaparte had already been revenging himself on Changarnier for some time by provoking the War Minister to a disciplinary quarrel with the troublesome protector. The last review at Satory finally caused the old animosity to erupt. Changarnier's constitutional indignation knew no bounds when he saw the cavalry regiments ride past with the unconstitutional cry: '*Vive l'empereur!*' To forestall any unpleasant debates about this in the coming session of the Chamber Bonaparte dismissed the War Minister, Hautpoul, by appointing him Governor of Algiers. In his place he put a reliable old general from the days of the Empire – Changarnier's complete equal in brutality. However, in order that Hautpoul's dismissal might not appear to be a concession to Changarnier, he transferred General Neumayer[77] – the great saviour of society's right hand – from Paris to Nantes. It had been Neumayer who, at the last review, had caused the whole infantry to march past

77. Maximilian-George Neumayer was a general and a supporter of the party of Order. He commanded the troops in Paris from 1848 to 1850.

Napoleon's successor in icy silence. Changarnier, feeling himself abused in the person of Neumayer, protested and threatened, but in vain. After negotiations lasting two days Neumayer's transfer orders appeared in the *Moniteur* and the hero of social order was left with the choice of either submitting to discipline or resigning.

Bonaparte's struggle with Changarnier is the continuation of his struggle with the party of Order. The re-opening of the National Assembly on 11 November is therefore overshadowed by dark omens. But it will be a storm in a teacup. Essentially, the old game cannot help but continue. In spite of the cries from the sticklers for principle in its various fractions the majority of the party of Order will be forced to prolong the power of the President. Similarly, despite all temporary protestations, Bonaparte will be obliged to accept this extension of power simply as a delegation from the National Assembly (if only for lack of money). Thus the solution will be postponed, the status quo preserved, one fraction of the party of Order compromised, weakened and rendered unacceptable to the other; the repression against the common enemy, the people, will be extended and exhausted, until the economic situation has again reached the point where a new explosion blows all these squabbling parties with their constitutional republic sky-high.

To reassure the bourgeoisie, it must be said that the scandal between Napoleon and the party of Order is resulting in many small capitalists being ruined on the Bourse and their wealth finding its way into the pockets of the big sharks there.

The Eighteenth Brumaire of Louis Bonaparte[1]

PREFACE TO THE SECOND EDITION (1869)

My friend Joseph Weydemeyer,[2] who died before his time, once had the intention of publishing a political weekly in New York, as from 1 January 1852. He invited me to provide a history of the coup d'état for this paper. Until the middle of February I therefore wrote him weekly articles under the title 'The Eighteenth Brumaire of Louis Bonaparte'. In the meantime Weydemeyer's original plan had fallen through. Instead he started a monthly, *Die Revolution*, in the spring of 1852, and its first number consists of my 'Eighteenth Brumaire'. A few hundred copies of this found their way into Germany at that time, without, however, entering the actual book trade. A German bookseller, who affected extremely radical airs, replied to my offer of the book with a truly virtuous horror at a 'presumption' so 'contrary to the times'.

It will be seen from these facts that the present work arose under the immediate pressure of events, and that its historical material does not extend beyond the month of February (1852). It is now republished, partly because of the demand of the book trade, and partly because my friends in Germany have urgently requested it.

Of the writings dealing with the same subject at about the *same time* as mine, only two are worthy of notice: Victor Hugo's *Napoléon le petit*[3] and Proudhon's *Coup d'état*.[4]

---

1. The circumstances in which the *Eighteenth Brumaire* was written and published are explained by Marx himself in the 'Preface' below. It is translated here from the text printed in *MEW* 8.

2. Joseph Weydemeyer was a member of the Communist League, a participant in the 1848 revolution, and the editor of the Frankfurt *Neue Deutsche Zeitung* from 1849 to 1850. In 1851 he emigrated to America. Marx's own footnote here reads, 'Military commander of the St Louis district during the American Civil War'.

3. London, 1852.

4. *La Révolution sociale demontrée par le coup d'état du 2 décembre*, Brussels, 1852. Pierre-Joseph Proudhon was a petty-bourgeois socialist whom Marx had criticized in *The Poverty of Philosophy* (1847).

Victor Hugo confines himself to bitter and witty invective against the responsible author of the coup d'état. With him the event itself appears like a bolt from the blue. He sees in it only a single individual's act of violence. He does not notice that he makes this individual great instead of little by ascribing to him a personal power of initiative which would be without precedent in world history. Proudhon, for his part, seeks to portray the coup as the result of the preceding historical development. But his historical construction of the coup imperceptibly turns into a historical apology for its hero. Thus he falls into the error of our so-called *objective* historians. I show how, on the contrary, the *class struggle* in France created circumstances and conditions which allowed a mediocre and grotesque individual to play the hero's role.

To revise the present work would be to rob it of its particular coloration. I have therefore merely corrected printer's errors and struck out allusions which are now no longer intelligible.

The closing sentence of my work: 'But when the emperor's mantle finally falls on the shoulders of Louis Bonaparte, the bronze statue of Napoleon will come crashing down from the top of the Vendôme Column', has already been fulfilled.[5]

Colonel Charras opened the attack on the cult of Napoleon in his work on the campaign of 1815.[6] Since then, and particularly in the last few years, French literature has knocked the Napoleonic legend on the head with the weapons of historical research, criticism, satire and wit. This violent rupture with traditional popular belief, this immense intellectual revolution, has been little noticed and less understood outside France.

Finally, I hope that my work will contribute towards eliminating the current German scholastic phrase which refers to a so-called *Caesarism*. This superficial historical analogy ignores the main point, namely that the ancient Roman class struggle was only fought out within a privileged minority, between the free rich and

5. This is meant in the metaphorical sense of the general attack on the Napoleon cult in the 1860s. In fact, the statue of Napoleon I came down two years later, in 1871, when the Paris Commune ordered its removal as a 'monument to barbarism and a symbol of brute force'.

6. *Histoire de la campagne de 1815, Waterloo*, Brussels, n.d. Jean-Baptiste Charras was a soldier and a moderate bourgeois republican. He took part in the suppression of the June insurrection and was a deputy in both Assemblies of the Second Republic. After attempting to resist Bonaparte's coup d'état, he was exiled from France.

the free poor, while the great productive mass of the population, the slaves, formed a purely passive pedestal for the combatants. People forget Sismondi's significant expression: the Roman proletariat lived at the expense of society, while modern society lives at the expense of the proletariat. The material and economic conditions of the ancient and the modern class struggles are so utterly distinct from each other that their political products also can have no more in common with each other than the Archbishop of Canterbury has with the High Priest Samuel.

London, 23 June 1869   KARL MARX

I

Hegel remarks somewhere that all the great events and characters of world history occur, so to speak, twice.[7] He forgot to add: the first time as tragedy, the second as farce. Caussidière in place of Danton, Louis Blanc in place of Robespierre, the Montagne of 1848–51 in place of the Montagne of 1793–5, the Nephew in place of the Uncle.[8] And we can perceive the same caricature in the circumstances surrounding the second edition of the eighteenth Brumaire![9]

Men make their own history, but not of their own free will; not under circumstances they themselves have chosen but under the given and inherited circumstances with which they are directly confronted. The tradition of the dead generations weighs like a nightmare on the minds of the living. And, just when they appear to be engaged in the revolutionary transformation of themselves and their material surroundings, in the creation of something which does not yet exist, precisely in such epochs of revolutionary crisis they timidly conjure up the spirits of the past to help them; they borrow their names, slogans and costumes so as to stage the new world-historical scene in this venerable disguise and borrowed language. Luther put on the mask of the apostle Paul; the Revolu-

7. It is doubtful whether Hegel ever wrote these words. This theme, which Marx elaborates on in the ensuing paragraphs, is an expansion of a number of hints thrown out by Engels in his letter to Marx of 3 December 1851. See *MECW 38*, p. 505: 'It really seems as if old Hegel in his grave were acting as World Spirit and directing history, ordaining most conscientiously that it should all be unrolled twice over, once as a great tragedy and once as a wretched farce.'

8. Louis Bonaparte was the nephew of Napoleon I.

9. Napoleon I's coup d'état against the Directory took place on 9 November 1799, i.e., on 18 Brumaire of the year VIII by the revolutionary calendar. Marx therefore described Louis Bonaparte's coup of 2 December 1851 as the second edition of the eighteenth Brumaire.

tion of 1789–1814 draped itself alternately as the Roman republic and the Roman empire; and the revolution of 1848 knew no better than to parody at some points 1789 and at others the revolutionary traditions of 1793–5. In the same way, the beginner who has learnt a new language always retranslates it into his mother tongue: he can only be said to have appropriated the spirit of the new language and to be able to express himself in it freely when he can manipulate it without reference to the old, and when he forgets his original language while using the new one.

If we reflect on this process of world-historical necromancy, we see at once a salient distinction. Camille Desmoulins, Danton, Robespierre, Saint-Just and Napoleon, the heroes of the old French Revolution, as well as its parties and masses, accomplished the task of their epoch, which was the emancipation and establishment of modern *bourgeois* society, in Roman costume and with Roman slogans. The first revolutionaries smashed the feudal basis to pieces and struck off the feudal heads which had grown on it. Then came Napoleon. Within France he created the conditions which first made possible the development of free competition, the exploitation of the land by small peasant property, and the application of the unleashed productive power of the nation's industries. Beyond the borders of France he swept away feudal institutions so far as this was necessary for the provision on the European continent of an appropriate modern environment for the bourgeois society in France. Once the new social formation had been established, the antediluvian colossi disappeared along with the resurrected imitations of Rome – imitations of Brutus, Gracchus, Publicola, the tribunes, the senators, and Caesar himself. Bourgeois society in its sober reality had created its true interpreters and spokesmen in such people as Say,[10] Cousin,[11] Royer-Collard,[12] Benjamin Constant[13] and Guizot. The real leaders of the bourgeois army

10. Jean-Baptiste Say was a French economist who popularized the doctrines of Adam Smith in the early nineteenth century.

11. Victor Cousin was a French philosopher, appointed Minister of Education in Thiers's short-lived cabinet of 1840. He endeavoured to combine the ideas of Descartes, Hume and Kant into a system he himself described as 'eclecticism'.

12. Pierre-Paul Royer-Collard was a political theorist and politician under the Restoration and the July monarchy. He supported constitutional monarchy as, quite explicitly, the organ of bourgeois rule.

13. Benjamin Constant was a liberal writer and politician, a leading figure in the opposition of the 1820s to the rule of Charles X and the ultras.

sat behind office desks while the fathead Louis XVIII served as the bourgeoisie's political head. Bourgeois society was no longer aware that the ghosts of Rome had watched over its cradle, since it was wholly absorbed in the production of wealth and the peaceful struggle of economic competition. But unheroic as bourgeois society is, it still required heroism, self-sacrifice, terror, civil war, and battles in which whole nations were engaged, to bring it into the world. And its gladiators found in the stern classical traditions of the Roman republic the ideals, art forms and self-deceptions they needed in order to hide from themselves the limited bourgeois content of their struggles and to maintain their enthusiasm at the high level appropriate to great historical tragedy. A century earlier, in the same way but at a different stage of development, Cromwell and the English people had borrowed for their bourgeois revolution the language, passions and illusions of the Old Testament. When the actual goal had been reached, when the bourgeois transformation of English society had been accomplished, Locke drove out Habakkuk.

In these revolutions, then, the resurrection of the dead served to exalt the new struggles, rather than to parody the old, to exaggerate the given task in the imagination, rather than to flee from solving it in reality, and to recover the spirit of the revolution, rather than to set its ghost walking again.

For it was only the ghost of the old revolution which walked in the years from 1848 to 1851, from Marrast, the *républicain en gants jaunes*[14] who disguised himself as old Bailly,[15] right down to the adventurer who is now hiding his commonplace and repulsive countenance beneath the iron death-mask of Napoleon.

An entire people thought it had provided itself with a more powerful motive force by means of a revolution; instead, it suddenly found itself plunged back into an already dead epoch. It was impossible to mistake this relapse into the past, for the old dates arose again, along with the old chronology, the old names, the old edicts, long abandoned to the erudition of the antiquaries, and the old minions of the law, apparently long decayed. The nation might well appear to itself to be in the same situation as that mad Englishman in Bedlam, who thought he was living in the time of the pharaohs. He moaned every day about the hard work he had to

14. Yellow-gloved republican.

15. Jean-Sylvain Bailly was a leader of the liberal and constitutionalist bourgeoisie in the first French revolution; guillotined in 1793.

perform as a gold-digger in the Ethiopian mines, immured in his subterranean prison, by the exiguous light of a lamp fixed on his own head. The overseer of the slaves stood behind him with a long whip, and at the exits was a motley assembly of barbarian mercenaries, who had no common language and therefore understood neither the forced labourers in the mines nor each other. 'And I, a freeborn Briton,' sighed the mad Englishman, 'must bear all this to make gold for the old pharaohs.' 'To pay the debts of the Bonaparte family,' sighed the French nation. As long as he was in his right mind, the Englishman could not free himself of the obsession of making gold. As long as the French were engaged in revolution, they could not free themselves of the memory of Napoleon. The election of 10 December 1848[16] proved this. They yearned to return from the dangers of revolution to the fleshpots of Egypt, and 2 December 1851 was the answer. They have not merely acquired a caricature of the old Napoleon, they have the old Napoleon himself, in the caricature form he had to take in the middle of the nineteenth century.

The social revolution of the nineteenth century can only create its poetry from the future, not from the past. It cannot begin its own work until it has sloughed off all its superstitious regard for the past. Earlier revolutions have needed world-historical reminiscences to deaden their awareness of their own content. In order to arrive at its own content the revolution of the nineteenth century must let the dead bury their dead. Previously the phrase transcended the content; here the content transcends the phrase.

The February revolution was a surprise attack; it took the old society *unawares*. The people proclaimed this unexpected *coup de main*[17] to be an historic deed, the opening of a new epoch. On 2 December the February revolution was conjured away by the sleight of hand of a cardsharper. It is no longer the monarchy that appears to have been overthrown but the liberal concessions extracted from it by a century of struggle. Instead of *society* conquering a new content for itself, it only seems that the *state* has returned to its most ancient form, the unashamedly simple rule of the military sabre and the clerical cowl. The answer to the coup *de main* of February 1848 was the *coup de tête*[18] of December

16. On 10 December 1848 Louis Bonaparte was elected President of the French Republic by a large majority.

17. Surprise attack.

18. Impulsive act.

1851. Easy come, easy go! However, the intervening period has not gone unused. Between 1848 and 1851 French society, using an abbreviated because revolutionary method, caught up on the studies and experiences which would in the normal or, so to speak, textbook course of development have had to precede the February revolution if it were to do more than merely shatter the surface. Society now appears to have fallen back behind its starting-point; but in reality it must first create the revolutionary starting-point, i.e., the situation, relations and conditions necessary for the modern revolution to become serious.

Bourgeois revolutions, such as those of the eighteenth century, storm quickly from success to success. They outdo each other in dramatic effects; men and things seem set in sparkling diamonds, and each day's spirit is ecstatic. But they are short-lived; they soon reach their apogee, and society has to undergo a long period of regret until it has learnt to assimilate soberly the achievements of its period of storm and stress. Proletarian revolutions, however, such as those of the nineteenth century, constantly engage in self-criticism, and in repeated interruptions of their own course. They return to what has apparently already been accomplished in order to begin the task again; with merciless thoroughness they mock the inadequate, weak and wretched aspects of their first attempts; they seem to throw their opponent to the ground only to see him draw new strength from the earth and rise again before them, more colossal than ever; they shrink back again and again before the indeterminate immensity of their own goals, until the situation is created in which any retreat is impossible, and the conditions themselves cry out:

Hic Rhodus, hic salta! Here is the rose, dance here![19]

In any case, every observer of any competence must have suspected, even without having followed the course of French development step by step, that the revolution was about to meet with an unheard-of humiliation. It was enough to hear the self-satisfied yelps of victory with which the gentlemen of the democratic party congratulated one another on the anticipated happy

19. The Latin phrase comes from one of Aesop's fables. It is the reply made to a boaster who claimed he had once made an immense leap in Rhodes: 'Rhodes is here. Leap here and now.' But the German phrase, '*Hier ist die Rose, hier tanze!*' ('here is the rose, dance here'), is Hegel's variant, in the Preface to the *Philosophy of Right*. The Greek '*Rhodos*' can mean both Rhodes and rose.

consequences of the second Sunday in May 1852.[20] In their minds the second Sunday in May 1852 had become an obsession, a dogma, like the day of Christ's Second Coming and the beginning of the millennium in the minds of the Chiliasts. As always, weakness had found its salvation in a belief in miracles. The democrats thought the enemy had been overcome when they had conjured him away in imagination, and lost all understanding of the present in their inactive glorification of the anticipated future, and of the deeds they had up their sleeves but did not yet wish to display publicly. Those heroes who seek to disprove their well-established incapability by presenting each other with their sympathy and gathering together in a crowd had tied up their bundles and grabbed their laurel wreaths as advance payment. They were just then engaged in discounting on the exchange market the republics of a purely titular character for which they had already quietly, modestly and providently organized the governing personnel. The second of December struck them like lightning from a clear sky, and the people who in periods of despondency willingly let their inner fears be drowned by those who could shout the loudest will now perhaps have convinced themselves that the time has gone by when the cackle of geese could save the Capitol.

The Constitution, the National Assembly, the dynastic parties,[21] the blue and the red republicans, the heroes of Africa,[22] the thunder from the platform, the sheet lightning of the daily press, all the other publications, the political names and intellectual reputations, the civil law and the penal code, *liberté, égalité, fraternité* and the second Sunday in May – all have vanished like a series of optical illusions before the spell of a man whom even his enemies do not claim to be a magician. Universal suffrage seems to have survived for a further moment[23] so as to sign its testament with its own hand before the eyes of the whole world,

20. On the second Sunday in May 1852 the presidential term was to end and new elections were to be held, according to the Constitution of 4 November 1848.

21. A common name for the Legitimists (supporters of a Bourbon restoration) and Orleanists (supporters of an Orleans restoration).

22. The republican generals, Cavaignac, Lamoricière and Bedeau, who had commanded in the colonial wars in Algeria in the 1830s and 1840s.

23. The plebiscite of 20 December 1851, which sanctioned the coup d'état of 2 December by 7,500,000 votes to 650,000, according to the official figures, was held on a basis of universal (male) suffrage.

and to declare in the name of the people themselves: *All that exists deserves to perish.*[24]

It is not sufficient to say, as the French do, that their nation was taken by surprise. A nation and a woman are not forgiven for the unguarded hour in which the first available adventurer is able to violate them. Expressions of that kind do not solve the problem; they merely give it a different formulation. It remains to be explained how a nation of thirty-six millions could be taken by surprise by three swindlers[25] and delivered without resistance into captivity.

Let us recapitulate in their general features the phases the French revolution passed through from 24 February 1848 to December 1851.

Three main periods are unmistakable: *the February period*; *the period of the constitution of the republic* or *of the Constituent National Assembly*, from 4 May 1848 to 28 May 1849; and *the period of the constitutional republic* or *of the Legislative National Assembly*, from 28 May 1849 to 2 December 1851.

The *first period*, from the fall of Louis Philippe on 24 February 1848 to the meeting of the Constituent Assembly on 4 May, the *February period* proper, can be described as the *prologue* to the revolution. Its character was officially expressed by the declaration of its own improvised government that it was merely *provisional*, and, like the government, everything that was suggested, attempted or enunciated in this period proclaimed itself to be merely *provisional*. Nobody and nothing took the risk of claiming the right to exist and take real action. The dynastic opposition, the republican bourgeoisie, the democratic and republican petty bourgeoisie, and the social-democratic working class, i.e., all the elements that had prepared or determined the revolution, provisionally found their place in the February government.

It could not have been otherwise. The original aim of the February days was electoral reform, to widen the circle of the politically privileged within the possessing class itself and to overthrow the exclusive domination of the aristocracy of finance. However, when it came to the actual conflict, when the people mounted the barricades, the National Guard maintained a passive attitude, the army offered no serious resistance, and the monarchy

---

24. A saying of Mephistopheles in the first part of Goethe's *Faust*.

25. The three swindlers were no doubt Bonaparte, his half-brother Morny, and Eugène Rouher, Minister of Justice from 1849 to 1852.

ran away, the republic appeared to be a matter of course. But every party interpreted it in its own way. The proletariat had secured the republic arms in hand and now imprinted it with its own hallmark, proclaiming it to be a *social republic*. In this way the general content of the modern revolution was indicated, but this content stood in the strangest contradiction with everything which could immediately and directly be put into practice in the given circumstances and conditions, with the material available and the level of education attained by the mass of the people. On the other hand, the claims of all the other elements which had contributed to the February revolution were recognized in that they secured the lion's share of the posts in the new government. In no period, therefore, do we find a more variegated mixture of elements, more high-flown phrases, yet more actual uncertainty and awkwardness; more enthusiastic striving for innovation, yet a more fundamental retention of the old routine; a greater appearance of harmony throughout the whole society, yet a more profound alienation between its constituent parts. While the Paris proletariat was still basking in the prospect of the wide perspectives which had opened before it and indulging in earnest discussions on social problems, the old powers of society regrouped themselves, assembled, reflected on the situation, and found unexpected support from the mass of the nation, the peasants and the petty bourgeoisie, who all rushed onto the political stage once the barriers of the July monarchy had collapsed.

The *second period*, from 4 May 1848 to the end of May 1849, was the period of the *constitution* or *foundation* of the *bourgeois republic*. Immediately after the February days, the dynastic opposition had been taken unawares by the republicans, and the republicans by the socialists. But France too had been taken unawares by Paris. The National Assembly which met on 4 May 1848 had emerged from elections held throughout the nation; it therefore represented the nation. It was a living protest against the pretensions of the February days and an attempt to reduce the results of the revolution to the standards of the bourgeoisie. In vain did the Paris proletariat (which had grasped the nature of this National Assembly straightaway) endeavour on 15 May, a few days after the Assembly had met, to deny its existence by force, to dissolve it, to tear apart the organic and threatening form taken on by the nation's counteracting spirit and to scatter its individual constituents to the winds.[26] As is well known, 15 May had no other result than to remove Blanqui and his comrades, i.e., the real leaders of the proletarian party, from the public stage for the entire duration of the cycle with which we are dealing.

The *bourgeois monarchy* of Louis Philippe could only be followed by a *bourgeois republic*. In other words, if a limited section of the bourgeoisie previously ruled in the name of the king, the whole of the bourgeoisie would now rule in the name of the people. The demands of the Paris proletariat are examples of utopian humbug, which must be finished with. The Paris proletariat replied to this declaration by the Constituent National Assembly with the *June insurrection*, the most colossal event in the history of European civil wars. The bourgeois republic was victorious. It had on its side the financial aristocracy, the industrial bourgeoisie, the middle class, the petty bourgeoisie, the army, the Mobile Guard (i.e., the organized lumpenproletariat), the intellectual celebrities, the priests and the rural population. On the side of the Paris proletariat stood no one but itself. Over 3,000 insurgents were butchered after the victory, and a further 15,000 were transported without having been convicted. With this defeat the proletariat passed into the *background* of the revolutionary stage. Whenever the movement appeared to be making a fresh start the proletariat tried to push forward again, but it displayed less and less strength and achieved ever fewer results. As soon as one of the higher social strata got into a revolutionary ferment, the proletariat would enter into alliance with it and so share all the defeats successively suffered by the different parties. But the wider the area of society that these additional blows affected, the weaker they became. One by one the proletariat's more important leaders in the Assembly and in the press fell victim to the courts, and ever more dubious figures stepped forward to lead it. In part it threw itself into *doctrinaire experiments, exchange banks and workers' associations,[27] i.e., into a movement which renounces the hope of overturning the old world by using the huge combination of means provided by the latter, and seeks rather to achieve its salvation in a private manner, behind the back of society, within its own limited conditions of existence; such a movement necessarily fails.* It seems

26. See p. 58.

27. Exchange banks based on 'labour money' were the Proudhonist panacea. The workers' associations referred to here were early craft unions, lacking broad revolutionary perspectives.

that until *all the classes* that the proletariat fought against in June themselves lie prostrate beside it, it will be unable either to recover its own revolutionary greatness or to win new energy from the alliances into which it has recently entered. But at least it was defeated with the honours attaching to a great world-historical struggle; not just France, but the whole of Europe trembled in face of the June earthquake, whereas the later defeats of the higher social classes were bought so cheaply that the victorious party had to exaggerate them impudently to make them pass for events at all, and were the more shameful the greater the distance between the defeated party and that of the proletariat.

The defeat of the June insurgents certainly prepared and flattened the ground on which the bourgeois republic could be founded and erected, but at the same time it showed that there are other issues at stake in Europe besides that of 'republic or monarchy'. It revealed that the bourgeois republic signified here only the unrestricted despotism of one class over other classes. It proved that in the older civilized countries, with their highly developed class formation, modern conditions of production, and their intellectual consciousness in which all traditional ideas have been dissolved through the work of centuries, *the republic is generally only the political form for the revolutionizing of bourgeois society*, and not its *conservative form of existence*, as for example in the United States of America. There, although classes already exist, they have not yet become fixed, but rather continually alter and mutually exchange their component parts; the modern means of production make up for the relative scarcity of heads and hands instead of coinciding with a stagnant surplus population; finally, the feverish and youthful movement of a material production which has to appropriate a new world has left neither time nor opportunity for the abolition of the old spiritual world.

During the June days all other classes and parties joined together to form the *party of Order*, in opposition to the proletarian class, the *party of Anarchy*, of socialism and communism. They 'saved' society from 'the enemies of society'. They handed out the catchphrases of the old society – 'property, family, religion, order' – among their soldiers as passwords, and proclaimed to the counter-revolutionary crusading army: 'In this sign shalt thou conquer.'[28] From this moment onwards, as soon as one of the

---

28. Christian legend has it that a cross appeared to the Emperor Constantine before the battle fought in 312 against Maxentius, bearing these words.

numerous parties which had assembled under this sign against the June insurgents sought to defend its own class interest on the revolutionary battlefield, it succumbed in face of the cry of 'property, family, religion, order'. Society was saved as often as the circle of its rulers contracted, as often as a more exclusive interest was upheld as against the wider interest. Every demand for the simplest bourgeois financial reform, every demand of the most ordinary liberalism, the most formal republicanism, or the most commonplace democracy, was simultaneously punished as an 'attack on society' and denounced as 'socialism'. And, finally, the high priests of the cult of 'religion and order' are themselves kicked off their Delphic stools, hauled from their beds at the dead of night, put in prison vans, and thrown into jail or sent into exile. Their temple is levelled to the ground, their mouths are sealed, their pens smashed, and their law torn to pieces in the name of religion, property, family and order. Bourgeois fanatics for order are shot down on their balconies by drunken bands of troops, their sacred domesticity is profaned, their houses are bombarded for the fun of it, all in the name of property, the family, religion and order. Last of all, the dregs of bourgeois society form themselves into the *holy phalanx of order*, and the hero Crapulinski[29] moves into the Tuileries as the 'saviour of society'.

II

Let us pick up the threads of this historical process once again.

After the June days, the history of the *Constituent National Assembly* was the *history of the domination and the dissolution of the republican fraction of the bourgeoisie*, that fraction which goes under the various names of tricolour republicans, pure republicans, political republicans, formal republicans, etc.

Under the bourgeois monarchy of Louis Philippe, this fraction had formed the *official* republican *opposition* and was therefore a recognized component of the contemporary political world. It had its representatives in parliament and a considerable field of influence in the press. Its Paris organ, *Le National*, was considered

29. 'Crapulinski' comes from the French word '*crapule*' (scoundrel) and was used by Heine as the name of the spendthrift Polish nobleman in his poem 'Two Knights'.

to be just as respectable in its own way as the *Journal des Débats*.[30] Its position under the constitutional monarchy was in accordance with its character. This was not a fraction of the bourgeoisie bound together by great common interests and demarcated from the rest by conditions of production peculiar to it; it was a coterie of republican-minded members of the bourgeoisie, writers, lawyers, officers and officials. Its influence rested on the personal antipathies of the country towards Louis Philippe, on memories of the old republic, on the republican faith of a number of enthusiasts, and, above all, on *French nationalism*, for it constantly kept alive hatred of the Vienna treaties[31] and the alliance with England. This concealed imperialism[32] accounted for a large part of the support the *National* possessed under Louis Philippe, but later, under the republic, it was to confront it as a deadly rival in the person of Louis Bonaparte. Like the rest of the bourgeois opposition, it fought the financial aristocracy. Polemics against the budget, which in France coincided exactly with the struggle against the financial aristocracy, provided popularity too cheaply and material for puritanical *leading articles*[33] too plentifully for the opposition not to exploit the issue. The industrial bourgeoisie was grateful to it for its slavish defence of the French system of protective tariffs, although it took up this defence more on nationalist than on economic grounds. The bourgeoisie as a whole was grateful for its venomous denunciations of communism and socialism. Apart from this, the party of the *National* was *purely republican*, i.e., it demanded a republican instead of a monarchical form of bourgeois rule, and it demanded above all the lion's share of this rule. It was absolutely unclear about the conditions of this transformation. What was as clear as day, and publicly declared at the reform banquets held in the last days of Louis Philippe, was that the official opposition was unpopular with the petty-bourgeois democrats and, more so, with the revolutionary proletariat. The oppositional pure republicans were already on the point of making

30. The leading Orleanist paper, which had a semi-official character under the July monarchy.

31. See above, p. 68, n. 65.

32. Marx uses the term 'imperialism' not in its present-day sense, but to refer to the form of French nationalism which looked back to the exploits of Napoleon I, i.e., to the First Empire, and expressed itself in support for Louis Bonaparte in the 1850s. Where the words 'imperialism' and 'imperialist' appear in this translation, they are used in this sense.

33. In English in the original.

do initially with a regency of the Duchess of Orleans[34] when the February revolution broke out and assigned their best-known representatives a place in the Provisional Government; in this they showed themselves to be typical of all pure republicans. They naturally possessed in advance the confidence of the bourgeoisie and the majority of the Constituent National Assembly. The *socialist* elements of the Provisional Government were straightaway excluded from the Executive Commission which the National Assembly formed when it met, and the party of the *National* made use of the outbreak of the June insurrection to dismiss the Executive Commission as well and thereby to free itself of its closest rivals, the *petty-bourgeois* or *democratic republicans* (Ledru-Rollin, etc.). Cavaignac, the general of the bourgeois republican party, who had commanded the June battle, replaced the Executive Commission with a kind of dictatorial authority. The former editor-in-chief of the *National*, Marrast, became the permanent chairman of the Constituent National Assembly, and the ministries, as well as all the other important posts, fell to the pure republicans.

The republican fraction of the bourgeoisie, which had long seen itself as the legitimate heir to the July monarchy, thus found its dearest expectations exceeded. But it had achieved power through the grape-shot which suppressed a rising of the proletariat against capital; not through a liberal revolt of the bourgeoisie against the throne. What it had imagined would be the *most revolutionary* event turned out to be in reality the *most counter-revolutionary*. The fruit fell into its lap from the tree of knowledge, not the tree of life.

The exclusive *rule of the bourgeois republicans* only lasted from 24 June to 10 December 1848. Its results can be summarized as the *drafting of a republican constitution* and the *state of siege in Paris*.

Fundamentally, the new Constitution was merely a republicanized version of the constitutional Charter of 1830.[35] The narrow electoral qualification of the July monarchy, which excluded even a large section of the bourgeoisie from political rule, was incom-

34. On the morning of 24 February 1848 Louis Philippe abdicated in favour of his young grandson, the comte de Paris. The child's mother, the duchesse d'Orléans, was to be regent for the time being.

35. The Charter of 1830 was the basic constitutional law of the July monarchy. It proclaimed the sovereignty of the people but retained the monarchy as well as the limited franchise of the previous regime, merely increasing the number eligible to vote to approximately two hundred thousand.

patible with the existence of the bourgeois republic. The February revolution had immediately proclaimed direct universal suffrage in place of the property qualification. The bourgeois republicans could not treat this event as not having happened. They had to content themselves with the addition of an ordinance limiting the electorate to those people who had resided for six months in the relevant constituency. The old organization of the administration, the municipalities, courts, the army, etc., continued to exist intact, or, where the Constitution did make a change, this change concerned the table of contents, not the content; the name, not the thing.

The inevitable general staff of the liberties of 1848, personal freedom, freedom of the press, speech, association, assembly, education, religion, etc., received a constitutional uniform which made it impossible to establish any cases where they might have been infringed. Each of these liberties is proclaimed to be the *unconditional* right of the French citizen, but there is always the marginal note that it is unlimited only in so far as it is not restricted by the '*equal rights of others* and the *public safety*', or by 'laws' which are supposed to mediate precisely this harmony of the individual liberties with each other and with the public safety. For example: 'Citizens have the right to form associations, to assemble peaceably and without weapons, to petition, and to express their opinions through the press or in any other manner. *The enjoyment of these rights has no other restriction than the equal rights of others and the public safety*' (Chapter II of the French Constitution, paragraph 8). Or: 'Education is free. Freedom of education shall be *enjoyed* under the conditions fixed by law and the supreme control of the state' (paragraph 9). Or: 'The domicile of every citizen is inviolable *except* in the forms laid down by law' (paragraph 3). And so on. The Constitution therefore constantly refers to future *organic* laws which are to implement the above glosses and regulate the enjoyment of these unrestricted liberties in such a way that they do not come up against each other or against the public safety. These organic laws were later brought into existence by the friends of order, and all liberties were regulated so as to make sure that the bourgeoisie was not hindered in its enjoyment of them by the equal rights of the other classes. Where the Constitution entirely forbade these liberties to the 'others' or allowed them to be enjoyed under conditions which were simply traps set by the police, this always happened solely in the interests of 'public safety', i.e., the safety of the bourgeoisie as laid down by the Constitution. In the period which followed, both sides had therefore a perfect right to appeal to the Constitution: the friends of order, who did away with all those liberties, and the democrats, who demanded their retention. For each paragraph of the Constitution contains its own antithesis, its own upper and lower house, namely, freedom in the general phrase, abolition of freedom in the marginal note. In this way, as long as the *name* of freedom was respected and only its actual implementation was prevented (in a legal way, it goes without saying), its constitutional existence remained intact and untouched however fatal the blows dealt to it in its actual physical existence.

This Constitution, so cleverly made inviolable, could nevertheless, like Achilles, be wounded at one point. Not in the heel, but in the head, or rather the two heads at its top – the Legislative Assembly on the one hand and the President on the other. If one skims through the Constitution, one finds that the only paragraphs which are absolute, positive, consistent, and incapable of distortion, are those which determine the relation between the President and the Legislative Assembly. For here the bourgeois republicans were concerned to secure their own position. Paragraphs 45 to 70 of the Constitution are drawn up in such a way that the National Assembly can remove the President constitutionally, whereas the President can only remove the National Assembly unconstitutionally, by sweeping away the Constitution itself. Here, therefore, the Constitution provokes its own forcible destruction. Not only does it sanctify the separation of powers, like the Charter of 1830; it extends this into an intolerable contradiction. The *game of constitutional powers*, as Guizot described the parliamentary squabble between the legislature and the executive, is continually played for the maximum possible stake in the 1848 Constitution. On one side are the seven hundred and fifty representatives of the people, who are elected by universal suffrage and are re-eligible; they form an uncontrollable, indissoluble, indivisible National Assembly, an all-powerful legislature which decides in the last instance on war, peace and commercial treaties, alone possesses the right of amnesty, and unceasingly holds the front of the stage owing to its permanent character. On the other side is the President, with all the attributes of royal power, with the authority to appoint and dismiss his ministers independently of the National Assembly, with all the instruments of executive power in his hands, and finally with the right of appointment to every post, which means in France the right to decide on the livelihood of at least a million and a half people, for this is the number who depend on the five hundred thousand officials and officers of every rank. He has the whole of the armed forces behind him. He has the privilege of pardoning individual criminals, suspending members of the National Guard, and, with the agreement of the Council of State,[36] dismissing the departmental, cantonal and municipal councils elected by the citizens themselves. The right to initiate and negotiate all treaties with foreign countries is reserved to him. While the Assembly constantly performs on the public stage and is exposed to the daylight of public criticism, the President lives a secluded life in the Elysian Fields,[37] though admittedly he has before his eyes and in his heart paragraph 45 of the Constitution, which daily calls out to him: '*Frère, il faut mourir.*'[38] Your power will cease on the second Sunday of the beautiful month of May in the fourth year after your election! Then your glory is at an end! The play will not be performed twice, and if you have debts make sure in good time that you pay them off with the 600,000 francs the Constitution has granted you, unless you prefer to move to Clichy[39] on the second Monday of the beautiful month of May!

Thus, if the Constitution assigns the real power to the President, it endeavours to secure moral power for the National Assembly. Leaving aside the fact that it is impossible to create moral authority by legislative fiat, the Constitution also provides for its own abolition by having the President elected by the direct suffrage of all Frenchmen. Whereas in the case of the National Assembly the votes of France are divided among its seven hundred and fifty members, they are here, on the contrary, concentrated on *one* individual. While each individual deputy represents only this or that party, this or that town, this or that bridgehead, or merely the necessity of electing some appropriate member of the seven

36. The Council of State was originally set up by Napoleon I, as a body of experts – administrative, scientific, diplomatic and military – to plan legislation. It has since found a place in most French regimes, being particularly important under the Second Empire and the Fifth Republic.

37. The President's palace is the Elysée, adjacent to the Avenue des Champs Elysées. The original Elysian Fields are the abode of the blessed after death in Greek mythology.

38. Brother, you must die.

39. Clichy was the Paris debtors' prison during the mid-nineteenth century.

hundred and fifty, in which case neither the issue nor the man is closely inspected, *he*, the President, is the elect of the nation, and the act of electing him is the great trump which the sovereign people plays once every four years. The elected National Assembly stands in a metaphysical relation to the nation, but the elected President stands in a personal relation to it. No doubt the National Assembly manifests in its individual deputies the multifarious aspects of the national spirit, but the President is its very incarnation. Unlike the Assembly, he possesses a kind of divine right; he is there by the grace of the people.

Thetis, the sea goddess, prophesied to Achilles that he would die in the bloom of youth. The Constitution, which, like Achilles, had its weak point, had also, like Achilles, a foreboding that it would have to go early to its death. The constitution-making pure republicans needed only to direct their gaze from the heavenly clouds of their ideal republic to the profane world in order to see how the insolence of the royalists, the Bonapartists, the democrats and the communists, as well as their own discredit, grew daily in the same measure that their great legislative artefact neared completion. They did not need Thetis to emerge from the sea and inform them of this secret. They endeavoured to cheat fate with constitutional cunning by inserting paragraph 111, according to which any motion for the *revision of the Constitution* had to be carried in three successive debates, with an interval of a whole month between each, by at least three quarters of the votes cast, and with no less than 500 members of the National Assembly voting. This was merely an impotent attempt to prolong their exercise of power as a parliamentary minority, which they prophetically saw their own future to be. Even at this time, when they had at their disposal a parliamentary majority and all the resources of governmental authority, power was daily slipping further from their feeble grasp.

Finally, in a melodramatic paragraph, the Constitution entrusts itself 'to the vigilance and the patriotism of the whole French people as well as every individual Frenchman', after it had previously, in a different paragraph, entrusted the 'vigilant' and 'patriotic' Frenchman to the tender and painstakingly penal care of the '*haute cour*', the special High Court invented for that very purpose.

This, then, was the Constitution of 1848, overthrown on 2 December 1851 not by a head, but by coming into contact with a mere hat; this hat was of course of the three-cornered Napoleonic variety.

Inside the Assembly the bourgeois republicans were engaged in discussing, voting and adding refinements to the Constitution; outside the Assembly Cavaignac was maintaining Paris in a *state of siege*. The state of siege in Paris was the midwife of the Constituent Assembly in its labour of creating the republic. If the Constitution was later put out of existence by bayonets, it should not be forgotten that it had to be protected in its mother's womb by bayonets, bayonets turned against the people, and brought into the world by them. The forefathers of the 'respectable republicans' had sent their symbol, the tricolour, on a grand tour round Europe. The republicans of 1848 in their turn made an invention which found its way unaided over the whole Continent, but returned to France with ever renewed love, so that by now it has obtained citizenship in half her departments – the *state of siege*. An excellent invention which has found periodic application in every successive crisis in the course of the French revolution. The barracks and the bivouac were thus periodically deposited on the head of French society in order to compress its brain and keep it quiet; the sabre and the musket were periodically made to judge and administer, to guard and to censor, to play the part of policeman and night-watchman; the military moustache and the service uniform were periodically trumpeted forth as the highest wisdom and the spiritual guide of society. Was it not inevitable that barracks and bivouac, sabre and musket, moustache and uniform, would finally hit on the idea of saving society once and for all by proclaiming the supremacy of their own regime and thus entirely freeing civil society from the trouble of ruling itself? They had the more reason to hit on this idea in that they could then expect a better cash payment in return for their elevated services, while the merely periodic states of siege and temporary rescues of society at the behest of this or that fraction of the bourgeoisie produced little solid payment apart from one or two dead and wounded and a few friendly bourgeois grimaces. Was the military not bound to finally play at state of siege in its own interests and for its own interests, and at the same time lay siege to the bourgeois purse? It should not be forgotten, by the way, that Colonel Bernard, the man who presided over the military commission which under Cavaignac deported 15,000 insurgents without trial, is at this moment again at the head of the military commissions active in Paris.

Although, with the state of siege in Paris, the respectable pure republicans founded the nursery in which the praetorian guards[40] of 2 December 1851 were to grow up, they nevertheless deserve our praise for one thing: instead of over-doing nationalist sentiment as they had done under Louis Philippe, now that they had control of the nation's armed forces they crawled before the foreigner, and instead of liberating Italy, they allowed the Austrians and Neapolitans to reconquer it.[41] The election of Louis Bonaparte as President on 10 December 1848 put an end to the dictatorship of Cavaignac and the Constituent Assembly.

It is stated in paragraph 44 of the Constitution that 'the President of the French Republic must never have lost his status as a French citizen'. The first President of the French Republic, L. N. Bonaparte, had, in addition to losing his status as a French citizen, been an English special constable, and he had even been naturalized in Switzerland.[42]

I have dealt elsewhere[43] with the significance of the election of 10 December, and I shall not return to the issue here. Suffice it to say that it was a *reaction of the peasants*, who had had to pay the costs of the February revolution, against the other classes of the nation, a *reaction of the country against the town*. It found great favour with the army, for which the republicans of the *National* had provided no glory and no extra pay, with the big bourgeoisie, who saw Bonaparte as a bridge to the monarchy, and with the proletarians and petty bourgeois, who hailed him as a scourge for Cavaignac. I shall find an opportunity later on to examine more closely the relation of the peasants to the French revolution.

The period from 20 December 1848[44] to the dissolution of the

40. A reference to the Society of 10 December (see below, p. 197). The original praetorian guards were attached to the person of the Roman emperors.

41. The Austrian victory of Custozza (25 July) was followed by the armistice of Vigevano (9 August) between Austria and Piedmont. On 25 August Cavaignac publicly rejected any idea of intervening against Austria, offering instead French mediation. The Neapolitan army reconquered half of Sicily in September 1848, but was compelled to conclude an armistice before the conquest was complete, as a result of joint Anglo-French pressure.

42. In 1832 Louis Bonaparte had adopted Swiss citizenship, and in 1848 he joined the special constabulary organized to defend London against the Chartists.

43. See above, p. 72–4.

44. On 20 December 1848 Cavaignac laid down his office, Louis Bonaparte was proclaimed President, and his first cabinet, under Odilon Barrot, was sworn in.

Constituent Assembly in May 1849 comprises the history of the fall of the bourgeois republicans. After they had founded a republic for the bourgeoisie, driven the revolutionary proletariat from the field, and temporarily reduced the democratic petty bourgeoisie to silence, they were themselves pushed aside by the mass of the bourgeoisie, which quite rightly confiscated the republic as being *its property*. This bourgeois mass was however *royalist*. One section of it, the great landowners, had ruled during the Restoration and was therefore Legitimist. The other, the aristocracy of finance and the big industrialists, had ruled under the July monarchy and was therefore Orleanist. The high dignitaries of the army, the university, the church, the bar, the academy and the press, were to be found on both sides, though in varying proportions. Here in the bourgeois republic, which bore neither the name 'Bourbon' nor the name 'Orleans', but the name 'Capital', they had found the form of state in which they could rule *jointly*. They had already been brought together into the 'party of Order' by the June insurrection. The first requirement now was the removal of the clique of bourgeois republicans who still occupied the seats in the National Assembly. These pure republicans had brutally misused physical force against the people; they were now just as cowardly, faint-hearted, spiritless, and incapable of resistance in their retreat as they had previously been brutal, when it was necessary to assert their republicanism and their legislative rights against the executive power and the royalists. I need not relate here the shameful history of their collapse. They did not go under; they faded away. Their history has been played out once and for all. In the following period they figured, whether inside or outside the Assembly, merely as memories, although these memories appeared to take on new life as soon as the mere name of Republic was at issue once more, and whenever the revolutionary conflict threatened to sink down to the lowest level. It might be pointed out in passing that the journal which gave this party its name, the *National*, was converted to socialism in the succeeding period.

Before we finish with this period we must cast a glance back at the two powers, one of which destroyed the other on 2 December 1851, although from 20 December 1848 to the exit of the Constituent Assembly they had lived in a conjugal relationship. We mean Louis Bonaparte, on the one hand, and the party of the royalist coalition, the party of Order, the party of the big bourgeoisie, on the other. At the beginning of his term of office Bonaparte immediately formed a ministry of the party of Order, placing at its head Odilon Barrot, the old leader – mark this well – of the most liberal fraction of the parliamentary bourgeoisie. Barrot had at last hunted down the ministerial position whose spectre had haunted him since 1830, and what is more, the premiership of that ministry; not, however, as he had imagined under Louis Philippe, as the most advanced leader of the parliamentary opposition, but with the task of killing off a parliament in alliance with all his arch-enemies, the Jesuits and Legitimists. He had finally brought his bride home, but only after she had become a prostitute. Bonaparte seemed to have completely effaced himself. The party of Order acted for him.

The Council of Ministers decided at its very first meeting on the expedition to Rome, agreeing that it should take place behind the back of the National Assembly. The means for the expedition were to be obtained from the Assembly on false pretences. It thus began with a fraud perpetrated on the National Assembly and a secret conspiracy with the absolutist powers abroad against the revolutionary Roman republic. In the same way and with the same manoeuvres Bonaparte was to prepare his coup of 2 December against the royalist Legislative Assembly and its constitutional republic. It should not be forgotten that the same party which formed Bonaparte's ministry on 20 December 1848 formed the majority of the Legislative Assembly on 2 December 1851.

The Constituent Assembly had decided in August that it would only dissolve when it had worked out and promulgated a whole series of organic laws which were to supplement the Constitution. The party of Order had the deputy Rateau propose on 6 January 1849 that the Assembly should forget the organic laws and instead resolve on its *own dissolution*. Odilon Barrot's ministry and all the royalist deputies bullied the National Assembly with the argument that its dissolution was necessary for the restoration of credit, for the consolidation of order, for the cessation of the indefinite provisional situation, for the establishment of a definitive state of affairs; that it hindered the new government's productivity and sought to prolong its existence out of mere spite; and that the country was tired of it. Bonaparte took note of all this invective against the legislative power, learnt it by heart, and on 2 December 1851 demonstrated to the parliamentary royalists that he had learnt his lessons well. He repeated their own catchwords against them.

The Barrot ministry and the party of Order went further. They were behind the *petitions to the National Assembly* which arrived from all over France, politely requesting the Assembly to disappear. Thus against the National Assembly, the constitutionally organized expression of the people, they led into the attack the unorganized masses. They taught Bonaparte to appeal from parliamentary assemblies to the people. Finally, on 29 January 1849, there came the day on which the Constituent Assembly was supposed to decide on its own dissolution. The Assembly found its meeting-place under military occupation; Changarnier, the party of Order's general who held the supreme command of both the National Guard and the troops of the line, held a big military review in Paris, as if in expectation of a battle, and the royalist coalition threatened the Constituent Assembly that force would be used if it was unwilling to submit. It was willing, but only obtained the very short extension of life it bargained for. What was 29 January if not the coup d'état of 2 December 1851, only carried out by the royalists in alliance with Bonaparte against the republican National Assembly? These gentlemen did not notice, or did not want to notice, that Bonaparte made use of 29 January 1849 by having a section of the troops march past him in front of the Tuileries, and eagerly seized on this first public display of the power of the military against the power of parliament to intimate that he would act the part of Caligula.[45] Of course, the royalists saw only their Changarnier.

One important factor which led the party of Order forcibly to cut short the Constituent Assembly's life was the question of the *organic* laws supplementing the Constitution, such as the laws on education, on religious worship, etc. It was of vital importance to the royalist coalition that it should make these laws itself and not allow them to be made by the now mistrustful republicans. Among these organic laws there was also a law on the responsibility of the President of the republic. In 1851, indeed, the Legislative Assembly was engaged in drafting a law of that kind when Bonaparte forestalled this coup with the coup of 2 December. What would the royalist coalition not have given in its parliamentary winter campaign of 1851 to find the law on responsibility ready

45. The Roman emperor Caligula (37–41) declared himself a god and established a regime of complete absolutism. He relied on the support of the military, and in particular on the praetorian guard.

and waiting, no matter that it had been drafted by a suspicious and malevolent republican Assembly?

After 29 January 1849, when the Constituent Assembly destroyed its own last weapon,[46] the Barrot ministry and the friends of order hounded it to death, did everything possible to humiliate it, and, making use of its weakness and self-despair, wrung from it laws which cost it its last remnant of public esteem. Bonaparte, occupied with his Napoleonic obsession, was impertinent enough to exploit this degradation of the power of parliament in public. When, on 8 May 1849, the National Assembly censured the ministry for Oudinot's occupation of Civitavecchia and gave orders for the Roman expedition to be brought back to its alleged purpose,[47] Bonaparte published a letter to Oudinot in the *Moniteur* the same evening, in which he congratulated him on his heroic deeds, and already acted the part of the magnanimous protector of the army against the pen-pushing parliamentarians. The royalists smiled at this. They simply considered Napoleon their dupe. Finally, when Marrast, the chairman of the Constituent Assembly, momentarily thought its safety was in danger and, basing himself on the Constitution, requisitioned a colonel with his regiment, the colonel refused the request with a reference to discipline, and referred Marrast to Changarnier, who scornfully turned him away with the remark that he did not like *bayonets which thought*. In November 1851, when the royalist coalition wanted to start the decisive struggle with Bonaparte, they tried to push through the principle of the direct requisition of troops by the chairman of the National Assembly, with their notorious Quaestors Bill.[48] One of their generals, Le Flô,[49] had signed the bill. Changarnier voted for it, and Thiers paid homage to the prudent wisdom of the former Constituent Assembly, but all to no purpose. The War Minister,

46. On 29 January 1849 the Constituent Assembly rejected a motion from Mathieu de la Drôme calling for the unconditional rejection of Rateau's motion of 6 January that the Assembly decree its own dissolution.

47. See above, pp. 85–7.

48. The name given, by analogy with the old Roman office, to the National Assembly's commissioners for finance and security. The quaestors Le Flô, Baze and Panat moved that the Assembly be given the exclusive right to command the troops. This motion was rejected on 17 November 1851 owing to the refusal of the Montagne to vote for it.

49. Adolphe Le Flô was a general and a diplomat. During the Second Republic he supported the party of Order.

Saint-Arnaud,[50] replied as Changarnier had replied to Marrast – and the Montagne applauded!

Thus when the party of Order did not yet control the National Assembly, when it was still only the ministry, it had itself stigmatized the parliamentary regime. And now it makes an outcry because 2 December 1851 has banished the parliamentary regime from France!

We wish it a pleasant journey.

III

The Legislative National Assembly met on 28 May 1849. It was dispersed on 2 December 1851. The period between these dates covers the life-span of the *constitutional* or *parliamentary republic*.

In the first French revolution the rule of the Constitutionalists was followed by the rule of the Girondins, and the rule of the Girondins by the rule of the Jacobins. Each of these parties leant on the more progressive party. As soon as it had brought the revolution to the point where it was unable to follow it any further, let alone advance ahead of it, it was pushed aside by the bolder ally standing behind it and sent to the guillotine. In this way the revolution moved in an ascending path.

In the revolution of 1848 this relationship was reversed. The proletarian party appeared as the appendage of petty-bourgeois democracy. It was betrayed and abandoned by the latter on 16 April,[51] on 15 May, and in the June days. The democratic party, for its part, leant on the shoulders of the bourgeois-republican party. As soon as the bourgeois republicans thought they had found their feet, they shook off this burdensome comrade and relied in turn on the shoulders of the party of Order. The party of Order hunched its shoulders, allowed the bourgeois republicans to tumble off, and threw itself onto the shoulders of the armed forces. It believed it was still sitting on those shoulders when it noticed one fine morning that they had changed into bayonets. Every party kicked out behind at the party pressing it forward

50. Armand de Saint-Arnaud was a Bonapartist general and an organizer of the coup d'état of 2 December. He was Minister of War from 1851 to 1854.

51. On 16 April 1848 a large body of workers was prevented by the National Guard from marching to the Hôtel de Ville to present a patriotic collection owing to the Provisional Government's fear that the demonstration might turn into a Blanquist coup directed against it.

and leant on the party in front, which was pressing backward. No wonder each party lost its balance in this ridiculous posture, and collapsed in the midst of curious capers, after having made the inevitable grimaces. In this way the revolution moved in a descending path. Before the last February barricade had been cleared away and the first revolutionary authority constituted, the parties found themselves enmeshed in this retrogressive process.

The period we have now to deal with contains the most variegated mixture of crying contradictions: constitutionalists who openly conspire against the Constitution; revolutionaries who are by their own admission constitutionalists; a National Assembly which aspires to supreme power but throughout remains parliamentary; a Montagne which finds its vocation in patience and parries its present defeats by prophesying future victories; royalists who are *patres conscripti*[52] of the republic and are compelled by the situation to keep the mutually hostile royal houses they support abroad and the republic they hate in France; an executive which draws strength from its very weakness and respectability from the contempt it inspires; a republic with imperialist trappings, which is nothing but the combined infamy of two monarchies, the Restoration and the July monarchy; alliances whose first condition is separation, and struggles whose first law is their indecisiveness; wild and empty agitation in the name of tranquillity, the most solemn preaching of tranquillity in the name of revolution; passions without truth, truths without passion; heroes without deeds of heroism, history without events; a course of development apparently only driven forward by the calendar, and made wearisome by the constant repetition of the same tensions and relaxations; antagonisms which seem periodically to press forward to a climax, but become deadened and fall away without having attained their resolution; exertions pretentiously put on show and bourgeois terror at the danger that the world may end, and at the same time the pettiest intrigues and courtly comedies played by the world's saviours, who in their *laissez-aller* are more reminiscent of the era of the Fronde[53] than of the Day of Judgement; the official collective genius of France brought to ruin by

52. The ancient Roman term for senators.
53. The movement of opposition on the part of the French nobility to the absolutism of the French monarchy, in the years 1648–53. The Fronde became a byword for aristocratic frivolity.

the cunning stupidity of a single individual; the collective will of the nation seeking its appropriate expression through the superannuated enemies of the interests of the masses, whenever it spoke through universal suffrage, until finally it found expression in the self-will of a freebooter. If any section of history has been painted grey on grey, it is this. Men and events appear as Schlemihls in reverse,[54] as shadows which have become detached from their bodies. The revolution paralyses its own representatives and endows only its opponents with passion and forcefulness. The 'red spectre' is continually conjured up and exorcized by the counter-revolutionaries; when it finally appears it is not with the Phrygian cap[55] of anarchy on its head, but in the uniform of order, in *red breeches*.

As we have seen, the ministry which Bonaparte installed on 20 December 1848, the day of his ascension into the Elysian Fields, was a ministry of the party of Order, of the Legitimist and Orleanist coalition. The Barrot-Falloux ministry outlasted the republican Constituent Assembly, whose life it had more or less violently curtailed, and was still at the helm when the Legislative Assembly met. Changarnier, the general of the royalist alliance, continued to combine in his own person the general command of the First Army Division and of the Paris National Guard. Finally, the general elections had secured for the party of Order the vast majority of the seats in the National Assembly. Here the former deputies and peers of Louis Philippe's reign met with a holy host of Legitimists, for whom many of the nation's voting cards had become transformed into cards of admission to the political stage. The Bonapartist deputies were too thin on the ground to be able to form an independent parliamentary party. They appeared only as the *mauvaise queue*[56] of the party of Order. Thus the party of Order was in possession of the power of government, of the army, and of the legislative body, in short, of all the power of the state. It had been morally strengthened by the general elections, which made it appear that it ruled by the will of the people, and also by the simultaneous victory of the counter-revolution all over the continent of Europe.

54. After the hero of *Peter Schlemihl*, by Adalbert von Chamisso. Schlemihl sold his shadow for a magic purse.

55. The conical peaked cap worn by the Jacobins; frequently used in the nineteenth century as a symbol of liberty.

56. Dubious hangers-on.

Never did a party open its campaign with greater resources or under more favourable auspices.

The shipwrecked *pure republicans* found that in the Legislative National Assembly they had shrunk to a clique of approximately fifty men, headed by the African generals Cavaignac, Lamoricière and Bedeau.[57] However, the main opposition party was formed by the Montagne. This was what the *social-democratic* party had baptized itself for parliamentary purposes. It had at its disposal more than 200 of the 750 votes in the National Assembly and was therefore at least as powerful as any one of the fractions of the party of Order taken in isolation. The fact that it was in a minority as against the royalist coalition as a whole seemed to be outweighed by special circumstances. It was not just that the elections in the departments showed that it had won considerable support among the rural population. It counted in its ranks almost all the deputies from Paris; the army had sworn its faith in democracy by electing three non-commissioned officers, and Ledru-Rollin, the leader of the Montagne, had, unlike any of the party of Order's deputies, been elected to parliament by five different departments. Thus on 28 May 1849 the Montagne seemed to possess all the requirements for success, in view of the inevitability of clashes between the rival royalists, and between Bonaparte and the party of Order in general. A fortnight later it had lost everything, including its honour.

Before we follow the parliamentary history any further, some remarks are necessary in order to avoid certain common delusions about the overall character of the epoch which lies before us. If we look at this in the fashion of the democrats, the issue during the period of the Legislative National Assembly was the same issue as in the period of the Constituent Assembly: a simple struggle between republicans and royalists. However, the democrats sum up the whole course of development itself in *one* slogan: '*reaction*' – a night in which all cats are grey and which allows them to reel off their useless platitudes. And of course an initial inspection reveals the party of Order to be a conglomeration of different royalist fractions, which not only intrigue against each other to

57. See above, p. 151. Christophe Juchault de Lamoricière was a deputy in both Assemblies, and War Minister in Cavaignac's government (June–December 1848). Marie-Adolphe Bedeau was vice-chairman of both Assemblies. Both generals actively participated in the suppression of the June insurrection.

raise their own pretender to the throne and exclude the pretender of the opposing fraction, but also unite together in a common hatred of the 'republic' and in common attacks on it. The Montagne for its part appears as the representative of the 'republic' in opposition to this royalist conspiracy. The party of Order appears to be constantly engaged in a 'reaction' directed, neither more nor less than in Prussia, against the press, the right of association, and similar things, and which is accomplished, as in Prussia, by means of the brutal police interventions of the bureaucracy, the *gendarmerie* and the courts. The Montagne for its part is just as continually engaged in fighting off these attacks and in this way defending the 'eternal rights of man', more or less in the same way as every so-called people's party has done for a century and a half. But this superficial appearance veils the *class struggle* and the peculiar physiognomy of this period, and it vanishes on a closer examination of the situation and the parties.

As we have said, Legitimists and Orleanists formed the two great fractions of the party of Order. Was it nothing but the *fleur-de-lis* and the tricolour, the House of Bourbon and the House of Orleans, the different shades of royalism, which held the fractions fast to their pretenders and apart from each other? Was it their royalist creed at all? Under the Bourbons, *big landed property* had ruled, with its priests and lackeys; under the July monarchy, it had been high finance, large-scale industry, large-scale trade, i.e., *capital*, with its retinue of advocates, professors and fine speech-makers. The legitimate monarchy was simply the political expression of the immemorial domination of the lords of the soil, just as the July monarchy was only the political expression of the usurped rule of the bourgeois parvenus. It was therefore not so-called principles which kept these fractions divided, but rather their material conditions of existence, two distinct sorts of property; it was the old opposition between town and country, the old rivalry between capital and landed property. Who would deny that at the same time old memories, personal enmities, fears and hopes, prejudices and illusions, sympathies and antipathies, convictions, articles of faith and principles bound them to one or the other royal house? A whole superstructure of different and specifically formed feelings, illusions, modes of thought and views of life arises on the basis of the different forms of property, of the social conditions of existence. The whole class creates and forms these out of its material foundations and the corresponding social relations.

The single individual, who derives these feelings, etc., through tradition and upbringing, may well imagine that they form the real determinants and the starting-point of his activity. The Orleanist and Legitimist fractions each tried to make out to their opponents and themselves that they were divided by their adherence to the two royal houses; facts later proved that it was rather the division between their interests which forbade the unification of the royal houses. A distinction is made in private life between what a man thinks and says of himself and what he really is and does. In historical struggles one must make a still sharper distinction between the phrases and fantasies of the parties and their real organization and real interests, between their conception of themselves and what they really are. Orleanists and Legitimists found themselves side by side in the republic, making equal claims. Each side wanted to secure the *restoration* of its *own* royal house against the other; this had no other meaning than that each of the *two great interests* into which the bourgeoisie is divided – landed property and capital – was endeavouring to restore its own supremacy and the subordination of the other interest. We refer to the two interests of the bourgeoisie because big landed property in fact has been completely bourgeoisified by the development of modern society, despite its feudal coquetry and racial pride. The Tories in England long imagined they were enthusiastic about the monarchy, the church, and the beauties of the old English constitution, until the day of danger wrung from them the confession that they were only enthusiastic about *ground rent*.[58]

The members of the royalist coalition intrigued against each other outside parliament: in the press, at Ems, and at Claremont.[59] Behind the scenes they dressed up again in their old Orleanist and Legitimist liveries and went back to their old tournaments. But on the public stage, in their grand national performances as a great parliamentary party, they put off their respective royal houses with mere bows and adjourned the restoration of the monarchy to an indefinite point in the future. They did their real business as

58. This is a reference to the effect of the abolition of the Corn Laws in 1846 on the Tory party: the party's name was changed to that of Protectionist, and for some years it campaigned on the single issue of the restoration of the Corn Laws, with a view to keeping ground rents at the highest possible level. (See 'Tories and Whigs', p. 257.)

59. Ems, near Wiesbaden, was the residence of the comte de Chambord (Henri V), the Legitimist claimant; Claremont, near London, was the residence of Louis Philippe.

the *party of Order*, i.e., under a *social* and not a *political* title, as representatives of the bourgeois world order, not as knights of errant princesses, as the bourgeois class against other classes, not as royalists against republicans. And as the party of Order they ruled over the other classes of society more harshly and with less restriction than ever they could under the Restoration or the July monarchy. This was only possible given the governmental form of the parliamentary republic, for the two great subdivisions of the French bourgeoisie could only unite under this form, thus placing on the agenda the rule of their class instead of the regime of a privileged fraction of it. If, nevertheless, as the party of Order, they also insulted the republic and expressed their abhorrence of it, this did not happen merely as a result of royalist memories. They realized instinctively that although the republic made their political rule complete it simultaneously undermined its social foundation, since they had now to confront the subjugated classes and contend with them without mediation, without being concealed by the Crown, without the possibility of diverting the national attention by their secondary conflicts amongst themselves and with the monarchy. It was a feeling of weakness which caused them to recoil when faced with the pure conditions of their own class rule and to yearn for the return of the previous forms of this rule, which were less complete, less developed and, precisely for that reason, less dangerous. But whenever the royalists in coalition came into conflict with the pretender who confronted them, with Bonaparte, whenever they thought the executive power was endangering their parliamentary omnipotence, whenever, in other words, they had to produce the political title-deeds of their domination, they came forward as *republicans*, not *royalists*, from the Orleanist Thiers, who warned the National Assembly that the republic divided them least, to the Legitimist Berryer, who, on 2 December 1851, swathed in the tricoloured sash, harangued the people assembled in front of the town hall of the tenth *arrondissement* as a tribune speaking in the name of the republic.[60] Admittedly a mocking echo called back to him: *Henri V! Henri V!*[61]

The petty bourgeoisie and the workers had formed their own coalition, the so-called *social-democratic* party, in opposition to the coalition of the bourgeoisie. The petty bourgeoisie saw that they had done badly out of the June days. Their material interests were in danger, and the counter-revolution called into question

60. See p. 233.   61. See p. 105, n. 12.

the democratic guarantees which were supposed to secure the assertion of those interests. They therefore drew closer to the workers. Their parliamentary representatives, on the other hand, the Montagne, had improved their position. After being pushed aside during the dictatorship of the bourgeois republicans, they had reconquered their lost popularity in the latter half of the session of the Constituent Assembly by their struggle with Bonaparte and the royalist ministers. They had concluded an alliance with the socialist leaders, celebrated in February 1849 with banquets of reconciliation. A joint programme was drafted, joint election committees were set up, and joint candidates put forward. The social demands of the proletariat lost their revolutionary point and gained a democratic twist, while the democratic claims of the petty bourgeoisie were stripped of their purely political form and had their socialist point emphasized. In this way arose *social-democracy*. Apart from some working-class extras, and a few members of the socialist sects, the new Montagne, the result of this combination, contained the same elements as the old Montagne, but more of them. However, it had changed along with the class it represented in the course of historical development. The peculiar character of social-democracy can be summed up in the following way: democratic republican institutions are demanded as a means of softening the antagonism between the two extremes of capital and wage labour and transforming it into harmony, not of superseding both of them. However varied the measures proposed for achieving this goal, however much it may be edged with more or less revolutionary conceptions, its content remains the same. This content is the reformation of society by democratic means, but a reformation within the boundaries set by the petty bourgeoisie. Only one must not take the narrow view that the petty bourgeoisie explicitly sets out to assert its egoistic class interests. It rather believes that the *particular* conditions of its liberation are the only *general* conditions within which modern society can be saved and the class struggle avoided. Nor indeed must one imagine that the democratic representatives are all *shopkeepers*[62] or their enthusiastic supporters. They may well be poles apart from them in their education and their individual situation. What makes them representatives of the petty bourgeoisie is the fact that their minds are restricted by the same barriers which the petty bourgeoisie fails to overcome in real life, and that

62. In English in the original.

they are therefore driven in theory to the same problems and solutions to which material interest and social situation drive the latter in practice. This is the general relationship between the *political and literary representatives* of a class and the class which they represent.

After the analysis we have given, it should be self-evident that the ultimate goal of the Montagne in its fight with the party of Order on behalf of the republic and the so-called rights of man was neither of these things; just as little as an army which resists those who want to deprive it of its weapons has joined battle in order to remain in possession of those weapons.

The party of Order provoked the Montagne as soon as the National Assembly met. The bourgeoisie now felt it necessary to settle accounts with the democratic petty bourgeoisie, just as, a year earlier, it had realized the necessity of dealing with the revolutionary proletariat. Only this time the situation of the opponent was different. The strength of the proletarian party lay in the streets; the strength of the petty-bourgeois party lay in the National Assembly. The petty bourgeoisie had, therefore, to be enticed out of the National Assembly and into the streets, so that they would themselves destroy their parliamentary power before there was time or opportunity to consolidate it. The Montagne rushed into the trap at a full gallop.

The bombardment of Rome by French troops[63] was the bait thrown to it. This violated paragraph V of the Constitution, which forbade the French republic to employ its armed forces against the liberties of another people. On top of this, paragraph 54 forbade the executive to declare war without the agreement of the National Assembly, and the Constituent Assembly had expressed its disapproval of the Roman expedition by the resolution of 8 May 1849. On these grounds, therefore, Ledru-Rollin introduced a bill of impeachment against Bonaparte and his ministers on 11 June 1849. Infuriated by the wasp-stings of Thiers, he allowed himself to be carried away to the point of threatening to defend the Constitution by all means, even with weapons. The Montagne rose to a man and repeated this call to arms. On 12 June the National Assembly rejected the bill of impeachment and the Montagne left the Assembly. The events of 13 June are well known: the proclamation of one section of the Montagne by which Bona-

---

63. The seige of Rome began on 3 June 1849. It mainly consisted of a bombardment of the city, which lasted throughout the month (see pp. 85–7).

parte and his ministers were declared to be 'outside the Constitution'; the street procession of the democratic National Guards, who, being unarmed, dispersed when they came up against Changarnier's troops, and so on. Some of the Montagne fled abroad, others were handed over to the High Court at Bourges, and a parliamentary regulation subjected the rest of them to the schoolmasterly supervision of the chairman of the National Assembly.[64] Paris was again placed in a state of siege and the democratic part of its National Guard was dissolved. In this way the influence of the Montagne in parliament was broken together with the power of the petty bourgeoisie in Paris.

Lyons, where 13 June had given the signal for a bloody workers' uprising, was similarly proclaimed in a state of siege, together with the five surrounding departments, and this situation has lasted up to the present time.

The bulk of the Montagne had left its vanguard in the lurch by refusing to sign its proclamation. The press had deserted, only two newspapers having dared to publish it. The individual petty bourgeois betrayed their representatives, for the National Guards either stayed away or, where they appeared, hindered the building of barricades. The petty bourgeois had in turn been deceived by their representatives, in that their alleged allies from the ranks of the army were nowhere to be seen. Finally, instead of gaining increased strength from the proletariat, the democratic party had infected it with its own weakness; as is usual with the exploits of the democrats, the leaders had the satisfaction of being able to charge their 'people' with desertion, and the people had the satisfaction of being able to charge its leaders with fraud.

Seldom had an action been announced more noisily than the impending campaign of the Montagne; seldom had an event been trumpeted with greater certainty or longer in advance than the inevitable victory of democracy. The democrats certainly believe in the trumpets whose blasts made the walls of Jericho collapse. Whenever they are confronted with the ramparts of despotism, they endeavour to imitate that miracle. If the Montagne wanted a parliamentary victory, it ought not to have given the call to arms. If it gave the call to arms in parliament, it ought not to have

64. A new order of business was adopted by the National Assembly under the impact of the events of 13 June. It gave the chairman of the Assembly the right to exclude deputies for infringing due parliamentary forms and provided for the loss of half a deputy's salary if he was censured three times in a month.

behaved in a parliamentary fashion in the streets. If the peaceful demonstration was meant seriously, it was foolish not to foresee that it would be received in a warlike manner. If a real struggle was intended, it was very odd to lay down the weapons with which it would have to be fought. But the revolutionary threats of the petty bourgeoisie and their democratic representatives are merely attempts to intimidate the opponent. And when they have run into a blind alley, when they have compromised themselves sufficiently to be compelled to carry out their threats, they do this in an ambiguous way, avoiding the means to the end like the plague and clutching at excuses for their failure. The blaring overture which announced the struggle dies away into a subdued grumbling as soon as it is due to begin, the actors cease to take themselves *au sérieux*, and the action totally collapses like a balloon pricked by a needle.

No party exaggerates the means at its disposal more than the democratic party; no party deludes itself more frivolously about the situation. Since part of the army had voted for it, the Montagne was now convinced that the army would revolt in its favour. And on what occasion was this supposed to happen? On an occasion which had no other meaning, from the troops' point of view, than that the revolutionaries had taken the side of Roman soldiers against French soldiers. On the other hand, the memory of June 1848 was still too fresh for the proletariat to feel anything but a deep aversion towards the National Guard, or for the leaders of the secret societies[65] to feel anything but complete mistrust for the democratic leaders. Important common interests had to be at stake to offset these differences, and the violation of an abstract paragraph of the Constitution did not provide a common interest of this kind. Did the democrats themselves not insist that the Constitution had been repeatedly violated? Had the most popular newspapers not branded it as a counter-revolutionary concoction? But because the democrat represents the petty bourgeoisie, a *transitional class* in which the interests of two classes meet and become blurred, he imagines he is elevated above class antagonisms generally. The democrats admit that they are confronted with a privi-

65. The organizations that Marx is referring to here are not, strictly speaking, the revolutionary secret societies that existed before the February revolution, but rather their open descendants, the 'Republican clubs' that were set up by revolutionary militants such as Blanqui, Barbès, etc., after February 1848.

leged class, but assert that they, along with all the rest of the nation, form the *people*. What they represent is the *right of the people*; what interests them is the *interest of the people*. Therefore, when a struggle approaches, they do not need to examine the interests and positions of the various classes. They do not need to weigh up the means at their disposal too critically. They have only to give the signal for the people, with all its inexhaustible resources, to fall upon the oppressors. If in the sequel their interests turn out to be uninteresting and their power turns out to be impotence, either this is the fault of dangerous sophists, who split the *indivisible people* into different hostile camps, or the army was too brutalized and deluded to understand that the pure goals of democracy were best for it too, or a mistake in one detail of implementation has wrecked the whole plan, or indeed an unforeseen accident has frustrated the game this time. In each case the democrat emerges as spotless from the most shameful defeat as he was innocent when he went into it, fresh in his conviction that he must inevitably be victorious, taking the view that conditions must ripen to meet his requirements, rather than that he and his party must abandon their old standpoint.

Consequently, we must not imagine that the Montagne felt particularly miserable, although it was decimated, broken and humiliated by the new parliamentary regulations. If 13 June had removed its leaders, it had nevertheless made room for men of an inferior stamp, who were flattered by this new position. If their powerlessness in parliament could no longer be doubted, they were now justified in confining their activities to outbursts of moral indignation and blustering declamation. The party of Order pretended to see all the horrors of anarchy embodied in them, as the last official representatives of the revolution; they could therefore be all the more insipid and modest in reality. Thus, they consoled each other for 13 June along the following lines: But if they dare to attack universal suffrage, then we shall show them what kind of people we are! *Nous verrons!*

As far as those members of the Montagne who fled abroad are concerned, it is sufficient here to point out that because Ledru-Rollin had succeeded, in barely two weeks, in irretrievably ruining the powerful party he headed, he now considered it his mission to form a French government *in partibus*.[66] As the level of the revolution sank and the official celebrities of official France be-

66. See p. 138, n. 74.

came more dwarf-like, Ledru-Rollin's figure in the distance, removed from the scene of action, seemed to increase in magnitude; he was able to figure as the republican pretender for 1852, periodically issuing circulars to the Wallachians and other peoples in which he threatened to take action, along with his confederates, against the continental despots. Was Proudhon completely wrong to exclaim to these gentlemen: '*Vous n'êtes que des blagueurs*'?[67]

The party of Order had broken the Montagne on 13 June; it had also succeeded in *subordinating the Constitution to the majority decision of the National Assembly*. That was its interpretation of the republic: the rule of the bourgeoisie in parliamentary forms, without the restrictions characteristic of a monarchy, such as the executive veto or the possibility of dissolving parliament. This was the *parliamentary republic*, as Thiers put it. But when, on 13 June, the bourgeoisie had secured its own supremacy within the parliament building, had it not also afflicted parliament itself with an incurable weakness *vis-à-vis* the executive and the people by expelling its most popular part? By surrendering numerous deputies on the demand of the courts, and without making a great deal of fuss, it abolished its own parliamentary immunity. The humiliating procedural rules to which it subjected the Montagne exalted the status of the President of the republic in the same measure as it degraded the individual deputies. By stigmatizing an insurrection for the protection of constitutional provisions as an anarchistic attempt to overthrow society, it forbade any appeal to the weapon of insurrection on its own part if ever the executive power should behave unconstitutionally towards it. And the irony of history would have it that Oudinot, the general who bombarded Rome on Bonaparte's instructions and so provided the immediate occasion for the constitutionalist revolt of 13 June, was the man vainly and imploringly offered to the people by the party of Order on 2 December 1851 as the general to defend the Constitution against Bonaparte. Another hero of 13 June was Vieyra,[68] who reaped a harvest of congratulations from the tribune of the National Assembly for the brutalities he had committed in the offices of democratic newspapers at the head of a band of National Guards belonging to high financial circles. This same Vieyra was a party

67. 'You are nothing but humbugs,' a phrase from an article of 20 July 1850; P.-J. Proudhon, *Correspondence*, vol. 14, p. 297.

68. Vieyra, a French colonel, was in 1851 the Chief of Staff of the National Guard and a Bonapartist. He took part in the coup d'état of 2 December.

to Bonaparte's conspiracy and played a very important part in depriving the National Assembly of any protection by the National Guard in the hour of its final agony.

13 June had yet another meaning. The Montagne had wanted to force the impeachment of Bonaparte. Its defeat was thus a direct victory for him, a personal triumph over his democratic enemies. The party of Order had won that victory; Bonaparte had only to cash in on it, and he did. On 14 June a proclamation could be read on the walls of Paris in which the President, reluctantly and almost against his will, compelled, as it were, by the sheer force of events, emerged from his cloistered seclusion as the incarnation of misunderstood virtue, and complained of the slanders of his opponents. While appearing to identify his person with the cause of order, he in fact identified the cause of order with his person. In addition to this, Bonaparte had himself taken the initiative in the matter of the expedition against Rome, whereas the National Assembly had only retrospectively approved it. After reinstalling the High Priest Samuel in the Vatican, he could hope to enter the Tuileries as King David.[69] He had won over the priests.

As we have seen, the revolt of 13 June was limited to a peaceful street procession. There were therefore no military laurels to be won against it. Despite this, the party of Order was able to transform a bloodless battle into a second Austerlitz[70] in this period so poor in heroes and events. On public platforms and in the press the army was praised as the force of order against the anarchic impotence of the popular masses, and Changarnier was praised as the 'bulwark of society'; in the end he believed in this mystification himself. Secretly, however, the corps that seemed doubtful were transferred from Paris, the regiments which had voted for democratic candidates at the elections were banished from France to Algeria, restless elements among the troops were assigned to penal detachments, and finally the press was systematically isolated from the barracks and the barracks from civil society.

We have now arrived at the decisive turning point in the history of the French National Guard. In 1830 its attitude had decided the fate of the Restoration. Under Louis Philippe every rebellion in which the National Guard stood on the side of the troops was a

69. Louis Bonaparte, it was rumoured, hoped to receive the French crown from the hands of Pius IX after he had restored the Pope's temporal power.

70. The first Austerlitz was the battle of that name in 1805, at which Napoleon I defeated the allied Russian and Austrian armies.

failure. In the February days of 1848, when the National Guard behaved passively towards the insurrection and ambiguously towards Louis Philippe, he admitted defeat, and indeed he was defeated. In this way the conviction became rooted that the revolution could not win *without* the National Guard, and that the army could not win *against* it. This was the army's superstitious belief in civilian omnipotence. The June days of 1848, when the whole National Guard put down the insurrection alongside the troops of the line, had strengthened this belief. After Bonaparte took office the importance of the National Guard was to some extent reduced by the unification of its command with that of the First Army Division in the person of Changarnier, in defiance of the Constitution.

Command of the National Guard thus appeared as an attribute of the military commander-in-chief, and the National Guard appeared as no more than an addition to the troops of the line. Its power was finally broken on 13 June. Not simply because of its partial dissolution, which was later to be repeated all over France, leaving only fragments behind. The demonstration of 13 June had been above all a demonstration by the democratic wing of the National Guard. To be sure, they had not confronted the army with their weapons, but only with their uniforms; however, the talisman lay precisely in the uniform. Once the army reached the conviction that it was a woollen rag like any other uniform, the charm lost its power. In the June days the bourgeoisie and petty bourgeoisie, as the National Guard, were united with the army against the proletariat; on 13 June 1849 the bourgeoisie let the army disperse the petty-bourgeois sections of the National Guard; on 2 December 1851 the bourgeois National Guard itself vanished, and Bonaparte merely bore witness to this fact when he subsequently signed the decree dissolving it. Thus the bourgeoisie smashed its own last weapon against the army. However, it was compelled to do so from the moment when the petty bourgeoisie ceased to stand behind it as its vassal, and instead stood before it as a rebel, just as, in general, it had to destroy all its instruments of defence against absolutism with its own hand as soon as it had itself become absolute.

In the meantime the party of Order celebrated the reconquest of a power only apparently lost in 1848, and recovered in 1849 free from its previous restrictions. It celebrated with invective against the republic and the Constitution, execration of all revolutions, whether present, past or future, including that made by its own leaders, and legislation muzzling the press, destroying the right of association, and establishing the state of siege as an organic institution. Then, after appointing a Standing Commission to sit in its absence, the National Assembly adjourned from the middle of August to the middle of October. During this recess the Legitimists intrigued with Ems, the Orleanists with Claremont, Bonaparte went on princely tours of the country, and the Departmental Councils discussed the possibility of revising the Constitution. These incidents regularly recurred every time the National Assembly went into recess, but I shall only discuss them where they became real events. Let us merely point out here that the National Assembly acted imprudently in disappearing from the stage for considerable intervals, leaving only *one* figure in sight at the head of the republic, even though it was the pitiful figure of Louis Bonaparte, at a time when the party of Order, to the scandal of the public, was splitting up into its royalist components and pursuing mutually contradictory desires for a restoration. As soon as the confusing din of the Assembly fell silent during these recesses, and its body merged into that of the nation, it became obvious that only *one thing* was needed to complete the true form of this republic: the *former's* recess must be made permanent, and the *latter's* motto, *liberté, égalité, fraternité*, must be replaced with the unambiguous words *infantry, cavalry, artillery!*

IV

The National Assembly resumed its sittings in the middle of October 1849. On 1 November[71] Bonaparte surprised it with a message announcing the dismissal of the Barrot-Falloux ministry and the formation of a new one. Lackeys have never been sacked with less ceremony than Bonaparte used with his ministers. For the time being Barrot and company received the kicks that were intended for the National Assembly.

As we have seen, the Barrot ministry had been made up of Legitimists and Orleanists; it was a ministry of the party of Order. Bonaparte had needed such a ministry so as to dissolve the republican Constituent Assembly, carry out the expedition against Rome, and break the democratic party. He had seemed to efface

---

71. The date of the dismissal of the Barrot-Falloux ministry and the formation of the Hautpoul ministry was in fact 31 October.

himself behind this ministry, resigning the power of government into the hands of the party of Order and assuming the modest character mask worn by responsible newspaper editors in the time of Louis Philippe, the mask of the *straw man*.[72] Now he threw away the mask, for it was no longer a light veil behind which he could hide his features, but an iron mask which prevented him from displaying any features of his own. He had appointed the Barrot ministry so as to disperse the republican National Assembly in the name of the party of Order; he dismissed it so as to declare his own name to be independent of the party of Order's National Assembly.

There was no shortage of plausible pretexts for this dismissal. The Barrot ministry even neglected to observe the proprieties which would have let the President of the republic appear as a power alongside the National Assembly. During the National Assembly's recess Bonaparte published a letter to Edgar Ney[73] in which he seemed to object to the illiberal attitude of the Pope; in the same way he had opposed the Constituent Assembly by publishing a letter commending Oudinot for the attack on the Roman republic. Now, when the National Assembly voted the budget for the Roman expedition, Victor Hugo brought this letter up for discussion, for supposedly liberal reasons. The party of Order drowned the idea that Bonaparte's notions might have any political weight with cries of scornful disbelief. None of the ministers took up the gauntlet on his behalf. On another occasion Barrot let fall from the platform, with his usual hollow pathos, words of indignation about the 'abominable machinations' which were going on, according to him, in the immediate entourage of the President. On top of this the ministry rejected any proposal for an increase in the presidential civil list, whilst it obtained a widow's pension for the Duchess of Orleans from the National Assembly. And the imperial pretender in Bonaparte was so intimately mingled with the adventurer who has fallen on bad times that his one great idea, that it was his destiny to restore the empire, was always supplemented by the other, that it was the mission of the French people to pay his debts.

72. The severe press law of September 1835 laid down that the responsible editor of a newspaper had personally to sign each issue. Since many of the real editors of republican journals were in prison, 'straw men' (*hommes de paille*) had to be employed, men who lent their names to the paper while in practice having nothing to do with it.

73. General Edgar Ney was Louis Bonaparte's military aide.

The Barrot-Falloux ministry was the first and last *parliamentary ministry* called to life by Bonaparte. Its dismissal therefore marked a decisive turning point. With it the party of Order lost the lever of executive power, an indispensable position for the maintenance of the parliamentary regime, and it never re-conquered it. In France the executive has at its disposal an army of more than half a million individual officials, and it therefore constantly maintains an immense mass of interests and livelihoods in a state of the most unconditional dependence; the state enmeshes, controls, regulates, supervises and regiments civil society from the most all-embracing expressions of its life down to its most insignificant motions, from its most general modes of existence down to the private life of individuals. This parasitic body acquires, through the most extraordinary centralization, an omnipresence, an omniscience, an elasticity and an accelerated rapidity of movement which find their only appropriate complement in the real social body's helpless irresolution and its lack of a consistent formation. One realizes immediately that in such a country the National Assembly lost all real influence when it lost control of the ministerial portfolios, because it failed at the same time to simplify the state administration, reduce the army of officials as much as possible, and finally let civil society and public opinion create their own organs independent of the power of the government. But the *material interest* of the French bourgeoisie is most intimately imbricated precisely with the maintenance of that extensive and highly ramified state machine. It is that machine which provides its surplus population with jobs, and makes up through state salaries for what it cannot pocket in the form of profits, interest, rents and fees. Its *political interest* equally compelled it daily to increase the repression, and therefore to increase the resources and the personnel of the state power; it had simultaneously to wage an incessant war against public opinion and mistrustfully mutilate and cripple society's independent organs of movement where it did not succeed in entirely amputating them. The French bourgeoisie was thus compelled by its class position both to liquidate the conditions of existence of all parliamentary power, including its own, and to make its opponent, the executive, irresistible.

The new ministry was known as the Hautpoul ministry. It was not that General Hautpoul had received the rank of Prime Minister. Bonaparte had abolished this dignitary when he removed

Barrot, for the existence of a Prime Minister condemned the President of the republic to the legal nullity of a constitutional monarch, though in this case a monarch with neither throne nor crown, neither sceptre nor sword, neither irresponsibility nor the indefeasible possession of the highest state dignity – worst of all, without a civil list. The Hautpoul ministry contained only one man with a parliamentary reputation, the moneylender Fould, one of the most notorious members of the clique of high financiers. The Ministry of Finance was allotted to him. Look up the quotations of the Paris Bourse, and you will find that from 1 November 1849 onwards, French government securities rose and fell with the rise and fall of the Bonapartist stocks. Bonaparte had found his ally in the Bourse; at the same time he gained control of the police through the appointment of Carlier as Prefect of Police in Paris.

The consequences of this change of ministries could only emerge in the further course of development. Bonaparte seemed to have first taken a step forwards only to be driven all the more conspicuously backwards. His blunt message was followed by the most servile declaration of allegiance to the National Assembly. Whenever his ministers dared to make the timid attempt to introduce his personal fads as proposals for legislation, it was apparent that they were being compelled by their position to unwillingly fulfil peculiar commissions which they were convinced in advance would be unsuccessful. His own ministers disavowed him from the platform of the National Assembly whenever he blurted out his intentions behind their backs, playing with his 'Napoleonic ideas'.[74] His desire to usurp power only seemed to be expressed aloud so that the malicious laughter of his opponents might never fall silent. He behaved like the misunderstood genius proclaimed by all the world to be a simpleton. He never enjoyed the hatred of all classes to a greater degree than in this period. The rule of the bourgeoisie was never more unconditional, and it never wore the insignia of domination more ostentatiously.

I do not need to write the history of the bourgeoisie's legislative activity here: it can be summed up for this period in two laws, the one restoring the *wine tax*[75] and the other abolishing unbelief:

74. Louis Bonaparte expressed his theory of government in a book entitled *Des idées napoléoniennes*, published in Paris in 1839.

75. The Constituent Assembly had resolved to abolish the wine tax as from 1 January 1850, but on 20 December 1849 the Legislative Assembly reintroduced the tax. On the political significance of this decision, see *The Class Struggles in France*, above, pp. 113–15.

the *education law*.[76] If wine-drinking was made harder for the French, they were endowed all the more richly with the water of true life. With the law on the wine tax the bourgeoisie declared the inviolability of the old and hated French tax system, but they endeavoured by means of the education law to ensure the continuance of the old state of mind which allowed the masses to tolerate it. It is astounding to see the Orleanists, liberal members of the bourgeoisie, old apostles of Voltaireanism and eclecticism in philosophy, entrusting the control of the French mind to their hereditary enemies, the Jesuits. However, although Orleanists and Legitimists might be deeply divided as regards the pretenders to the throne, they understood that they now needed to unite the repressive instruments of two epochs in order to secure their joint domination, supplementing and strengthening the means of subjugation characteristic of the July monarchy with those of the Restoration.

The peasants had been disappointed in all their hopes; they were oppressed more than ever, on the one hand, by the low level of grain prices, on the other hand, by the growing burden of taxes and mortgage debts, and they started to stir in the departments. The government replied by starting a campaign against schoolmasters, who were made subject to the priests, a campaign against mayors, who were made subject to the prefects, and a system of informers, to which everyone was subject. In Paris and the big towns the reaction itself bears the features of its epoch, and challenges more than it strikes down. In the countryside it becomes dull, common, petty, fatiguing and plodding; it becomes, in one word, a *gendarme*. It is understandable how three years of rule by the *gendarme*, consecrated by the rule of the priests, were bound to demoralize the immature peasant masses.

Whatever quantity of passion and declamation the party of Order employed against the minority from the tribune of the National Assembly, its actual speech remained as monosyllabic as that of the Christian, with his 'yea, yea, nay, nay'. The party of Order was as monosyllabic in parliament as in the press, and as boring as a riddle whose solution is known in advance. One slogan constantly recurred, one theme always stayed the same, one

76. The education law (*loi Falloux*), which was adopted on 15 March 1850, placed all state schools under the joint supervision of the clergy and the mayors, as well as making numerous other provisions designed to strengthen clerical influence in the educational system.

verdict was always ready, whether it was a question of the right of petition, the tax on wine, the freedom of the press, trade, the clubs, or the charter of a municipality, the protection of personal freedom or the regulation of the state budget: the invariable word '*socialism*'. Even bourgeois liberalism was declared *socialist*, as well as bourgeois enlightenment and bourgeois financial reform. It was socialist to build a railway where a canal already existed, and it was socialist to defend oneself with a stick when attacked with a rapier.

This was not merely a figure of speech, a fashion or a piece of party tactics. The bourgeoisie correctly saw that all the weapons it had forged against feudalism were turning their points against the bourgeoisie itself, that all the means of education it had produced were rebelling against its own civilization, and that all the gods it had created had abandoned it. It understood that all the so-called bourgeois liberties and organs of progress were attacking and threatening its *class rule* both at the social foundation and the political summit, and had therefore become '*socialist*'. It rightly discerned the secret of socialism in this threat and this attack.

The bourgeoisie judges the meaning and tendency of socialism more correctly than so-called socialism itself can; this is why the latter cannot understand the bourgeoisie's obdurate resistance to it, whether it snivels sentimentally about the sufferings of mankind, prophesies the millennium and universal brotherly love in the Christian manner, drivels about the mind, education and freedom in the humanistic style, or, finally, in doctrinaire fashion, cooks up a system for the reconciliation and welfare of all classes.[77] However, what the bourgeoisie did not grasp was the logical conclusion that its *own parliamentary regime*, its *political rule* in general, must now succumb to the general verdict of condemnation for being *socialist*. As long as the rule of the bourgeois class was not completely organized and had not attained its pure political expression, the antagonism of the other classes could not emerge in its pure form, and, when it did emerge, it could not take the dangerous turn which transforms every struggle against the

77. In the 1848 period the term 'socialism' generally referred to the various middle-class schools of social reform, while 'communism' referred to the revolutionary working-class movement. See *Manifesto of the Communist Party*, section III, in *The Revolutions of 1848*, pp. 87–97; Engels's preface to the English edition, ibid., pp. 64–5; and *The Class Struggles in France*, p. 122.

state power into a struggle against capital. If it saw 'tranquillity' endangered by every sign of life in society, how could it want to retain a *regime of unrest*, its own *parliamentary regime*, at the head of society? A regime which lives in struggle and by struggle, as one of its orators expressed it. If the parliamentary regime lives by discussion, how can it forbid discussion? In it all interests and social institutions are transformed into general ideas, and debated in that form. How can any interest or institution then assert itself to be above thought, and impose itself as an article of faith? The struggle of the parliamentary orators calls forth the struggle of the scribblers of the press; the parliamentary debating club is necessarily supplemented by debating clubs in the salons and alehouses; the deputies, by constantly appealing to the opinion of the people, give the people the right to express their real opinion in petitions. The parliamentary regime leaves everything to the decision of majorities; why then should the great majority outside parliament not want to make the decisions? When you play the fiddle at the summit of the state, what else is there to expect than that those down below should dance?

Thus, by now branding as 'socialist' what it had previously celebrated as 'liberal', the bourgeoisie confesses that its own interest requires its deliverance from the peril of its own self-government; that to establish peace and quiet in the country its bourgeois parliament must first of all be laid to rest; that its political power must be broken in order to preserve its social power intact; that the individual bourgeois can only continue to exploit the other classes and remain in undisturbed enjoyment of property, family, religion and order on condition that his class is condemned to political insignificance along with the other classes; and that in order to save its purse the crown must be struck off its head and the sword which is to protect it must be hung over it like the sword of Damocles.

The National Assembly proved to be so unproductive in the area of the general interests of the bourgeoisie that its proceedings on the Paris–Avignon railway, for example, which began in the winter of 1850, were still not ready to be concluded on 2 December 1851. Wherever it was not engaged in measures of repression or reaction, the Assembly was cursed with incurable barrenness.

While his ministry partly seized the initiative in proposing laws in the spirit of the party of Order, and partly even outdid its severity in implementing and administering them, Bonaparte also sought to win popularity in another direction, to demonstrate his opposition to the National Assembly and hint at a secret reserve which was only temporarily prevented by the situation from making its hidden treasures available to the French people, by making childishly absurd proposals, such as the proposal to decree a pay increase of four sous a day for non-commissioned officers, or the proposal to establish a bank which would loan money to workers on the security of their honour. Money as a gift and money on tick, these were the perspectives with which he hoped to entice the masses. The financial science of the lumpenproletariat, of both the genteel and the common variety, is restricted to gifts and loans. These were the only springs Bonaparte knew how to set in motion. Never has a pretender speculated in a more vulgar fashion on the gullibility of the masses.

The National Assembly repeatedly became enraged at these unmistakable attempts to gain popularity at its expense, and at the growing danger that this adventurer, whipped on by his debts and not held back by an established reputation, would risk a desperate stroke. The discord between the party of Order and the President had assumed a threatening character when an unexpected occurrence threw him back, repentant, into its arms. We are referring to the *by-elections of 10 March 1850*. These elections took place in order to fill the seats made vacant after 13 June either by imprisonment or exile. The only candidates elected in Paris were social-democrats. Indeed, most of the Parisian votes went to de Flotte, one of the insurgents of June 1848. In this way the petty bourgeoisie of Paris, in alliance with the proletariat, had its revenge for the defeat of 13 June 1849. It seemed to have disappeared from the battlefield at the moment of danger only in order to return at more favourable opportunity with fighting forces of a more mass character and a bolder battle-cry. There was one circumstance that appeared to heighten the danger of this electoral victory: the army voted in Paris for the June insurgent and against La Hitte, one of Bonaparte's ministers, and in the departments largely for the Montagnards, who maintained their numerical preponderance over their opponents here as well, though not so decisively as in Paris.

Bonaparte suddenly saw himself confronted once again with the revolution. As on 29 January and 13 June 1849, so also on 10 March 1850 he disappeared behind the party of Order. He bowed to it submissively, he humbly begged its pardon, he offered to appoint any ministry whatsoever at the command of the parliamentary majority, he even implored the Orleanist and Legitimist party leaders such as Thiers, Berryer, de Broglie[78] and Molé, in short the so-called burgraves,[79] to seize the helm of state themselves. This moment was irretrievable, but the party of Order did not know how to make use of it. Instead of boldly taking possession of the power offered, it did not even force Bonaparte to reinstate the ministry dismissed on 1 November. It contented itself with humiliating him with its forgiveness and attaching M. Baroche to the Hautpoul ministry. This Baroche had twice put on a rabid performance as public prosecutor before the High Court at Bourges, once against the revolutionaries of 15 May [1848], the other time against the democrats of 13 June [1849], each time because of an attack on the National Assembly's position. Yet none of Bonaparte's ministers later contributed more greatly to the degradation of the National Assembly, and after 2 December we rediscover him as the duly installed and highly paid vice-chairman of the Senate. He had spat in the soup of the revolutionaries so that Bonaparte might eat it up.

The social-democratic party, for its part, seemed to be simply straining after pretexts to put its own victory in question again and take the sting out of it. Vidal, one of the newly elected representatives for Paris, had been elected simultaneously in Strasbourg. He was persuaded to decline the Paris mandate and accept that of Strasbourg. And so, instead of giving its electoral victory a definitive character and thereby compelling the party of Order immediately to contest it in parliament, instead of driving its opponent into a conflict at a moment of enthusiasm among the people and favour among the army, the democratic party bored Paris during the months of March and April with renewed electoral agitation, allowed the excited passions of the people to be worn out in this repetition of the provisional voting game, allowed the energy of the revolution to be satiated with constitutional successes and wasted on petty intrigues, empty declamations and sham movements, allowed the bourgeoisie to rally and make its preparations, and finally allowed the subsequent election of April to weaken the significance of the March elections by making

78. Achille, duc de Broglie was an Orleanist politician, Prime Minister from 1835 to 1836, and a deputy in the Legislative Assembly from 1849 to 1851.

79. See p. 132, n. 63.

a sentimental commentary on them in the form of the election of Eugène Sue. To put it succinctly, the democratic party made an April fool of 10 March.

The parliamentary majority knew its opponent's weaknesses. Bonaparte had left it to direct the attack and take responsibility for it, and its seventeen burgraves worked out a new electoral law to be proposed by M. Faucher, who had begged for the honour of being entrusted with it. On 8 May he introduced the law, which abolished universal suffrage, imposed a three-year residence requirement for the electors, and made proof of residence dependent in the case of workers on a certificate from their employers.

The democrats had stormed and raged in a revolutionary fashion during the constitutional electoral contest; but now, when it was necessary to demonstrate the seriousness of that electoral victory arms in hand, they preached in a constitutional fashion, in favour of order, majestic calm (*calme majestueux*) and lawful behaviour, i.e., blind subjection to the will of the counter-revolution which had imposed itself as law. During the debate the Montagne shamed the party of Order by upholding the dispassionate attitude of the philistine who sticks to the legal basis as against the revolutionary passion of the upholders of order, and struck them down with the frightful reproach that their acts were revolutionary. Even the newly elected deputies took care to show by their respectable and discreet behaviour how wrong it was to decry them as anarchists and interpret their election as a victory for revolution. The new electoral law went through on 31 May. The Montagne was content to smuggle a protest into the chairman's pocket. The electoral law was followed by a new press law, which completely got rid of the revolutionary newspapers.[80] They had deserved their fate. The *National* and the *Presse*, both bourgeois organs, were left behind after this deluge as the most extreme outposts of the revolution.

We have seen how the democratic leaders had done everything to embroil the people of Paris in a sham fight throughout March and April, and how they did all they could to hold them back from a real struggle after 8 May. In addition to this, we should not forget that 1850 was a year of the most splendid industrial and commercial prosperity, and the Paris proletariat was therefore

80. The press law of 16 July 1850 increased the amount of caution money required for any newspaper to 24,000 francs and imposed a stamp duty on all periodicals of less than ten sheets.

fully employed. But it was excluded from any share in political power by the electoral law of 31 May 1850. This barred the proletariat from the very arena of the struggle. It threw the workers back into the position they had occupied before the February revolution: they were again outcasts. By allowing themselves to be led by the democrats in face of such an event, by their ability to forget their revolutionary class interest in a situation which was momentarily comfortable, they renounced the honour of being a conquering power, gave themselves up to their fate, and proved that the defeat of June 1848 had rendered them incapable of fighting for years; they proved that, for the time being, the historical process would again have to go forward *over* their heads. As for the petty-bourgeois democrats, who on 13 June had exclaimed, 'But if they touch universal suffrage, then we'll show them,' they now consoled themselves with the assertion that the counter-revolutionary blow they had been struck was not a blow and that the law of 31 May was not a law. On the second Sunday of May 1852, they said, every Frenchman would appear at the polling station with a voting card in one hand and a sword in the other. They thought this prophecy was sufficient. Lastly, the army was punished by its superiors for the elections of March and April 1850, just as it had been punished for the elections of 29 May 1849. This time, however, it said to itself emphatically, 'The revolution will not swindle us a third time.'

The law of 31 May 1850 was the bourgeoisie's coup d'état. All its previous victories over the revolution had only a provisional character. They were put in question as soon as the existing National Assembly withdrew from the stage. They depended on the chance result of a new general election, and the history of elections since 1848 proved irrefutably that the moral domination of the bourgeoisie over the masses declined in direct proportion to the development of its physical domination. On 10 March universal suffrage declared directly against the rule of the bourgeoisie, and the bourgeoisie replied by outlawing it. The law of 31 May was therefore a necessity of the class struggle. Moreover, the Constitution required a minimum of two million votes to make the election of a President of the republic valid. If none of the presidential candidates received this minimum, the National Assembly was to choose the President from among the three candidates who received the most votes. At the time when the Constituent Assembly made this law, ten million electors were registered on the voting lists. In the Constituent Assembly's sense, then, a fifth of the voting strength was sufficient to make the election of the President valid. The law of 31 May struck at least three million electors from the voting lists, reducing the number of people entitled to vote to seven million, but it nevertheless retained the legal minimum of two million for the election of the President. It therefore raised the legal minimum from a fifth to nearly a third of the possible votes, i.e., it did everything to smuggle the election of the President out of the hands of the people and into the hands of the National Assembly. Thus the party of Order seemed to have made its rule doubly secure by the electoral law of 31 May; it placed both the election of the National Assembly and the election of the President of the republic in the hands of the stationary part of society.

V

The struggle between the National Assembly and Bonaparte broke out again immediately after the revolutionary crisis had been weathered and universal suffrage abolished.

The Constitution had fixed Bonaparte's salary at 600,000 francs. Hardly six months after his installation he had succeeded in doubling this sum of money. For Odilon Barrot had extracted from the Constituent Assembly an annual supplement of 600,000 francs for so-called official expenses. After 13 June 1849 Bonaparte had had similar requests aired, but this time Barrot did not give them a hearing. Now, after 31 May 1850, he immediately made use of the favourable moment and made his ministers propose a civil list of three million in the National Assembly. In the course of a long and adventurous life of vagabondage he had developed very sensitive feelers for sensing the weak moments when he might extort money from the bourgeoisie. He practised real *chantage*.[81] The National Assembly had violated popular sovereignty with his aid and his connivance; he threatened to denounce its crime to the tribunal of the people if it did not open its purse and buy his silence with three million a year. It had robbed three million Frenchmen of their franchise; he demanded a franc in circulation for every Frenchman withdrawn from circulation, precisely three million francs. Six million had voted for him; he demanded compensation for the votes of which he had been retrospectively

81. Blackmail.

cheated. The Commission of the National Assembly sent this importunate person away; the Bonapartist press began to make threats.
Could the National Assembly break with the President of the republic at a time when it had broken fundamentally with the mass of the
nation? Admittedly, it rejected the annual civil list, but it granted an
allowance, which was intended to be unique, of 2,160,000 francs. It
thus made itself guilty of the double weakness of granting the money
and simultaneously showing, by its annoyance, its unwillingness to
grant it. Later on we shall see what Bonaparte needed the money for.

After this tiresome sequel to the abolition of universal suffrage,
in which Bonaparte exchanged his humble bearing during the crisis
of March and April for an impertinent provocation of the usurping
parliament, the National Assembly adjourned for three months, from
11 August to 11 November. It left behind it a Standing Commission
of twenty-eight members, which contained no Bonapartists at all but
did include some moderate republicans. The Standing Commission
of 1849 had only included gentlemen of order and Bonapartists.
But at that time the party of Order had declared itself in permanent
session against the revolution. This time the parliamentary republic
declared itself in permanent session against the President. After the
law of 31 May the President was the only rival still confronting the
party of Order.

The National Assembly met again in November 1850. It now
seemed that in place of the previous petty skirmishes a great and
ruthless struggle with the President, a life-and-death struggle between
the two powers, had become inevitable.

During the parliamentary recess of 1850, just as in 1849, the
party of Order had split up into its separate fractions, each busy
with its own restorationist intrigues; these had now been reinforced by the death of Louis Philippe.[82] Henri V, the king of the
Legitimists, had even appointed a formal ministry which resided in
Paris, and which included members of the Standing Commission.
Bonaparte was therefore justified for his part in making circular tours through the French departments, canvassing votes for
himself and blurting out his own restorationist plans, sometimes
publicly and sometimes in secret, according to the mood of the
town he happened to be favouring with his presence. On these
expeditions, which the grand official *Moniteur* and the small
private *Moniteurs* belonging to Bonaparte naturally had to cele-

82. On 26 August 1850.

brate as triumphs, he was constantly accompanied by affiliates of the Society of 10 December.[83] This society dated from 1849. Under the pretext of founding a charitable organization, the Paris lumpen-proletariat had been organized into secret sections, each section led by Bonapartist agents and the whole headed by a Bonapartist general. Alongside decayed roués of doubtful origin and uncertain means of subsistence, alongside ruined and adventurous scions of the bourgeoisie, there were vagabonds, discharged soldiers, discharged criminals, escaped galley slaves, swindlers, confidence tricksters, *lazzaroni*, pickpockets, sleight-of-hand experts, gamblers, *maquereaux*,[84] brothel-keepers, porters, pen-pushers, organ-grinders, rag-and-bone merchants, knife-grinders, tinkers and beggars: in short, the whole indeterminate fragmented mass, tossed backwards and forwards, which the French call *la bohème*; with these elements, so akin to himself, Bonaparte formed the backbone of the Society of 10 December. This was a 'charitable organization' in that all its members, like Bonaparte, felt the need to provide themselves with charity at the expense of the nation's workers. This Bonaparte, who has set himself up as the *head of the lumpenproletariat*, who can only in that class find a mass reflection of the interests he himself pursues, who perceives in the scum, the leavings, the refuse of all classes the only class which can provide him with an unconditional basis, this is the real Bonaparte, the Bonaparte *sans phrase*.[85] An old, cunning roué, he conceives the historical life of nations and their state proceedings as comedy in the most vulgar sense, as a masquerade in which the grand costumes, words and postures merely serve as a cover for the most petty trickery. On his expedition to Strasbourg a trained Swiss vulture represented the Napoleonic eagle. For his landing in Boulogne he put some London flunkeys into French uniforms to represent the army.[86] In his Society of 10 December he assembled ten thousand rogues, who were supposed to represent the people in the way that Snug the joiner represented the lion.[87] At a time when the bourgeoisie

83. Founded by Carlier, the Paris Prefect of Police, and headed by Louis Bonaparte's friend, General Piat.

84. Pimps.

85. Unextenuated.

86. In October 1836 Louis Bonaparte attempted to seize the town of Strasbourg and was expelled from France; in August 1840 he landed at Boulogne and tried to start a Bonapartist mutiny in the Boulogne garrison.

87. In *A Midsummer Night's Dream*.

itself was playing the most complete comedy, but in the most serious manner in the world, without infringing any of the pedantic requirements of French dramatic etiquette, and was itself half duped and half convinced of the serious character of its own state proceedings, the adventurer had to win, because he treated the comedy simply as a comedy. Only now that he has removed his solemn opponent, now that he himself takes his imperial role seriously and imagines that the Napoleonic mask represents the real Napoleon, does he become the victim of his own conception of the world, the serious clown who no longer sees world history as a comedy but his comedy as world history. What the National Workshops[88] were for the socialist workers, what the Mobile Guard was for the bourgeois republicans, the Society of 10 December was for Bonaparte: the characteristic fighting force of his party. On his journeys detachments of the Society had to pack the trains and improvise a public for him, had to stage public enthusiasm, scream the words *vive l'empereur*, insult and beat up republicans, all with the protection of the police, of course. When he returned to Paris they had to form the advance guard and forestall or disperse counter-demonstrations. The Society of 10 December belonged to him, it was *his* work, his very own idea. Whatever else he laid hold of was put into his hands by the force of circumstances, whatever else he did either circumstances did for him or he copied from the deeds of others; but he himself became an original author when he combined official turns of phrase about order, religion, family and property, spoken publicly before the citizens, with the secret society of the Schufterles and the Spiegelbergs,[89] the society of disorder, prostitution and theft, behind him. The history of the Society of 10 December is his own history.

Now it happened by way of exception that some deputies belonging to the party of Order got in the way of the Decembrists' sticks. There was worse to come. Police Commissioner Yon, who was assigned to the National Assembly with the job of looking after its security, informed the Standing Commission, acting on the deposition of a certain Allais, that a section of the Decembrists had resolved to assassinate General Changarnier and the Chairman of the National Assembly, Dupin, and had already

88. See pp. 53–4.
89. Two characters from Schiller's drama *The Robbers*, who were portrayed as complete rogues, lacking all moral principles.

chosen the individuals who were to accomplish this. One can well understand how terrified Monsieur Dupin was. A parliamentary investigation into the Society of 10 December, i.e., the profanation of the secret world of Bonapartism, seemed unavoidable. Just before the National Assembly met Bonaparte prudently dissolved his society, only on paper of course, for even at the end of 1851 Police Prefect Carlier sent him an exhaustive memorandum in which he vainly endeavoured to persuade him to break up the Decembrists in actual fact.

The Society of 10 December was to remain Bonaparte's private army until he succeeded in turning the public army into a Society of 10 December. He made the first attempt at this shortly after the adjournment of the National Assembly, and indeed with the money he had just extracted from it. As a fatalist he believed that there are certain higher powers which man, and the soldier in particular, cannot withstand. Among these powers he counted above all cigars and champagne, cold poultry and garlic sausage. He therefore began by entertaining officers and NCOs in the Elysée apartments with cigars and champagne, cold poultry and garlic sausage. On 3 October he repeated this manoeuvre with the mass of the troops at a review held at St Maur, and on 10 October, on a still larger scale, at a review held at Satory. The uncle recalled the campaigns of Alexander in Asia, the nephew recalled the conquests of Bacchus in the same land. Alexander was of course a demigod; but Bacchus was a god, in fact he was the god of the Society of 10 December.

After the review of 3 October the Standing Commission summoned the War Minister, Hautpoul, to appear before it. He promised that these acts of indiscipline would not recur. We know how on 10 October Bonaparte kept Hautpoul's word. Changarnier had been in command at both reviews, as commander-in-chief of the Paris army. He was simultaneously a member of the Standing Commission and the head of the National Guard, the 'saviour' of 29 January and 13 June, the 'bulwark of society', the party of Order's presidential candidate, and the anticipated Monk[90] of two monarchies. So far he had never recognized that he was subordinate to the Minister of War; he had always openly scoffed at the republican Constitution and clothed Bonaparte with an

90. Changarnier had been expected both by the Legitimists and the Orleanists to invite their king back to the throne, as General Monk had invited Charles II in 1660.

ambiguously lordly protection. Now he was eager to uphold discipline against the Minister of War and the Constitution against Bonaparte. Whereas a section of the cavalry raised the cry '*Vive Napoléon! Vivent les saucissons!*'[91] on 10 October, Changarnier arranged that the infantry at least, which was marching past under the command of his friend Neumayer, should observe an icy silence. As a punishment, and at Bonaparte's instigation, the Minister of War relieved General Neumayer of his post in Paris, on the pretext of installing him as commanding general of the Fourteenth and Fifteenth Army Divisions. Neumayer rejected this exchange of commands and had therefore simply to take his leave.

Changarnier for his part published an order of the day on 2 November in which he forbade the troops to shout political slogans or engage in demonstrations of any kind while bearing arms. The Elysée newspapers attacked Changarnier; the newspapers of the party of Order attacked Bonaparte; the Standing Commission held repeated secret sessions and it was repeatedly proposed that a state of emergency be declared; the army seemed to be divided into two antagonistic camps with two antagonistic general staffs, one in the Elysée, Bonaparte's residence, the other in the Tuileries, Changarnier's residence. Only the meeting of the National Assembly seemed necessary and the signal for battle would resound. The French public judged this friction between Bonaparte and Changarnier like the English journalist who characterized it in the following words:

> The political housemaids of France are sweeping away the glowing lava of the revolution with old brooms and squabbling while they work.

Meanwhile Bonaparte quickly removed his Minister of War, dispatching him precipitately to Algeria, and appointing General Schramm[92] in his place. On 12 November he sent the National Assembly a message of American elaborateness, overloaded with details, reeking of order, anxious for conciliation, resigned to the Constitution, dealing with every possible question except the *questions brûlantes*[93] of the hour. As if in passing, he let fall the remark that, according to the express provisions of the Constitu-

91. Long live Napoleon! Long live the sausages!
92. Jean-Paul Schramm was a Bonapartist general, and Minister of War from October 1850 to 1851.
93. Burning questions.

tion, the President alone had the army at his disposal. The message closed with this solemn declaration:

Above all else France demands tranquillity . . . I alone am bound by my oath, and I shall keep within the narrow limits the Constitution has drawn for me. . . . As far as I am concerned, I am elected by the people and owe my power to them alone, and I shall always submit to their lawfully expressed will. Should you resolve at this session on a revision of the Constitution, a Constituent Assembly will regulate the position of the executive power. If not, then the nation will solemnly proclaim its decision in 1852. But whatever the solutions of the future may be, let us come to an understanding, so that passion, surprise, or violence will never decide the destiny of a great nation . . . My attention is claimed not by the question of who is to rule France in 1852 but by the question of how to employ the time at my disposal so that the intervening period may pass by without agitation or disturbance. I have opened my heart to you with sincerity; you will answer my frankness with your trust, my good endeavours with your cooperation, and God will do the rest.

The respectable, hypocritically moderate, virtuously commonplace language of the bourgeoisie revealed its deepest level of meaning when used by the autocrat of the Society of 10 December, the picnic hero of St Maur and Satory.

The burgraves of the party of Order were not for a moment deluded about the kind of confidence this outpouring deserved. They had long been cynical about oaths; they could count veterans and virtuosos of political perjury in their midst, and they had not failed to overhear the passage about the army. They noticed with indignation that in its long-winded enumeration of the latest laws the message had passed over the most important law, the electoral law, with an affected silence and, moreover, that the election of the President in 1852 was left to the hands of the people, provided there was no revision of the Constitution in the meantime. The electoral law was the party of Order's ball and chain, which prevented it from walking and, *a fortiori*, from storming forward! Moreover, with the official dissolution of the Society of 10 December and the dismissal of War Minister Hautpoul, Bonaparte had sacrificed the scapegoats with his own hand on the altar of the country. He had taken the sting out of the expected conflict. Finally, the party of Order itself anxiously sought to avoid, mitigate or conceal any decisive conflict with the executive. It allowed its rival to win the fruits of its victories over the revolution, out of its own fear of losing them. 'Above all else, France demands tranquillity': the party of Order had proclaimed this to the revolution ever since February, and now Bonaparte's message proclaimed it to the party of Order. 'Above all else, France demands tranquillity': Bonaparte committed acts which aimed at usurpation, but the party of Order upset the 'tranquillity' if it raised the alarm about these acts and interpreted them in hypochondriac fashion. The sausages of Satory were as quiet as mice if no one referred to them. 'Above all else, France demands tranquillity.' Bonaparte thus demanded to be left alone to do as he liked, and the parliamentary party was paralysed by a double fear – by the fear of conjuring up new revolutionary disorders, and by the fear of appearing in the eyes of the bourgeoisie, in the eyes of its own class, as itself the instigator of unrest. Since France demanded tranquillity above all else, the party of Order did not dare to answer 'war' after Bonaparte had spoken in his message of 'peace'. The public, which had looked forward to seeing great scenes of scandal at the opening of the National Assembly, was disappointed in its hopes. The opposition deputies, who demanded that the minutes of the Standing Commission's discussions on the October events be laid on the table, were outvoted by the majority. On principle, all debates that could cause excitement were avoided. The activities of the National Assembly during November and December 1850 were without interest.

At last, towards the end of December, guerrilla warfare began over some particular parliamentary prerogatives. The movement could only get bogged down in such petty quarrels over the prerogatives of the two powers because the bourgeoisie had done away with the class struggle for the time being by abolishing universal suffrage.

A verdict of debt had been obtained against a deputy, Mauguin.[94] The Minister of Justice, Rouher,[95] replied to an inquiry from the president of the court that a warrant for the debtor's arrest should be made out without further formalities. Mauguin was therefore thrown into the debtors' prison. The National Assembly was furious when it learnt of this outrage. It not only ordered Mauguin's immediate release, but also had

94. François Mauguin was a lawyer and a deputy in both Assemblies.

95. Eugène Rouher was a Bonapartist deputy in both Assemblies, intermittently Minister of Justice between 1849 and 1852, and later a leading official of the Second Empire.

him forcibly brought back from Clichy the same evening by its *greffier*.[96] But in order to show its faith in the sacredness of private property, and with the *arrière pensée* of providing an asylum for troublesome Montagnards in case of need, it declared that deputies could be imprisoned for debt with the prior consent of the National Assembly. It forgot to decree that the President could also be locked up for debts incurred. It destroyed the last appearance of immunity surrounding its own members.

It will be recalled that Police Commissioner Yon, acting on the deposition of a certain Allais, had denounced a section of the Decembrists for planning the murder of Dupin and Changarnier. In relation to this, the quaestors proposed at the Assembly's very first sitting that it should form its own parliamentary police force, paid out of its private budget and completely independent of the Prefect of Police. The Minister of the Interior, Baroche, protested against this encroachment on his province. At this point a wretched compromise was concluded, by which the Assembly's police commissioner was to be paid out of its private budget and appointed and dismissed by its quaestors, but only after previous agreement with the Ministry of the Interior. Meanwhile the government had taken criminal proceedings against Allais, and here it was easy to present his deposition as an invention, and to put Dupin, Changarnier, Yon and the whole National Assembly in a ridiculous light through the speeches of the public prosecutor. On 29 December Baroche wrote a letter to Dupin demanding Yon's dismissal. The bureau of the National Assembly decided to retain Yon in his position, but the Assembly itself, alarmed by its own violence in the Mauguin affair and accustomed to receiving two blows in return for every one it ventured to strike at the executive power, failed to sanction this decision. As a reward for his professional zeal Yon was dismissed, and the Assembly robbed itself of a parliamentary prerogative indispensable against a man who, rather than deciding by night and striking by day, decides by day and strikes by night.[97]

We have already seen how during the months of November and December the National Assembly circumvented or suppressed any struggle with the executive over important and striking issues. We now see it forced to take up the struggle over the pettiest

96. The clerk to the Assembly, a fairly lowly position. In fact, however, it was Jean-Didier Baze, a quaestor, who was sent to fetch Mauguin.

97. Bonaparte's coup d'état took place on the night of 1–2 December 1851.

questions. In the Mauguin affair it confirmed in principle the liability of deputies to imprisonment for debt, but it reserved the right to have it applied only to deputies it disliked, and wrangled over this infamous privilege with the Minister of Justice. Instead of utilizing the alleged murder plot to start an investigation into the Society of 10 December and utterly discredit Bonaparte before France and Europe by revealing his true character as the head of the Paris lumpenproletariat, it let the conflict sink down to a level at which the only point at issue between itself and the Minister of Interior was the question of competence to appoint and dismiss a police commissioner. So, throughout the whole of this period we see the party of Order compelled by its ambiguous position to dissipate and fragment its struggle with the executive into petty conflicts of competence, chicaneries, legalistic hair-splitting and demarcation disputes, and to make the most preposterous formal questions about the content of its activity. It did not dare take up the conflict at a moment when it would have had a principled significance, when the executive had really compromised itself and the cause of the National Assembly would have been the cause of the nation, because by doing that it would have given the nation its marching orders, and a nation on the move was what it feared most of all. It accordingly rejected the motions put forward by the Montagne on such occasions, and proceeded to the order of the day. Having thus escaped the broader dimensions of the issue, the executive calmly awaited the time when it could take up the disputed question again in connection with some petty and insignificant issue, one of merely local parliamentary interest as it were. Then the pent-up rage of the party of Order could break out, they could tear down the stage curtains, they could denounce the President, they could declare the republic in danger, but then too their passion would appear absurd and the occasion of the struggle a hypocritical pretext, not worth fighting for. The parliamentary storm became a storm in a teacup, the fight became an intrigue, the confrontation became a scandal. The revolutionary classes gloated with malicious joy over the humiliation of the National Assembly, for they were as enthusiastically in favour of its parliamentary prerogatives as the Assembly was in favour of public liberties; the bourgeoisie outside parliament did not understand how the bourgeoisie inside parliament could waste its time on such petty squabbles and compromise public tranquillity over such pitiful rivalries with the President. The bourgeoisie was confused by a strategy which made peace at the moment when all the world expected battles, and launched an attack at the moment when all the world thought peace had been made.

On 20 December Pascal Duprat[98] questioned the Minister of the Interior about the Gold Bars lottery. This lottery was a 'daughter of Elysium'. Bonaparte had brought it into the world with the aid of his faithful followers, and Police Prefect Carlier had placed it under his official protection, although in France the law forbids all lotteries with the exception of raffles for charitable purposes. Seven million lottery tickets were to be sold at one franc each. The profits were supposedly earmarked for the transportation of Parisian vagabonds to California. In part, this was an attempt to supplant the Paris proletariat's dreams of socialism with dreams of gold, the doctrinaire right to work with the seductive prospect of the big win. The Paris workers naturally did not recognize the inconspicuous francs enticed out of their own pockets when they saw the glitter of the Californian gold bars. However, the main object was a straightforward swindle. The vagabonds who wanted to open the gold mines of California without bothering to leave Paris were Bonaparte himself and his debt-ridden knights of the round table. The three million francs granted by the National Assembly had been squandered in riotous living; the coffers had to be refilled in one way or another. In vain had Bonaparte opened a national subscription for the building of so-called *cités ouvrières*,[99] with himself figuring at the top of the list for a substantial sum. The hard-hearted members of the bourgeoisie suspiciously awaited the payment of his share in hard cash, and as this was naturally not forthcoming, the speculation in socialist castles in the air fell flat on the ground. The gold bars were a better draw. It was not enough for Bonaparte and his confederates to pocket part of the surplus of seven millions over the value of the bars to be given out as prizes; they manufactured false lottery tickets; they issued ten, fifteen, even twenty tickets with the same number. This was a financial operation in the spirit of the Society of 10 December! Here the National Assembly was confronted not with the nominal President of the republic but with the flesh and blood Bonaparte. It could catch him red-handed, transgressing not the Constitution but the Code Pénal. If it proceeded with the

98. Pascal Duprat was a republican journalist and politician, and a deputy in both Assemblies.
99. Workers' settlements.

day's agenda, ignoring Duprat's question, this did not just happen because Girardin's motion that the Assembly should declare itself '*satisfait*' reminded the party of Order of its own systematic corruption. The bourgeois, and above all the bourgeois puffed up into a statesman, supplements his practical vulgarity with theoretical extravagance. As a statesman, he becomes a higher being, like the state power which confronts him, and a higher being can only be fought in a higher, consecrated fashion.

Precisely because Bonaparte was a bohemian, a princely lumpen-proletarian, he had the advantage over the bourgeois scoundrels that he could wage the struggle in vulgar fashion. He now saw that the moment had come, after the Assembly had led him with its own hand over the treacherous ground of the military banquets, the reviews, the Society of 10 December and the Code Pénal, to go over from the apparent defensive to the real offensive. He was hardly embarrassed by the minor defeats sustained in the meantime by the Ministers of Justice, War, the Navy and Finance, through which the National Assembly displayed its irritation and dissatisfaction. Not only did he prevent the ministers from resigning and thus recognizing the subjection of the executive to parliament; he was now able to finish off what he had begun during the National Assembly's recess: the severance of the military power from parliament, the *dismissal of Changarnier*.

An Elysée newspaper published an order of the day, allegedly directed to the First Army Division during the month of May, and therefore proceeding from Changarnier, in which officers were recommended to give no quarter to traitors in their own ranks in case of an insurrection, to shoot them immediately and to refuse troops to the National Assembly if it should requisition them. The cabinet was questioned about this order of the day on 3 January 1851. It demanded first three months, then a week, and finally only twenty-four hours for the consideration and examination of the matter. The Assembly insisted on an immediate explanation. Changarnier got up and declared that this order of the day had never existed. He added that he would always hasten to comply with any summons the Assembly made and that it could count on him in case of a conflict. It received his declaration with a huge ovation and passed a vote of confidence in him. By placing itself under the private protection of a general, the Assembly abdicated: it decreed its own powerlessness and the army's omnipotence. But the general was deceiving himself when he put at the Assembly's disposal against Bonaparte a power he only held in fief from that same Bonaparte, when he himself expected protection from this parliament which needed him to protect it. However, Changarnier believed in the mysterious power which the bourgeoisie had vested in him on 29 January 1849. He held himself to be the third power, existing alongside the two other powers in the state. He shared the fate of the other heroes, or rather saints, of that epoch, whose greatness consisted precisely in the high opinion of them which was spread abroad by their party in its own interests, and who collapsed into ordinary mortals as soon as the situation required them to perform miracles. Scepticism is generally the deadly enemy of these presumed heroes and real saints. This is the reason for their dignified moral indignation at unenthusiastic wits and scoffers.

The same evening the ministers were ordered to go to the Elysée. Bonaparte insisted on Changarnier's dismissal, which five ministers refused to sign; the *Moniteur* announced that there was a ministerial crisis, and the press supporting the party of Order threatened to form a parliamentary army under the command of Changarnier. The party of Order had the constitutional authority to take this step. It only needed to appoint Changarnier as Chairman of the National Assembly and requisition any number of troops it pleased for its protection. It could do this all the more safely in that Changarnier was still in fact the head of the army and the Paris National Guard, and was only waiting for the opportunity to be requisitioned along with the army. The Bonapartist press did not as yet even dare to question the right of the National Assembly to requisition troops directly, in view of the likely lack of success, under the given circumstances, of legalistic discussions of this kind. It appears likely that the army would have obeyed the orders of the National Assembly, if one bears in mind that Bonaparte had to search the whole of Paris for eight days to find two generals – Baraguay d'Hilliers and Saint-Jean d'Angely[1] – who were ready to countersign Changarnier's dismissal. But it appears more than doubtful whether the party of Order would have found the necessary number of votes in its own ranks and in parliament, when one considers that eight days later 286 votes separated themselves from that party, and that the

1. Auguste, comte Regnault de Saint-Jean d'Angely was a Bonapartist general and a deputy in both Assemblies. He was made Minister of War in January 1851.

Montagne rejected a proposal of this nature even in December 1851, at the final and decisive hour. Nevertheless, the burgraves might perhaps have succeeded in inspiring the mass of their party to a heroism consisting in feeling secure behind a forest of bayonets and accepting the services of an army which had deserted to their camp. Instead, these gentlemen proceeded to the Elysée on the evening of 6 January[2] to make Bonaparte forgo the sacking of Changarnier by using diplomatic phrases and objections. He who seeks to persuade someone acknowledges him as the master of the situation. Bonaparte was therefore reassured by this action, and on 12 January[3] he appointed a new ministry in which the leaders of the old ministry, Fould and Baroche, retained their seats. Saint-Jean d'Angely became Minister of War, the *Moniteur* published the decree dismissing Changarnier, and his command was divided between Baraguay d'Hilliers, who received the First Army Division, and Perrot,[4] who received the National Guard. The bulwark of society had been dismissed, and while this did not cause a great stir, it did cause the quotations on the Bourse to rise.

By rejecting the army which was placed at its disposal in the person of Changarnier, and so irrevocably delivering it into the hands of the President, the party of Order declared that the bourgeoisie had lost its vocation to rule. The parliamentary ministry had already ceased to exist. Since it had now lost its grip on the army and the National Guard, what instruments of power remained for it to maintain both the usurped power of the Assembly over the people and its constitutional power against the President? None. All it had left now was the appeal to principles without the support of force, principles it had always interpreted as general rules to be prescribed for others so as to improve one's own freedom of movement. With the dismissal of Changarnier and the devolution of military power into Bonaparte's hands we come to the end of the first section of the period we are considering, the period of the struggle between the party of Order and the executive. The war between the two powers was now openly declared and openly waged, but only after the party of Order had lost both weapons and soldiers. Without a ministry, without an army, without the people, without public opinion, no longer the repre-

2. The correct date is 8 January 1851.
3. The correct date is 10 January 1851.
4. Benjamin-Pierre Perrot was a general who took part in the suppression of the June insurrection.

sentative of the sovereign nation since its electoral law of 31 May, sans teeth, sans eyes, sans taste, sans everything, the National Assembly had gradually become transformed into an old French *parlement*,[5] which had to leave action to the government and make do with growling and remonstrating after the deed was done.

The party of Order received the new ministry with a storm of indignation. General Bedeau reminded the Assembly of the meekness of the Standing Commission during the recess and the excessive consideration for the President which had led it to give up the idea of publishing its proceedings. The Minister of the Interior himself now insisted on the publication of these minutes, which had of course become as dull as ditchwater, revealed no new facts, and made no impact whatsoever on a bored public. The National Assembly accepted Rémusat's[6] proposal to withdraw into its offices and appoint a 'Committee for Extraordinary Measures'. The dislocation of Parisian daily routine caused by the Assembly was the less effective in that trade was now prosperous, factories and workshops were fully employed, the price of corn was low, foodstuffs were available in abundance, and the saving banks received new deposits every day. The 'extraordinary measures' announced so noisily by the parliament fizzled out into a vote of no confidence against the ministers on 18 January, a vote in which General Changarnier was not even mentioned. The party of Order had been forced to word its resolution in this way in order to secure the republican vote, as the dismissal of Changarnier was the single one of all the ministry's measures that the republicans approved of, whereas the party of Order could not reproach the ministry with any of its other acts, since it had dictated them itself.

The no-confidence resolution of 18 January was passed by 415 votes to 286. In other words, it was carried only by a *coalition* between the staunch Legitimists and Orleanists, the pure republicans, and the Montagne. This demonstrated that in its conflicts with Bonaparte the party of Order had lost not only the ministry and the army, but also its independent parliamentary majority, that a detachment of representatives had deserted its camp out of

5. The regional assembly of magistrates in the France of the *ancien régime*. It registered the king's decrees and had the right to refuse registration if the decree went against the customs of the realm. In practice the king was able to override such a refusal, although this power was disputed by the parlements in the eighteenth century.

6. Charles, comte de Rémusat was a writer and an Orleanist politician, Minister of the Interior in 1840. He sat in both Assemblies.

fear of struggle, fanaticism for compromise, boredom, family regard for relatives holding state salaries, speculation on coming vacancies in ministerial positions (Odilon Barrot), and finally the simple egoism which always inclines the ordinary bourgeois citizen to sacrifice the general interest of his class to this or that private motive. From the beginning, the Bonapartist representatives had belonged to the party of Order only in its struggle against the revolution. The leader of the Catholic party, Montalembert, had already thrown his influence onto the scales on Bonaparte's side, since he despaired of the Assembly's prospects of survival. Finally, the parliamentary leaders, the Orleanist Thiers and the Legitimist Berryer, were compelled to proclaim openly that they were republicans, to admit that though their hearts were royalist their minds were republican, since the parliamentary republic was the only possible form for the rule of the bourgeoisie as a whole. They were thus forced, before the eyes of the bourgeois class itself, to brand the plans for restoration which they unwearyingly continued to pursue behind the Assembly's back as intrigues as dangerous as they were thoughtless.

The no-confidence resolution of 18 January struck at the ministers, not the President. But it was the President, not the ministers, who had dismissed Changarnier. Should the members of the party of Order impeach Bonaparte himself? What for? For his desire to carry out a restoration? This only supplemented their own. For conspiracy, in the matter of the military reviews and the Society of 10 December? They had buried these themes long ago beneath the normal order of business. For the dismissal of the hero of 29 January and 13 June 1849, the man who in May 1850 threatened to set fire to all four corners of Paris in case of an uprising? Their allies, the supporters of the Montagne and of Cavaignac, did not even allow them to set the fallen bulwark of society on his feet with an official declaration of sympathy. Indeed, they could not deny that the President had the constitutional authority to dismiss a general. They were only furious because he made an unparliamentary use of his constitutional right. But had they not repeatedly made an unconstitutional use of their parliamentary prerogative, in particular when they abolished universal suffrage? They were therefore thrown back onto manoeuvres which took place entirely within parliamentary bounds. This attitude was supported by that peculiar epidemic which has prevailed over the whole continent of Europe since 1848, *parliamentary cretinism*, which holds its victims spellbound in an imaginary world and robs them of all sense, all memory, and all understanding of the rough external world. It required this parliamentary cretinism to make the party of Order view its parliamentary victories as real victories and imagine it was touching the President when it struck at his ministers, for its members had themselves destroyed the whole basis of parliamentary power with their own hands, indeed had been forced to destroy it in their struggle with the other classes. They merely gave Bonaparte the opportunity of humiliating the National Assembly once again in the eyes of the nation. On 20 January the *Moniteur* announced that the resignation of the entire ministry had been accepted. On the pretext that no parliamentary party had a majority any longer, as demonstrated by the vote of 18 January, this fruit of a coalition between the Montagne and the royalists, and in expectation of the later formation of a new majority, Bonaparte appointed a so-called transitional ministry which contained not a single member of parliament and consisted exclusively of entirely unknown and insignificant individuals, a ministry of mere clerks and copyists. The party of Order could now wear itself out in playing games with these puppets; the executive no longer saw the point of being seriously represented in the National Assembly. The more his ministers were reduced to playing mere walk-on parts, the more obviously did Bonaparte concentrate the whole executive power in his own person and the more latitude did he have to exploit it for his own purposes.

The party of Order, in coalition with the Montagne, revenged itself by rejecting the presidential grant of 1,800,000 francs which the head of the Society of 10 December had forced his ministerial clerks to propose. This time the issue was decided by a majority of only 102 votes; another twenty-seven votes had therefore fallen away since 18 January. The dissolution of the party of Order was proceeding apace. At the same time, in order to make sure that there was not even a momentary mistake made about the meaning of its coalition with the Montagne, it disdained even to take into consideration a proposal signed by 189 members of the Montagne for a general amnesty of political offenders. It was sufficient for the Minister of the Interior, a certain Vaïsse,[7] to declare that the present tranquillity was only apparent, and that

7. Claude-Marius Vaïsse, a typical nonentity in Bonaparte's 'ministry of clerks'.

in secret a great agitation was going on, secret societies were being organized everywhere, the democratic papers were making arrangements to reappear, the reports from the departments sounded unfavourable, the exiles in Geneva were leading a conspiracy which was spreading via Lyons over the whole of southern France, that France stood on the edge of an industrial and commercial crisis, that the manufacturers of Roubaix had reduced the hours of work, that the prisoners of Belle Isle[8] were in revolt – even a mere Vaïsse could conjure up the red spectre and make the party of Order reject without discussion a proposal which would have won immense popularity for the National Assembly and thrown Bonaparte back into its arms. Instead of letting itself be intimidated by the executive's perspective of new disorders, it should rather have allowed the class struggle some latitude, so as to keep the executive dependent on itself. But it did not feel equal to the task of playing with fire.

The so-called transitional ministry continued to vegetate until the middle of April. Bonaparte wearied and teased the National Assembly with constantly renewed ministerial combinations. Sometimes he seemed to want to form a republican ministry with Lamartine and Billault,[9] at other times a parliamentary ministry with the inevitable Odilon Barrot, whose name is always there when a dupe is needed, at other times a Legitimist ministry with Vatimesnil[10] and Benoist d'Azy,[11] and at still other times an Orleanist ministry with Maleville.[12] While he maintained the tension between the different fractions of the party of Order in this way, and alarmed them all with the prospect of a republican ministry and the return of universal suffrage which would inevitably follow, he simultaneously created among the bourgeoisie as a whole the conviction that his honest endeavours to form a parliamentary ministry were being wrecked by the irreconcilability of the royalist

8. The revolutionaries arrested during the previous three years had been imprisoned on the island of Belle Isle, off the west coast of France.

9. August-Adolphe Billault was a lawyer and an Orleanist, who sat in both Assemblies and became a Bonapartist after the coup d'état. He was Minister of the Interior from 1854 to 1858.

10. Antoine Lefebvre de Vatimesnil was a Legitimist politician, Minister of Education under Charles X. He sat in the Legislative Assembly.

11. Denis, comte Benoist d'Azy was a financier and industrialist, and a Legitimist deputy and vice-chairman in the Legislative Assembly, 1849–51.

12. Léon de Maleville was an Orleanist deputy in both Assemblies, and Minister of the Interior in December 1848.

fractions. The bourgeoisie cried out all the more loudly for a 'strong government'. It found it all the more unforgivable to leave France 'without administration' in that a general commercial crisis now seemed to be setting in, winning recruits for socialism in the towns while the ruinously low price of corn did the same for the countryside. Trade became daily more stagnant, and the number of hands without work increased noticeably. In Paris at least 10,000 workers were without bread; in Rouen, Mulhouse, Lyons, Roubaix, Tourcoing, St Etienne, Elbeuf, etc., innumerable factories stood idle. Under these circumstances Bonaparte could take the risk, on 11 April, of restoring the ministry of 18 January, i.e., Messrs Rouher, Fould, Baroche, etc., reinforced by Monsieur Léon Faucher, whom the Constituent Assembly at the end of its life had unanimously (with the exception of five ministerial votes) branded with a vote of no confidence for the dissemination of false dispatches by telegraph.[13] In other words, the National Assembly had won a victory over the ministry of 18 January, and it had struggled with Bonaparte for three months, only for Fould and Baroche to admit the puritan Faucher as the third member of their ministerial alliance on 11 April.

In November 1849 Bonaparte had been satisfied with an *unparliamentary* ministry; in January 1851 he had been satisfied with an *extra-parliamentary* ministry; now, on 11 April 1851, he felt strong enough to form an *anti-parliamentary* ministry, which harmoniously combined within itself the votes of no confidence passed by both Assemblies, the Constituent and the Legislative, the Assembly of the republicans and the Assembly of the royalists. This graduated scale of ministries was the thermometer with which the Assembly could measure the decline in its own vital heat. This thermometer had fallen so low by the end of April that Persigny[14] could invite Changarnier in a personal interview to go over to the presidential camp. He assured him that Bonaparte regarded the influence of the National Assembly as completely annihilated and that a proclamation had already been prepared

13. On 11 May 1849 the Constituent Assembly rebuked Faucher for announcing in a dispatch that the deputies who had voted against the government were 'just waiting to mount the barricades and start the June business again'.

14. Jean Fialin, duc de Persigny was a Bonapartist and a deputy in the Legislative Assembly. He helped to organize the coup d'état of 2 December and was Minister of the Interior from 1852 to 1854 and again from 1860 to 1863.

for publication after the coup d'état, which was his constant aim but which had to be postponed again for accidental reasons. Changarnier informed the leaders of the party of Order of this obituary notice, but who believes that the bites of a bed-bug are fatal? And the Assembly, in its defeated, disintegrated and putrescent condition, could not bring itself to see in its duel with the grotesque head of the Society of 10 December anything other than a duel with a bed-bug. But Bonaparte answered the party of Order as Agesilaus answered King Agis: 'I seem an ant to you, but one day I shall be a lion.'[15]

VI

In its vain endeavours to maintain possession of the military and to reconquer supreme control of the executive, the party of Order was condemned to remain in coalition with the Montagne and the pure republicans. This proved incontrovertibly that it had lost its independent *parliamentary majority*. The mere power of the calendar, of the hour hand of the clock, gave the signal for its complete disintegration on 28 May. The last year of the National Assembly's life began on 28 May. It had now to decide whether the Constitution was to continue unchanged or be revised. But the revision of the Constitution did not just involve the question of bourgeois rule or petty-bourgeois democracy, democracy or proletarian 'anarchy', parliamentary republic or Bonaparte, it also posed the question of Orleans or Bourbon! Thus there fell into the Assembly's midst the apple of discord which would openly arouse the conflict of interests and split the party of Order into opposing fractions. The party of Order was a combination of heterogeneous social substances. The question of revision produced a level of political temperature at which the mixture decomposed into its original constituents.

The Bonapartists' interest in revision was simple. For them it was above all a question of the abolition of paragraph 45, which forbade Bonaparte's re-election, and the prolongation of his authority. The position of the republicans was just as simple. They were unconditionally opposed to any revision; they saw in revision a general conspiracy against the republic. As they disposed of

15. From Athenaeus' *Deipnosophistai*. In fact it was Tachos, king of Egypt, whom Agesilaus, king of Sparta, answered in that way, and he referred to a mouse rather than an ant.

more than a quarter of the votes in the National Assembly, and as, according to the Constitution, three quarters of the votes were required for a resolution in favour of revision to be legally valid and for the convocation of a special revising Assembly, they only needed to count their votes to be sure of victory. And they were sure of victory.

As against these clear positions, the party of Order found itself involved in inextricable contradictions. If it rejected revision, it endangered the status quo by leaving Bonaparte only one way out, the way of force, and by abandoning France at the moment of decision, the second Sunday of May 1852, to revolutionary anarchy, with a President who had lost his authority, a parliament which had long lacked authority, and a people which meant to reconquer its authority. It knew that to cast its vote for revision as the Constitution laid down was a waste of time, as it would be defeated, in accordance with the Constitution, by the veto of the republicans. If it unconstitutionally declared a simple majority vote to be binding, it could only hope to master the revolution by subordinating itself unconditionally to the domination of the executive. In that case, it would make Bonaparte the master of the Constitution, of its revision, and of the party of Order itself. A merely partial revision, prolonging the authority of the President, would pave the way to imperialist usurpation. A general revision, cutting short the existence of the republic, would inevitably bring the dynastic claims into conflict, for the conditions of a Bourbon and an Orleanist restoration were not just different, but mutually exclusive.

The *parliamentary republic* was more than the neutral territory where the two fractions of the French bourgeoisie, Legitimists and Orleanists, big landed property and industry, could live side by side with equal rights. It was the inescapable condition of their *joint* rule, the only form of state in which both the claims of these particular fractions and the claims of all other classes of society were subjected to the general interest of the bourgeois class. As royalists, they fell back into their old antagonism, into the struggle between landed property and money for supremacy, and their kings and dynasties formed the highest expression of this antagonism, its personification. Hence the opposition of the party of Order to the *recall of the Bourbons*.

Between 1849 and 1851 the Orleanist deputy Creton had periodically introduced a motion to rescind the decree exiling the royal families. The Assembly just as regularly offered the spectacle of an assembly of royalists obstinately barring the door through which their exiled kings could return home. Richard III had murdered Henry VI, remarking that he was too good for this world and belonged in heaven.[16] They, in turn, declared that France was too bad to have her kings back. They had become republicans under the compulsion of circumstances, and they repeatedly sanctioned the popular decision that banished their kings from France.

A revision of the Constitution – and the circumstances compelled them to consider this possibility – would put in question not only the republic but also the joint rule of the two bourgeois fractions, and the possibility of a monarchy recalled to life the rivalry of the interests it had preferentially represented by turns, and the struggle for the supremacy of one fraction over the other. The party of Order's diplomats thought they could settle the conflict by merging the two dynasties, by a so-called *fusion* of the royalist parties and their respective houses. The genuine fusion of the Restoration and July monarchies was the parliamentary republic, in which the Orleanist and the Legitimist colours were extinguished and the various species of bourgeois disappeared into the bourgeois as such, the bourgeois genus. But now the Orleanist was supposed to become a Legitimist and the Legitimist an Orleanist. Royalty, the personification of their antagonism, was now to embody their unity; the expression of their exclusive fractional interests was to become the expression of their common class interest; the monarchy was to accomplish what could only be, and had been, accomplished by the abolition of two monarchies, i.e., the republic. This was the philosophers' stone the doctors of the party of Order racked their brains to produce. As if the Legitimist monarchy could ever become the monarchy of the industrial bourgeoisie or the bourgeois monarchy could ever become the monarchy of the hereditary landed aristocracy! As if landed property and industry could fraternize beneath a *single* crown which could only be placed on a single head, the head of the elder brother or the younger! As if industry could make a compromise with landed property at all, as long as landed property did not decide to become industrial

16. Marx's reference here is to Shakespeare rather than historical fact. In *Henry VI*, V, vi Gloucester (later Richard III) kills Henry VI, and in *Richard III*, I, ii he justifies his action with the line that Henry 'was fitter for that place than Earth'.

itself! If Henri V were to die tomorrow, the comte de Paris[17] would not for that reason become the king of the Legitimists, unless he ceased to be the king of the Orleanists. However, the philosophers of fusion, who became more prominent as the question of revision came further into the foreground, who had created their own official daily organ in the shape of the *Assemblée nationale*,[18] and who are again at work even at this very moment (February 1852), explain the whole problem as a result of the antagonism and rivalry between the two dynasties. The attempts to reconcile the Orleans family with Henri V had begun with the death of Louis Philippe, but, like all the dynastic intrigues, they were games played only during the recesses of the National Assembly, in the intervals of the drama and behind the scenes, more a case of sentimental coquetry with old superstitions than seriously meant business. Now, however, these intrigues became important state proceedings, performed by the party of Order on the public stage, instead of in amateur theatricals, as hitherto. The couriers rushed from Paris to Venice,[19] from Venice to Claremont, from Claremont to Paris. The comte de Chambord issued a manifesto announcing not his, but the 'national' restoration, 'with the help of all members of his family'. The Orleanist Salvandy[20] threw himself at the feet of Henri V. The Legitimist leaders Berryer, Benoist d'Azy and Saint-Priest[21] travelled to Claremont in order to persuade the Orleans clique, but without success. Too late the fusionists realized that the interests of the two fractions of the bourgeoisie did not lose in exclusiveness or gain in flexibility when brought to their quintessential form of family interests, the interests of two royal houses. If Henri V were to recognize the comte de Paris as his successor – the only success fusion could achieve in the best circumstances – the House of Orleans would not win any claim not already secured by the childlessness of Henri V, but it would lose all the claims conquered by the July revolution. It would have abandoned its original claims, all the titles it had

17. Louis-Philippe-Albert, the grandson of Louis Philippe.

18. A newspaper of a Legitimist tendency, which appeared in Paris between 1848 and 1857.

19. The comte de Chambord, 'Henri V', lived in Venice in the 1850s.

20. Narcisse, comte de Salvandy was an Orleanist politician of the 1830s and 1840s, and Minister of Education from 1837 to 1839 and from 1845 to 1848.

21. Louis, vicomte de Saint-Priest was a general and a diplomat, and a deputy in the Legislative National Assembly.

wrung from the elder branch of the Bourbons in almost a hundred years of struggle, it would have exchanged its historical prerogative, the prerogative of the modern monarchy, for the prerogative of its lineage. Fusion was therefore nothing but a voluntary abdication by the House of Orleans, its resignation in face of legitimism, a repentant withdrawal from the Protestant state church back into the Catholic. Moreover, this withdrawal would not even bring it to the throne it had lost but to the steps of the throne, where it had been born. The old Orleanist ministers (Guizot, Duchâtel,[22] etc.), who also hastened to Claremont to put in their word for fusion, only represented the retrospective regret felt for the July revolution, the despair felt for the bourgeois monarchy and the monarchical character of the ordinary citizen, and the superstitious belief in legitimacy as the last charm against anarchy. They imagined they were mediators between Orleans and Bourbon; in fact they were merely Orleanists who had abandoned Orleans, and the prince de Joinville[23] received them as such. On the other hand, the lively and combative section of the Orleanists, Thiers, Baze,[24] etc., found it so much the easier to convince the family of Louis Philippe that if any direct restoration of the monarchy presupposed the fusion of the two dynasties, and if any such fusion presupposed the abdication of the House of Orleans, it corresponded entirely to the traditions of their predecessors to recognize the republic provisionally and to wait until events permitted the transformation of the President's chair into a throne. Rumours of Joinville's candidature were spread abroad, public curiosity was kept in suspense, and a few months later, in September, after the rejection of revision, his candidature was publicly proclaimed.

The attempt at a royalist fusion between Orleanists and Legitimists had thus not only failed; it had broken up their *parliamentary fusion*, their common republican form, and disintegrated the party of Order into its original constituents; but as the estrangement between Claremont and Venice grew, their attempted compromise collapsed, and agitation in favour of Joinville gained

22. Charles, comte Duchâtel had been Minister of Trade in 1834–6 and Minister of the Interior in 1839 and 1840–48.

23. François, duc d'Orléans, prince de Joinville was the son of Louis Philippe and the cousin of the Orleanist pretender.

24. Jean-Didier Baze was a lawyer and an Orleanist politician. He sat in both Assemblies.

ground, so the negotiations between Bonaparte's minister Faucher and the Legitimists became all the more eager and serious.

The dissolution of the party of Order did not stop short when its original elements had re-emerged. Each of the two great fractions itself underwent a new decomposition. It was as if all the old nuances which had previously fought and pressed against each other within each of the two circles, whether Legitimist or Orleanist, had become reactivated through contact with water, like dried infusoria, as if they had regained enough vital energy to form their own groups and indulge in their own independent antagonisms. The Legitimists dreamed they were back among the disputes between the Tuileries and the Pavillon Marsan,[25] between Villèle and Polignac,[26] while the Orleanists relived the golden epoch of the jousting matches between Guizot, Molé, de Broglie, Thiers and Odilon Barrot.[27]

The section of the party of Order which was eager for revision, but divided on the limits of this revision – a section composed of the two groups of Legitimists led respectively by Berryer and Falloux, and by La Rochejaquelein, together with the war-weary Orleanists such as Molé, Broglie, Montalembert and Odilon Barrot – agreed with the Bonapartist representatives on the following indefinite and broadly framed motion: 'The undersigned representatives move that the Constitution be revised, with the aim of restoring to the nation the full exercise of its sovereignty.'

However, at the same time they unanimously declared through their *rapporteur*, de Tocqueville,[28] that the National Assembly did not have the right to propose the *abolition of the republic*, for

25. The disputes of the period between 1815 and 1824 between Louis XVIII, who resided in the Tuileries, and the comte d'Artois, later Charles X, who resided at the Pavillon Marsan.

26. Jean-Baptiste, comte de Villèle, Prime Minister from 1822 to 1827, was regarded as representing the main body of the ultra-royalists, and Auguste, prince de Polignac, Prime Minister from 1829 to 1830, as representing the most reactionary and politically naïve faction of that party.

27. The 1830s were a period of confused faction-fighting, while the continuous presence of Guizot as Prime Minister from 1840 to 1848 later provided the elements of a division between right and left, with Thiers and Barrot representing different currents of the Orleanist 'left' against the other politicians mentioned by Marx.

28. Alexis de Tocqueville was an historian and a constitutional monarchist politician, a supporter of the Orleanist 'third party' in the 1840s, Foreign Minister from June to October 1849, and a deputy in both Assemblies.

this right belonged exclusively to the Revising Chamber.[29] In any case, the Constitution could only be revised in a '*legal*' manner, only if the constitutionally prescribed three quarters of the votes cast were in favour of revision. On 19 July, after six days of stormy debate, the motion for revision failed to secure the necessary majority, as was only to be expected. 446 votes were cast in favour and 278 against. The rigid Orleanists such as Thiers, Changarnier, etc., voted with the republicans and the Montagne.

Thus a majority of the Assembly had proclaimed its opposition to the Constitution, but the Constitution itself opted in favour of the minority, and declared its decision to be binding. But had not the party of Order subordinated the Constitution to the parliamentary majority on 13 June 1849 and again on 31 May 1850? Did not its whole previous policy rest on the subordination of paragraphs of the Constitution to the decisions of a parliamentary majority? Had it not left the Old Testament-style faith in the letter of the law to the democrats, and punished them for that faith? At the present moment, however, the revision of the Constitution meant nothing but the continuation of the President's authority, just as the continued existence of the Constitution meant nothing but the deposition of the President. Bonaparte was therefore acting in accordance with the will of the Assembly when he tore up the Constitution, and he followed the spirit of the Constitution when he broke up the Assembly.

The Assembly had declared the Constitution to be 'beyond the province of a majority', and its own rule along with it; by its vote it had abolished the Constitution and prolonged the President's power, while declaring at the same time that it was impossible either for the former to die or for the latter to live as long as it, the Assembly, continued to exist. The feet of its intended gravediggers could be heard just outside the door. While it debated the question of revision, Bonaparte removed General Baraguay d'Hilliers, who had shown himself to be irresolute, from the command of the First Army Division. He appointed instead General Magnan,[30] the victor of Lyons and the hero of the December days, one of his

29. This would be a new Constituent Assembly, elected for the purpose of revising the 1848 Constitution.

30. Bernard-Pierre Magnan was a Bonapartist general, prominent in suppressing the Lyons risings of 1831 and 1849 and the Paris rising of June 1848. He sat in both Assemblies and helped to organize the coup d'état of 2 December.

creatures, who had already more or less compromised himself for him in the days of Louis Philippe in connection with the Boulogne expedition.

By its decision on revision, the party of Order proved that it could neither rule nor serve, neither live nor die, neither tolerate the republic nor overthrow it, neither uphold the Constitution nor throw it overboard, neither cooperate with the President nor break with him. From whom, then, did it expect the resolution of all these contradictions? The calendar, the course of events, was supposed to bring the solution. The party of Order no longer had the impertinence to claim that it controlled events, and it therefore challenged the events to assume control over it, for the events were the power to which it had surrendered one position after another in the struggle against the people, until it stood impotent before it. It now chose this critical moment to retire from the stage and adjourn for three months, from 10 August to 4 November. The result was that the head of the executive was able to draw up his plan of campaign without disturbance, to strengthen his means of attack, select his instruments of attack, and fortify his positions.

Not only was the parliamentary party of Order split into its two great fractions, and each of these fractions divided within itself, but the party of Order within the parliament had also fallen out with the party of Order *outside* parliament. The spokesmen and writers of the bourgeoisie, its platform and its press, to put it briefly the ideologists of the bourgeoisie, had become alienated from the bourgeoisie itself. Representatives and represented faced each other in mutual incomprehension.

The Legitimists in the provinces, with their limited horizons and unlimited enthusiasm, censured their parliamentary leaders, Berryer and Falloux, for deserting to the Bonapartist camp and abandoning Henri V. Their understanding restricted to the level of the *fleur-de-lis*, they believed in the fall of man but not in diplomacy.

The commercial bourgeoisie's break with its politicians was far more fateful and decisive. The bourgeoisie did not reproach its representatives, as the Legitimists had reproached theirs, with having abandoned principles, but rather with having clung to principles which had become useless.

I pointed out earlier that after Fould's entry into the ministry the section of the commercial bourgeoisie which had held the lion's share of power under Louis Philippe, the *financial aristocracy*, had become Bonapartist. Fould represented Bonaparte's interests in the Bourse and the Bourse's interests before Bonaparte. A quotation from the European organ of the financial aristocracy, the London *Economist*, portrays its position most strikingly. In the issue of 1 February 1851, its Paris correspondent had this to say:

Now we have it stated from numerous quarters that France wishes above all things for repose. The President declares it in his message to the Legislative Assembly; it is echoed from the tribune; it is asserted in the journals; it is announced from the pulpit; *it is demonstrated by the sensitiveness of the public funds at the least prospect of disturbance, and their firmness the instant it is made manifest that the executive is victorious.*

In the issue of 29 November 1851, the *Economist* declared in its own name: '*The President is the guardian of order, and is now recognized as such on every Stock Exchange of Europe.*'[31]

The financial aristocracy thus condemned the party of Order's parliamentary struggle against the executive as a *disturbance of order*, and celebrated every victory of the President over its own supposed representatives as a *victory of order*. By the 'financial aristocracy' must be understood not merely the big loan promoters and speculators in public funds, whose interests, it is immediately apparent, coincide with the interests of the state power. The whole of the modern money market, the whole of the banking business, is most intimately interwoven with public credit. A part of their business capital is necessarily put out at interest in short-term public funds. Their deposits, the capital put at their disposal by merchants and industrialists and distributed by them among the same people, flow in part from the dividends of holders of government bonds. If in every epoch the stability of the state power has constituted the most essential requirement for the entire money market and its high priests, why should this not be even truer today, when every deluge threatens to sweep away the old state debts along with the old states?

The *industrial bourgeoisie* shared this fanaticism for order, and was also angered by the bickering between the parliamentary party of Order and the executive power. After their vote on 18 January, in connection with the dismissal of Changarnier,

---

31. The italics in these quotations are Marx's own.

Thiers, Anglès, Sainte-Beuve,[32] etc., received public admonitions in which their coalition with the Montagne was particularly scourged as a betrayal of order – criticism received indeed precisely from the industrial districts. As we have seen, the ostentatious bantering and petty intrigues which marked the struggle of the party of Order with the President deserved no better reception than this. Equally, however, this bourgeois party, which demanded that its representatives should let military power slip from its own parliament to an adventurer and pretender without the slightest resistance, was not even worth the intrigues which were wasted in its interests. The struggle to maintain its *public* interests, its own *class interests*, its *political power*, only troubled and upset it, as it was a disturbance of private business.

With scarcely any exception, the bourgeois dignitaries of the chief departmental towns, the municipal authorities, the judges of the commercial courts, etc., received Bonaparte in the most servile manner wherever his tours carried him, even when, as in Dijon, he roundly attacked the National Assembly, and the party of Order in particular.

When trade was good, as it still was at the beginning of 1851, the commercial bourgeoisie raged against any parliamentary struggle, lest trade be put out of sorts. When trade was bad, as it was continuously from the end of February 1851, the commercial bourgeoisie accused the parliamentary struggles of being the cause of stagnation and screamed for them to fall silent so that the voice of trade could again be heard. The revision debates fell precisely in this bad period for trade. Since it was the existence or non-existence of the present form of the state which was at stake here, the bourgeoisie felt it had all the more justification for demanding that its representatives finish with this excruciating interregnum and yet simultaneously maintain the status quo. There was no contradiction here. The end of the interregnum was understood to mean precisely its continuation, the postponement to a remote future of the moment of decision. The status quo could only be maintained in two ways: by the prolongation of Bonaparte's authority or by his retirement in accordance with the Constitution and the election of Cavaignac. One section of the bourgeoisie desired the latter solution and could give its representatives no

32. François-Ernest Anglès was a landed proprietor, and a deputy in the Legislative National Assembly. Pierre-Henri Sainte-Beuve was a manufacturer and landed proprietor, and a deputy in both Assemblies.

better advice than to keep quiet and steer clear of the burning question. They took the view that if their representatives did not speak, Bonaparte would not act. They wanted a parliamentary ostrich which would hide its head in order to remain invisible. Another section of the bourgeoisie wanted to leave Bonaparte sitting in the presidential chair because he was already there, and thus keep everything in the same old rut. They were indignant that their parliament had not openly broken the Constitution and abdicated without further ado.

The General Councils of the departments, those provincial representative bodies of the big bourgeoisie, met during the recess of the National Assembly from 25 August onwards. They declared for revision almost unanimously, thus against the Assembly and for Bonaparte.

The bourgeoisie demonstrated its anger with its literary representatives, its own press, even more unambiguously than its break with its *parliamentary representatives*. Not only France but the whole of Europe was astonished by the sentences of ruinous fines and shameless terms of imprisonment inflicted, on verdicts brought in by bourgeois juries, for every attack by bourgeois journalists on Bonaparte's usurpationist desires, and for every attempt by the press to defend the political rights of the bourgeoisie against the executive power.

As I have shown, the *parliamentary party of Order* condemned itself to acquiescence by its clamour for tranquillity. It declared the political rule of the bourgeoisie to be incompatible with the bourgeoisie's own safety and existence by destroying with its own hands the whole basis of its own regime, the parliamentary regime, in the struggle against the other classes of society. Similarly, the *extra-parliamentary mass of the bourgeoisie* invited Bonaparte to suppress and annihilate its speaking and writing part, its politicians and intellectuals, its platform and its press, by its own servility towards the President, its vilification of parliament, and its brutal mistreatment of its own press. It hoped that it would then be able to pursue its private affairs with full confidence under the protection of a strong and unrestricted government. It declared unequivocally that it yearned to get rid of its own political rule so as to be free of the attendant troubles and dangers.

And this bourgeoisie, which had already rebelled against the purely parliamentary and literary struggle for the rule of its own class and betrayed the leaders of that struggle, now dares to indict the proletariat retrospectively for failing to rise in a bloody life-and-death struggle on its behalf! This bourgeoisie, which had at every moment sacrificed its general class interests, i.e., its political interests, to the narrowest and most sordid private interests, and expected its representatives to make a similar sacrifice, now bewails the fact that the proletariat has sacrificed the bourgeoisie's ideal political interests to its own material interests. It poses as a pure soul, misunderstood and deserted at the decisive hour by a proletariat led astray by socialists. And it finds a general echo in the bourgeois world. Here I am not speaking, of course, of obscure German politicians or riff-raff of similar opinions. I refer, for example, to the *Economist*, as already quoted, which declared as late as 29 November 1851, that is, four days before the coup d'état, that Bonaparte was the 'guardian of order' and Thiers and Berryer were 'anarchists', and which on 27 December, after Bonaparte had quietened down these anarchists, was already screaming of the betrayal committed by the 'masses of ignorant, untrained, and stupid *proletaires*' against 'the skill, knowledge, discipline, mental influence, intellectual resources and moral weight of the middle and upper ranks'. The stupid, ignorant and vulgar mass was nothing other than the bourgeoisie itself.

In the year 1851 France had admittedly undergone a kind of minor trade crisis. At the end of February it emerged that there was a decline in exports in comparison with 1850; in March trade suffered and factories closed down; in April the position of the industrial departments appeared to be as desperate as after the February days; in May business had still not revived; as late as 28 June the portfolio of the Bank of France showed by the immense growth of deposits and the similarly great decrease in advances on bills of exchange that production was at a standstill. It was not until the middle of October that a progressive improvement of business again set in. The French bourgeoisie attributed this stagnation in trade to purely political causes, to the struggle between the legislature and the executive, to the insecurity of a merely provisional form of state, to the terrifying prospect of the second Sunday in May 1852. I do not wish to deny that all these circumstances had a depressing effect on a number of branches of industry in Paris and the provinces. But in every case the impact of political conditions was only local and inconsiderable. Does this need any other proof than the fact that the improvement of trade occurred towards the middle of October, at the precise moment when the political situation grew worse, the political horizon darkened, and a thunderbolt from Elysium was expected at any time? Let it be said in passing that the French bourgeois, whose 'skill, knowledge, mental insight and intellectual resources' reach no further than the end of his nose, could have found the cause of his commercial misery right under his nose for the whole duration of the Great Exhibition in London. While factories were closed down in France, commercial bankruptcies broke out in England. The industrial panic reached a climax in France in April and May; the commercial panic reached a climax in England in April and May. The English woollen industry suffered alongside the French woollen industry; English silk manufacture suffered alongside French silk manufacture. The English cotton mills continued to operate, but without producing the same profits as in 1849 and 1850. The only difference was that the crisis in France was industrial, in England commercial; that in France the factories stood still, while in England they extended their operations, but under less favourable conditions than in the preceding years; that in France it was exports which received the fiercest blows, in England imports. The reason for both situations was obvious, although not to be found within the confines of the French political horizon. 1849 and 1850 were years of very great material prosperity, and of an overproduction which only made itself apparent in 1851. At the beginning of the year this trend was very much strengthened by the prospect of the Industrial Exhibition.[33] Special circumstances also made their contribution: the initial partial failure of the cotton crop in 1850 and 1851, followed by the certainty that there would be a bigger cotton crop than expected; the initial rise followed by the sudden fall, in other words, the fluctuations, in the price of cotton; the fact that the raw silk crop, in France at least, had turned out below the average yield; and finally the fact that woollen manufacture had expanded so much since 1848 that wool production could not keep up with it, so that the price of raw wool rose out of all proportion to the price of woollen manufactures. Here, then, in the raw material of three industries producing for the world market we already have three reasons for a stagnation in trade. Leaving aside these special circumstances, the apparent crisis of 1851 was simply the halt which overproduction and excessive speculation always have to come to in the course of the industrial cycle, before they collect together all their

33. The London 'Great Exhibition' of 1851.

reserves of strength in order to drive feverishly through the final phase of the cycle and return to their starting-point, the *general trade crisis*. During such interruptions in the course of trade commercial bankruptcies break out in England, while in France industry itself is reduced to immobility, partly because it is forced into retreat by the competition of the English in all markets, which becomes intolerable at precisely such moments, partly because, producing luxury goods, it is a preferential target of attack in every business stagnation. Thus, apart from the general crises, France undergoes her own national trade crises, which are nevertheless determined and conditioned far more by the general state of the world market than by French local influences. It will not be without interest to contrast the sober judgement of the English bourgeois with the prejudiced view of the French bourgeois. One of the biggest Liverpool trading firms wrote in its annual trading report for 1851:

Few years have more thoroughly belied the anticipations formed at their commencement than the one just closed; instead of the great prosperity which was almost unanimously looked for it has proved one of the most discouraging that has been seen for the last quarter of a century – this, of course, refers to the mercantile, not the manufacturing classes. And yet there certainly were grounds for anticipating the reverse at the beginning of the year – stocks of produce were moderate, money was abundant, and food was cheap, a plentiful harvest well secured, unbroken peace on the Continent, and no political or fiscal disturbances at home; indeed, the wings of commerce were never more unfettered ... To what source, then, is this disastrous result to be attributed? We believe to *over-trading* both in imports and exports. Unless our merchants will put more stringent limits to their freedom of action, nothing but a triennial panic can keep us in check.[34]

Now imagine the French bourgeois, imagine how in the midst of this business his trade-crazy brain is tortured, whirled around and stunned by rumours of a coup d'état, by rumours that universal suffrage will be restored, by the struggle between parliament and the executive, by the Fronde-like war between Orleanists and Legitimists, by the communist conspiracies in southern France, by alleged *jacqueries* in the departments of Nièvre and Cher, by the publicity campaigns of the various presidential candidates, by the cheap and showy slogans of the newspapers, by the threats of the republicans to uphold the Constitution and universal suffrage

34. *Economist*, 10 January 1852.

by force of arms, by the preaching of the *émigré* heroes *in partibus*, who announced that the world would come to an end on the second Sunday in May 1852 – think of all this, and you will understand why the bourgeois, in this unspeakable, clamorous chaos of fusion, revision, prorogation, constitution, conspiration, coalition, emigration, usurpation and revolution, madly snorts at his parliamentary republic: *Rather an end with terror than a terror without end.*

Bonaparte understood this cry. His powers of comprehension had been sharpened by the growing vehemence of creditors who saw in every sunset a movement of the stars in protest against their terrestrial bills of exchange, since every sunset brought nearer settlement day, the second Sunday in May 1852. They had turned into veritable astrologers. The National Assembly had deprived Bonaparte of any hope of a constitutional prolongation of his authority; the candidature of the prince de Joinville did not permit any further hesitation.

If ever an event cast its shadow forward well in advance of its occurrence, it was Bonaparte's coup d'état. Scarcely a month after his election, on 29 January, he had already made a proposal to Changarnier to this effect. His own Prime Minister, Odilon Barrot, had secretly denounced the policy of coup d'état in the summer of 1849, and Thiers had denounced it openly in the winter of 1850. In May 1851 Persigny had tried once more to win Changarnier for the coup; the *Messager de l'Assemblée*[35] had published a report of this negotiation. During every parliamentary storm, the Bonapartist newspapers threatened a coup d'état, and the nearer the crisis approached, the louder their tone became. In the orgies at which Bonaparte celebrated every night in company with the men and women of the *swell mob*,[36] when the hour of midnight approached and rich libations had loosened tongues and heated imaginations, the coup d'état was fixed for the following morning. Swords were drawn, glasses clinked, deputies were thrown out of the window, and the imperial mantle fell on Bonaparte's shoulders, until the following morning once more exorcized the ghost, and an astounded Paris learnt of the danger it had once again escaped from vestals who lacked reserve and paladins who lacked discretion. During the months of September and October rumours of a coup came thick and fast.

35. A newspaper which appeared in Paris from February to December 1851.
36. In English in the original.

At the same time the shadow took on colour, like a variegated daguerreotype. If one looks up the European daily newspapers for the months of September and October one finds, word for word, suggestions like the following: 'Paris is full of rumours of a coup d'état. The capital is to be filled with troops during the night, and the next morning decrees will be issued dissolving the National Assembly, declaring the department of Seine in a state of siege, restoring universal suffrage and appealing to the people. Bonaparte is said to be looking for ministers who will execute these illegal decrees.' The news reports which brought this information always closed with the fateful word '*postponed*'. The coup d'état was always Bonaparte's obsession. It was with this idea in his mind that he had again set foot on French soil. He was possessed by it to such an extent that he repeatedly betrayed it and blurted it out. He was so weak that he gave it up just as often. The shadow of the coup had become so familiar to the Parisians as a spectre that they were unwilling to believe in it when it finally appeared as flesh and blood. It was therefore neither the discreet reticence of the head of the Society of 10 December nor the unexpected nature of the attack on the National Assembly which allowed the coup d'état to succeed. If it succeeded, it was as a necessary and inevitable result of the previous course of development, which occurred in spite of Bonaparte's indiscretion and with the Assembly's foreknowledge.

On 10 October Bonaparte announced to his ministers his decision to restore universal suffrage; on 16 October they resigned, and on 26 October Paris learnt of the formation of the Thorigny[37] ministry. At the same time Carlier was replaced by Maupas[38] as Prefect of Police, and the head of the First Army Division, Magnan, concentrated the most reliable regiments in the capital. On 4 November the National Assembly resumed its sittings. It could do no more than repeat the course it had gone through in a short, succinct summary, and prove that it was buried only after it had died.

The first outpost it had lost in the struggle with the executive was the ministry. It had solemnly to admit this loss by accepting at full value the Thorigny ministry, which was a ministry in

37. Pierre-François Thorigny was a lawyer and a Bonapartist, appointed Minister of the Interior in October 1851.

38. Charlemagne de Maupas was a lawyer and a Bonapartist, Paris Prefect of Police in 1851, one of the organizers of the coup d'état of 2 December, and later Minister of Police.

appearance only. The Standing Commission received Monsieur Giraud[39] with laughter when he presented himself in the name of the new ministers. Such a weak ministry for such strong measures as the restoration of universal suffrage! But that was precisely the intention, to accomplish nothing *in* the Assembly and to accomplish everything *against* the Assembly.

On the very first day of the new session, the National Assembly received Bonaparte's message demanding the restoration of universal suffrage and the abolition of the law of 31 May 1850. On the same day his ministers introduced a decree to this effect. The Assembly immediately rejected the ministers' motion of urgency, and on 13 November rejected the law itself by 355 votes to 348. Thus it tore up its mandate once more; it confirmed once again that it had transformed itself from the freely elected representation of the people into the usurping parliament of a class; and it acknowledged once again that the muscles which connected the parliamentary head with the body of the nation had been cut in two by the parliament itself.

While the executive appealed from the National Assembly to the people with its motion to restore universal suffrage, the legislature appealed from the people to the army by its Quaestors Bill. The aim of the Quaestors Bill was to establish its right to requisition troops directly and to set up a parliamentary armed force. But by appointing the army as arbitrator between itself and the people, between itself and Bonaparte, by recognizing the army as the decisive power in the state, the Assembly only confirmed the fact that it had long since abandoned any claim to rule over the army. By debating its right to requisition troops, instead of immediately requisitioning them, it revealed its doubts about its own power. By rejecting the Quaestors Bill it publicly admitted its powerlessness. The bill was defeated by 108 votes, and it was the Montagne which decided the issue. It found itself in the position of Buridan's ass, though in this case it had not to decide which was the more attractive of two bundles of hay but which was the harder of two showers of blows. On the one side there was the fear of Changarnier; on the other side there was the fear of Bonaparte. One must admit that the circumstances were not conducive to heroism.

39. Charles-Joseph Giraud was a lawyer who was made Minister of Education in the Thorigny cabinet.

On 18 November an amendment was moved to the law on municipal elections introduced by the party of Order, providing for a
reduction of the residence requirement for municipal electors from
three years to one year. The amendment was defeated by a single
vote, but it immediately became apparent that this single vote had
been a mistake. By splitting up into its hostile fractions, the party
of Order had long ago lost its independent parliamentary majority.
It now showed that there was no longer any parliamentary majority
at all. The National Assembly had become *incapable of transacting
business*. Its atomized constituents were no longer held together by
any cohesive force; it had used up its last supply of breath. It was
dead.

Finally, a few days before the catastrophe, the extra-parliamentary
mass of the bourgeoisie once more solemnly confirmed its breach
with the bourgeoisie in parliament. Thiers, as a parliamentary hero,
had received an exceptionally strong dose of the incurable sickness
of parliamentary cretinism. After the Assembly itself had died, he
devised a new parliamentary intrigue together with the Council of
State. This was a law of responsibility, which was supposed to confine
the President firmly within the limits of the Constitution. Bonaparte,
however, had other ideas. On 15 September, when he laid the foundation stone of the new market halls in Paris, he had, like a second
Masaniello,[40] enchanted the *dames des halles*, the fishwives – of
course, one fishwife outweighed seventeen burgraves in real power.
A little later, after the introduction of the Quaestors Bill, he roused
the enthusiasm of the lieutenants being entertained in the Elysée.
And now, on 25 November, he swept off their feet the members of
the industrial bourgeoisie who had assembled at the Circus to receive
from his hands prize medals for the London Industrial Exhibition. I
give here the significant section of his speech, in the version given by
the *Journal des Débats*:

With such unhoped-for successes, I am justified in saying once more
how great the French republic would be if it were permitted to pursue
its real interests and reform its institutions, instead of being constantly
disturbed by demagogues on one side and monarchical hallucinations
on the other. [*Loud, stormy and repeated applause from all parts of the
amphitheatre.*] The monarchical hallucinations hinder all progress and
all important branches of industry. In place of progress there is only

40. Masaniello was a Neapolitan fisherman, leader of a popular rising against Spanish rule in 1647.

struggle. One sees men who were previously the most zealous upholders of the royal authority and prerogative become partisans of a Convention merely in order to weaken the authority that has sprung from universal suffrage. [*Loud and repeated applause.*] We see men who have suffered most from the revolution, and have deplored it most, provoke a new one, and do this merely in order to fetter the will of the nation . . . I promise you tranquillity for the future, *etc. etc.* [*Cries of bravo, stormy acclamations.*]

The industrial bourgeoisie thus applauded the coup d'état on 2 December, the destruction of the Assembly, the downfall of its own rule, and the dictatorship of Bonaparte, with servile cries of bravo. The thunder of applause on 25 November was answered by the thunder of cannon on 4 December, and it was on the house of Monsieur Sallandrouze,[41] who had clapped most, that they clapped most of the bombs.

When Cromwell dissolved the Long Parliament, he went alone into its midst, drew out his watch so that it should not exist a minute beyond the time limit he had set, and drove out the members of parliament individually with jovial and humorous invective. Napoleon, though smaller than his model, at least went to the Council of the Five Hundred on 18 Brumaire and read out its sentence of death, albeit in an uneasy voice. The second Bonaparte, who, by the way, found himself in possession of an executive power very different from that of Cromwell or Napoleon, sought his model not in the annals of world history but in the annals of the Society of 10 December, in the annals of the criminal courts. He robbed the Bank of France of twenty-five million francs; he bought General Magnan with a million and the soldiers with fifteen francs each and liquor; he held a meeting with his accomplices in secret, like a thief in the night; he had the houses of the most dangerous parliamentary leaders broken into and Cavaignac, Lamoricière, Le Flô, Changarnier, Charras, Thiers, Baze, etc., dragged from their beds; he had the main squares of Paris and the parliament buildings occupied by troops; and then, early in the morning, he had ostentatious placards put up on all the walls, proclaiming the dissolution of the National Assembly and the Council of State, the restoration of universal suffrage, and the imposition of a state of siege in the Seine depart-

41. Charles Sallandrouze de Lamornais was an industrialist, and a deputy in the Constituent Assembly; at first an Orleanist, he later supported the coup d'état.

ment. Shortly afterwards he also inserted a false document in the *Moniteur*, purporting to show that some influential parliamentary names had grouped themselves around him and formed a consultative commission.

The rump parliament, assembled in the *mairie* of the tenth arrondissement and composed mainly of Legitimists and Orleanists, voted the deposition of Bonaparte amid repeated cries of 'Long live the republic', vainly harangued the gaping crowds in front of the building, and was finally dragged away, escorted by a company of the African infantry, first to the d'Orsay barracks, and later, after being packed into prison vans, to the prisons of Mazas, Ham and Vincennes. Thus ended the party of Order, the Legislative Assembly, and the February revolution. Before we hurry on to our conclusion, let us give a short summary of the history of the February revolution:

1. *First period*. From 24 February to 4 May 1848. February period. Prologue. Universal brotherhood swindle.

2. *Second period*. Period of the establishment of the republic and of the Constituent National Assembly.

(a) 4 May to 25 June 1848. Struggle of all classes against the proletariat. Defeat of the proletariat in the June days.

(b) 25 June to 10 December 1848. Dictatorship of the pure bourgeois republicans. Drafting of the Constitution. Proclamation of a state of siege in Paris. The bourgeois dictatorship ended on 10 December by the election of Bonaparte as President.

(c) 20 December 1848 to 28 May 1849. Struggle of the Constituent Assembly with Bonaparte and with the party of Order in alliance with him. End of the Constituent Assembly. Fall of the republican bourgeoisie.

3. *Third period*. Period of the *constitutional republic* and the *Legislative National Assembly*.

(a) 28 May 1849 to 13 June 1849. Struggle of the petty bourgeoisie with the bourgeoisie and with Bonaparte. Defeat of petty-bourgeois democracy.

(b) 13 June 1849 to 31 May 1850. Parliamentary dictatorship of the party of Order. It completes its supremacy by abolishing universal suffrage but loses the parliamentary ministry.

(c) 31 May 1850 to 2 December 1851. Struggle between the parliamentary bourgeoisie and Bonaparte.

(i) 31 May 1850 to 12 January 1851. The Assembly loses the supreme command of the army.

(ii) 12 January 1851 to 11 April 1851. It fails in its attempts to regain the administrative power. The party of Order loses its independent parliamentary majority. Its coalition with the republicans and the Montagne.

(iii) 11 April to 9 October 1851. Attempts at revision, fusion and prorogation. The party of Order dissolves into its individual components. The breach between the bourgeois parliament and press and the mass of the bourgeoisie is consolidated.

(iv) 9 October to 2 December 1851. Open breach between the Assembly and the executive. The Assembly performs its dying act and succumbs, left in the lurch by its own class, by the army, and by all other classes. End of the parliamentary regime and of bourgeois rule. Victory of Bonaparte. The empire is restored as a parody.

VII

The *social republic* appeared on the threshold of the February revolution as a phrase, as a prophecy. In the June days of 1848 it was drowned in the blood of the Paris proletariat, but it haunted the succeeding acts of the drama like a ghost. The *democratic republic* also announced its appearance on the stage. On 13 June 1849 it fizzled out, together with its *petty-bourgeois* supporters, who took flight, but at the same time advertised themselves with redoubled boastfulness. The *parliamentary republic*, together with the bourgeoisie, took possession of the entire stage and enjoyed its existence to the full, but it was buried on 2 December 1851 while the coalition of royalists cried out in anguish: 'Long live the republic!'

The French bourgeoisie revolted at the prospect of the rule of the labouring proletariat; it has brought the lumpenproletariat into power, led by the head of the Society of 10 December. The bourgeoisie held France in breathless fear of the future terrors of red anarchy; Bonaparte discounted this future for it when, on 4 December, he had the refined bourgeois citizens of the Boulevard Montmartre and the Boulevard des Italiens shot down at their windows in alcoholic enthusiasm by the army of order. It deified the sword; it is ruled by the sword. It destroyed the revolutionary press; its own press has been destroyed. It placed popular meetings under police supervision; its salons are under the supervision of the police. It dissolved the democratic National Guard; its own National Guard has been dissolved. It imposed a state of siege; a state of siege has been imposed upon it. It replaced juries with military commissions; its juries have been replaced with military commissions. It subjected the education of the people to the priests; the priests have subjected it to their own education. It transported without trial; it is being transported without trial. It suppressed every stirring in society by means of the state power; every stirring in its society is crushed by means of the state power. It rebelled against its own politicians and intellectuals out of enthusiasm for its purse; its politicians and intellectuals have been swept away, but its purse is being plundered now that its mouth is gagged and its pen broken. The bourgeoisie indefatigably cried out to the revolution what Saint Arsenius cried out to the Christians: '*Fuge, tace, quiesce!*' 'Run away, keep quiet, and don't make a disturbance!'[42] Bonaparte cries to the bourgeoisie: '*Fuge, tace, quiesce!*' 'Run away, keep quiet, and don't make a disturbance!'

The French bourgeoisie long ago solved Napoleon's dilemma: '*Dans cinquante ans l'Europe sera républicaine ou cosaque.*'[43] Their solution was the 'Cossack republic'. That work of art, the bourgeois republic, has not been distorted into a monstrous shape by the black magic of a Circe. It has lost nothing but the appearance of respectability. The parliamentary republic contained present-day France in finished form. It only required a bayonet thrust for the abscess to burst and the monster to spring forth before our eyes.

Why did the Paris proletariat not rise in revolt after 2 December?

As yet, the overthrow of the bourgeoisie had only been decreed, the decree had not been carried out. Any serious proletarian rising would at once have revived the bourgeoisie, reconciled it with the army, and ensured a second June defeat for the workers.

On 4 December the proletariat was incited to fight by the bourgeois and the *épicier*.[44] On the evening of that day several legions of the National Guard promised to appear on the scene of battle armed and uniformed. For the bourgeois and the shop-

42. This was the advice given by Arsenius when he left Rome to become a hermit in the Egyptian desert in the early fifth century.

43. In fifty years Europe will be republican or Cossack.

44. Shopkeeper – a rather pejorative term.

keeper had found out that in one of the decrees of 2 December Bonaparte had abolished the secret ballot and advised them to record their 'yes' or their 'no' in the official registers after their names. Bonaparte was intimidated by the resistance of 4 December. During the night he had placards posted on all the street corners of Paris, announcing the restoration of the secret ballot. The bourgeois and the shopkeeper believed they had achieved their aim. It was the bourgeois and the shopkeeper who failed to appear next morning.

Bonaparte had robbed the Paris proletariat of its leaders, the barricade commanders, by a surprise attack during the night of 1–2 December. The proletariat was an army without officers, and it was in any case unwilling to fight under the banner of the Montagnards because of the memories of June 1848, June 1849, and May 1850. It left its vanguard, the secret societies, to save the insurrectional honour of Paris, which the bourgeoisie had so unresistingly abandoned to the soldiery, so that Bonaparte was later able to disarm the National Guard with the derisive justification that he was afraid its weapons would be misused against itself by the anarchists!

'*C'est le triomphe complet et définitif du socialisme.*'[45] This was Guizot's characterization of 2 December. But if the overthrow of the parliamentary republic contains within itself the germ of the triumph of the proletarian revolution, its first tangible result was *the victory of Bonaparte over the Assembly, of the executive over the legislature, of force without words over the force of words*. In the Assembly the nation raised its general will to the level of law, i.e., it made the law of the ruling class its general will. It then renounced all will of its own in face of the executive and subjected itself to the superior command of an alien will, to authority. The opposition between executive and legislature expresses the opposition between a nation's heteronomy and its autonomy. France therefore seems to have escaped the despotism of a class only to fall back beneath the despotism of an individual, and indeed beneath the authority of an individual without authority. The struggle seems to have reached the compromise that all classes fall on their knees, equally mute and equally impotent, before the rifle butt.

But the revolution is thorough. It is still on its journey through purgatory. It goes about its business methodically. By 2 December

45. It is the complete and final triumph of socialism.

1851 it had completed one half of its preparatory work; it is now completing the other half. First of all it perfected the parliamentary power, in order to be able to overthrow it. Now, having attained this, it is perfecting the *executive power*, reducing it to its purest expression, isolating it, and pitting itself against it as the sole object of attack, in order to concentrate all its forces of destruction against it. And when it has completed this, the second half of its preliminary work, Europe will leap from its seat and exultantly exclaim: 'Well worked, old mole!'[46]

The executive power possesses an immense bureaucratic and military organization, an ingenious and broadly based state machinery, and an army of half a million officials alongside the actual army, which numbers a further half million. This frightful parasitic body, which surrounds the body of French society like a caul and stops up all its pores, arose in the time of the absolute monarchy, with the decay of the feudal system, which it helped to accelerate. The seignorial privileges of the landowners and towns were transformed into attributes of the state power, the feudal dignitaries became paid officials, and the variegated medieval pattern of conflicting plenary authorities became the regulated plan of a state authority characterized by a centralization and division of labour reminiscent of a factory. The task of the first French revolution was to destroy all separate local, territorial, urban and provincial powers in order to create the civil unity of the nation. It had to carry further the centralization that the absolute monarchy had begun, but at the same time it had to develop the extent, the attributes and the number of underlings of the governmental power. Napoleon perfected this state machinery. The Legitimist and July monarchies only added a greater division of labour, which grew in proportion to the creation of new interest groups, and therefore new material for state administration, by the division of labour within bourgeois society. Every *common* interest was immediately detached from society, opposed to it as a higher, *general* interest, torn away from the self-activity of the individual members of society and made a subject for governmental activity, whether it was a bridge, a schoolhouse, the communal property of a village community, or the railways, the

46. Hamlet's actual words in *Hamlet* I, v, 162, are, 'Well said old mole, canst work i' th' ground so fast?' Marx's '*Brav gewühlt, alter Maulwurf*' is a condensation, with the twist that *wühlen*, besides meaning to work, grub, burrow, also means to agitate, stir up, foment discontent. See below, p. 300.

national wealth and the national university of France. Finally, the parliamentary republic was compelled in its struggle against the revolution to strengthen by means of repressive measures the resources and centralization of governmental power. All political upheavals perfected this machine instead of smashing it. The parties that strove in turn for mastery regarded possession of this immense state edifice as the main booty for the victor.

However, under the absolute monarchy, during the first French revolution, and under Napoleon, bureaucracy was only the means of preparing the class rule of the bourgeoisie. Under the Restoration, Louis Philippe, and the parliamentary republic, on the other hand, it was the instrument of the ruling class, however much it strove for power in its own right.

Only under the second Bonaparte does the state seem to have attained a completely autonomous position. The state machine has established itself so firmly *vis-à-vis* civil society that the only leader it needs is the head of the Society of 10 December, an adventurer who has rushed in from abroad and been chosen as leader by a drunken soldiery, which he originally bought with liquor and sausages, and to which he constantly has to throw more sausages. This explains the shamefaced despair, the feeling of terrible humiliation and degradation which weighs upon France's breast and makes her catch her breath. France feels dishonoured.

But the state power does not hover in mid-air. Bonaparte represents a class, indeed he represents the most numerous class of French society, the *small peasant proprietors*.

Just as the Bourbons were the dynasty of big landed property and the Orleans the dynasty of money, so the Bonapartes are the dynasty of the peasants, i.e., of the mass of the French people. The chosen hero of the peasantry is not the Bonaparte who submitted to the bourgeois parliament but the Bonaparte who dispersed it. For three years the towns succeeded in falsifying the meaning of the election of 10 December and swindling the peasants out of the restoration of the empire. The election of 10 December 1848 was completed only with the coup d'état of 2 December 1851.

The small peasant proprietors form an immense mass, the members of which live in the same situation but do not enter into manifold relationships with each other. Their mode of operation isolates them instead of bringing them into mutual intercourse. This isolation is strengthened by the wretched state of France's means of communication and by the poverty of the peasants.

Their place of operation, the smallholding, permits no division of labour in its cultivation, no application of science and therefore no diversity of development, variety of talent, or wealth of social relationships. Each individual peasant family is almost self-sufficient; it directly produces the greater part of its own consumption and therefore obtains its means of life more through exchange with nature than through intercourse with society. The smallholding, the peasant and the family; next door, another smallholding, another peasant and another family. A bunch of these makes up a village, and a bunch of villages makes up a department. Thus the great mass of the French nation is formed by the simple addition of isomorphous magnitudes, much as potatoes in a sack form a sack of potatoes. In so far as millions of families live under economic conditions of existence that separate their mode of life, their interests and their cultural formation from those of the other classes and bring them into conflict with those classes, they form a class. In so far as these small peasant proprietors are merely connected on a local basis, and the identity of their interests fails to produce a feeling of community, national links or a political organization, they do not form a class. They are therefore incapable of asserting their class interest in their own name, whether through a parliament or through a convention.[47] They cannot represent themselves; they must be represented. Their representative must appear simultaneously as their master, as an authority over them, an unrestricted governmental power that protects them from the other classes and sends them rain and sunshine from above. The political influence of the small peasant proprietors is therefore ultimately expressed in the executive subordinating society to itself.

Historical tradition produced the French peasants' belief that a miracle would occur, that a man called Napoleon would restore all their glory. And an individual turned up who pretended to be that man, because he bore the name of Napoleon, thanks to the stipulation of the Code Napoléon that '*la récherche de la paternité est interdite*'.[48] After twenty years of vagabondage and a series of grotesque adventures the prophecy was fulfilled and the man became Emperor of the French. The nephew's obsession was realized, because it coincided with the obsession of the most numerous class of the French people.

47. I.e., a revolutionary assembly like that of 1792–5.
48. Inquiry into paternity is forbidden.

But the objection will be made: What about the peasant risings in half of France, the army's murderous forays against them, and their imprisonment and transportation *en masse*?

Since Louis XIV, France has experienced no corresponding persecution of the peasants 'for demagogic practices'.

This point should be clearly understood: the Bonaparte dynasty represents the conservative, not the revolutionary peasant: the peasant who wants to consolidate the condition of his social existence, the smallholding, not the peasant who strikes out beyond it. It does not represent the country people who want to overthrow the old order by their own energies, in alliance with the towns, but the precise opposite, those who are gloomily enclosed within this old order and want to see themselves and their small-holdings saved and given preferential treatment by the ghost of the Empire. It represents the peasant's superstition, not his enlightenment; his prejudice, not his judgement; his past, not his future; his modern Vendée, not his modern Cevennes.[49]

Three years of hard rule by the parliamentary republic had freed some of the French peasants from the Napoleonic illusion and revolutionized them, if only superficially, but they were violently suppressed by the bourgeoisie whenever they started to move. Under the parliamentary republic the modern consciousness of the peasant fought with his traditional consciousness. The process moved forward in the form of an unceasing struggle between the schoolmasters and the priests. The bourgeoisie struck down the schoolmasters. For the first time the peasants endeavoured to take up an independent attitude in face of the government's activities. This was shown in the continual conflict between the mayors and the prefects. The bourgeoisie deposed the mayors. Finally, during the period of the parliamentary republic the peasants of various localities rose against their own offspring, the army. The bourgeoisie punished them with states of siege and military expeditions. And this same bourgeoisie is now exclaiming over the stupidity of the masses, the *vile multitude*[50] which allowed them to betray it to Bonaparte. The bourgeoisie itself violently strength-

49. Vendée, in Brittany, was the focus of royalist revolt during the first French revolution. Cevennes was the area of southern France in which the peasant rising of the years 1702–5 took place, the 'revolt of the Camisards'. It was a rising of Protestants for freedom of conscience, and also against feudal dues.

50. In English in the original.

ened the imperialist leanings of the peasant class and kept in being the conditions that form the breeding-ground of this peasant religion. The bourgeoisie is naturally bound to fear the stupidity of the masses as long as they remain conservative, and the discernment of the masses as soon as they become revolutionary.

In the risings after the coup d'état a section of the French peasantry protested, arms in hand, against its own vote of 10 December 1848. The school these peasants had gone through since 1848 had sharpened their wits. But they had signed themselves away to the underworld of history, and history kept them to their word. Moreover, the majority was still so prejudiced that the peasant population of precisely the reddest departments voted openly for Bonaparte. In its view the National Assembly had hindered his progress. He had now merely broken the fetters imposed by the towns on the will of the country. Here and there the peasants even entertained the grotesque idea that a convention could co-exist with Napoleon.

After the first revolution had transformed the peasants from a state of semi-serfdom into free landed proprietors, Napoleon confirmed and regulated the conditions under which they could exploit undisturbed the soil of France, which had now devolved on them for the first time, and satisfy their new-found passion for property. But the French peasant is now succumbing to his smallholding itself, to the division of the land, the form of property consolidated in France by Napoleon. It was the material conditions which made the feudal French peasant a small proprietor and Napoleon an emperor. Two generations have been sufficient to produce the inevitable consequence: a progressive deterioration of agriculture and a progressive increase in peasant indebtedness. The 'Napoleonic' form of property, which was the condition for the liberation and enrichment of the French rural population at the beginning of the nineteenth century, has developed in the course of that century into the legal foundation of their enslavement and their poverty. And precisely this law is the first of the 'Napoleonic ideas' which the second Bonaparte has to uphold. If he still shares with the peasants the illusion that the cause of their ruin is to be sought, not in the smallholding itself, but outside it, in the influence of secondary circumstances, his experiments will burst like soap bubbles at their first contact with the relations of production.

The economic development of the smallholding has profoundly

distorted the relation of the peasants to the other classes of society. Under Napoleon the fragmentation of landed property in the countryside supplemented free competition and the beginning of large industry in the towns. The peasant class was the ubiquitous protest against the landed aristocracy which had just been overthrown. The roots which the smallholding struck in French soil deprived feudalism of all nutriment. Its fences formed the bourgeoisie's system of natural fortifications against surprise attacks on the part of its old overlords. But in the course of the nineteenth century the urban usurer replaced the feudal lord; the mortgage on the land replaced its feudal obligations; bourgeois capital replaced aristocratic landed property. The peasant's smallholding is now only the pretext that allows the capitalist to draw profits, interest and rent from the soil, while leaving the tiller himself to work out how to extract the wage for his labour. The mortgage debt burdening the soil of France imposes on the French peasantry an interest payment equal to the annual interest on the entire British national debt. Owing to this enslavement by capital, inevitably brought about by its own development, small peasant property has transformed the mass of the French nation into troglodytes. Sixteen million peasants (including women and children) live in hovels, many of which have only one opening, others only two, and the rest, the most fortunate cases, only three. Windows are to a house what the five senses are to a head. The bourgeois order, which at the beginning of the century made the state do sentry duty over the newly arisen smallholding, and manured it with laurels, has become a vampire that sucks out its blood and brains and throws them into the alchemist's cauldron of capital. The Code Napoléon is now merely the lawbook for distraints on chattels, forced sales and compulsory auctions. To the four million (including children, etc.) officially admitted paupers, vagabonds, criminals and prostitutes in France must be added five million who totter on the precipice of non-existence and either wander around the countryside itself or, with their rags and their children, continually desert the country for the towns and the towns for the country. The interests of the peasants are therefore no longer consonant with the interests of the bourgeoisie, as they were under Napoleon, but in opposition to those interests, in opposition to capital. They therefore find their natural ally and leader in the *urban proletariat*, whose task is the overthrow of the bourgeois order. But the *strong and unrestricted government* – and this is the second '*Napoleonic idea*' which the second Napoleon has to implement – is required to defend this 'material' order by force. This '*ordre matériel*' also serves as the catchword in all Bonaparte's proclamations against the rebellious peasants.

Besides the mortgage which capital imposes on it, the small-holding is burdened by *taxation*. Taxation is the source of life for the bureaucracy, the army, the priests and the court; in short, it is the source of life for the whole executive apparatus. Strong government and heavy taxes are identical. By its very nature, small peasant property is suitable to serve as the foundation of an all-powerful and innumerable bureaucracy. It creates a uniform level of relationships and persons over the whole surface of the land. Hence it also allows a uniformity of intervention from a supreme centre into all points of this uniform mass. It annihilates the aristocratic intermediate levels between the mass of the people and the state power. On all sides, therefore, it calls forth the direct interference of this state power and the interposition of its organs without mediation. Finally, it produces an unemployed surplus population which can find room neither on the land nor in the towns, and which accordingly grasps at state office as providing a kind of respectable charity, thus provoking the creation of state posts. Napoleon repaid the forced taxes with interest by the new markets he opened with the bayonet, and by plundering the European continent. Previously these taxes were an incentive to peasant industry, but now they rob it of its last resources and put the finishing touch to the peasant's inability to resist pauperism. And an enormous bureaucracy, with gold braid and a fat belly, is the 'Napoleonic idea' which is most congenial of all to the second Bonaparte. It could not be otherwise, for he has been forced to create, alongside the real classes of society, an artificial caste for which the maintenance of his regime is a question of self-preservation. One of his first financial operations was therefore to raise officials' salaries to their old level and to create new sinecures.

Another 'Napoleonic idea' is the rule of the *priests* as an instrument of government. But if the newly arisen smallholding was naturally religious in its accord with society, its dependence on natural forces, and its subjection to the authority protecting it from on high, it is naturally irreligious when ruined by debts, at variance with society and authority, and driven beyond its own limitations. Heaven was a very nice addition to the narrow strip of land just obtained, especially as it produced the weather; it becomes an insult as soon as it is offered as a substitute for the small-holding. The priest then appears as merely the anointed bloodhound of the terrestrial police – another 'Napoleonic idea'. Next time the expedition against Rome will take place in France itself, but in a sense opposite to that of Monsieur Montalembert.[51]

Lastly, the culminating point of the 'Napoleonic idea' is the predominance of the *army*. The army was the small peasant proprietors' *point d'honneur*, the peasant himself transformed into a hero, defending his new possessions against external enemies, glorifying his recently won nationhood, and plundering and revolutionizing the world. The uniform was the peasant's national costume, the war was his poetry, the smallholding, extended and rounded off in imagination, was his fatherland, and patriotism was the ideal form of his sense of property. But the French peasant now has to defend his property, not against the Cossacks, but against the *huissier*[52] and the tax collector. The smallholding lies no longer in the so-called fatherland, but in the register of mortgages. The army itself is no longer the flower of peasant youth, but the dregs of the peasant lumpenproletariat. To a large extent it consists of *remplaçants*, substitutes, just as the second Bonaparte is himself only a substitute for Napoleon. It now performs its deeds of valour by driving and hunting the peasants like chamois or pheasants, in the course of *gendarme* duty, and if the internal contradictions of his system drive the head of the Society of 10 December to send his army over the French border, it will reap not laurels but a sound thrashing, after committing a few acts of brigandage.

All the 'Napoleonic ideas' are ideas of the undeveloped small-holding in its heyday. So much is evident. It is equally true that they are an absurdity for the smallholding that has outlived its day. They are only the hallucinations of its death agony, words made into phrases, spirits made into ghosts. But this parody of the empire was necessary to free the mass of the French nation from the burden of tradition and to bring out the antagonism between the state power and society in its pure form. With the progressive disintegration of small peasant property the state structure erected upon it begins to collapse. The political centraliza-

---

51. Montalembert was a leading supporter of the expedition to crush the Roman republic and restore the temporal power of the Pope (April–July 1849).

52. Bailiff.

tion that modern society requires can arise only on the debris of the military and bureaucratic government machinery originally forged in opposition to feudalism.[53]

The situation of the French peasantry reveals the solution to the riddle of the *general elections of 20 and 21 December*, which bore the second Bonaparte onto Mount Sinai, not to receive laws, but to make them.

Clearly, the bourgeoisie now had no other choice than to elect Bonaparte. When the puritans at the Council of Constance[54] complained of the dissolute lives of the Popes and moaned about the necessity of moral reform, Cardinal Pierre d'Ailly thundered at them: 'The Catholic Church can only be saved now by the Devil in person, and you ask for angels.' Similarly, after the coup d'état, the French bourgeoisie cried, 'Bourgeois society can only be saved now by the head of the Society of 10 December! Only theft can save property; perjury, religion; bastardy, the family; disorder, order!'

Bonaparte is the executive authority which has attained power in its own right, and as such he feels it to be his mission to safeguard 'bourgeois order'. But the strength of this bourgeois order lies in the middle class. He therefore sees himself as the representative of the middle class and he issues decrees in this sense. However, he is only where he is because he has broken the political power of this middle class, and breaks it again daily. He therefore sees himself as the opponent of the political and literary power of the middle class. But by protecting its material power he recreates its political power. The cause must accordingly be kept alive, but the effect must be done away with wherever it appears. However, this cannot occur without slight confusions of cause and effect, since both lose their distinguishing characteristics when they interact. New decrees are issued that obliterate the boundary between the

53. In the first edition this paragraph ended with the following lines, which Marx omitted from the 1869 edition: 'The destruction of the state machine will not endanger centralization. Bureaucracy is only the low and brutal form of a centralization still burdened with its opposite, feudalism. In despair and disappointment at the Napoleonic restoration, the French peasant will abandon his faith in his smallholding, the entire state edifice erected on the smallholding will fall to the ground, and *the proletarian revolution will obtain the chorus without which its solo will prove a requiem* in all peasant countries.'

54. A council of the Catholic Church, held between 1414 and 1418, at which the position of the Pope was restored after the disturbances of the previous century, and the doctrines of the reformers Wycliffe and Hus were declared heretical.

two. As against the bourgeoisie, Bonaparte sees himself simultaneously as the representative of the peasants and of the people in general, as the man who wants to make the lower classes happy within the framework of bourgeois society. New decrees are issued that swindle the 'true socialists'[55] out of their statecraft in advance. But, above all, Bonaparte sees himself as the head of the Society of 10 December, as the representative of the lumpenproletariat to which he himself, his entourage, his government and his army belong, and whose chief concern is to do well for himself and extract California lottery prizes from the treasury. And he confirms that he is the head of the Society of 10 December with decrees, without decrees and despite decrees.

The contradictory task facing the man explains the contradictions of his government, the confused and fumbling attempts to win and then to humiliate first one class and then another, the result being to array them all in uniform opposition to him. This practical uncertainty forms a highly comic contrast to the peremptory and categorical style of the government's decrees, a style faithfully copied from the uncle.

Industry and trade, i.e., the business affairs of the middle class, are to flourish under the strong government as in a hothouse. Hence the grant of innumerable railway concessions. But the Bonapartist lumpenproletariat is to enrich itself. Hence fraudulent manipulation of the Bourse with the railway concessions, by those already initiated. But no capital is forthcoming for the railways. Hence the Bank is obliged to make advances on the railway shares. But the Bank must simultaneously be exploited by Bonaparte, and therefore must be cajoled. Hence it is released from the obligation to publish its report every week. The government makes a leonine agreement[56] with the Bank. The people are to be given employment. Hence instructions are issued for public works. But the public works raise the tax burden on the people. Hence the taxes are reduced by attacking the *rentiers*, by conversion of the 5 per cent bonds to 4½ per cent. But the middle class must again receive a sop. Hence the wine tax is doubled for the people, who

55. A reference to the ideas of the German socialists of the 1840s, who preached a sentimental and humanistic variety of socialism, subjected to a devastating critique by Engels in the second part of *The German Ideology*. (See also *The Manifesto of the Communist Party*, section III in *The Revolutions of 1848*, pp. 90–93.)

56. An agreement from which one partner secures all the gains, the other partner suffers all the losses. From Aesop's fable of the lion.

buy it in small quantities, and halved for the middle class, who drink it in bulk. The existing workers' associations are dissolved, but miracles of association are promised for the future. The peasants are to be helped. Hence mortgage banks are set up to accelerate their indebtedness, on the one hand, and the concentration of capital, on the other. But these banks are to be used to make money out of the confiscated estates of the House of Orleans, and no capitalist wishes to accept this condition, which is not contained in the decree. Hence the mortgage bank remains a mere decree, etc., etc.

Bonaparte would like to appear as the patriarchal benefactor of all classes. But he cannot give to one class without taking from another. At the time of the Fronde, it was said of the duc de Guise that he was the most obliging man in France, because he had turned all his estates into obligations of his supporters towards himself. In the same way Bonaparte would like to be the most obliging man in France and turn all the property and labour of the country into a personal obligation towards himself. He would like to steal the whole of France in order to be able to give it back to France, or rather to be able to buy France again with French money, for as the head of the Society of 10 December he must buy what ought to belong to him. And all the institutions of the state, the Senate,[57] the Council of State, the Legislative Body,[58] the Legion of Honour, the military medals, the wash-houses, the public works, the railways, the general staff of the National Guard (without privates) and the confiscated estates of the House of Orleans – all these things become part of the Institute of Purchase. Every place in the army and the government apparatus becomes a means of purchase. But the most important aspect of this process of taking France in order to give France back is the percentage that finds its way into the pockets of the head and the members of the Society of 10 December during the transaction. The *bon mot* with which Countess L., the mistress of Monsieur de Morny,[59]

57. The Senate was the upper house set up by the constitution of 14 January 1852, with the task of protecting the constitution and the power to modify it if the President (as 'Napoleon III' still regarded himself) proposed this. Its members were appointed by the President.

58. The Legislative Body (Corps Législatif) of the Second Empire was elected by universal suffrage, but had very restricted power.

59. Charles, duc de Morny was the half-brother of Louis Bonaparte, a deputy in the Legislative National Assembly and one of the organizers of the coup of 2 December.

characterized the confiscation of the Orleans estates, '*C'est le premier vol*[60] *de l'aigle*,'[61] fits every flight of this *eagle*, which is more like a *raven*. Every day he and his adherents call out to each other like that Carthusian monk in Italy who said to the miser ostentatiously counting up the goods he could live on for years to come, '*Tu fai conto sopra i beni, bisogna prima far il conto sopra gli anni.*'[62] So as not to get the years wrong, they count in minutes. A gang of shady characters pushes its way forward to the court, into the ministries, to the chief positions in the administration and the army. Of even the best of them it must be said that no one knows where they come from. They are a noisy, disreputable, rapacious crowd of bohemians, crawling into gold-braided coats with the same grotesque dignity as the high dignitaries of Soulouque's empire.[63] One can gain a shrewd idea of this upper stratum of the Society of 10 December if one bears in mind that Véron-Crevel[64] preaches its morals and Granier de Cassagnac is its thinker. When Guizot utilized this Granier at the time of his ministry in an obscure provincial paper against the dynastic opposition, he used to boast of him with the phrase, '*C'est le roi des drôles*' – 'he is the king of buffoons.' It would be a mistake to call to mind the Regency[65] or Louis XV in connection with the court and the clan of Louis Bonaparte. For 'France has often experienced a government of mistresses, but never before a government of kept men.'[66]

Driven on by the contradictory demands of his situation, Bonaparte, like a conjuror, has to keep the eyes of the public fixed on himself, as Napoleon's substitute, by means of constant surprises, that is to say by performing a coup d'état in miniature every day. He thereby brings the whole bourgeois economy into confusion, violates everything that seemed inviolable to the revolution of 1848, makes some tolerant of revolution and others

60. *Vol* means flight and theft. [*Footnote by Marx.*]

61. It is the first flight of the eagle.

62. You are reckoning up your goods, but you should first reckon your years. [*Footnote by Marx.*]

63. See p. 75, n. 71.

64. In the character of Crevel in *Cousine Bette*, drawn after Dr Véron, the owner of *Le Constitutionnel*, Balzac portrayed the thoroughly dissolute Parisian philistine. [*Footnote by Marx.*]

65. The regency of Philippe of Orleans, during the minority of Louis XV (1715–23).

66. Madame Girardin's remark. [*Footnote by Marx.*]

desirous of revolution, creates anarchy itself in the name of order, and at the same time strips the halo from the state machine, profaning it and making it both disgusting and ridiculous. He repeats the cult of the Holy Tunic at Trier[67] in the form of the cult of the Napoleonic imperial mantle in Paris. But when the emperor's mantle finally falls on the shoulders of Louis Bonaparte, the bronze statue of Napoleon will come crashing down from the top of the Vendôme Column.

67. One of the sacred relics exhibited in Trier Cathedral in 1844 as part of the Catholic revival of the 1840s.

Articles on Britain

It is the intention of Monsieur Guizot's pamphlet to demonstrate why Louis Philippe and the policies of Guizot should not really have been overthrown on 24 February 1848, and how the shameful character of the French is to blame for the fact that the July monarchy collapsed ignominiously after eighteen troubled years and did not achieve that durability which the English monarchy has enjoyed since 1688.

We can see from this pamphlet how even the most able figures of the *ancien régime*, even those whom in their way possess an unquestionable talent for history, have been so completely bewildered by the fateful events of February that they have lost all historical understanding, even of their own earlier actions. Instead of the February revolution bringing him to recognize the completely different historic conditions, the completely different situation of the social classes under the French monarchy of 1830 and the English monarchy of 1688, M. Guizot resolves the difference in a few moral phrases and asserts in conclusion that the policy overthrown on 24 February 'can overcome revolutions, just as it preserves states'.

Clearly formulated, the question which M. Guizot is trying to answer is this: Why has bourgeois society in England developed in the form of a constitutional monarchy longer than in France?

The following passage serves to characterize M. Guizot's familiarity with bourgeois development in England:

Under the reigns of George I and George II public attention turned elsewhere: foreign policy ceased to be its main consideration; domestic

---

1. François Guizot, *Pourquoi la révolution d'Angleterre a-t-elle réussi?* Paris, 1850. Marx wrote this review for the February 1850 issue of the *Neue Rheinische Zeitung Revue*, and it is translated here from the text printed in *MEW* 7.

administration, the maintenance of peace, financial, colonial, commercial questions, parliamentary development and parliamentary struggles became the main preoccupation of government and public (p. 168).

In the reign of William III M. Guizot finds only two factors worthy of mention: the maintenance of the balance of power between Parliament and the Crown, and the maintenance of the European balance of power in the struggle against Louis XIV. Suddenly, during the Hanoverian dynasty, 'public attention turned elsewhere'; we do not know how or why. It is evident here how M. Guizot transfers the most commonplace phrases from French parliamentary debate to English history and how, by doing so, he imagines that he has provided an explanation. In precisely the same way M. Guizot imagined, as a minister, that he could carry on his shoulders both the equilibrium between parliament and Crown and the European equilibrium, whereas in reality he did nothing except sell off the whole French state and the whole of French society, piece by piece, to the financial sharks of the Paris Bourse.

M. Guizot does not regard it as worth mentioning that the wars against Louis XIV were wars of competition, pure and simple, aimed at destroying French trade and French sea-power; that under William III the rule of the financial bourgeoisie was given its first legitimation with the establishment of the Bank of England and the introduction of the national debt;[2] and that the manufacturing bourgeoisie was given a new impetus by the consistent application of the protective tariff system. Only political phrases have any meaning for him. He does not even mention that under Queen Anne the ruling parties were able to preserve themselves and the constitutional monarchy only by force, by extending the life of Parliament to seven years, and thus almost destroying the influence of the people upon the government.[3]

Under the Hanoverian dynasty England had already developed to such an extent that it was able to conduct the war of competition against France in the modern fashion. England itself continued to fight France only in America and the East Indies, while contenting itself on the Continent with financing foreign princes like

2. The charter of the Bank of England, granted in 1694, was conditional on its providing loans to the government.
3. The Septennial Act was not in fact passed until May 1716, by which time George I had succeeded to the throne.

Frederick II in their wars against France. And because foreign wars thus assumed another form, M. Guizot says that 'foreign policy ceased to be the main consideration' and that its place was taken by 'the maintenance of peace'. The extent to which 'parliamentary development and parliamentary struggles became the main preoccupation of government and public' should be measured against the cases of bribery under Walpole's ministry,[4] which, it must be said, resemble to a 'T' the scandals which were the order of the day under M. Guizot.

M. Guizot ascribes the fact that the English revolution fared better than the French to two particular causes: the first is that the English revolution had a distinctly religious character and thus by no means broke with all the traditions of the past; the second is that from its inception it operated not as a destructive but as a conservative force, in that Parliament was defending old existing laws against the encroachments of the Crown.

As far as the first point is concerned, M. Guizot forgets that free thought, which causes his flesh to creep so badly in connection with the French revolution, was exported to France from England, no less. Locke had been its father, and in Shaftesbury and Bolingbroke it had already assumed that intellectually acute form which was later developed so brilliantly in France. We thus come to the strange conclusion that this same free thought which, according to M. Guizot, caused the French revolution to come to grief, was one of the most important products of the religious revolution in England.

As for the second point, M. Guizot completely forgets that the French revolution began just as conservatively, if not more so, than the English revolution. Absolutism, particularly as it finally manifested itself in France, was also an innovation there, and the *parlements* rose up against this innovation in defence of the old laws, the *us et coutumes*[5] of the old monarchy based on the estates. And whereas the first step taken by the French revolution was to revive the Estates General, which had lain dormant since Henri IV and Louis XIII, the English revolution does not reveal any evidence of the same classical conservatism.

According to M. Guizot, the main result of the English revolution was that it became impossible for the king to govern against the will of Parliament, in particular the House of Commons. The

---

4. Sir Robert Walpole was Whig Prime Minister from 1721 to 1742.

5. Practices and customs.

significance of the whole revolution, as he sees it, lies in the fact that initially both sides, Crown and Parliament, overstepped the limits of their power and went too far until, finally, under William III, they found the right balance and neutralized each other. M. Guizot finds it superfluous to mention that the subjection of the monarchy to Parliament amounts to its subjection to the rule of a class. He is therefore also absolved from having to investigate how this class finally acquired the necessary power to make the Crown its servant. In his account the whole struggle between Charles I and Parliament turned around purely political privileges. As to why Parliament and the class which it represents needed these privileges, we hear not a word. No more does M. Guizot speak of Charles I's direct interference in free competition, which made things increasingly impossible for English commerce and industry, or of Charles I's dependence upon Parliament, which resulted from his continual financial difficulties and which increased the more he tried to defy Parliament. Thus, for M. Guizot, the whole revolution is to be explained simply by the malevolence and religious fanaticism of individual troublemakers, who could not content themselves with moderate freedom. He is equally unable to enlighten us about the connection between the religious movement and the development of bourgeois society. The Commonwealth, of course, is likewise merely the work of a few ambitious, fanatical and malevolent individuals. That around the same time in Lisbon, Naples and Messina attempts were also made to establish republics,[6] and that, as in England, this was under the influence of the Dutch example, is a fact which goes without mention. Although M. Guizot never loses sight of the French revolution, he never once comes to the simple conclusion that everywhere the transition from an absolute to a constitutional monarchy only comes about after a violent struggle and by way of a form of republic, and that even then the old obsolete dynasty has to make way for a usurpatory collateral branch. Consequently, he is only able to produce the most trivial commonplaces about the overthrow of the English Restoration monarchy. He does not even mention the most immediate causes: the fear felt among the new great landowners created by the Reformation of the re-establishment of Catholicism, in which case they would, of course, have had to surrender all their stolen Church property, as a result

6. Republican uprisings against the Spanish monarchy took place in Lisbon in 1640, in Naples in 1647–8 and in Messina (Sicily) in 1674–6.

of which seven tenths of the total acreage of England would have changed owners; the fear of Catholicism felt by the commercial and industrial bourgeoisie, since it by no means suited their business interests; the nonchalance with which the Stuarts, to their own advantage and that of their court nobility, sold the whole of English industry and commerce to the government of France – the only country which at that time was endangering England with its competition, in many respects successfully. Consequently, as M. Guizot everywhere omits the most important factors, there is nothing left for him but to present a highly unsatisfactory and banal narration of the merely political events.

The great puzzle of the conservative character of the English revolution, which M. Guizot can solve only by attributing it to the superior intelligence of the English, is in fact explained by the lasting alliance of the bourgeoisie with the great landowners, an alliance which fundamentally distinguishes the English from the French revolution, the latter having destroyed large landed property by dividing it up into smallholdings. This class of large landowners allied with the bourgeoisie, which, it may be added, had already arisen under Henry VIII, was not, as were the French feudal landowners of 1789, in conflict with the vital interests of the bourgeoisie, but rather in complete harmony with them. Their estates were indeed not feudal but bourgeois property. On the one hand, they provided the industrial bourgeoisie with the population necessary to operate the manufacturing system, and, on the other hand, they were in a position to raise agricultural development to the level corresponding to that of industry and commerce. Hence their common interests with the bourgeoisie; hence their alliance.

As far as M. Guizot is concerned, English history comes to an end with the consolidation of the constitutional monarchy. Subsequent events are limited to a pleasant interchange between Whigs and Tories, on the lines of the great debate between M. Guizot and M. Thiers. In reality, however, the momentous development and transformation of bourgeois society in England only began with the consolidation of the constitutional monarchy. Where M. Guizot sees only a gentle tranquillity and an idyllic peace, in reality the most tremendous conflicts and far-reaching revolutions were taking place. At first, manufacturing expanded under the constitutional monarchy to an extent hitherto unknown, later making way for large-scale industry, the steam-engine and the gigantic factories. Whole classes disappeared from the population, new classes taking their place with a new basis of existence and new needs. A new bourgeoisie of colossal proportions arose; while the old bourgeoisie struggled with the French revolution, the new one conquered the world market. It became so omnipotent that, even before it gained direct political power as a result of the Reform Bill,[7] it forced its opponents to legislate in *its* interests and in accordance with *its* requirements. It captured direct representation in Parliament and used this to destroy the last remnants of real power left to the landed proprietors. Finally, at this moment, it is busy completely demolishing the beautiful edifice of the English constitution before which M. Guizot stands in admiration.

And while M. Guizot compliments the English on the failure of republicanism and socialism – those base, tumorous growths of French society – to shake the foundations of an infinitely beneficent monarchy, class conflicts in English society have reached a pitch unequalled in any other country: a bourgeoisie with unprecedented wealth and productive forces is confronted here by a proletariat which equally has no precedent in power and concentration. So the respectful tribute which M. Guizot pays to England really amounts to this: that under the protection of the constitutional monarchy elements of social revolution have developed which are far more radical and far greater in number than in all other countries of the world put together. Whenever the strands which make up the course of English history become intertwined in a conjunctural knot, which he cannot even give the appearance of severing with mere political phrases, M. Guizot takes refuge in religious phrases, in the armed intervention of God. Thus the spirit of God, for instance, moves over the army and prevents Cromwell from proclaiming himself king, etc., etc. Guizot seeks refuge from his conscience in God; he seeks refuge from a profane public in style.

Indeed, it is not merely that *les rois s'en vont*, but also that *les capacités de la bourgeoisie s'en vont*.[8]

---

7. Of 1831–2.
8. Not only do kings disappear, but so do the leading authorities of the bourgeoisie.

TORIES AND WHIGS[9]

London, 6 August 1852

The results of the general election for the British Parliament are now known. These results I shall analyse more fully in my next letter.[10]

What were the parties which during this electioneering agitation opposed or supported each other?

Tories, Whigs, Liberal Conservatives (Peelites), Free Traders, *par excellence* (the men of the Manchester School, Parliamentary and Financial Reformers),[11] and lastly, the Chartists.

Whigs, Free Traders and Peelites coalesced to oppose the Tories. It was between this coalition on one side, and the Tories on the other, that the real electoral battle was fought. Opposed to Whigs, Peelites, Free Traders and Tories, and thus opposed to entire official England, were the Chartists.

The political parties of Great Britain are sufficiently known in the United States. It will be sufficient to bring to mind, in a few strokes of the pen, the distinctive characteristics of each of them.

Up to 1846 the Tories passed as the guardians of the traditions of Old England. They were suspected of admiring in the British

9. The following three articles were Marx's first authentic contributions to the *New York Daily Tribune*, although Engels's articles on 'Germany: Revolution and Counter-Revolution' had been appearing since October 1851 under Marx's name. As Marx had not yet mastered the English language sufficiently, he drafted these articles in German, and Engels translated them into English and sent them to New York. A small number of obvious mistranslations and grammatical mistakes have here been corrected. Within a few months, however, Marx was able to write fluently in English. This article appeared in the *New York Daily Tribune* of 21 August 1852.

10. Marx's article 'Result of the Elections' was published in the *New York Daily Tribune* of 11 September 1852.

11. The name 'Manchester School', which strictly speaking denoted the economists who ideologically represented the industrial bourgeoisie, was often used by extension for the Free Trade party of Liberals and Radicals. The significance of Marx's tag '*par excellence*' is that Whigs and Peelites also supported free trade and in particular the repeal of the Corn Laws, but without this being the guiding principle of their politics. The National Association for Parliamentary and Financial Reform was founded in 1849 by Cobden and Bright, and lasted until 1855. Its programme, the 'Little Charter', included household suffrage, triennial parliaments and the ballot. The Association was supported by the Free Traders, and also by the reformist wing of the Chartists.

Constitution the eighth wonder of the world; to be *laudatores temporis acti*,[12] enthusiasts for the throne, the High Church, the privileges and liberties of the British subject. The fatal year, 1846, with its repeal of the Corn Laws, and the shout of distress which this repeal forced from the Tories, proved that they were enthusiasts for nothing but the rent of land, and at the same time disclosed the secret of their attachment to the political and religious institutions of Old England. These institutions are the very best institutions, with the help of which *large landed property* – the landed interest – has hitherto ruled England, and even now seeks to maintain its rule. The year 1846 brought to light in its nakedness the *substantial class interest* which forms the *real base* of the Tory party. The year 1846 tore down the traditionally venerable lion's hide, under which Tory class interest had hitherto hidden itself. The year 1846 transformed the Tories into *Protectionists*.[13] Tory was the sacred name, Protectionist is the profane one; Tory was the political battle-cry, Protectionist is the economical shout of distress; Tory seemed an idea, a principle, Protectionist is an interest. Protectionists of what? Of their own revenues, of the rent of their own land. Then the Tories, in the end, are bourgeois as much as the remainder, for where is the bourgeois who is not a protectionist of his own purse? They are distinguished from the other bourgeois in the same way as rent of land is distinguished from commercial and industrial profit. Rent of land is conservative, profit is progressive; rent of land is national, profit is cosmopolitical; rent of land believes in the State Church, profit is a dissenter by birth. The repeal of the Corn Laws in 1846 merely recognized an already accomplished fact, a change long since enacted in the elements of British civil society, viz., the subordination of the landed interest to the moneyed interest, of property to commerce, of agriculture to manufacturing industry, of the country to the city. Could this fact be doubted since the country population stands, in England, to the towns' population in the proportion of one to three? The substantial foundation of the power of the Tories was the rent of land. The rent of land is regulated by the price of food. The price of food,

12. Those who extol the past.

13. In 1846 Sir Robert Peel, the Tory Prime Minister, split his party by repealing the Corn Laws with Whig and Radical support. The majority fraction of the Tory party (anti-Peelite) campaigned in the 1852 election under the 'Protectionist' banner.

then, was artificially maintained at a high rate by the Corn Laws. The repeal of the Corn Laws brought down the price of food, which in its turn brought down the rent of land, and with sinking rent broke down the real strength upon which the political power of the Tories reposed.

What, then, are they trying to do now? To maintain a political power, the social foundation of which has ceased to exist. And how can this be attained? By nothing short of a *counter-revolution*, that is to say, by a reaction of the state against society. They strive to retain forcibly institutions and a political power which were condemned from the very moment at which the rural population found itself outnumbered three times by the population of the towns. And such an attempt must necessarily end with their destruction; it must accelerate and make more acute the social development of England; it must bring on a crisis.

The Tories recruit their army from the farmers, who have either not yet lost the habit of following their landlords as their natural superiors, or who are economically dependent upon them, or who do not yet see that the interest of the farmer and the interest of the landlord are no more identical than the respective interests of the borrower and of the usurer. They are followed and supported by the Colonial Interest, the Shipping Interest, the State Church party, in short, by all those elements which consider it necessary to safeguard their interests against the necessary results of modern manufacturing industry, and against the social revolution prepared by it.

Opposed to the Tories, as their hereditary enemies, stand the Whigs, a party with whom the American Whigs have nothing in common but the name.

The British Whig, in the natural history of politics, forms a species which, like all those of the amphibious class, exists very easily, but is difficult to describe. Shall we call them, with their opponents, Tories out of office or, as continental writers love it, take them for the representatives of certain *popular* principles? In the latter case we should get embarrassed in the same difficulty as the historian of the Whigs, Mr Cooke, who, with great naiveté, confesses in his *History of Parties*[14] that it is indeed a certain number of 'liberal, moral and enlightened principles' which constitutes the Whig party, but that it was greatly to be regretted

14. G. W. Cooke, *The History of the Parties* (3 volumes), London, 1836–7.

that during the more than a century and a half that the Whigs have existed, they have been, when in office, always prevented from carrying out these principles. So that in reality, according to the confession of their own historian, the Whigs represent something quite different from their professed 'liberal and enlightened principles'. Thus they are in the same position as the drunkard brought up before the Lord Mayor who declared that he represented the temperance principle but from some accident or other always got drunk on Sundays.

But never mind their principles; we can better make out what they are in historical fact; what they carry out, not what they once believed, and what they now want other people to believe with respect to their character.

The Whigs, as well as the Tories, form a fraction of the large landed proprietors of Great Britain. Nay, the oldest, richest and most arrogant portion of English landed property is the very nucleus of the Whig party.

What, then, distinguishes them from the Tories? The Whigs are the *aristocratic representatives* of the bourgeoisie, of the industrial and commercial middle class. Under the condition that the bourgeoisie should abandon to them, to an oligarchy of aristocratic families, the monopoly of government and the exclusive possession of office, they make to the middle class, and assist it in conquering, all those concessions which in the course of social and political development have shown themselves to have become *unavoidable* and *undelayable*. Neither more nor less. And as often as such an unavoidable measure has been passed, they declare loudly that herewith the end of historical progress has been obtained; that the whole social movement has carried its ultimate purpose, and then they 'cling to finality'.[15] They can support more easily than the Tories a decrease of their rental revenues, because they consider themselves as the heaven-born farmers of the revenues of the British Empire. They can renounce the monopoly of the Corn Laws, as long as they maintain the monopoly of government as their family property. Ever since the 'Glorious Revolution' of 1688 the Whigs, with short intervals caused principally by the first French revolution and the consequent reaction, have found themselves in the enjoyment of the public offices.

15. In 1837 Lord John Russell, the Whig leader, had characterized the Reform Bill of 1832 as the final point of constitutional reform. The Radicals thereupon nicknamed him 'Finality John'.

Whoever recalls to his mind this period of English history will find no other distinctive mark of Whigdom but the maintenance of their family oligarchy. The interests and principles which they represent besides, from time to time, do not belong to the Whigs; they are forced upon them by the development of the industrial and commercial class, the bourgeoisie. After 1688 we find them united with the Bankocracy, just then rising into importance, as we find them in 1846 united with the Millocracy. The Whigs as little carried the Reform Bill of 1831 as they carried the Free Trade Bill of 1846. Both reform movements, the political as well as the commercial, were movements of the bourgeoisie. As soon as either of these movements had ripened into irresistibility, as soon as, at the same time, it had become the safest means of turning the Tories out of office, the Whigs stepped forward, took up the direction of the government, and secured to themselves the governmental part of the victory. In 1831 they extended the political portion of reform as far as was necessary in order not to leave the middle class entirely dissatisfied; after 1846 they confined their free-trade measures so far as was necessary in order to save to the landed aristocracy the greatest possible amount of privileges. Each time they took the movement in hand in order to prevent its forward march, and to recover their own posts at the same time.

It is clear that from the moment when the landed aristocracy is no longer able to maintain its position as an independent power, to fight, as an independent party, for the government position, in short, that from the moment when the Tories are definitively overthrown, British history has no longer any room for the Whigs. The aristocracy once destroyed, what is the use of an aristocratic representation of the bourgeoisie against this aristocracy?

It is well known that in the Middle Ages the German emperors put the just then arising towns under imperial governors, '*advocati*', to protect these towns against the surrounding nobility. As soon as growing population and wealth gave them sufficient strength and independence to resist, and even to attack the nobility, the towns also drove out the noble governors, the *advocati*.

The Whigs have been these *advocati* of the British middle class, and their governmental monopoly must break down as soon as the landed monopoly of the Tories is broken down. In the same measures as the middle class has developed its independent strength, they have shrunk down from a party to a coterie.

It is evident what a distastefully heterogeneous mixture the character of the British Whigs must turn out to be: feudalists, who are at the same time Malthusians, money-mongers with feudal prejudices, aristocrats without point of honour, bourgeois without industrial activity, finality-men with progressive phrases, progressists with fanatical conservatism, traffickers in homeopathical fractions of reforms, fosterers of family-nepotism, grand masters of corruption, hypocrites of religion, Tartuffes of politics. The mass of the English people have a sound aesthetical common sense. They have an instinctive hatred against everything motley and ambiguous, against bats and Russellites. And then, with the Tories, the mass of the English people, the urban and rural proletariat, has in common the hatred against the 'money-monger'. With the bourgeoisie it has in common the hatred against aristocrats. In the Whigs it hates the one and the other, aristocrats and bourgeois, the landlord who oppresses, and the money lord who exploits it. In the Whig it hates the oligarchy which has ruled over England for more than a century, and by which the people is excluded from the direction of its own affairs.

The Peelites (Liberal Conservatives) are no party; they are merely the souvenir of a partyman, of the late Sir Robert Peel. But Englishmen are too prosaical for a souvenir to form, with them, the foundation for anything but elegies. And now that the people have erected brass and marble monuments to the late Sir Robert Peel in all parts of the country, they believe they are able so much the more to do without those perambulant Peel monuments, the Grahams, the Gladstones, the Cardwells, etc.[16] The so-called Peelites are nothing but this staff of bureaucrats which Robert Peel had schooled for himself. And because they form a pretty complete staff, they forget for a moment that there is no army behind them. The Peelites, then, are old supporters of Sir Robert Peel, who have not yet come to a conclusion as to what party to attach themselves to. It is evident that a similar scruple is not a sufficient means for them to constitute an independent power.

Remain the Free Traders and the Chartists, the brief delineation of whose character will form the subject of my next.

---

16. William Gladstone, the future Liberal Prime Minister, had been President of the Board of Trade in Peel's second ministry of 1841–6. Edward Cardwell and Sir James Graham, who had been respectively Secretary to the Treasury and Home Secretary, were also to hold ministerial office as Liberals.

THE CHARTISTS[17]

London, 10 August 1852

While the Tories, the Whigs, the Peelites – in fact, all the parties we have hitherto commented upon – belong more or less to the past, the Free Traders (the men of the Manchester School, the Parliamentary and Financial Reformers) are the *official representatives of modern English society*, the representatives of that England which rules the market of the world. They represent the party of the self-conscious bourgeoisie, of industrial capital striving to make available its social power as a political power as well, and to eradicate the last arrogant remnants of feudal society. This party is led on by the most active and most energetic portion of the English bourgeoisie – the *manufacturers*. What they demand is the complete and undisguised ascendancy of the bourgeoisie, the open, official subjection of society at large to the laws of modern, bourgeois production, and to the rule of those men who are the directors of that production. By free trade they mean the unfettered movement of capital; freed from all political, national and religious shackles. The soil is to be a marketable commodity, and the exploitation of the soil is to be carried on according to the common commercial laws. There are to be manufacturers of food as well as manufacturers of twist and cottons, but no longer any lords of the land. There are, in short, not to be tolerated any political or social restrictions, regulations or monopolies, unless they proceed from 'the eternal laws of political economy', that is, from the conditions under which capital produces and distributes. The struggle of this party against the old English institutions, products of a superannuated, an evanescent stage of social development, is resumed in the watchword: *Produce as cheap as you can, and do away with all the* faux frais *of production* (with all superfluous, unnecessary expenses in production). And this watch-word is addressed not only to the private individual, but to the *nation at large* principally.

Royalty, with its 'barbarous splendors', its court, its civil list and its flunkeys – what else does it belong to but to the *faux frais* of production? The nation can produce and exchange without royalty; away with the crown. The sinecures of the nobility, the House of Lords? *Faux frais* of production. The large standing army? *Faux frais* of production. The colonies? *Faux frais* of production. The State Church, with its riches, the spoils of plunder or of mendicity? *Faux frais* of production. Let parsons compete freely with each other, and everyone pay them according to his own wants. The whole circumstantial routine of English law, with its Court of Chancery? *Faux frais* of production. National wars? *Faux frais* of production. England can exploit foreign nations more cheaply while at peace with them.

You see, to these champions of the British bourgeoisie, to the men of the Manchester School, every institution of Old England appears in the light of a piece of machinery as costly as it is useless, and which fulfils no other purpose but to prevent the nation from producing the greatest possible quantity at the least possible expense, and to exchange its products in freedom. Necessarily, their last word is the bourgeois republic, in which free competition rules supreme in all spheres of life; in which there remains altogether that *minimum* only of government which is indispensable for the administration, internally and externally, of the common class interest and business of the bourgeoisie; and where this minimum of government is as soberly, as economically organized as possible. Such a party, in other countries, would be called *democratic*. But it is necessarily revolutionary, and the complete annihilation of Old England as an aristocratic country is the end which it follows up with more or less consciousness. Its nearest object, however, is the attainment of a parliamentary reform which should transfer to its hands the legislative power necessary for such a revolution.

But the British bourgeois are not excitable Frenchmen. When they intend to carry a parliamentary reform they will not make a February revolution. On the contrary. Having obtained, in 1846, a grand victory over the landed aristocracy by the repeal of the Corn Laws, they were satisfied with following up the material advantages of this victory, while they neglected to draw the necessary political and economic conclusions from it, and thus enabled the Whigs to reinstate themselves into their hereditary monopoly of government. During all the time from 1846 to 1852, they exposed themselves to ridicule by their battle-cry: Broad principles and practical (read *small*) measures. And why all this? Because in every violent movement they are obliged to appeal to the *working class*. And if the aristocracy is their vanishing opponent, the working class is their arising enemy. They prefer to compromise with the vanishing opponent rather than to strengthen the arising enemy, to whom the future belongs, by concessions of a more than apparent importance. Therefore, they strive to avoid every forcible collision with the aristocracy; but historical necessity and the Tories press them onwards. They cannot avoid fulfilling their mission, battering to pieces Old England, the England of the past; and the very moment when they will have conquered exclusive political dominion, when political dominion and economic supremacy will be united in the same hands, when, therefore, the struggle against capital will no longer be distinct from the struggle against the existing government – from that very moment will date the *social revolution of England*.

We now come to the Chartists, the politically active portion of the British *working class*. The six points of the Charter which they contend for contain nothing but the demand of universal suffrage, and of the conditions without which universal suffrage would be illusory for the working class, such as the ballot, payment of members, annual general elections. But universal suffrage is the equivalent for political power for the working class of England, where the proletariat forms the large majority of the population, where, in a long, though underground, civil war, it has gained a clear consciousness of its position as a class, and where even the rural districts know no longer any peasants, but only landlords, industrial capitalists (farmers) and hired labourers. The carrying of universal suffrage in England would, therefore, be a far more socialistic measure than anything which has been honoured with that name on the Continent.

Its inevitable result, here, is *the political supremacy of the working class*.

I shall report, on another occasion, on the revival and the reorganization of the Chartist party. For the present I have only to treat of the recent election.

To be a voter for the British Parliament, a man must occupy, in the boroughs, a house rated at £10 for the poor rate, and, in the counties, he must be a freeholder to the annual amount of 40 shillings, or a leaseholder to the amount of £50. From this statement alone it follows that the Chartists could take, officially, but little part in the electoral battle just concluded. In order to explain the actual part they took in it, I must recall to mind a peculiarity of the British electoral system:

Nomination day and declaration day! Show of hands and poll!

When the candidates have made their appearance on the day of election, and have publicly harangued the people, they are elected, in the first instance, by the show of hands, and every hand has the right to be raised, the hand of the non-elector as well as that of the elector. For whomsoever the majority of the hands are raised, that person is declared, by the returning officer, to be (provisionally) elected by show of hands. But now the medal shows its reverse. The election by show of hands was a mere ceremony, an act of formal politeness towards the 'sovereign people', and the politeness ceases as soon as privilege is menaced. For if the show of hands does not return the candidates of the privileged electors, these candidates demand a poll; only the privileged electors can take part in the poll, and whosoever has there the majority of votes is declared duly elected. The first election, by show of hands, is a show satisfaction allowed, for a moment, to public opinion, in order to convince it, the next moment, the more strikingly of its impotency.

It might appear that this election by show of hands, this danger-ous formality, had been invented in order to ridicule universal suffrage, and to enjoy some little aristocratic fun at the expense of the 'rabble' (expression of Major Beresford, Secretary at War). But this would be a delusion, and the old usage, common originally to all Teutonic nations, could drag itself traditionally down to the nineteenth century, because it gave to the British class-parliament, cheaply and without danger, an appearance of popularity. The ruling classes drew from this usage the satisfaction that the mass of the people took part, with more or less passion, in their sectional interests as its national interests. And it was only since the bour-geoisie took an independent station at the side of the two official parties, the Whigs and Tories, that the working masses stood up on the nomination days in their own name. But in no former year the contrast of show of hands and poll, of nomination day and declara-tion day, has been so serious, so well defined by opposed principles, so threatening, so general, upon the whole surface of the country, as in this last election of 1852.

And what a contrast! It was sufficient to be named by show of hands in order to be beaten at the poll. It was sufficient to have had the majority at a poll, in order to be saluted by the people with rotten apples and brickbats. The duly elected members of Parliament, before all [else], had a great deal to do in order to keep their own parliamentary bodily selves in safety. On one side the majority of the people, on the other the twelfth part of the whole population, and the fifth part of the sum total of the male adult inhabitants of the country. On one side enthusiasm, on the other bribery. On one side parties disowning their own distinctive signs, liberals pleading the conservatism, conservatives proclaiming the liberalism of their views; on the other, the people, proclaiming their presence and pleading their own cause. On one side a worn-out engine which, turning incessantly in its vicious circle, is never able to move a single step forward, and the impotent process of friction by which all the official parties gradually grind each other into dust; on the other, the advancing mass of the nation, threatening to blow up the vicious circle and to destroy the official engine.

I shall not follow up, over all the surface of the country, this contrast between nomination and poll, between the threatening electoral demonstration of the working class and the timid electioneering manoeuvres of the ruling classes. I take one borough from the mass, where the contrast is concentrated in a focus: the Halifax election. Here the opposing candidates were: [Henry] Edwards (Tory); Sir Charles Wood (late Whig Chancellor of the Exchequer, brother-in-law to Earl Grey); Frank Crossley (Manchester man); and finally Ernest Jones, the most talented, consistent and energetic representative of Chartism. Halifax being a manufacturing town, the Tory had little chance. The Manchester man, Crossley, was leagued with the Whigs. The serious struggle, then, lay only between Wood and Jones, between the Whig and the Chartist.[18]

Sir Charles Wood made a speech of about half an hour, perfectly inaudible at the commencement and during its latter half for the disapprobation of the immense multitude. His speech, as reported by the reporter, who sat close to him, was merely a recapitulation of the free-trade measures passed, an attack on Lord Derby's government,[19] and a laudation of '*the unexampled prosperity of the country and the people!*' ('Hear, hear.') He did not propound one single new measure of reform; and but faintly, in very few words, hinted at Lord John Russell's bill for the franchise.[20]

18. The following passages are quoted from the *People's Paper*, 14 July 1852.

19. Edward Stanley, Earl of Derby, was the leader of the Tory party from 1846 until his death in 1869, and Prime Minister in 1852, 1858–9 and 1866–8.

20. In February 1852 Russell announced a bill for further electoral reform, but he never introduced it.

I give a more extensive abstract of E. Jones's speech, as you will not find it in any of the great London ruling-class papers.

Ernest Jones, who was received with immense enthusiasm, then spoke as follows:

'Electors and non-electors, you have met upon a great and solemn festival. Today the constitution recognizes universal suffrage in theory, that it may perhaps deny it in practice on the morrow [. . .] Today the representatives of two systems stand before you, and you have to decide beneath which you shall be ruled for seven years. Seven years – a little life! [. . .] I summon you to pause upon the threshold of those seven years: today they shall pass slowly and calmly in review before you: today decide, you 20,000 men!, that perhaps five hundred may undo your will tomorrow.' ('Hear, hear.') 'I say the representatives of two systems stand before you. Whig, Tory, and money-monger are on my left, it is true, but they are all as one. The money-monger says, buy cheap and sell dear. The Tory says, buy dear, sell dearer. Both are the same for labour. But the former system is in the ascendant, and pauperism rankles at its root. That system is based on foreign competition. Now I assert that under the buy-cheap-and-sell-dear principle, brought to bear on foreign competition, the ruin of the working and small trading classes must go on. Why? Labour is the creator of all wealth. A man must work before a grain is grown, or a yard is woven. But there is no self-employment for the working man in this country. Labour is a hired commodity – labour is a thing in the market that is bought and sold; consequently, as labour creates all wealth, labour is the first thing bought – "Buy cheap! Buy cheap!" Labour is bought in the cheapest market. But now comes the next: "Sell dear! Sell dear!" Sell what? *Labour's produce*. To whom? To the foreigner – aye! and to *the labourer himself* – for labour, not being self-employed, the labourer is *not* the partaker of the first fruits of his toil. "Buy cheap, sell dear." How do you like it? "Buy cheap, sell dear." Buy the working man's labour cheaply, and sell back to that very working man the produce of his own labour dear! The principle of inherent loss is in the bargain. The employer buys the labour cheap – he sells, and on the sale he must make a profit; he sells to the working man himself – and thus every bargain between employer and employed is a deliberate cheat on the part of the employer. Thus labour has to sink through eternal loss, that capital may rise through lasting fraud. But the system stops not here. *This is brought to bear on foreign competition – which means, we must ruin the trade of other countries, as we have ruined the labour of our own.*[21] How does it work? The high-taxed country has to undersell the low-taxed. Competition abroad is constantly increasing – consequently cheapness must increase constantly also. Therefore, wages in England must keep constantly falling. And how do they effect the fall? By *surplus labour*. How do they obtain the surplus labour? By monopoly of the land, which drives more hands than are wanted into the factory. By monopoly of machinery, which drives those hands into the street – by woman labour which drives the man from the shuttle – by child labour, which drives the woman from the loom. Then planting their foot upon that living base of surplus, they press its aching heart beneath their heel, and cry "Starvation! Who'll work? A half loaf is better than no bread at all" – and the writhing mass grasps greedily at their terms.' (Loud cries of 'Hear, hear.') 'Such is the system for the working man. But electors! How does it operate on you? How does it affect home trade, the shopkeeper, poor rate and taxation? For every increase of competition abroad, there must be an increase of cheapness at home. Every increase of cheapness in labour is based on increase of labour surplus – and this surplus is obtained by an increase of machinery. I repeat, how does this operate on you? The Manchester Liberal on my left establishes a new patent, and throws three hundred men as a surplus in the streets. Shopkeepers! Three hundred customers less. Ratepayers! Three hundred paupers more.' (Loud cheers.) 'But mark me! The evil stops not there. These three hundred men operate first to bring down the wages of those who remain at work in their own trade. The employer says, "Now I reduce your wages." The men demur. Then he adds: "Do you see those three hundred men who have *just* walked out – you *may change places if you like*, they're sighing to come in on any terms, for they're starving." The men feel it, and are crushed. Ah! You Manchester Liberal! Pharisee of politics! those men are listening – have I got you now? But the evil stops not yet. Those men, driven from their own trade, seek employment in others, when they swell the surplus, and bring wages down. The low-paid trades of today were the high-paid once – the high paid of today will be the low paid soon. Thus the purchasing power of the working classes is diminished every day, and with it dies home trade. Mark

21. Marx's italics.

it, shopkeepers! Your customers grow poorer, and your profits less, while your paupers grow more numerous and your poor rates and your taxes rise. Your receipts are smaller, your expenditure is more large. You get less and pay more. How do you like the system? On you the rich manufacturer and landlord throw the weight of poor rate and taxation. Men of the middle class! You are the tax-paying machine of the rich. They create the poverty that creates their riches, and they make you pay for the poverty they have created. The landlord escapes it by privilege, the manufacturer by repaying himself out of the wages of his men, and that reacts on you. How do you like the system? Well, that is the system upheld by the gentlemen on my left. What then do I propose? I have shown the wrong. That is something. But I do more; I stand here to show the right, and prove it so.' (Loud cheers.)

Ernest Jones then went on to expose his own views on political and economic reform, and continued as follows:

'Electors and non-electors, I have now brought before you some of the social and political measures, the immediate adoption of which I advocate now, as I did in 1847. But, because I tried to extend *your* liberties, *mine* were curtailed.' ('Hear, hear.') 'Because I tried to rear the temple of freedom for you all, I was thrown into the cell of a felon's jail;[22] and there, on my left, sits one of my chief jailers.' (Loud and continued groans, directed towards the left.) 'Because I tried to give voice to truth, I was condemned to silence. For two years and one week he cast me into a prison in solitary confinement on the silent system, without pen, ink or paper, but oakum picking as a substitute. [. . .] Ah!' (turning to Sir Charles Wood) 'it was your turn for two years and one week; it is mine this day. I summon the angel of retribution from the heart of every Englishman here present.' (An immense burst of applause.) 'Hark! you feel the fanning of his wings in the breath of this vast multitude!' (Renewed cheering, long continued.) [. . .] 'You may say this is not a public question. But it is!' ('Hear, hear.') 'It is a public question, for the man who cannot feel for the wife of the prisoner will not feel for the wife of the working man. He who will not feel for the children of the captive will not feel for the children of the labour-slave.' ('Hear, hear,' and cheers.) 'His past life proves it, his promise of today does not contradict it.

22. Ernest Jones and other leaders of the revolutionary wing of the Chartist party were imprisoned in 1850; two of Jones's comrades died of the mistreatment they received.

Who voted for Irish coercion,[23] the gagging bill,[24] and tampering with the Irish press? The Whig! There he sits! Turn him out! Who voted fifteen times against Hume's motion for the franchise; Locke King's on the counties; Ewart's for short Parliaments; and Berkeley's for the ballot?[25] The Whig, there he sits; turn him out! Who voted against the release of Frost, Williams and Jones?[26] The Whig, there he sits; turn him out! Who voted against inquiry into colonial abuses and in favour of Ward and Torrington, the tyrants of Ionia and Ceylon?[27] The Whig, there he sits; turn him out! Who voted against reducing the Duke of Cambridge's salary of £12,000,[28] against all reductions in the army and navy, against the repeal of the window-tax, and forty-eight times against every other reduction of taxation, his own salary included? The Whig, there he sits; turn him out! Who voted against a repeal of the paper duty, the advertisement duty, and the taxes on knowledge? The Whig, there he sits; turn him out! Who voted for the batches of new bishops, vicar rate, the Maynooth grant,[29] against its reduction, and against absolving dissenters from paying Church rates? The Whig, there he sits; turn him out! Who voted against all inquiry into the adulteration of food? The Whig, there he sits; turn him out! Who voted against lowering the duty on sugar, and repealing the tax on malt? The Whig, there he sits; turn him out! Who voted against shortening the nightwork of bakers, against inquiry into the condition of framework knitters, against medical inspectors of workhouses, against preventing little children from working before six in the morning, against parish relief for preg-

23. This refers to the act of April 1833 which gave the Lord Governor of Ireland arbitrary powers of repression.

24. The 'gagging bill' was the popular name for Castlereagh's 'six acts' passed in winter 1819, which among other repressive measures banned public meetings and imposed a heavy tax on newspapers.

25. These bills were all introduced as part of the campaign for the Parliamentary and Financial Reformers' 'Little Charter'.

26. John Frost and Zephaniah Williams were Chartist militants transported to Australia for life for their part in the Welsh miners' revolt of 1839.

27. Henry George Ward and George Byng, Viscount Torrington, were both Whig politicians, respectively Lord High Commissioner of the Ionian Islands (1849–55) and Governor of Ceylon (1847–50).

28. The Duke of Cambridge was Queen Victoria's cousin, a general, and Commander-in-Chief of the British army from 1856 to 1895.

29. This was a government grant to an Irish Catholic college, part of the British government's attempt to win the Irish clergy away from the national movement.

nant women of the poor, and against the Ten Hours Bill?[30] The Whig, there he sits; turn him out! Turn him out, in the name of humanity and of God! Men of Halifax! Men of England! The two systems are before you. Now judge and choose!' (It is impossible to describe the enthusiasm kindled by this speech, and especially at the close; the voice of the vast multitude, held in breathless suspense during each paragraph, came at each pause like the thunder of a returning wave, in execration of the representative of Whiggery and class rule. Altogether, it was a scene that will long be unforgotten in Halifax. On the show of hands being taken, very few, and those chiefly of the hired or intimidated, were held up for Sir C. Wood; [. . .] but almost every one present raised both hands for Ernest Jones, amidst cheering and enthusiasm it would be impossible to describe.)

The Mayor declared Mr Ernest Jones and Mr Henry Edwards to be elected by show of hands. Sir C. Wood and Mr Crossley then demanded a poll.

What Jones had predicted took place; he was nominated by 20,000 votes, but the Whig Sir Charles Wood and the Manchester man Crossley were elected by 500 votes.

CORRUPTION AT ELECTIONS[31]

London, 20 August 1852

Just before the late House of Commons separated, it resolved to heap up as many difficulties as possible for its successors in their way to Parliament. It voted a Draconian law against bribery, corruption, intimidation, and electioneering sharp practices in general.

A long list of questions is drawn up, which, by this enactment, may be put to petitioners of sitting members, the most searching and stringent that can be conceived. They may be required on oath to state who were their agents, and what communications they held with them. They may be asked and compelled to state, not only what they know, but what they 'believe, conjecture, and

30. The Ten Hours Bill, passed in 1847, set a statutory limit on the working day of women and young people under eighteen, and thereby indirectly affected the working hours of many adult male workers as well. See Engels's article 'The Ten Hours Bill' in *MECW* 10, pp. 288–300.

31. From the *New York Daily Tribune*, 4 September 1852.

suspect,' as to money expended either by themselves or anyone else acting – authorized or not authorized – on their behalf. In a word, no member can go through the strange ordeal without risk of perjury, if he have the slightest idea that it is possible or likely that anyone has been led to overstep on his behalf the limits of the law.

Now, even supposing this law to take it for granted that the new legislators will use the same liberty as the clergy, who only believe *some* of the Thirty-Nine Articles, yet contrive to sign them *all*, yet there remain, nevertheless, clauses sufficient to make the new Parliament the most virginal assembly that ever made speeches and passed laws for the three kingdoms. And in juxtaposition with the general election immediately following, this law secures to the Tories the glory that under their administration the greatest purity of election has been theoretically proclaimed, and the greatest amount of electoral corruption has been practically carried out.

A fresh election is proceeded with, and here a scene of *bribery, corruption, violence, drunkenness and murder* ensues, *unparalleled* since the times when old Tory monopoly reigned supreme before. We actually hear of soldiers with loaded guns, and bayonets fixed, taking liberal electors by force, dragging them under the landlords' eyes to vote against their own consciences, and those soldiers shooting with deliberate aim, the people who dared to sympathize with the captive electors, and committing wholesale murder on the unresisting [. . .] people! [Allusion to the event at Six Mile Bridge, Limerick, County Clare.] It may be said: That was in Ireland! Aye! and in England they have employed their police to break the stalls of those opposed to them; they have sent their organized gangs of midnight ruffians prowling through the streets to intercept and intimidate the Liberal electors; they have opened the cesspools of drunkenness; they have showered the gold of corruption, as at Derby, and in almost every contested place they have exercised systematic intimidation.

Thus far Ernest Jones's *People's Paper.*[32] Now, after this Chartist weekly paper, hear the weekly paper of the opposite party, the most sober, the most rational, the most moderate organ of the industrial bourgeoisie, the London *Economist:*[33]

We believe we may affirm, at this general election, there has been more *truckling*, more *corruption*, more *intimidation*, more *fanaticism* and more *debauchery*[34] than on any previous occasion. It is reported

32. 14 August 1852. 33. 7 August 1852. 34. Marx's italics.

that bribery has been more extensively resorted to at this election than for many previous years . . . Of the amount of intimidation and undue influence of every sort which has been practised at the late election, it is probably impossible to form an exaggerated estimate . . . And when we sum up all these things – the brutal drunkenness, the low intrigues, the wholesale corruption, the barbarous intimidation, the integrity of candidates warped and stained, the honest electors who are ruined, the feeble ones who are suborned and dishonoured; the lies, the stratagems, the slanders which stalk abroad in the daylight, naked and not ashamed; the desecration of holy words; the soiling of noble names – we stand aghast at the holocaust of victims – of destroyed bodies and lost souls – on whose funeral pile a new Parliament is reared.

The means of corruption and intimidation were the usual ones: direct government influence. Thus on an electioneering agent at Derby, arrested in the flagrant act of bribing, a letter was found from Major Beresford, the Secretary at War, wherein that same Beresford opens a credit upon a commercial firm for electioneering monies. The *Poole Herald* publishes a circular from Admiralty House to the half-pay officers, signed by the commander-in-chief of a naval station, requesting their votes for the ministerial candidates. Direct force of arms has also been employed, as at Cork, Belfast, Limerick (at which latter place eight persons were killed). Threats of ejection by landlords against their farmers, unless they voted with them. The land agents of Lord Derby herein gave the example to their colleagues. Threats of exclusive dealing against shopkeepers, of dismissal against workmen, intoxication, etc., etc. To these *profane* means of corruption *spiritual* ones were added by the Tories; the royal proclamation against Roman Catholic processions was issued in order to inflame bigotry and religious hatred; the No Popery cry was raised everywhere. One of the results of this proclamation were the Stockport riots.[35] The Irish priests, of course, retorted with similar weapons.

The election is hardly over, and already a single Queen's Counsel has received from twenty-five places instructions to invalidate the returns to Parliament on account of bribery and intimidation. Such petitions against elected members have been signed, and the expenses of the proceedings raised, at Derby, Cockermouth, Barnstaple, Harwich, Canterbury, Yarmouth, Wakefield, Boston, Huddersfield, Windsor and a great number of

35. On 29–30 June 1852, at Stockport, Cheshire, a Protestant mob conducted a terrorist attack on the local Irish population, with police connivance.

other places. Of eight to ten Derbyite members it is proved that, even under the most favourable circumstances, they will be rejected on petition.

The principal scenes of this bribery, corruption and intimidation were, of course, the agricultural counties and the peers' boroughs; for the conservation of the greatest possible number of the latter the Whigs had expended all their acumen in the Reform Bill of 1831. The constituencies of large towns and of densely populated manufacturing counties were, by their peculiar circumstances, very unfavourable ground for such manoeuvres.

Days of general election are in Britain traditionally the bacchanalia of drunken debauchery, conventional stock-jobbing terms for the discounting of political consciences, the richest harvest times of the publicans. As an English paper says, 'These recurring saturnalia never fail to leave enduring traces of their pestilential presence.'[36] Quite naturally so. They are saturnalia in the ancient Roman sense of the word. The master then turned servant, the servant turned master. If the servant be master for one day, on that day brutality will reign supreme. The masters were the grand dignitaries of the ruling classes, or sections of classes, the servants formed the mass of these same classes, the privileged electors encircled by the mass of the non-electors, of those thousands that had no other calling than to be mere hangers-on, and whose support, vocal or manual, always appeared desirable, were it only on account of the theatrical effect.

If you follow up the history of British elections for a century past or longer, you are tempted to ask not why British Parliaments were so bad, but on the contrary, how they managed to be even as good as they were, and to represent as much as they did, though in a dim refraction, the actual movement of British society. Just as opponents of the representative system must feel surprised on finding that legislative bodies in which the abstract majority, the accident of the mere number, is decisive, yet decide and resolve according to the necessities of the situation – at least during the period of their full vitality. It will always be impossible, even by the utmost straining of logical deductions, to derive from the relations of mere numbers the necessity of a vote in accordance with the actual state of things; but from a given state of things the necessity of certain relations of numbers will always follow as of itself. The traditional bribery of British elections, what else was

36. *Economist*, 7 August 1852.

it but another form, as brutal as it was popular, in which the relative strength of the contending parties showed itself? Their respective means of influence and of dominion, which on other occasions they used in a *normal* way, were here enacted for a few days in an abnormal and more or less burlesque manner. But the premise remained, that the candidates of the rivalling parties represented the interests of the mass of the electors, and that the privileged electors again represented the interests of the nonvoting mass, or rather, that this voteless mass had, as yet, no specific interest of its own. The Delphic priestesses had to become intoxicated by vapours to enable them to find oracles; the British people must intoxicate itself with gin and porter to enable it to find its oracle-finders, the legislators. And where these oracle-finders were to be looked for, that was a matter of course.

This relative position of classes and parties underwent a radical change from the moment the industrial and commercial middle classes, the bourgeoisie, took up its stand as an official party at the side of the Whigs and Tories, and especially from the passing of the Reform Bill in 1831. These bourgeois were in no wise fond of costly electioneering manoeuvres, of *faux frais* of general elections. They considered it cheaper to compete with the landed aristocracy by general moral, than by personal pecuniary means. On the other hand they were conscious of representing a universally predominant interest of modern society. They were, therefore, in a position to demand that electors should be ruled by their common national interests, not by personal and local motives, and the more they recurred to this postulate, the more the latter species of electoral influence was, by the very composition of constituencies, centred in the landed aristocracy but withheld from the middle classes. Thus the bourgeoisie contended for the principle of moral elections and forced the enactment of laws in that sense, intended, each of them, as safeguards against the local influence of the landed aristocracy; and indeed, from 1831 down, bribery adopted a more civilized, more hidden form, and general elections went off in a more sober way than before. When at last the mass of the people ceased to be a mere chorus, taking a more or less impassioned part in the struggle of the official heroes, drawing lots among them, rioting, in bacchantic carouse, at the creation of parliamentary divinities, like the Cretan centaurs at the birth of Jupiter, and taking pay and treat for such participation in their glory – when the Chartists surrounded in threatening

masses the whole circle within which the official election struggle must come off, and watched with scrutinizing mistrust every
movement taking place within it – then an election like that
of 1852 could not but call for universal indignation, and elicit
even from the conservative *Times*, for the first time, some words
in favour of general suffrage, and make the whole mass of the
British proletariat shout as with one voice: The foes of Reform,
they have given Reformers the best arguments; such is an election
under the class system; such is a House of Commons with such a
system of election!

In order to comprehend the character of bribery, corruption and
intimidation, such as they have been practised in the late election,
it is necessary to call attention to a fact which operated in a parallel
direction.

If you refer to the general elections since 1831, you will find
that, in the same measure as the pressure of the voteless majority
of the country upon the privileged body of electors was increasing,
as the demand was heard louder, from the middle classes, for an
extension of the circle of constituencies, from the working class,
to extinguish every trace of a similar privileged circle – that in the
same measure the number of electors who actually voted grew less
and less, and the constituencies thus more and more contracted
themselves. Never was this fact more striking than in the late
election.

Let us take, for instance, London. In the City the constituency
numbers 26,728; only 10,000 voted. The Tower Hamlets number
23,534 registered electors; only 12,000 voted. In Finsbury, of 20,025
electors, not one half voted. In Liverpool, the scene of one of the
most animated contests, of 17,433 registered electors, only 13,000
came to the polls.

These examples will suffice. What do they prove? The apathy
of the privileged constituencies. And this apathy, what proves it?
That they have outlived themselves – that they have lost every
interest in their own political existence. This is in no wise apathy
against politics in general, but against a species of politics, the
result of which, for the most part, can only consist in helping the
Tories to oust the Whigs, or the Whigs to conquer the Tories. The
constituencies feel instinctively that the decision lies no longer
either with Parliament, or with the making of Parliament. Who
repealed the Corn Laws? Assuredly not the voters who had elected
a Protectionist Parliament, still less the Protectionist Parliament

itself, but only and exclusively the pressure from without. In this pressure from without, in other means of influencing Parliament than by voting, a great portion even of electors now believe. They consider the hitherto lawful mode of voting as an antiquated formality, but from the moment Parliament should make front against the pressure from without, and dictate laws to the nation in the sense of its narrow constituencies, they would join the general assault against the whole antiquated system of machinery.

The bribery and intimidation practised by the Tories were, then, merely violent experiments for bringing back to life dying electoral bodies which have become incapable of production, and which can no longer create decisive electoral results and really national Parliaments. And the result? The old Parliament was dissolved, because at the end of its career it had dissolved into sections which brought each other to a complete standstill. The new Parliament begins where the old one ended; it is paralytic from the hour of its birth.

LETTER TO THE LABOUR PARLIAMENT[37]

London, 9 March 1854

I regret deeply to be unable, for the moment at least, to leave London, and thus to be prevented from expressing verbally my feelings of pride and gratitude on receiving the invitation to sit as Honorary Delegate at the Labour Parliament. The mere assembling of such a Parliament marks a new epoch in the history of the world. The news of this great fact will arouse the hopes of the working classes throughout Europe and America.

Great Britain, of all other countries, has seen developed on the greatest scale the despotism of capital and the slavery of labour. In no other country have the intermediate stations between the millionaire commanding whole industrial armies and the wage slave living only from hand to mouth so gradually been swept away from the soil. There exist here no longer, as in continental countries, large classes of peasants and artisans almost equally

37. The Labour Parliament held in Manchester from 6 to 18 March 1854 was part of an unsuccessful attempt by the Chartist left wing to create a broad workers' organization out of the widespread strike movement of 1853–4. Marx was elected an honorary delegate, no doubt on Ernest Jones's proposal. His 'Letter' was read to the Labour Parliament on 10 March, and published in the *People's Paper* on 18 March 1854.

dependent on their own property and their own labour. A complete divorce of property from labour has been effected in Great Britain. In no other country, therefore, the war between the two classes that constitute modern society has assumed so colossal dimensions and features so distinct and palpable.

But it is precisely from these facts that the working classes of Great Britain, before all others, are competent and called for to act as leaders in the great movement that must finally result in the absolute emancipation of labour. Such they are from the conscious clearness of their position, the vast superiority of their numbers, the disastrous struggles of their past, and the moral strength of their present.

It is the working millions of Great Britain who first have laid down the real basis of a new society – modern industry, which transformed the destructive agencies of nature into the productive power of man. The English working classes, with invincible energies, by the sweat of their brows and brains, have called into life the material means of ennobling labour itself, and of multiplying its fruits to such a degree as to make general abundance possible.

By creating the inexhaustible productive powers of modern industry they have fulfilled the first condition of the emancipation of labour. They have now to realize its other condition. They have to free those wealth-producing powers from the infamous shackles of monopoly, and subject them to the joint control of the producers, who, till now, allowed the very products of their hands to turn against them and be transformed into as many instruments of their own subjugation.

The labouring classes have conquered nature; they have now to conquer man. To succeed in this attempt they do not want strength, but the organization of their common strength, organization of the labouring classes on a national scale – such, I suppose, is the great and glorious end aimed at by the Labour Parliament.

If the Labour Parliament proves true to the idea that called it into life, some future historian will have to record that there existed in the year 1854 two parliaments in England, a parliament at London, and a parliament at Manchester – a parliament of the rich, and a parliament of the poor – but that men sat only in the parliament of the men and not in the parliament of the masters.

Yours truly,

KARL MARX

PARTIES AND CLIQUES[38]

London, 5 February

The duration of the present government crisis[39] is more or less normal, as such crises in England have in the past lasted an average of nine to ten days. In his famous work *On Man and the Development of his Faculties*[40] [Adolphe] Quételet amazes the reader with the demonstration that the annual number of accidents, crimes, etc., in civilized countries can be determined in advance with almost mathematical accuracy. There is nothing amazing, however, about the normal duration of the English government crises typical of various periods of the nineteenth century; it is well known that a definite series of ministerial permutations must be attempted, a definite number of offices must be haggled over, and a definite number of intrigues must be allowed to cancel each other out. Only the character of the present political permutations is unusual, a character that is due to the dissolution of the old parties. It was, indeed, this very dissolution which made possible and inevitable the formation of the Coalition ministry which has now collapsed. The governing caste, which in England is by no means identical with the ruling class, will now be driven from one coalition to the next until it has given conclusive proof that it is no longer destined to govern. As is known, the Derbyites had declared their opposition to coalitions in highly solemn tones. Yet Lord Derby's first step, as soon as the Queen had charged him with the formation of a new Cabinet, was to try to form a coalition, not only with Palmerston (and Disraeli had explicitly declared during the Roebuck debate that the vote of censure which had been moved was no longer directed against the Duke of Newcastle[41] or Aberdeen but against Palmerston himself),

38. The following five articles were written by Marx in 1855 for the *Neue Oder-Zeitung*, a German newspaper with democratic leanings published in Breslau. They are translated here from the texts printed in *MEW* 11. 'Parties and Cliques' first appeared in the *Neue Oder-Zeitung* of 8 February 1855.

39. This government crisis followed the resignation of Lord Aberdeen's Coalition ministry (of Whigs and Peelites) on 29 January 1855. The Aberdeen ministry was defeated in the Commons over the 'Roebuck motion', which appointed a Select Committee to investigate the government departments responsible for the mismanagement of the British army in the Crimea.

40. English translation published in Edinburgh, 1842.

41. The Duke of Newcastle was Minister of War in the Aberdeen ministry.

but also with Gladstone and Sidney Herbert – that is, with the Peelites. The Tories pursued the Peelites with particular hatred as they saw in them the most immediately identifiable instruments of their party's dissolution. Russell was then charged with the formation of a Cabinet, and he attempted a coalition with the same Peelites whose presence in the old ministry had served as a pretext for his resignation and who had deserted him in a solemn parliamentary sitting. When Palmerston finally forms his ministry he will only produce a second, slightly altered version of the old Coalition ministry. The Whig Grey clan will perhaps replace the Whig Russell clan, and so on.

The old parliamentary parties with their monopoly on government exist now only in the form of coteries; but the same causes which have robbed these coteries of the power to form parties, to distinguish themselves from each other, also rob them of the power to unite. As a result, no period of English parliamentary history has demonstrated such a fragmentation into a mass of insignificant and fortuitous cliques as the period of the Coalition ministry. Only two of these cliques, the Derbyites and the Russellites, are numerically significant. Their followers include an extremely ramified group of powerful old families with a wide patronage. But it is precisely this numerical strength which constitutes the weakness of the Derbyites and Russellites. They are too small to form an independent parliamentary majority; yet they are too large and nourish too many careerists at their breasts to be able to purchase sufficient support from outside their ranks by bestowing important positions. The numerically weak cliques of Peelites, Greyites, Palmerstonians, etc., are therefore more suited to form coalition ministries. But the very thing that enables them to form ministries – the weakness of each of these cliques individually – makes their parliamentary majority a matter of chance, which can be broken any day, whether by an alliance of Derbyites and Russellites or by a combination of the Derbyites with the Manchester School.

The recent attempts to form ministries have been equally interesting from another point of view. In all these ministerial combinations members of the old Cabinet have been included, and the most important member of this Cabinet now heads the latest combination. Yet does not the passage of the Roebuck motion, which censured all the members of the old Coalition, imply that the vote of no confidence will be followed by a committee of inquiry, as Palmerston himself declared in his answer to Disraeli?

Are the accused to take over the helm of state again before the committee has been appointed, before the investigation has opened? But although Parliament has the power to bring down the ministry, the ministry has the power to *dissolve* Parliament. How the prospect of a dissolution must affect the present Parliament can be seen from the statement made on 1 March 1853 by Sir John Trollope, who observed that as many as fourteen Commons committees were already sitting to investigate the cases of corruption in the last parliamentary elections. If this continued, every Member of Parliament would be fully occupied with committees of inquiry. Indeed, the number of members accused was so overwhelming that the rest, whose election was not contested, would not suffice to pass judgement on them, or even to conduct an inquiry.

It would be a bitter blow if the seats so dearly bought were to be lost at the very beginning of the third parliamentary session – for patriotism's sake.

THE BRITISH CONSTITUTION[42]

London, 2 March

While the British Constitution has failed all along the line wherever the war has put it to the test, on the home front the Coalition ministry – the most constitutional in English history – has disintegrated. 40,000 British soldiers have died on the shores of the Black Sea, victims of the British Constitution! Officers, Command Headquarters, Commissariat, Medical Corps, Transport Corps, Admiralty, Horse Guards, Ordnance Department, the Army and Navy – all have collapsed. They have completely ruined their reputation in the eyes of the world; but all have the satisfaction of knowing that they were only doing their duty in the eyes of the British Constitution! *The Times* spoke truer than it knew when it declared that it was the British Constitution itself that was on trial. It has stood trial and has been found guilty.

But what is this British Constitution? Are its essential features to be found in the laws governing representation and the limitations imposed on the executive power? These characteristics distinguish it neither from the Constitution of the United States nor from the constitutions of the countless joint-stock companies in England which know 'their business'. The British Constitution

---

42. From the *Neue Oder-Zeitung*, 6 March 1855.

is, in fact, only an antiquated and obsolete compromise made between the bourgeoisie, which rules in actual practice, although *not officially*, in all the decisive spheres of bourgeois society, and the landed aristocracy, which forms the *official government*. After the 'Glorious Revolution' of 1688 only one section of the bourgeoisie, the *financial aristocracy*, was originally included in the compromise. The Reform Bill of 1831 opened the door to another group – the *millocracy*, as they are called in England: the high dignitaries of the *industrial* bourgeoisie. Legislative history since 1831 is the history of concessions made to the industrial bourgeoisie, from the Poor Law Amendment Act[43] to the repeal of the Corn Laws, and from the repeal of the Corn Laws to the Succession Duty on landed property.[44]

Although the bourgeoisie – itself only the highest social stratum of the middle classes – thus also gained general *political* recognition as the *ruling class*, this only happened on one condition; namely that the whole business of government in all its details – including even the executive branch of the legislature, that is, the actual making of laws in both Houses of Parliament – remained the guaranteed domain of the landed aristocracy. In 1830 the bourgeoisie preferred a renewal of the compromise with the landed aristocracy to a compromise with the mass of the English people. Now, subjected to certain principles laid down by the bourgeoisie, the aristocracy (which enjoys exclusive power in the Cabinet, in Parliament, in the Civil Service, in the Army and Navy, and which is thus one half, and comparatively the most important one, of the British nation) is being forced at this very moment to sign its own death warrant and to admit before the whole world that it is no longer destined to govern England. Observe the attempts being made to galvanize the corpses of the aristocracy into life! Ministry after ministry is formed, only to dissolve itself after governing for a few weeks. The crisis is permanent; the government only provisional. All political action has been suspended, and everyone admits that his only concern is to keep the political machine adequately oiled so that it does not come to a complete standstill. Not even the House of Commons recognizes itself in the ministries which are created in its own image.

43. The Poor Law Amendment Act of 1834 abolished outdoor relief and set up a standardized system of poor relief based on workhouses.
44. Succession Duty was introduced in 1853.

In this general state of helplessness there is not only a war to be waged but an enemy even more dangerous than Tsar Nicholas to be fought. This enemy is the *commercial* and *industrial* crisis, which since last September has been increasing in force and scope with every day that passes. Its iron hand has stopped the mouths of the superficial apostles of free trade who have been preaching for years that, since the repeal of the Corn Laws, saturated markets and social crises have been banished for ever into the shadowy realm of the past. The markets are saturated again, and no one is decrying the lack of caution which has prevented manufacturers from curbing production louder than the same economists who were lecturing us five months ago, with dogmatic infallibility, that it was impossible to produce too much.

The sickness appeared in a chronic form at the time of the Preston strike.[45] Shortly afterwards saturation of the American market brought the crisis to a head in the United States. Although saturated, India and China, just like California and Australia, continued to function as outlets for overproduction. As the English manufacturers could no longer sell their goods on the domestic markets without forcing down prices, they resorted to the dangerous expedient of sending their products abroad on consignment, particularly to India, China, Australia and California. These evasive measures enabled trade to continue for a while with less disruption than if the goods had been dumped on the market all at once. But as soon as these goods arrived at their destination they immediately affected prices, and towards the end of September the effects were also felt here in England.

The crisis then moved from a chronic to an acute stage. The first firms to collapse were calico printers, among them old-established firms in and around Manchester. It was next the turn of the ship-owners, the Australian and Californian traders, then the Chinese and finally the Indian firms. Everyone was hit, and most suffered heavy losses; many firms have had to suspend business, and the danger is not over for any of them in this area of commerce. On the contrary, it continues to grow. Silk manu-

45. The strike of cotton spinners and weavers in Preston and the surrounding districts, which began in August 1853, was one of the largest strikes of the 1850s. The workers' basic demand was a wage rise of 10 per cent. The manufacturers responded with a lock-out, which lasted until February 1854. The Chartists played a prominent role in the strike, which was eventually broken by the arrest of its leaders in March 1854 and the importing of Irish strike-breakers.

facturers have been similarly hit; for the moment their industry
has almost come to a standstill, and the districts where silk is
manufactured are suffering terrible hardships. It is now the turn
of the cotton spinners and manufacturers: some have already
succumbed and a good many more will inevitably share their
fate. We have already mentioned[46] that the fine-spun producers
are still working short time and the manufacturers of coarse-spun
will soon have to resort to the same measures. Even now some of
them are only working for a few days per week. How long will
they be able to last?

Another few months and the crisis in the manufacturing districts
will reach the severity of 1842, if it does not exceed it. But as soon
as its effects are generally felt among the working classes there
will be a revival of the political movements which for six years
have been more or less dormant among these classes and have
only left behind the cadres for new agitation. The conflict between
the industrial proletariat and the bourgeoisie will begin again at
the same time as the conflict between bourgeoisie and aristocracy reaches its climax. The mask will then drop, which until now
has hidden from the foreigner the real features of Great Britain's
political physiognomy. However, only those who are unacquainted
with this country's rich human and material resources will doubt
that it will emerge victorious and rejuvenated from the impending
great crisis.[47]

46. In an article in the *Neue Oder-Zeitung* of 20 February 1855; see *MEW* 11,
pp. 66–8.

47. In a variant of this article published in the *New York Daily Tribune* on 24
March 1855, this paragraph is replaced by the following: 'A few months more
and the crisis will be at a height which it has not reached in England since 1846,
perhaps not since 1842. When its effects begin to be fully felt among the working
classes, then will that political movement begin again, which has been dormant for
six years. Then will the working men of England rise anew, menacing the middle
classes at the very time that the middle classes are finally driving the aristocracy
from power. Then will the mask be torn off which has hitherto hid the real political features of Great Britain. Then will the two real contending parties in that
country stand face to face – the middle class and the working class, the bourgeoisie
and the proletariat – and England will at last be compelled to share in the general social evolutions of European society. When England entered into the French
alliance she finally abandoned that isolated character which her insular position
had created for her, but which the commerce of the world, and the increasing
facilities for intercourse, had long since undermined. Henceforth she can hardly
help undergoing the great internal movements of the other European nations.' 'The
Crisis in England', *MECW* 14, pp. 61–2.

THE CHARACTER OF THE WHIGS AND TORIES[48]

London, 14 May

The *anti-aristocratic* movement in England[49] can only have one *immediate* result: to bring the Tories, that is, the *specifically aristocratic party, to power*. If not, it is bound, first of all, to peter out in a few Whig platitudes, a few administrative sham reforms not worth mentioning. Layard's[50] announcement of his resolutions on the 'State of the Nation' and the reception given to this announcement in the House of Commons led to the holding of the City meetings. But hot on the heels of the City meetings came Ellenborough's motion in the House of Lords by means of which the Tories have taken control of the new Reform agitation and have transformed it into a ladder for their rise to government power. In his motion Layard himself has changed the words '*aristocratic influence*' to '*family influence*' – a concession to the Tories. Every movement outside the House assumes *within* the House the form of a squabble between the two fractions of the ruling class. In the hands of the Whigs the Anti-Corn-Law League became a means of overthrowing the Tories. In the hands of the Tories the Administrative Reform Association has become a means of overthrowing the Whigs.[51] It must not be forgotten that in this way both fractions in turn have sacrificed one basic element of the old regime after another, while, it may be added, the regime itself has been preserved. We have already expressed our view that only the Tories can be forced into making large concessions because only under them does the pressure from outside assume a threatening, and even a revolutionary, character. The Whigs represent the actual oligarchy in England, the rule of a few great families such as the Sutherlands, the Bedfords, the Carlisles, the

48. From the *Neue Oder-Zeitung*, 18 May 1855. This is the second part of a composite article originally entitled '*Morning Post* against Prussia; Character of the Whigs and Tories'.

49. This anti-aristocratic movement was the Association for Administrative Reform, founded in May 1855 by City business circles. It attempted to use the unrest due to the Crimean catastrophe, and the exposures of official incompetence by the Roebuck Committee, to promote the appointment of more representatives of the commercial and financial bourgeoisie to official positions.

50. Sir Austen Henry Layard, an archaeologist and the Radical MP, was a member of the Roebuck Committee investigating the conduct of the Crimean War.

51. The Whig government of Palmerston in fact survived until 1858.

Devonshires, etc.; the Tories represent the squireocracy, the Junker party, one might say, although broad lines of distinction must be drawn between the English squire and the north German Junker. The Tories, therefore, are the vehicles of all the Old English prejudices with regard to Church and state, patronage and anti-Catholicism. The Whigs, the oligarchs, are *enlightened* and have never hesitated to cast off prejudices which stand in the way of their hereditary tenure of state office. The Whigs have always prevented any movement within the middle classes by offering their friendship; the Tories have always driven the mass of the people into the arms of the middle classes with their friendship, having already placed the middle classes at the disposal of the Whigs. At this moment there is no longer any difference between Whigs and Tories except that the latter represent the plebs of the aristocracy, and the former its cream. The old aristocratic phrases are on the side of the aristocratic plebs; the liberal phrases on the side of the aristocratic upper crust. Indeed, since the decline of the old Tories (Lord Bolinbroke, etc.) the Tory party has always been ruled by parvenus, Pitt, Addington, Perceval, Canning, Peel and Disraeli. The *homines novi*[52] have always been found among the ranks of the Tories. When Lord Derby (himself a Whig turncoat) formed his ministry it contained besides him perhaps two other old names. All the rest were simple squires, apart from one man of letters. The Whigs, on the other hand, who have never hesitated for a second to change their coats and views with the times, who apparently can always rejuvenate and metamorphose themselves, have not needed any new people. They have been able to perpetuate the family names. If one reviews the whole of English history since the 'Glorious Revolution' of 1688, one finds that all the laws directed against the mass of the people have been initiated by the Whigs, from the Septennial Act to the most recent Poor Law and factory legislation. But Whig reaction has always been in harmony with the middle classes. Tory reaction has been directed even more against the middle classes than against the mass of the people. Hence the liberal reputation of the Whigs.

ON THE REFORM MOVEMENT[53]

London, 21 May

Today all the London newspapers have published an address from

52. New men.   53. From the *Neue Oder-Zeitung*, 24 May 1855.

the City Reformers, or rather from their executive committee, to the 'People of England'. The style of the document is dry, business-like and not quite as fulsome as the trade circulars which periodically appear from the same source offering to the world at large coffee, tea, sugar, spices and other tropical products wrapped up in tastefully arranged verbiage. The Association promises to produce material for a thorough physiological examination of the different government departments and to reveal all the mysteries of Downing Street and its heritage of wisdom. That is what it promises. What it demands in return is that, instead of sending candidates to Parliament who, as hitherto, have been imposed on them by aristocratic clubs, the English electorates should elect candidates of their own choosing, who recommend themselves solely by their merit. Thus the Association recognizes as normal those same privileged electorates which – with their corruption, their dependence upon a few clubs and their total lack of freedom – it admits to be the birthplace of the present House of Commons and therefore of the government. The members of the Association have no desire to abolish these exclusive electoral bodies nor even to widen them; they merely wish to exercise a moral influence on them. Why do they not have done with it and appeal to the conscience of the oligarchy instead of threatening to abolish its privileges? It must surely be an easier task to convert the heads of the oligarchy than its electoral bodies. Evidently the City Association would like to provoke an anti-aristocratic movement, but a movement *within* the bounds of *legality* (as Guizot put it), a movement within official England. And how does it intend to stir up the stagnant morass of the constituencies? How does it intend to bring about their emancipation from interests and practices which make them the vassals of a few select clubs and the supporting pillars of the governing oligarchy? By means of a physiology of Downing Street? Not quite; but nevertheless by means of *pressure from without*, mass meetings and the like. And how does the Association intend to mobilize the unofficial and unfranchised masses, in order to exert pressure on the privileged electoral circle? By inviting them to abandon the People's Charter (which basically contains nothing less than the demand for *universal suffrage* and the necessary conditions for its genuine realization in England); by inviting them to acknowledge the privileges of these electorates, which, as the City Reformers themselves admit, are in the process of decay. The City Association has before it the example of the Parliamentary and Financial Reformers. It knows that this movement, led by Hume, Bright, Cobden, Walmsley and Thompson, failed because it tried to replace the People's Charter by the so-called 'Little Charter', because it tried to make a compromise with the masses, because it tried to fob them off with mere concessions. Does the Association imagine that it can achieve *without* concessions what these men were not able to achieve *despite* concessions? Or does it conclude from the Anti-Corn-Law movement that it is possible to mobilize the English people for partial reforms? The object of that movement was very general, very popular, very palpable. The symbol of the Anti-Corn-Law League was, of course, a large and substantial loaf of bread, in contrast to the diminutive loaf of the Protectionists. The popular idiom naturally responded more readily to the idea of a loaf of bread – particularly in the famine year of 1845 – than it would to the notion of a 'physiology of Downing Street'. We need not remind our readers of a famous brochure, *The City; or, the Physiology of London Business*,[54] which demonstrated with the greatest accuracy that no matter how well the gentlemen of the City conduct their individual business, in the management of their *common* business, like all *insurance companies*, they follow more or less faithfully the official line laid down by Downing Street. Their management of the *railways*, with its blatant fraud, swindling and total neglect of safety precautions, is so notorious that more than once the question has been raised in and outside Parliament, and in the press, as to whether the railways should not be put under direct state control and taken out of the hands of the private capitalists! The physiology of Downing Street, therefore, will not 'do', as the English say. '*This will not do, sir!*'[55]

AGITATION AGAINST THE SUNDAY TRADING BILL[56]

London, 25 June

Obsolete social forces, nominally still in possession of all the attributes of power long after the basis of their existence has rotted away under their feet, continue to vegetate as their heirs begin to quarrel over their claims to the inheritance – even before

54. By D. M. Evans, London, 1845.   55. In English in the original.
56. From the *Neue Oder-Zeitung*, 28 June 1855.

the obituary notice has been printed and the testament unsealed; and it is an old maxim, borne out by history, that before their final death agony these social forces summon up their strength once more and move from the defensive to the offensive, issuing challenges instead of giving ground, and attempting to draw the most extreme conclusions from premises which have not only been called into question but have already been condemned. Such is the case today with the English oligarchy; and such is the case with its twin sister, the Church. There have been innumerable attempts at reorganization within the Established Church, both High and Low, and attempts to come to terms with the dissenters so that the profane masses can be confronted with a compact force. Measures of religious coercion have followed each other in rapid succession – in the House of Lords the pious Lord Ashley bewailed the fact that in England alone five million people had become estranged not only from the Church but from Christianity. The Established Church replies, '*Compelle intrare*'.[57] It leaves it to Lord Ashley and similar dissenting, sectarian and hysterical pietists to pull out of the fire the chestnuts which it intends to eat itself.

The Beer Bill, which closed all places of public amusement on Sundays except between 6 and 10 p.m., was the first example of religious coercion. It was smuggled through a sparsely attended House at the end of a sitting, after the pietists had bought the support of the larger London publicans by guaranteeing them the continuation of the licensing system – the continued monopoly of big capital. Then came the Sunday Trading Bill, which has now passed its third reading in the Commons and which has just been debated clause by clause by the Committee of the Whole House. In this new coercive measure, too, the interest of big capital has been heeded, as only small shopkeepers do business on Sundays and the big shops are quite willing to eliminate the Sunday competition of the small traders by parliamentary means. In both cases we find a conspiracy between the Church and the capitalist monopolies, and in both religious penal laws aimed at the lower classes to set at rest the conscience of the privileged classes. The aristocratic clubs were no more hit by the Beer Bill than the Sunday occupations of fashionable society are by the Sunday Trading Bill. The working class receives its wages late on Satur-

57. From the biblical phrase, 'Compel them to come in, that my house may be filled.'

days; Sunday trading, therefore, exists solely for them. They are the only section of the population forced to make their small purchases on Sundays, and the new bill is directed against them alone. In the eighteenth century the French aristocracy said, 'For us, Voltaire; for the people, mass and tithes.' In the nineteenth century the English aristocracy says, 'For us, pious phrases; for the people, Christian practice.' The classical saints of Christianity mortified their bodies to save the souls of the masses; the modern, educated saints mortify the *bodies of the masses* to save their own souls.

This alliance between a degenerate, dissipated and pleasure-seeking aristocracy and the Church – built on a foundation of filthy and calculated profiteering on the part of the beer magnates and monopolistic wholesalers – gave rise to a *mass demonstration* in Hyde Park yesterday, such as London has not seen since the death of George IV, the 'first gentleman of Europe'. We witnessed the event from beginning to end and believe we can state without exaggeration that *yesterday in Hyde Park the English revolution began*. The latest news from the Crimea acted as an important ferment in this *'unparliamentary'*, *'extra-parliamentary'* and *'anti-parliamentary'* demonstration.

The instigator of the Sunday Trading Bill, Lord Robert Grosvenor, had answered the objection that his bill was directed only against the poor and not against the rich classes by saying that the aristocracy was largely refraining from employing its servants and horses on Sundays. At the end of last week the following poster issued *by the Chartists* could be seen on all the walls in London announcing in large print:

New Sunday Bill prohibiting newspapers, shaving, smoking, eating and drinking and all other kinds of recreation and nourishment both corporal and spiritual, which the *poor people* still enjoy at the present time. *An open-air meeting* of artisans, workers and *'the lower orders'* generally of the capital will take place in Hyde Park on Sunday afternoon to see how religiously the aristocracy is observing the Sabbath and how anxious it is not to employ its servants and horses on that day, as Lord Robert Grosvenor said in his speech. The meeting is called for three o'clock on the right bank of the Serpentine, on the side towards Kensington Gardens. Come and bring your wives and children in order that they may profit by the example their 'betters' set them!

It should be realized that what Longchamps means to the Parisians, the road along the Serpentine means to English high society:

it is the place where in the afternoons, particularly on Sundays, they parade their magnificent carriages with all their trappings and exercise their horses followed by swarms of lackeys. It will be evident from the poster quoted above that the struggle against clericalism, like every serious struggle in England, is assuming the character of a *class struggle* waged by the poor against the rich, by the people against the aristocracy, by the 'lower orders' against their 'betters'.

At 3 o'clock about 50,000 people had gathered at the appointed spot on the right bank of the Serpentine in the huge meadows of Hyde Park. Gradually the numbers swelled to at least 200,000 as people came from the left bank too. Small knots of people could be seen being jostled from one spot to another. A large contingent of police was evidently attempting to deprive the organizers of the meeting of what Archimedes had demanded in order to move the earth: a fixed place to stand on. Finally, a large crowd made a firm stand and the Chartist [James] Bligh constituted himself chairman on a small rise in the middle of the crowd. No sooner had he begun his harangue than Police Inspector Banks at the head of forty truncheon-swinging constables explained to him that the Park was the private property of the Crown and that they were not allowed to hold a meeting in it. After some preliminary exchanges, in the course of which Bligh tried to demonstrate that the Park was public property and Banks replied he had strict orders to arrest him if he persisted in his intention, Bligh shouted amidst the tremendous roar of the masses around him: 'Her Majesty's police declare that Hyde Park is the private property of the Crown and that Her Majesty is not inclined to lend her land to the people for their meetings. So let us adjourn to Oxford Market.'

With the ironic cry of '*God save the Queen!*' the throng dispersed in the direction of Oxford Market. But meanwhile [James] Finlen, a member of the Chartist leadership, had rushed to a tree some distance away. A crowd followed him and surrounded him instantly in such a tight and compact circle that the police abandoned their attempts to force their way through to him. 'We are enslaved for six days a week', he said, 'and Parliament wants to rob us of our bit of freedom on the seventh. These oligarchs and capitalists and their allies, the sanctimonious clerics, want to do *penance* – not by mortifying themselves but by mortifying us – for the unconscionable murder committed against the sons of the people sacrificed in the Crimea.'

We left this group to approach another where a speaker, stretched out on the ground, was haranguing his audience from this horizontal position. Suddenly from all sides came the cry: 'Let's go to the road. Let's go to the carriages.' Meanwhile people had already begun heaping insults on the carriages and riders. The constables, who were steadily receiving reinforcements, drove the pedestrians back from the road. They thus helped to form a dense avenue of people on either side which extended for more than a quarter of an hour's walk from Aspley House, up Rotten Row, and along the Serpentine as far as Kensington Gardens. The public gathering consisted of about two thirds workers and one third members of the middle class, all with their wives and children. The reluctant actors – elegant gentlemen and ladies, 'commoners and lords' in high coaches-and-four with liveried servants in front and behind, elderly gentlemen alone on horseback, a little flushed from their port wine – this time did not pass by in review. They ran the gauntlet. A babel of jeering, taunting and discordant noises – in which no language is so rich as the English – soon closed in upon them from all sides. As the concert was improvised there was a lack of instrumental accompaniment. The chorus, therefore, had to make use of its own organs and to confine itself to vocal music. And what a diabolical concert it was: a cacophony of grunting, hissing, whistling, squawking, snarling, growling, croaking, yelling, groaning, rattling, shrieking, gnashing sounds. Music to drive a man out of his mind, music to move a stone. Added to this came outbursts of genuine Old English humour strangely mixed with boiling and long-constrained anger. 'Go to church!' was the only recognizable articulate sound. In a conciliatory fashion one lady stretched out an orthodoxly bound prayerbook from the coach. 'Give it to your horses to read!' the thunder of a thousand voices echoed back. When the horses shied, reared, bucked and bolted, endangering the lives of their elegant burdens, the mocking cries became louder, more menacing, more implacable. Noble lords and ladies, among them Lady Granville, wife of the President of the Privy Council, were forced to alight and make use of their feet. When elderly gentlemen rode by whose dress – in particular the broad-brimmed hat – envinced a special claim to purity of faith, all the sounds of fury were extinguished, as at a command – by inextinguishable laughter. One of these gentlemen lost his patience. Like Mephistopheles he made an indecent gesture: he stuck his tongue out at the enemy. 'He is a wordcatcher! a parliamentary man! He fights with his own weapons!' someone called out from one side of the road. 'He is a saint! he is psalm singing!' came the antistrophe from the other side. Meanwhile the metropolitan electric telegraph had announced to all police stations that a riot was imminent in Hyde Park and ordered the police to the theatre of war. So at short intervals one police detachment after another marched between the two rows of people from Aspley House to Kensington Garden, each being met with the popular ditty:

> Where are the geese?
> Ask the police!

This refers to a notorious theft of geese which a constable recently committed in Clerkenwell.

The spectacle lasted for three hours. Only English lungs are capable of such a feat. During the performance opinions such as 'This is only the beginning!' 'This is the first step!' 'We hate them!' etc., could be heard from various groups. While hatred could be read in the faces of the workers we have never seen such smug, self-satisfied smiles as those that covered the faces of the middle classes. Just before the end the demonstration increased in violence. Sticks were shaken at the carriages, and through the endless discordant din the cry could be heard: 'You rascals!' Zealous Chartist men and women battled their way through the crowds throughout these three hours, distributing leaflets which declared in large type:

Reorganization of Chartism! A big public meeting will take place next Tuesday, 26 June, in the Literary and Scientific Institute in Friar Street, Doctor's Commons, to elect delegates to a conference for the reorganization of Chartism in the capital. Admission free.

Today's London papers carry on average only a short account of the events in Hyde Park. There have been no leading articles yet with the exception of Lord Palmerston's *Morning Post*. This paper writes:

A scene, in the highest degree disgraceful and dangerous, was enacted yesterday in Hyde Park ... [an] outrage on law and decency ... It was distinctly illegal to interfere, by physical force, in the free action of the legislature ... We must have no repetition of violence on Sunday next, as has been threatened.

But at the same time it declares that the 'fanatical' Lord Grosvenor is solely 'responsible' for the trouble and that he has provoked the 'just indignation of the people'! As if Parliament has not given Lord Grosvenor's Bill its three readings! Has he perhaps also exerted pressure 'by physical force in the free action of the legislature'?

II[58]

London, 2 July

The demonstration against the Sunday Bill was repeated in Hyde Park yesterday on a larger scale, under a more ominous sign and with more serious consequences, as is witnessed by the sombre but agitated mood in London today.

The posters calling for the repetition of the meeting also contained an invitation to assemble on Sunday at 10 a.m. before the house of the pious Lord Grosvenor and to accompany him to church. The pious gentleman, however, had left London on Saturday in a private carriage – in order to travel incognito. That he is by nature destined to make martyrs of others rather than to be a martyr himself had been demonstrated by his circular in all the London newspapers, in which he on the one hand upheld his Bill and on the other took pains to show that it is without meaning, function or significance. On Sunday his house was occupied all day not by psalm singers but by constables, 200 in number. Such was the case, too, at the house of his brother, the Marquess of Westminster, a man famous for his wealth.

On Saturday the head of the London police, Sir Richard Mayne, had posters stuck on all the walls in London in which he '*prohibited*' not only a meeting in Hyde Park but also the gathering of any 'large numbers' and the manifestation of any signs of approval or disapproval. The result of these decrees was that as early as 3 o'clock – even according to the report of the *Police Gazette* – 150,000 people of *every* age and social position were milling about. Gradually the crowds swelled to gigantic proportions unbelievable even by London standards. Not only did London appear *en masse*; an avenue of spectators formed again on both sides of the road along the Serpentine; only this time the crowd was denser and deeper than last Sunday. High society, however, stayed away. Altogether perhaps twenty vehicles put in

58. From the *Neue Oder-Zeitung*, 5 July 1855.

an appearance, most of them gigs and phaetons, which drove by without hindrance. Their more stately and better upholstered brethren, who displayed larger paunches and more livery, were greeted with the old shouts and with the old babel of noise; and this time the sound waves made the air vibrate for at least a mile around. The police decrees were given a rebuttal by the mass gathering and by the chorus of noise from a thousand throats. High society had avoided the field of battle, and by its absence it had acknowledged the sovereignty of the *vox populi*.

It was 4 o'clock. The demonstration seemed to be fizzling out into a harmless Sunday outing for want of any combustible elements. But the police had other plans. Were they to withdraw to the accompaniment of general laughter, casting wistful parting glances at their own posters, which could be read in large print at the entrance to the park? Besides, their high dignitaries were present: Sir Richard Mayne and Superintendents Gibbs and Walker on horseback, Inspectors Banks, Darkin and Brennan on foot. 800 constables had been strategically deployed, for the most part hidden in buildings and concealed in ambush. Stronger detachments had been stationed in neighbouring districts as reinforcements. At a point of intersection where the road along the Serpentine crosses a path leading towards Kensington Gardens, the Ranger's Lodge, the Magazine and the premises of the Royal Humane Society had been transformed into improvised blockhouses manned by a strong police contingent; each building had been prepared to accommodate prisoners and wounded. Cabs stood at the ready at the police station in Vine Street, Piccadilly, waiting to drive to the scene of battle and to take away the defeated demonstrators under safe escort. In short, the police had drawn up a plan of campaign 'more vigorous', as *The Times* said, 'than any of which we have yet had notice in the Crimea'. The police needed bloody heads and arrests so as not to stumble straight from the sublime into the ridiculous. So, as soon as the avenue of spectators had cleared somewhat, and the masses had dispersed away from the road into different groups on the huge expanse of the park, their senior officers took up positions in the middle of the road, between the rows of people, and from their horses they issued pompous orders right and left, supposedly for the protection of the carriages and horsemen passing by. As there were no carriages or horsemen, however, and therefore nothing to protect, they began to pick out individuals from the crowd 'on false pretexts' and to have them arrested on the pretext that they were pickpockets. As these experiments increased in number and the pretext lost its credibility the crowds raised a general cry, and the contingents of police broke out from their hiding places. Drawing their truncheons from their pockets they beat heads bloody, tore people out of the crowd here and there – altogether there were 104 such arrests – and dragged them to the improvised blockhouses. The left side of the road is separated only by a narrow piece of ground from the Serpentine. By manoeuvring his gang of constables a police officer managed to drive the spectators close to the edge of the water, where he threatened them with a cold bath. In order to escape the police truncheons one man swam across the Serpentine to the other bank; a policeman gave chase in a boat, caught him and brought him back in triumph.

How the scene had changed since the previous Sunday! Instead of elegant coaches-and-four, dirty cabs, which drove back and forth between the police station at Vine Street and the improvised jails in Hyde Park. Instead of lackeys on the boxes of carriages, constables sitting next to drunken cab drivers. Inside the vehicles, instead of elegant gentlemen and ladies, prisoners with bloody heads, dishevelled hair, half undressed and with torn clothes, guarded by dubious conscripts from the Irish lumpenproletariat who had been pressed into the London police. Instead of the wafting of fans, a hail of truncheons. Last Sunday the ruling classes had shown their fashionable face; this time the face they displayed was that of the state. In the background – behind the affably grinning old gentlemen, the fashionable dandies, the elegantly infirm widows and the perfumed beauties in their cashmeres, ostrich feathers, and garlands of flowers and diamonds – stood the constable with his waterproof coat, greasy oilskin hat and truncheon – the reverse side of the coin. Last Sunday the ruling classes had confronted the masses as individuals. This time they assumed the form of state power, law and truncheon. This time resistance amounted to insurrection, and the Englishman must be subjected to long, slow provocation before he is moved to insurrection. Thus, the counter-demonstration was limited, on the whole, to hissing, grunting and whistling at the police vehicles, to isolated attempts to free the prisoners but, above all, to passive resistance, as the crowds phlegmatically stood their ground on the field of battle.

Soldiers – partly from the Guard, partly from the 66th Regiment – assumed a characteristic role in this spectacle. They had appeared in force. Twelve of them, some decorated with medals from the Crimea, stood among a group of men, women and children on whom the police truncheons were descending. An old man fell to the ground, struck by a blow. 'The London stiffstaffs' (a term of abuse for the police) 'are worse than the Russians at Inkerman,' called out one of the Crimean heroes. The police seized him. He was immediately freed to the accompaniment of shouts from the crowd: 'Three cheers for the army!' The police deemed it advisable to move off. Meanwhile, a number of Grenadiers had arrived; the soldiers fell into line and with the crowd milling about them shouting, 'Hurrah for the army, down with the police, down with the Sunday Bill,' they paraded up and down in the park. The police stood about irresolutely, when a sergeant of the Guard appeared and loudly called them to account for their brutality, calmed the soldiers and persuaded some of them to follow him to the barracks to avoid more serious collisions. But the majority of the soldiers remained behind, and from among the people they gave vent to their anger at the police in no uncertain terms. In England the opposition between the police and the army is an old one. The present moment, when the army is the 'pet child' of the masses, is certainly not likely to reduce this opposition.

An old man named Russell is said to have died today as a result of the wounds he suffered yesterday; half a dozen people are in St George's Hospital suffering from injuries. During the demonstration different attempts were again made to hold smaller meetings. In one of them, near the Albert Gate outside the section of the park originally occupied by the police, an anonymous speaker harangued his public something like this:

Men of Old England! Awake, rise up from your slumber or fall for ever; resist the government every Sunday! Observe the Sunday Bill as you have done today. Do not be afraid to demand those rights to which you are entitled. Cast off the fetters of oligarchical oppression and tyranny. If you do not, you will be hopelessly crushed. Is it not outrageous that the inhabitants of this great metropolis, the greatest in the civilized world, must surrender their freedom into the hands of a Lord Grosvenor or a man like Lord Ebrington! His Lordship feels obliged to drive us to Church and to make us religious by means of an act of Parliament. His attempts are in vain. Who are we, and who are they? Look at the war which is being fought. Is it not being waged at the expense and with the blood of the productive classes? And what about the unproductive classes? They have bungled it from start to finish.

Speaker and meeting were, of course, interrupted by the police.

In Greenwich, near the Observatory, Londoners also held a meeting of ten to fifteen thousand people, which was likewise broken up by the police.

Speech at the Anniversary of the *People's Paper*[1]

The so-called revolutions of 1848 were but poor incidents – small fractures and fissures in the dry crust of European society. However, they denounced the abyss. Beneath the apparently solid surface they betrayed oceans of liquid matter, only needing expansion to rend into fragments continents of hard rock. Noisily and confusedly they proclaimed the emancipation of the proletarian, i.e., the secret of the nineteenth century, and of the revolution of that century. That social revolution, it is true, was no novelty invented in 1848. Steam, electricity, and the self-acting mule were revolutionists of a rather more dangerous character than even citizens Barbès, Raspail and Blanqui. But, although the atmosphere in which we live weighs upon every one with a 20,000 lb. force, do you feel it? No more than European society before 1848 felt the revolutionary atmosphere enveloping and pressing it from all sides. There is one great fact, characteristic of this our nineteenth century, a fact which no party dares deny. On the one hand, there have started into life industrial and scientific forces which no epoch of former human history had ever suspected. On the other hand, there exist symptoms of decay, far surpassing the horrors recorded of the latter times of the Roman empire. In our days everything seems pregnant with its contrary. Machinery, gifted with the wonderful power of shortening and fructifying human labour, we behold starving and overworking it. The newfangled sources of wealth, by some strange weird spell, are turned into sources of want. The victories of art seem bought by the loss of character. At the same pace that mankind masters nature, man seems to become enslaved to other men or to his own infamy. Even the pure light of science seems unable to shine but on the

1. Marx delivered this speech at a dinner commemorating the fourth anniversary of Ernest Jones's *People's Paper*, in London on 14 April 1856. It was published in the *People's Paper* on 19 April 1856.

dark background of ignorance. All our invention and progress seem to result in endowing material forces with intellectual life, and in stultifying human life into a material force. This antagonism between modern industry and science on the one hand, modern misery and dissolution on the other hand; this antagonism between the productive powers and the social relations of our epoch is a fact, palpable, overwhelming, and not to be controverted. Some parties may wail over it; others may wish to get rid of modern arts, in order to get rid of modern conflicts. Or they may imagine that so signal a progress in industry wants to be completed by as signal a regress in politics. On our part, we do not mistake the shape of the shrewd spirit that continues to mark all these contradictions. We know that to work well the new-fangled forces of society, they only want to be mastered by new-fangled men – and such are the working men. They are as much the invention of modern time as machinery itself. In the signs that bewilder the middle class, the aristocracy and the poor prophets of regression, we do recognize our brave friend, Robin Good-fellow, the old mole that can work in the earth so fast, that worthy pioneer – the Revolution.[2] The English working men are the first-born sons of modern industry. They will then, certainly, not be the last in aiding the social revolution produced by that industry, a revolution which means the emancipation of their own class all over the world, which is as universal as capital-rule and wages-slavery. I know the heroic struggles the English working class have gone through since the middle of the last century – struggles [no] less glorious because they are shrouded in obscurity, and burked by the middle-class historian. To revenge the misdeeds of the ruling class, there existed in the Middle Ages, in Germany, a secret tribunal called the 'Vehmgericht'. If a red cross was seen marked on a house, people knew that its owner was doomed by the 'Vehm'. All the houses of Europe are now marked with the mysterious red cross. History is the judge – its executioner, the proletarian.

2. Robin Goodfellow is a character of English folklore, used by Shakespeare in *A Midsummer Night's Dream*. On the 'old mole', see above, p. 237, n. 46.

Articles on India and China

THE BRITISH RULE IN INDIA[1]

London, 10 June 1853

Hindustan is an Italy of Asiatic dimensions, the Himalayas for the Alps, the Plains of Bengal for the Plains of Lombardy, the Deccan for the Apennines, and the Isle of Ceylon for the Island of Sicily. The same rich variety in the products of the soil, and the same dismemberment in the political configuration. Just as Italy has, from time to time, been compressed by the conqueror's sword into different national masses, so do we find Hindustan, when not under the pressure of the Mohammedan, or the Mogul, or the Briton, dissolved into as many independent and conflicting states as it numbered towns, or even villages. Yet, in a social point of view, Hindustan is not the Italy, but the Ireland of the East. And this strange combination of Italy and Ireland, of a world of voluptuousness and a world of woes, is anticipated in the ancient traditions of the religion of Hindustan. That religion is at once a religion of sensualist exuberance and a religion of self-torturing asceticism; a religion of the Lingam and of the Juggernaut; the religion of the monk, and of the bayadere.

I share not the opinion of those who believe in a golden age of Hindustan, without recurring, however, like Sir Charles Wood,[2] for the confirmation of my view, to the authority of Khuli Khan.[3] But take, for example, the times of Aurungzeb;[4] or the epoch when the Mogul appeared in the north, and the Portuguese in the

1. For this article Marx made use of ideas expressed by Engels in his letter to Marx of 6 June 1853 (*MECW* 39, pp. 335–41). The article first appeared in the *New York Daily Tribune* of 25 June 1853.

2. Sir Charles Wood, later Lord Halifax, was President of the Board of Control, the British minister responsible for the supervision of the East India Company. Marx refers to a speech by Wood in the House of Commons on 3 June 1853.

3. Khuli Khan, also known as Nadir Shah, invaded India from Afghanistan in 1739 and dealt the Mogul empire its death blow.

4. Aurungzeb, the sixth Mogul emperor, reigned from 1658 to 1707.

south;[5] or the age of Mohammedan invasion, and of the heptarchy in southern India;[6] or, if you will, go still more back to antiquity, take the mythological chronology of the Brahmin himself, who places the commencement of Indian misery in an epoch even more remote than the Christian creation of the world.

There cannot, however, remain any doubt but that the misery inflicted by the British on Hindustan is of an essentially different and infinitely more intensive kind than all Hindustan had to suffer before. I do not allude to European despotism, planted upon Asiatic despotism, by the British East India Company, forming a more monstrous combination than any of the divine monsters startling us in the Temple of Salsette.[7] This is no distinctive feature of British colonial rule, but only an imitation of the Dutch, and so much so that in order to characterize the working of the British East India Company, it is sufficient to literally repeat what Sir Stamford Raffles, the *English* Governor of Java, said of the old Dutch East India Company.

The Dutch Company, actuated solely by the spirit of gain, and viewing their Javan subjects with less regard or consideration than a West India planter formerly viewed the gang upon his estate, because the latter had paid the purchase money of human property, which the other had not, employed all the pre-existing machinery of despotism to squeeze from the people their utmost mite of contribution, the last dregs of their labour, and thus aggravated the evils of a capricious and semi-barbarous government, by working it with all the practised ingenuity of politicians, and all the monopolizing selfishness of traders.[8]

All the civil wars, invasions, revolutions, conquests, famines, strangely complex, rapid and destructive as the successive action in Hindustan may appear, did not go deeper than its surface. England has broken down the entire framework of Indian society, without any symptoms of reconstitution yet appearing. This loss

5. This would be the early sixteenth century. The Portuguese annexed Goa in 1510. Babar, the founder of the Mogul empire, conquered the Punjab in 1525.

6. The Islamic conquest of India began with Mahmud's invasion of Lahore in 1001. This first wave of Islamic rule decomposed in the mid-fourteenth century. By 'heptarchy' Marx refers to the fragmentation that preceded the Islamic conquest. The original heptarchy was England of the sixth to eighth century, divided into seven kingdoms.

7. The Isle of Salsette, north of Bombay, is celebrated for its 109 cave temples.

8. T. S. Raffles, *The History of Java*, London, 1871, vol. 1, p. 168.

of his old world, with no gain of a new one, imparts a particular kind of melancholy to the present misery of the Hindu, and separates Hindustan, ruled by Britain, from all its ancient traditions, and from the whole of its past history.

There have been in Asia, generally, from immemorial times, but three departments of government: that of finance, or the plunder of the interior; that of war, or the plunder of the exterior; and, finally, the department of public works. Climate and territorial conditions, especially the vast tracts of desert, extending from the Sahara, through Arabia, Persia, India and Tartary, to the most elevated Asiatic highlands, constituted artificial irrigation by canals and waterworks the basis of Oriental agriculture. As in Egypt and India, inundations are used for fertilizing the soil of Mesopotamia, Persia, etc.; advantage is taken of a high level for feeding irrigative canals. This prime necessity of an economical and common use of water, which in the Occident drove private enterprise to voluntary association, as in Flanders and Italy, necessitated in the Orient, where civilization was too low and the territorial extent too vast to call into life voluntary association, the interference of the centralizing power of government. Hence an economical function devolved upon all Asiatic governments, the function of providing public works. This artificial fertilization of the soil, dependent on a central government, and immediately decaying with the neglect of irrigation and drainage, explains the otherwise strange fact that we now find whole territories barren and desert that were once brilliantly cultivated, as Palmyra, Petra, the ruins in Yemen, and large provinces of Egypt, Persia and Hindustan; it also explains how a single war of devastation has been able to depopulate a country for centuries, and to strip it of all its civilization.

Now, the British in East India accepted from their predecessors the departments of finance and of war, but they have neglected entirely that of public works. Hence the deterioration of an agriculture which is not capable of being conducted on the British principle of free competition, of *laissez-faire* and *laissez-aller*. But in Asiatic empires we are quite accustomed to see agriculture deteriorating under one government and reviving again under some other government. There the harvests correspond to good or bad governments, as they change in Europe with good or bad seasons. Thus the oppression and neglect of agriculture, bad as it is, could not be looked upon as the final blow dealt to Indian society by the

British intruder, had it not been attended by a circumstance of quite different importance, a novelty in the annals of the whole Asiatic world. However changing the political aspect of India's past must appear, its social condition has remained unaltered since its remotest antiquity, until the first decennium of the nineteenth century. The hand-loom and the spinning-wheel, producing their regular myriads of spinners and weavers, were the pivots of the structure of that society. From immemorial times Europe received the admirable textures of Indian labour, sending in return for them her precious metals, and furnishing thereby his material to the goldsmith, that indispensable member of Indian society, whose love of finery is so great that even the lowest class, those who go about nearly naked, have commonly a pair of golden earrings and a gold ornament of some kind hung round their necks. Rings on the fingers and toes have also been common. Women as well as children frequently wore massive bracelets and anklets of gold or silver, and statuettes of divinities in gold and silver were met with in the households. It was the British intruder who broke up the Indian hand-loom and destroyed the spinning-wheel. England began with driving the Indian cottons from the European market; it then introduced twist into Hindustan and in the end inundated the very mother country of cotton with cottons. From 1818 to 1836 the export of twist from Great Britain to India rose in the proportion of 1 to 5,200. In 1824 the export of British muslins to India hardly amounted to 1,000,000 yards, while in 1837 it surpassed 64,000,000 yards. But at the same time the population of Dacca decreased from 150,000 inhabitants to 20,000. This decline of Indian towns celebrated for their fabrics was by no means the worst consequence. British steam and science uprooted, over the whole surface of Hindustan, the union between agriculture and manufacturing industry.

These two circumstances – the Hindu, on the one hand, leaving, like all Oriental peoples, to the central government the care of the great public works, the prime condition of his agriculture and commerce, dispersed, on the other hand, over the surface of the country, and agglomerated in small centres by the domestic union of agricultural and manufacturing pursuits – these two circumstances had brought about, since the remotest times, a social system of particular features – the so-called *village system*, which gave to each of these small unions their independent organization and distinct life. The peculiar character of this system may be judged from the following description, contained in an old official report of the British House of Commons on Indian affairs:[9]

A village, geographically considered, is a tract of country comprising some hundred or thousand acres of arable and waste lands; politically viewed it resembles a corporation or township. Its proper establishment of officers and servants consists of the following descriptions: the *potail*, or head inhabitant, who has generally the superintendence of the affairs of the village, settles the disputes of the inhabitants, attends to the police, and performs the duty of collecting the revenue within his village, a duty which his personal influence and minute acquaintance with the situation and concerns of the people render him the best qualified for this charge. The *kurnum* keeps the accounts of cultivation, and registers everything connected with it. The *tallier* and the *totie*, the duty of the former of which consists in gaining information of crimes and offences, and in escorting and protecting persons travelling from one village to another; the province of the latter appearing to be more immediately confined to the village, consisting, among other duties, in guarding the crops and assisting in measuring them. The *boundaryman*, who preserves the limits of the village, or gives evidence respecting them in cases of dispute. The superintendent of tanks and watercourses distributes the water for the purposes of agriculture. The Brahmin, who performs the village worship. The schoolmaster, who is seen teaching the children in a village to read and write in the sand. The calendar-Brahmin, or astrologer, etc. These officers and servants generally constitute the establishment of a village; but in some parts of the country it is of less extent; some of the duties and functions above described being united in the same person; in others it exceeds the above-named number of individuals. Under this simple form of municipal government, the inhabitants of the country have lived from time immemorial. The boundaries of the villages have been but seldom altered; and though the villages themselves have been sometimes injured, and even desolated by war, famine or disease, the same name, the same limits, the same interests, and even the same families, have continued for ages. The inhabitants gave themselves no trouble about the breaking up and divisions of kingdoms; while the village remains entire, they care not to what power it is transferred, or to what sovereign it devolves; its internal economy remains unchanged. The *potail* is still the head inhabitant, and still acts as the petty judge or magistrate, and collector or rentor of the village.

These small stereotype forms of social organism have been to the greater part dissolved, and are disappearing, not so much

9. Marx quotes this report of 1812 from G. Campbell, *Modern India: A Sketch of the System of Civil Government*, London, 1852, pp. 84–5.

through the brutal interference of the British tax-gatherer and the British soldier, as to the working of English steam and English free trade. Those family-communities were based on domestic industry, in that peculiar combination of hand-weaving, hand-spinning and hand-tilling agriculture which gave them self-supporting power. English interference having placed the spinner in Lancashire and the weaver in Bengal, or sweeping away both Hindu spinner and weaver, dissolved these small semi-barbarian, semi-civilized communities by blowing up their economical basis, and thus produced the greatest and, to speak the truth, the only *social* revolution ever heard of in Asia.

Now, sickening as it must be to human feeling to witness those myriads of industrious patriarchal and inoffensive social organizations disorganized and dissolved into their units, thrown into a sea of woes, and their individual members losing at the same time their ancient form of civilization and their hereditary means of subsistence, we must not forget that these idyllic village communities, inoffensive though they may appear, had always been the solid foundation of Oriental despotism, that they restrained the human mind within the smallest possible compass, making it the unresisting tool of superstition, enslaving it beneath traditional rules, depriving it of all grandeur and historical energies. We must not forget the barbarian egotism which, concentrating on some miserable patch of land, had quietly witnessed the ruin of empires, the perpetration of unspeakable cruelties, the massacre of the population of large towns, with no other consideration bestowed upon them than on natural events, itself the helpless prey of any aggressor who deigned to notice it at all. We must not forget that this undignified, stagnatory and vegetative life, that this passive sort of existence evoked on the other part, in contradistinction, wild, aimless, unbounded forces of destruction, and rendered murder itself a religious rite in Hindustan. We must not forget that these little communities were contaminated by distinctions of caste and by slavery, that they subjugated man to external circumstances instead of elevating man to be the sovereign of circumstances, that they transformed a self-developing social state into never-changing natural destiny, and thus brought about a brutalizing worship of nature, exhibiting its degradation in the fact that man, the sovereign of nature, fell down on his knees in adoration of Kanuman, the monkey, and Sabbala, the cow.

England, it is true, in causing a social revolution in Hindustan was actuated only by the vilest interests, and was stupid in her manner of enforcing them. But that is not the question. The question is, can mankind fulfil its destiny without a fundamental revolution in the social state of Asia? If not, whatever may have been the crimes of England she was the unconscious tool of history in bringing about that revolution.

Then, whatever bitterness the spectacle of the crumbling of an ancient world may have for our personal feelings, we have the right, in point of history, to exclaim with Goethe:

> *Sollte diese Qual uns quälen,*
> *Da sie unsre Lust vermehrt,*
> *Hat nicht Myriaden Seelen*
> *Timurs Herrschaft aufgezehrt?*[10]

THE EAST INDIA COMPANY – ITS HISTORY AND RESULTS[11]

London, 24 June 1853

The debate on Lord Stanley's motion to postpone legislation for India has been deferred until this evening.[12] For the first time since 1783 the Indian question has become a ministerial one in England.[13] Why is this?

The true commencement of the East India Company cannot be dated from a more remote epoch than the year 1702, when the different societies, claiming the monopoly of the East India trade, united together in one single company. Till then the very existence of the original East India Company was repeatedly endangered, once suspended for years under the protectorate of Cromwell, and once threatened with utter dissolution by parliamentary interference under the reign of William III. It was under the ascendancy of that Dutch prince when the Whigs became the farmers

10.   'Should this torture then torment us
                      Since it brings us greater pleasure?
                      Were not through the rule of Timur
                      Souls devoured without measure?'
From Goethe's *Westöstlicher Diwan. An Suleika.*

    11. From the *New York Daily Tribune*, 11 July 1853.

    12. The motion proposed by Lord Stanley, a Tory, was designed to block the further progress of the Aberdeen Coalition's Government of India Bill, which with its minor reforms satisfied neither the Tories nor the Radicals.

    13. In 1783 Fox had proposed the transfer of the East India Company's political powers to the Crown, and his government had been defeated on this issue.

of the revenues of the British Empire, when the Bank of England sprang into life, when the protective system was firmly established in England and the balance of power in Europe was definitively settled, that the existence of an East India Company was recognized by Parliament. That era of apparent liberty was in reality the era of monopolies not created by royal grants, as in the times of Elizabeth and Charles I, but authorized and nationalized by the sanction of Parliament. This epoch in the history of England bears, in fact, an extreme likeness to the epoch of Louis Philippe in France, the old landed aristocracy having been defeated, and the bourgeoisie not being able to take its place except under the banner of moneyocracy, or the *haute finance*. The East India Company excluded the common people from the commerce with India, at the same time that the House of Commons excluded them from parliamentary representation. In this, as well as in other instances, we find the first decisive victory of the bourgeoisie over the feudal aristocracy coinciding with the most pronounced reaction against the people, a phenomenon which has driven more than one popular writer, like Cobbett, to look for popular liberty rather in the past than in the future.

The union between the constitutional monarchy and the monopolizing moneyed interest, between the Company of East India and the 'Glorious Revolution' of 1688 was fostered by the same force by which the liberal interests and a liberal dynasty have at all times and in all countries met and combined, by the force of corruption, that first and last moving power of constitutional monarchy, the guardian angel of William III and the fatal demon of Louis Philippe. So early as 1693, it appeared from parliamentary inquiries that the annual expenditure of the East India Company, under the head of 'gifts' to men in power, which had rarely amounted to above £1,200 before the revolution, reached the sum of £90,000. The Duke of Leeds was impeached for a bribe of £5,000, and the virtuous king himself convicted of having received £10,000. Besides these direct briberies, rival companies were thrown out by tempting the government with loans of enormous sums at the lowest interest, and by buying off rival directors.

The power the East India Company had obtained by bribing the government, as did also the Bank of England, it was forced to maintain by bribing again, as did the Bank of England. At every epoch when its monopoly was expiring, it could only effect a renewal of its charter by offering fresh loans and by fresh presents made to the government.

The events of the Seven Years' War[14] transformed the East India Company from a commercial into a military and territorial power. It was then that the foundation was laid of the present British empire in the East. Then East India stock rose to £263, and dividends were then paid at the rate of 12½ per cent. But then there appeared a new enemy to the Company, no longer in the shape of rival societies, but in the shape of rival ministers and a rival people. It was alleged that the Company's territory had been conquered by the aid of British fleets and British armies, and that no British subjects could hold territorial sovereignties independent of the Crown. The ministers of the day and the people of the day claimed their share in the 'wonderful treasures' imagined to have been won by the last conquests. The Company only saved its existence by an agreement made in 1767 that it should annually pay £400,000 into the national exchequer.

But the East India Company, instead of fulfilling its agreement, got into financial difficulties and, instead of paying a tribute to the English people, appealed to Parliament for pecuniary aid. Serious alterations in the charter were the consequence of this step. The Company's affairs failing to improve, notwithstanding their new condition, and the English nation having simultaneously lost their colonies in North America, the necessity of elsewhere regaining some great colonial empire became more and more universally felt. The illustrious Fox thought the opportune moment had arrived, in 1783, for bringing forward his famous India Bill, which proposed to abolish the Courts of Directors and Proprietors, and to vest the whole Indian government in the hands of seven commissioners appointed by Parliament. By the personal influence of the imbecile king[15] over the House of Lords, the bill of Mr Fox was defeated, and made the instrument of breaking down the then Coalition government of Fox and Lord North, and of placing the famous Pitt at the head of the government. Pitt carried in 1784 a bill through both Houses, which directed the establishment of the Board of Control, consisting of six members of the Privy Council, who were 'to check, superintend

14. For England, the dominant theatre of the Seven Years' War (1756–63) was in the colonial territories. Among other English gains France was forced to abandon her conquests in India.

15. George III.

and control all acts, operations and concerns which in any wise related to the civil and military Government, or revenues of the territories and possessions of the East India Company'.

On this head, Mill, the historian, says:

> In passing that law two objects were pursued. To avoid the imputation of what was represented as the heinous object of Mr Fox's bill, it was necessary that the principal part of the power should *appear* to remain in the hand of the Directors. For ministerial advantage it was necessary that it should in *reality* be all taken away. Mr Pitt's bill professed to differ from that of his rival, chiefly in this very point, that while the one destroyed the power of the Directors, the other left it almost entire. Under the act of Mr Fox the powers of the ministers would have been avowedly held. Under the act of Mr Pitt, they were held in secret and by fraud. The bill of Fox transferred the power of the Company to Commissioners appointed by Parliament. The bill of Mr Pitt transferred it to Commissioners appointed by the King.[16]

The years of 1783 and 1784 were thus the first, and till now the only years, for the Indian question to become a ministerial one. The bill of Mr Pitt having been carried, the charter of the East India Company was renewed, and the Indian question set aside for twenty years. But in 1813 the Anti-Jacobin war, and in 1833 the newly introduced Reform Bill, superseded all other political questions.

This, then, is the first reason of the Indian question's having failed to become a great political question, since and before 1784; that before that time the East Indian Company had first to conquer existence and importance; that after that time the oligarchy absorbed all of its power which it could assume without incurring responsibility; and that afterwards the English people in general were at the very epochs of the renewal of the charter, in 1813 and in 1833, absorbed by other questions of overbearing interest.

We will now take a different view. The East India Company commenced by attempting merely to establish factories for their agents and places of deposit for their goods. In order to protect them they erected several forts. Although they had, even as early as 1689, conceived the establishment of a dominion in India, and of making territorial revenue one of their sources of emolument, yet, down to 1744, they had acquired but a few unimportant districts around Bombay, Madras and Calcutta. The war which

16. James Mill, *The History of the British India*, London, 1826, vol. IV, p. 488 & vol. V, pp. 68, 75, 150–51.

subsequently broke out in the Carnatic[17] had the effect of rendering them, after various struggles, virtual sovereigns of that part of India. Much more considerable results arose from the war in Bengal and the victories of Clive. These results were the real occupation of Bengal, Bihar and Orissa. At the end of the eighteenth century, and in the first years of the present one, there supervened the wars with Tippoo Sahib,[18] and in consequence of them a great advance of power and an immense extension of the subsidiary system.[19] In the second decennium of the nineteenth century the first convenient frontier, that of India within the desert, had at length been conquered. It was not till then that the British empire in the East reached those parts of Asia which had been, at all times, the seat of every great central power in India. But the most vulnerable points of the empire, from which it had been overrun as often as old conquerors were expelled by new ones, the barriers of the western frontier, were not in the hands of the British. During the period from 1838 to 1849, in the Sikh and Afghan wars, British rule subjected to definitive possession the ethnographical, political and military frontiers of the East Indian continent, by the compulsory annexation of the Punjab and of Scinde. These were possessions indispensable to repulse any invading force issuing from Central Asia, and indispensable against Russia advancing to the frontiers of Persia. During this last decennium there have been added to the British Indian territory 167,000 square miles, with a population of 8,572,630 souls. As to the interior, all the native states now became surrounded by British possessions, subjected to British *suzeraineté* under various forms, and cut off from the sea-coast, with the sole exception of Gujarat and Scinde. As to its exterior, India was now finished. It is only since 1849 that the one great Anglo-Indian empire has existed.

17. The war between England and France in India, which broke out in 1744 and ended in 1761 with the complete withdrawal of the French, was fought mainly in the Carnatic (the south-eastern coastal region).

18. Tippoo was the Sultan of Mysore. The defeat of Tippoo in 1799 and the Second Mahratta War of 1803 left Britain the paramount power in the Indian subcontinent.

19. The system of 'subsidiary treaties' developed by the British to secure their position in India involved the British government guaranteeing a native ruler protection against attack in return for a sum of money. The British would raise, train and command the necessary number of sepoys, and leave internal affairs in the ruler's hands. States that accepted these treaties were known as 'native states', by far the largest being Hyderabad.

Thus the British government has been fighting, under the Company's name, for two centuries, till at last the natural limits of India were reached. We understand now, why during all this time all parties in England have connived in silence, even those which had resolved to become the loudest with their hypocritical peace cant, after the *arrondissement*[20] of the one Indian empire should have been completed. Firstly, of course, they had to get it, in order to subject it afterwards to their sharp philanthropy. From this view we understand the altered position of the Indian question in the present year, 1853, compared with all former periods of charter renewal.

Again, let us take a different view. We shall still better understand the peculiar crisis in Indian legislation on reviewing the course of British commercial intercourse with India through its different phases.

At the commencement of the East India Company's operations, under the reign of Elizabeth, the Company was permitted, for the purpose of profitably carrying on its trade with India, to export an annual value of £30,000 in silver, gold and foreign coin. This was an infraction against all the prejudices of the age, and Thomas Mun was forced to lay down in *A Discourse of Trade, from England unto the East-Indies*,[21] the foundation of the 'mercantile system', admitting that the precious metals were the only real wealth a country could possess, but contending at the same time that their exportation might be safely allowed, provided the *balance of payments* was in favour of the exporting nation. In this sense, he contended that the commodities imported from East India were chiefly re-exported to other countries, from which a much greater quantity of bullion was obtained than had been required to pay for them in India. In the same spirit, Sir Josiah Child wrote *A Treatise Wherein Is Demonstrated I. That the East India Trade Is the Most National of all Foreign Trades*.[22] By and by the partisans of the East India Company grew more audacious, and it may be noticed as a curiosity, in this strange Indian history, that the Indian monopolists were the first preachers of free trade in England.

Parliamentary intervention, with regard to the East India Company, was again claimed, not by the commercial but by the

20. Rounding off.
21. London, 1621, published under the initials T.M.
22. London, 1681, published under the pseudonym Philopatros.

industrial class, at the latter end of the seventeenth century, and during the greater part of the eighteenth, when the importation of East Indian cotton and silk stuffs was declared to ruin the poor British manufacturers, an opinion put forward in John Pollexfen's *England and East-India Inconsistent in Their Manufactures*, London, 1697,[23] a title strangely verified a century and a half later, but in a very different sense. Parliament did then interfere. By the Act 11 and 12, William III, cap. 10, it was enacted that the wearing of wrought silks and of printed or dyed calicoes from India, Persia and China should be prohibited, and a penalty of £200 imposed on all persons having or selling the same. Similar laws were enacted under George I, II and III, in consequence of the repeated lamentations of the afterwards so 'enlightened' British manufacturers. And thus, during the greater part of the eighteenth century, Indian manufactures were generally imported into England in order to be sold on the Continent, and to remain excluded from the English market itself.

Besides this parliamentary interference with East India, solicited by the greedy home manufacturer, efforts were made at every epoch of the renewal of the charter, by the merchants of London, Liverpool and Bristol, to break down the commercial monopoly of the Company and to participate in that commerce, estimated to be a true mine of gold. In consequence of these efforts, a provision was made in the Act of 1773 prolonging the Company's charter till 1 March 1814, by which private British individuals were authorized to export from, and the Company's Indian servants permitted to import into, England almost all sorts of commodities. But this concession was surrounded with conditions annihilating its effects, in respect to the exports to British India by private merchants. In 1813 the Company was unable to further withstand the pressure of general commerce, and, except the monopoly of the Chinese trade, the trade to India was opened, under certain conditions, to private competition. At the renewal of the Charter in 1833, these last restrictions were at length superseded, the Company forbidden to carry on any trade at all – their commercial character destroyed, and their privilege of excluding British subjects from the Indian territories withdrawn.

Meanwhile the East Indian trade had undergone very serious

23. This book was published anonymously.

revolutions, altogether altering the position of the different class interests in England with regard to it. During the whole course of the eighteenth century the treasures transported from India to England were gained much less by comparatively insignificant commerce than by the direct exploitation of that country, and by the colossal fortunes there extorted and transmitted to England. After the opening of the trade in 1813 the commerce with India more than trebled in a very short time. But this was not all. The whole character of the trade was changed. Till 1813 India had been chiefly an exporting country, while it now became an importing one; and in such a quick progression that already in 1823 the rate of exchange, which had generally been 2s. 6d. per rupee, sunk down to 2s. per rupee. India, the great workshop of cotton manufacture for the world since immemorial times, became now inundated with English twists and cotton stuffs. After its own produce had been excluded from England, or only admitted on the most cruel terms, British manufactures were poured into it at a small and merely nominal duty, to the ruin of the native cotton fabrics once so celebrated. In 1780 the value of British produce and manufactures [exported to India] amounted only to £386,152, the bullion exported during the same year to £15,041, the total value of exports during 1780 being £12,648,616, so that the Indian trade amounted to only one thirty-second of the entire foreign trade. In 1850 the total exports to India from Great Britain and Ireland were £8,024,000, of which cotton goods alone amounted to £5,220,000, so that it reached more than one eighth of the whole export, and more than one quarter of the foreign cotton trade. But the cotton manufacture also employed now one eighth of the population of Britain, and contributed one twelfth of the whole national revenue. After each commercial crisis the East Indian trade grew of more paramount importance for the British cotton manufacturers, and the East Indian continent became actually their best market. At the same rate at which the cotton manufactures became of vital interest for the whole social frame of Great Britain, East India became of vital interest for the British cotton manufacture.

Till then the interests of the moneyocracy which had converted India into its landed estates, of the oligarchy who had conquered it by their armies, and of the millocracy who had inundated it with their fabrics, had gone hand in hand. But the more the industrial interest became dependent on the Indian market, the more it felt the necessity of creating fresh productive powers in India, after having ruined her native industry. You cannot continue to inundate a country with your manufactures, unless you enable it to give you some produce in return. The industrial interest found that their trade declined instead of increasing. For the four years ending with 1846, the imports to India from Great Britain were to the amount of 261 million rupees, for the four years ending 1850 they were only 253 millions, while the exports for the former period [were] 274 million rupees, and for the latter period, 254 millions. They found out that the power of consuming their goods was contracted in India to the lowest possible point, that the consumption of their manufactures by the British West Indies was of the value of about 14s. per head of the population per annum, by Chile of 9s. 3d., by Brazil of 6s. 5d., by Cuba of 6s. 2d., by Peru of 5s. 7d., by Central America of 10d., while it amounted in India only to about 9d. Then came the short cotton crop in the United States, which caused them a loss of £11,000,000 in 1850, and they were exasperated at depending on America, instead of deriving a sufficiency of raw cotton from the East Indies. Besides, they found that in all attempts to apply capital to India they met with impediments and chicanery on the part of the Indian authorities. Thus India became the battlefield in the contest of the industrial interest on the one side, and of the moneyocracy and oligarchy on the other. The manufacturers, conscious of their ascendancy in England, ask now for the annihilation of these antagonistic powers in India, for the destruction of the whole ancient fabric of Indian government, and for the final eclipse of the East India Company.

And now to the fourth and last point of view, from which the Indian question must be judged. Since 1784 Indian finances have got more and more deeply into difficulty. There exists now a national debt of £50 million, a continual decrease in the resources of the revenue, and a corresponding increase in the expenditure, dubiously balanced by the gambling income of the opium tax, now threatened with extinction by the Chinese beginning themselves to cultivate the poppy, and aggravated by the expenses to be anticipated from the senseless Burmese war.[24]

'As the case stands,' says Mr Dickinson, 'as it would ruin

24. As Marx wrote this, a new Burmese war was anticipated as a result of the Burmese refusal to recognize the British annexation of Pegu in the Second Burmese War (1852). In the event, peace with Burma was signed before Marx's article was published.

England to lose her Empire in India, it is stretching our own finances with ruin, to be obliged to keep it.'[25]

I have shown thus, how the Indian question has become for the first time since 1783 an English question and a ministerial question.

INDIAN AFFAIRS[26]

London, 19 July 1853

The progress of the India Bill through the committee has little interest. It is significant that all amendments are thrown out now by the Coalition[27] coalescing with the Tories against their own allies of the Manchester School.

The actual state of India may be illustrated by a few facts. The home establishment absorbs 3 per cent of the net revenue, and the annual interest for home debt and dividends 14 per cent – together 17 per cent. If we deduct these annual remittances from India to England, the *military charges* amount to about two thirds of the whole expenditure available for India, or to 66 per cent, while the charges for *public works* do not amount to more than 2¾ per cent of the general revenue, or for Bengal 1 per cent, Agra 7¾, Punjab ⅛, Madras ½, and Bombay 1 per cent of their respective revenues. These figures are the official ones of the Company itself.

On the other hand nearly three fifths of the whole net revenue is derived from the *land*, about one seventh from *opium*, and upwards of one ninth from *salt*. These resources together yield 85 per cent of the whole receipts.

As to minor items of expenditure and charges, it may suffice to state that the *moturpha* revenue maintained in the Presidency of Madras and levied on shops, looms, sheep, cattle, sundry professions, etc., yields somewhat about £50,000 while the yearly dinners of the East India House cost about the same sum.

The great bulk of the revenue is derived from the land. As the various kinds of Indian land tenure have recently been described

25. John Dickinson, *The Government of India under a Bureaucracy*, London and Manchester, 1853, p. 50. Dickinson was a founder of the radical Indian Reform Association.

26. This is the final part of a composite article originally entitled 'The War Questions – Doings of Parliament – India'. From the *New York Daily Tribune*, 5 August 1853.

27. The same Coalition ministry referred to above, p. 279.

in so many places, and in popular style, too, I propose to limit my observations on the subject to a few general remarks on the *zemindari* and *ryotwari* systems.

The zemindari and the ryotwari were both of them agrarian revolutions, effected by British ukases, and opposed to each other: the one aristocratic, the other democratic; the one a caricature of English landlordism, the other of French peasant proprietorship; but pernicious, both combining the most contradictory character – both made not for the people who cultivate the soil, nor for the holder who owns it, but for the government that taxes it.

By the zemindari system, the people of the Presidency of Bengal were depossessed at once of their hereditary claims to the soil, in favour of the native tax-gatherers called *zemindars*. By the ryotwari system introduced into the Presidencies of Madras and Bombay, the native nobility, with their territorial claims, *merassis, jagirs*, etc., were reduced with the common people to the holding of minute fields, cultivated by themselves, in favour of the Collector[28] of the East India Company. But a curious sort of English landlord was the zemindar, receiving only one tenth of the rent, while he had to make over nine tenths of it to the government. A curious sort of French peasant was the *ryot*, without any permanent title in the soil, and with the taxation changing every year in proportion to his harvest. The original class of zemindars, notwithstanding their unmitigated and uncontrolled rapacity against the dispossessed mass of the ex-hereditary landholders, soon melted away under the pressure of the Company, in order to be replaced by mercantile speculators who now hold all the land of Bengal, with exception of the estates returned under the direct management of the government. These speculators have introduced a variety of the zemindari tenure called *patni*. Not content to be placed with regard to the British Government in the situation of middlemen, they have created in their turn a class of 'hereditary' middlemen called *patnidars*, who created again their subpatnidars, etc., so that a perfect scale of hierarchy of middlemen has sprung up, which presses with its entire weight on the unfortunate cultivator. As to the ryots in Madras and Bombay, the system soon degenerated into one of forced cultivation, and the land lost all its value.

28. A Collector was an official of the East India Company who combined the functions of tax collector, governor and judge.

'The land', says Mr Campbell, 'would be sold for balances by the Collector, as in Bengal, but generally is not, for a very good reason, viz.: that nobody will buy it.'[29]

Thus, in Bengal, we have a combination of English landlordism, of the Irish middleman system, of the Austrian system, transforming the landlord into the tax-gatherer, and of the Asiatic system, making the state the real landlord. In Madras and Bombay we have a French peasant proprietor who is at the same time a serf and a *métayer* of the state. The drawbacks of all these various systems accumulate upon him without his enjoying any of their redeeming features. The ryot is subject, like the French peasant, to the extortion of the private usurer; but he has no hereditary, no permanent title in his land, like the French peasant. Like the serf he is forced to cultivation, but he is not secured against want like the serf. Like the *métayer* he has to divide his produce with the state, but the state is not obliged, with regard to him, to advance the funds and the stock, as it is obliged to do with regard to the *métayer*. In Bengal, as in Madras and Bombay, under the zemindari as under the ryotwari, the ryots – and they form eleven twelfths of the whole Indian population – have been wretchedly pauperized; and if they are, morally speaking, not sunk as low as the Irish cottiers, they owe it to their climate, the men of the south being possessed of less wants, and of more imagination, than the men of the north.

Conjointly with the land tax we have to consider the salt tax. Notoriously, the Company retains the monopoly of that article which they sell at three times its mercantile value – and this in a country where it is furnished by the sea, by the lakes, by the mountains and the earth itself. The practical working of this monopoly was described by the Earl of Albemarle in the following words[30]: 'A great proportion of the salt for inland consumption throughout the country is purchased from the Company by large wholesale merchants at less than 4 rupees per *maund*;[31] these mix a fixed proportion of sand, chiefly got a few miles to the southwest of Dacca, and send the mixture to a second, or counting the government as the first, to a third monopolist at about 5 or 6 rupees. This dealer adds more earth or ashes, and thus passing

29. G. Campbell, *Modern India: A Sketch of the System of Civil Government.*

30. In a speech in the House of Lords on 18 July 1853.

31. An Indian dry measure of approximately twenty-six pounds.

through more hands, from the large towns to villages, the price is still raised from 8 to 10 rupees and the proportion of adulteration from 25 to 40 per cent. It appears then that the people pay from £21 17s. 2d. to £27 6s. 2d. for their salt, or in other words, from thirty to thirty-six times as much as the wealthy people of Great Britain.'

As an instance of English bourgeois morals, I may allege that Mr Campbell defends the opium monopoly because it prevents the Chinese from consuming too much of the drug, and that he defends the brandy monopoly (licences for spirit-selling in India) because it has wonderfully increased the consumption of brandy in India.

The zemindar tenure, the ryotwar and the salt tax, combined with the Indian climate, were the hotbeds of the cholera – India's ravages upon the Western world – a striking and severe example of the solidarity of human woes and wrongs.

THE FUTURE RESULTS OF THE BRITISH RULE IN INDIA[32]

London, 22 July 1853

I propose in this letter to conclude my observations on India. How came it that English supremacy was established in India? The paramount power of the Great Mogul was broken by the Mogul viceroys. The power of the viceroys was broken by the Mahrattas.[33] The power of the Mahrattas was broken by the Afghans, and while all were struggling against all, the Briton rushed in and was enabled to subdue them all. A country not only divided between Mohammedan and Hindu, but between tribe and tribe, between caste and caste; a society whose framework was based on a sort of equilibrium, resulting from a general repulsion and constitutional exclusiveness between all its members. Such a country and such a society, were they not the predestined prey of conquest? If we knew nothing of the past history of Hindustan, would there not be the one great incontestable fact, that even at

32. From the *New York Daily Tribune*, 8 August 1853.
33. The Mahrattas were a people from the north-western Deccan, who rose up against Mogul rule in the mid-seventeenth century and formed the Mahratta Confederacy. The Mahrattas' power was broken by the Afghan invasion of 1761 under Ahmad Khan, which also broke up the Mogul empire and created the conditions for British supremacy over the whole of India established after the Anglo-Mahratta war of 1803–5.

this moment India is held in English thraldom by an Indian army maintained at the cost of India? India, then, could not escape the fate of being conquered, and the whole of her past history, if it be anything, is the history of the successive conquests she has undergone. Indian society has no history at all, at least no known history. What we call its history is but the history of the successive intruders who founded their empires on the passive basis of that unresisting and unchanging society. The question, therefore, is not whether the English had a right to conquer India, but whether we are to prefer India conquered by the Turk, by the Persian, by the Russian, to India conquered by the Briton.

England has to fulfil a double mission in India: one destructive, the other regenerating – the annihilation of old Asiatic society, and the laying of the material foundations of Western society in Asia.

Arabs, Turks, Tartans, Moguls, who had successively overrun India, soon became *Hinduized*, the barbarian conquerors being, by an eternal law of history, conquered themselves by the superior civilization of their subjects. The British were the first conquerors superior and therefore inaccessible to Hindu civilization. They destroyed it by breaking up the native communities, by uprooting the native industry, and by levelling all that was great and elevated in the native society. The historic pages of their rule in India report hardly anything beyond that destruction. The work of regeneration hardly transpires through a heap of ruins. Nevertheless, it has begun.

The political unity of India, more consolidated and extending further than it ever did under the Great Moguls, was the first condition of its regeneration. That unity, imposed by the British sword, will now be strengthened and perpetuated by the electric telegraph. The native army, organized and trained by the British drill-sergeant, was the *sine qua non* of Indian self-emancipation, and of India ceasing to be the prey of the first foreign intruder. The free press, introduced for the first time into Asiatic society, and managed principally by the common offspring of Hindus and Europeans, is a new and powerful agent of reconstruction. The zemindari and ryotwari themselves, abominable as they are, involve two distinct forms of private property in land – the great desideratum of Asiatic society. From the Indian natives, reluctantly and sparingly educated at Calcutta under English superintendence, a fresh class is springing up, endowed with the requirements for government and imbued with European science. Steam has brought India into regular and rapid communication with Europe, has connected its chief ports with those of the whole south-eastern ocean, and has revindicated it from the isolated position which was the prime law of its stagnation. The day is not far distant when, by a combination of railways and steam vessels, the distance between England and India, measured by time, will be shortened to eight days, and when that once fabulous country will thus be actually annexed to the Western world.

The ruling classes of Great Britain have had, till now, but an accidental, transitory and exceptional interest in the progress of India. The aristocracy wanted to conquer it, the moneyocracy to plunder it, and the millocracy to undersell it. But now the tables are turned. The millocracy have discovered that the transformation of India into a reproductive country has become of vital importance to them, and that, to that end, it is necessary, above all, to gift her with means of irrigation and of internal communication. They intend now drawing a net of railways over India. And they will do it. The results must be inappreciable.

It is notorious that the productive powers of India are paralysed by the utter want of means for conveying and exchanging its various produce. Nowhere more than in India do we meet with social destitution in the midst of natural plenty, for want of the means of exchange. It was proved before a Committee of the British House of Commons, which sat in 1848, that 'when grain was selling from 6s. to 8s. a quarter at Khandesh, it was sold at 64s. to 70s. at Poona, where the people were dying in the streets of famine, without the possibility of gaining supplies from Khandesh, because the clay roads were impracticable'.

The introduction of railways may be easily made to subserve agricultural purposes by the formation of tanks, where ground is required for embankment, and by the conveyance of water along the different lines. Thus irrigation, the *sine qua non* of farming in the East, might be greatly extended, and the frequently recurring local famines, arising from the want of water, would be averted. The general importance of railways, viewed under this head, must become evident when we remember that irrigated lands, even in the districts near Ghauts, pay three times as much in taxes, afford ten or twelve times as much employment, and yield twelve or fifteen times as much profit, as the same area without irrigation.

Railways will afford the means of diminishing the amount and the cost of the military establishments. Col. Warren, Town Major of the Fort St William, stated before a Select Committee of the House of Commons: 'The practicability of receiving intelligence from distant parts of the country in as many hours as at present it requires days and even weeks, and of sending instructions with troops and stores, in the more brief period, are considerations which cannot be too highly estimated. Troops could be kept at more distant and healthier stations than at present, and much loss of life from sickness would by this means be spared. Stores could not to the same extent be required at the various depots, and the loss by decay, and the destruction incidental to the climate, would also be avoided. The number of troops might be diminished in direct proportion to their effectiveness.'

We know that the municipal organization and the economical basis of the village communities have been broken up, but their worst feature, the dissolution of society into stereotype and disconnected atoms, has survived their vitality. The village isolation produced the absence of roads in India, and the absence of roads perpetuated the village isolation. On this plan a community existed with a given scale of low conveniences, almost without intercourse with other villages, without the desires and efforts indispensable to social advance. The British having broken up this self-sufficient *inertia* of the villages, railways will provide the new want of communication and intercourse. Besides, 'one of the effects of the railway system will be to bring into every village affected by it such knowledge of the contrivances and appliances of other countries, and such means of obtaining them, as will first put the hereditary and stipendiary village artisanship of India to full proof of its capabilities, and then supply its defects.' (Chapman, *The Cotton and Commerce of India*.)[34]

I know that the English millocracy intend to endow India with railways with the exclusive view of extracting at diminished expenses the cotton and other raw materials for their manufacturers. But when you have once introduced machinery into the locomotion of a country which possesses iron and coals, you are unable to withhold it from its fabrication. You cannot maintain a net of railways over an immense country without introducing all those industrial processes necessary to meet the immediate and

---

34. John Chapman, *The Cotton and Commerce of India* . . ., London, 1851.

current want of railway locomotion, and out of which there must grow the application of machinery to those branches of industry not immediately connected with railways. The railway system will therefore become, in India, truly the forerunner of modern industry. This is the more certain as the Hindus are allowed by British authorities themselves to possess particular aptitude for accommodating themselves to entirely new labour, and acquiring the requisite knowledge of machinery. Ample proof of this fact is afforded by the capacities and expertness of the native engineers in the Calcutta mint, where they have been for years employed in working the steam machinery, by the natives attached to the several steam-engines in the Hurdwar coal districts, and by other instances. Mr Campbell himself, greatly influenced as he is by the prejudices of the East India Company, is obliged to avow 'that the great mass of the Indian people possesses a great *industrial energy*, is well fitted to accumulate capital, and remarkable for a mathematical clearness of head and talent for figures and exact sciences'. 'Their intellects', he says, 'are excellent.'[35]

Modern industry, resulting from the railway system, will dissolve the hereditary divisions of labour, upon which rest the Indian castes, those decisive impediments to Indian progress and Indian power.

All the English bourgeoisie may be forced to do will neither emancipate nor materially mend the social condition of the mass of the people, depending not only on the development of the productive powers, but on their appropriation by the people. But what they will not fail to do is to lay down the material premises for both. Has the bourgeoisie ever done more? Has it ever effected a progress without dragging individuals and peoples through blood and dirt, through misery and degradation?

The Indians will not reap the fruits of the new elements of society scattered among them by the British bourgeoisie till in Great Britain itself the now ruling classes shall have been supplanted by the industrial proletariat, or till the Hindus themselves shall have grown strong enough to throw off the English yoke altogether. At all events, we may safely expect to see, at a more or less remote period, the regeneration of that great and interesting country, whose gentle natives are, to use the expression of Prince Saltykov, even in the most inferior classes, '*plus fins et plus*

---

35. George Campbell, *Modern India: A Sketch of the System of Civil Government*, London, 1852, pp. 59–60.

adroits que les Italiens',[36] whose submission even is counterbalanced by a certain calm nobility, who, notwithstanding their natural languor, have astonished the British officers by their bravery, whose country has been the source of our languages, our religions, and who represent the type of the ancient German in the Jat and the type of the ancient Greek in the Brahmin.

I cannot part with the subject of India without some concluding remarks.

The profound hypocrisy and inherent barbarism of bourgeois civilization lies unveiled before our eyes, turning from its home, where it assumes respectable forms, to the colonies, where it goes naked. They are the defenders of property, but did any revolutionary party ever originate agrarian revolutions like those in Bengal, in Madras, and in Bombay? Did they not, in India, to borrow an expression of that great robber, Lord Clive himself, resort to atrocious extortion, when simple corruption could not keep pace with their rapacity? While they prated in Europe about the inviolable sanctity of the national debt, did they not confiscate in India the dividends of the rajahs, who had invested their private savings in the Company's own funds? While they combated the French revolution under the pretext of defending 'our holy religion', did they not forbid, at the same time, Christianity to be propagated in India, and did they not, in order to make money out of the pilgrims streaming to the temples of Orissa and Bengal, take up the trade in the murder and prostitution perpetrated in the temple of Juggernaut? These are the men of 'Property, Order, Family and Religion'.

The devastating effects of English industry, when contemplated with regard to India, a country as vast as Europe and containing 150 millions of acres, are palpable and confounding. But we must not forget that they are only the organic results of the whole system of production as it is now constituted. That production rests on the supreme rule of capital. The centralization of capital is essential to the existence of capital as an independent power. The destructive influence of that centralization upon the markets of the world does but reveal, in the most gigantic dimensions, the inherent organic laws of political economy now at work in every civilized town. The bourgeois period of history has to create the material basis of the new world – on the one hand the universal

36. 'More subtle and adroit than the Italians.' Marx is quoting from A. D. Saltykov, *Lettres sur l'Inde*, Paris, 1848, p. 61.

intercourse founded upon the mutual dependency of mankind, and the means of that intercourse; on the other hand the development of the productive powers of man and the transformation of material production into a scientific domination of natural agencies. Bourgeois industry and commerce create these material conditions of a new world in the same way as geological revolutions have created the surface of the earth. When a great social revolution shall have mastered the results of the bourgeois epoch, the market of the world and the modern powers of production, and subjected them to the common control of the most advanced peoples, then only will human progress cease to resemble that hideous pagan idol, who would not drink the nectar but from the skulls of the slain.

REVOLUTION IN CHINA AND IN EUROPE[37]

A most profound yet fantastic speculator on the principles which govern the movements of humanity[38] was wont to extol as one of the ruling secrets of nature what he called the law of the contact of extremes. The homely proverb that 'extremes meet' was, in his view, a grand and potent truth in every sphere of life; an axiom with which the philosopher could as little dispense as the astronomer with the laws of Kepler or the great discovery of Newton.

Whether the 'contact of extremes' be such a universal principle or not, a striking illustration of it may be seen in the effect the Chinese revolution[39] seems likely to exercise upon the civilized world. It may seem a very strange and a very paradoxical assertion that the next uprising of the people of Europe, and their next movement for republican freedom and economy of government, may depend more probably on what is now passing in the Celestial

37. This article was written by Marx on 20 May 1853, and printed in the *New York Daily Tribune* as an unsigned leader on 14 June 1853.

38. Hegel.

39. Marx is referring here to the Taiping Heavenly Kingdom, a broadly based peasant revolt against the Manchu dynasty which broke out in Kwangsi province in 1851 and spread to include the central provinces of China and the lower and middle Yangtse region. The Taiping rebellion abolished the Manchu system of taxation, land tenure and political control, and also attacked, in the name of religion, the Buddhist monasteries which were a base of Manchu power. In the conditions of mid-nineteenth-century China a new feudal ruling class rapidly formed within the Taiping movement which was ready to compromise with the Manchus, and, thus weakened, the Heavenly Kingdom was finally defeated by English, American and French intervention in 1864.

Empire, the very opposite of Europe, than on any other political cause that now exists – more even than on the menaces of Russia and the consequent likelihood of a general European war. But yet it is no paradox, as all may understand by attentively considering the circumstances of the case.

Whatever be the social causes, and whatever religious, dynastic or national shape they may assume, that have brought about the chronic rebellions subsisting in China for about ten years past, and now gathered together in one formidable revolution, the occasion of this outbreak has unquestionably been afforded by the English cannon forcing upon China that soporific drug called opium.[40] Before the British arms the authority of the Manchu dynasty fell to pieces; the superstitious faith in the eternity of the Celestial Empire broke down; the barbarous and hermetic isolation from the civilized world was infringed; and an opening was made for that intercourse which has since proceeded so rapidly under the golden attractions of California and Australia. At the same time the silver coin of the Empire, its lifeblood, began to be drained away to the British East Indies.

Up to 1830, the balance of trade being continually in favour of the Chinese, there existed an uninterrupted importation of silver from India, Britain and the United States into China. Since 1833, and especially since 1840, the export of silver from China to India has become almost exhausting for the Celestial Empire. Hence the strong decrees of the emperor against the opium trade, responded to by still stronger resistance to his measures. Besides this immediate economical consequence, the bribery connected with opium smuggling has entirely demoralized the Chinese state officers in the southern provinces. Just as the emperor was wont to be considered the father of all China, so his officers were looked upon as sustaining the paternal relation to their respective districts. But this patriarchal authority, the only moral link embracing the vast machinery of the state, has gradually been corroded by the corruption of those officers, who have made great gains by conniving at opium smuggling. This has occurred principally in the

40. The first Opium War was precipitated by the Chinese government's burning shipments of opium in Canton harbour in 1839. Three years later, Britain forced on China the treaty of Nanking (August 1842), which opened five major ports to British trade, ceded Britain Hongkong island in perpetuity, exacted from China a war indemnity, and was supplemented the following year by an agreement granting Westerners the right of extra-territoriality.

same southern provinces where the rebellion commenced. It is almost needless to observe that, in the same measure in which opium has obtained the sovereignty over the Chinese, the emperor and his staff of pedantic mandarins have become dispossessed of their own sovereignty. It would seem as though history had first to make this whole people drunk before it could rouse them out of their hereditary stupidity.

Though scarcely existing in former times, the import of English cottons, and to a small extent of English woollens, has rapidly risen since 1833, the epoch when the monopoly of trade with China was transferred from the East India Company to private commerce, and on a much greater scale since 1840, the epoch when other nations, and especially our own,[41] also obtained a share in the Chinese trade. This introduction of foreign manufactures has had a similar effect on the native industry to that which it formerly had on Asia Minor, Persia and India. In China the spinners and weavers have suffered greatly under this foreign competition, and the community has become unsettled in proportion.

The tribute to be paid to England after the unfortunate war of 1840, the great unproductive consumption of opium, the drain of the precious metals by this trade, the destructive influence of foreign competition on native manufactures, the demoralized condition of the public administration, produced two things: the old taxation became more burdensome and harassing, and new taxation was added to the old. Thus in a decree of the emperor, dated Peking, 5 January 1853, we find orders given to the viceroys and governors of the southern provinces of Wuchang and Hanyang[42] to remit and defer the payment of taxes and especially not in any case to exact more than the regular amount; for otherwise, says the decree, 'how will the poor people be able to bear it?' 'And thus, perhaps,' continues the emperor, 'will my people, in a period of general hardship and distress, be exempted from the evils of being pursued and worried by the tax-gatherer.'

Such language as this, and such concessions, we remember to have heard from Austria, the China of Germany, in 1848.

41. I.e., the United States. This is presumably an interpolation by the *Tribune* editor. Marx frequently had occasion to complain of editorial distortion of his contributions, especially when, as with the present piece, they were used as leading articles.

42. Wuchang and Hanyang are in fact cities in Hupei province.

All these dissolving agencies, acting together on the finances, the morals, the industry and political structure of China, received their full development under the English cannon in 1840, which broke down the authority of the emperor and forced the Celestial Empire into contact with the terrestrial world. Complete isolation was the prime condition of the preservation of old China. That isolation having come to a violent end by the medium of England, dissolution must follow as surely as that of any mummy carefully preserved in a hermetically sealed coffin whenever it is brought into contact with the open air. Now, England having brought about the revolution of China, the question is how that revolution will in time react on England, and through England on Europe. This question is not difficult of solution.

The attention of our readers has often been called to the unparalleled growth of British manufactures since 1850. Amid the most surprising prosperity, it has not been difficult to point out the clear symptoms of an approaching industrial crisis. Notwithstanding California and Australia,[43] notwithstanding the immense and unprecedented emigration, there must ever, without any particular accident, in due time arrive a moment when the extension of the markets is unable to keep pace with the extension of British manufactures, and this disproportion must bring about a new crisis with the same certainty as it has done in the past. But if one of the great markets suddenly becomes contracted, the arrival of the crisis is necessarily accelerated thereby. Now, the Chinese rebellion must, for the time being, have precisely this effect upon England. The necessity for opening new markets, or for extending the old ones, was one of the principal causes of the reduction of the British tea duties, as, with an increased importation of tea, an increased exportation of manufactures to China was expected to take place. Now, the value of the annual exports from the United Kingdom to China amounted, before the repeal in 1833 of the trading monopoly possessed by the East India Company, to only £600,000; in 1836 it reached the sum of £1,326,388; in 1845 it had risen to £2,394,827; in 1852 it amounted to about £3,000,000. The quantity of tea imported from China did not exceed, in 1793, 16,167,331 lb.; but in 1845 it amounted to 50,714,657 lb.; in 1846 to 57,584,561 lb.; it is now above 60,000,000 lb.

The tea crop of the last season will not prove short, as shown

---

43. I.e., the gold discoveries of 1848 and 1851 respectively.

already by the export lists from Shanghai, of 2,000,000 lb. above the preceding year. This excess is to be accounted for by two circumstances. On one hand, the state of the market at the close of 1851 was much depressed, and the large surplus stock left has been thrown into the export of 1852. On the other hand, the recent accounts of the altered British legislation with regard to imports of tea reaching China have brought forward all the available teas to a ready market, at greatly enhanced prices. But with respect to the coming crop the case stands very differently. This is shown by the following extracts from the correspondence of a large tea firm in London:

In Shanghai the terror is extreme. Gold has advanced upward of 25 per cent, *being eagerly sought for hoarding*; silver has so far disappeared that *none could be obtained* to pay the China dues on the British vessels requiring port clearance; and in consequence of which Mr Alcock[44] has consented to become responsible to the Chinese authorities for the payment of these dues, on receipt of East India Company's bills, or other approved securities. *The scarcity of the precious metals* is one of the most unfavourable features, when viewed in reference to the immediate future of commerce, as this abstraction occurs precisely at that period when their use is most needed, to enable the tea and silk buyers to go into the interior and effect their purchases, for which a *large portion of bullion is paid in advance, to enable the producers to carry on their operations* . . . At this period of the year it is usual to begin making arrangements for the new teas, whereas at present nothing is talked of but the means of protecting person and property, all transactions being at a stand . . . If the means are not applied to secure the leaves in April and May, the early crop, which includes all the finer descriptions, both of black and green teas, will be as much lost as unreaped wheat at Christmas.[45]

Now the means for securing the tea leaves will certainly not be given by the English, American or French squadrons stationed in the Chinese seas, but these may easily, by their interference, produce such complications as to cut off all transactions between the tea-producing interior and the tea-exporting sea ports. Thus, for the present crop, a rise in the prices must be expected – speculation has already commenced in London – and for the crop to come a large deficit is as good as certain. Nor is this all. The Chinese, ready though they may be, as are all people in

44. Sir Rutherford Alcock was the British consul at Peking.
45. This is quoted from a circular of Moffat & Co., published in the *Economist*, 21 May 1853. The italics are Marx's.

periods of revolutionary convulsion, to sell off to the foreigner all the bulky commodities they have on hand, will, as the Orientals are used to do in the apprehension of great changes, set to hoarding, not taking much in return for their tea and silk except hard money. England has accordingly to expect a rise in the price of one of her chief articles of consumption, a drain of bullion, and a great contraction of an important market for her cotton and woollen goods. Even the *Economist*, that optimist conjuror of all things menacing the tranquil minds of the mercantile community, is compelled to use language like this: 'We must not flatter ourselves with finding as extensive a market for our exports to China as hitherto . . . It is more probable that our export trade to China should suffer, and that there should be a diminished demand for the produce of Manchester and Glasgow.'[46]

It must not be forgotten that the rise in the price of so indispensable an article as tea, and the contraction of so important a market as China, will coincide with a deficient harvest in western Europe and, therefore, with rising prices of meat, corn, and all other agricultural produce. Hence contracted markets for manufactures, because every rise in the prices of the first necessaries of life is counterbalanced, at home and abroad, by a corresponding reduction in the demand for manufactures. From every part of Great Britain complaints have been received on the backward state of most of the crops. The *Economist* says on this subject:

> In the South of England not only will there be left much land unsown, until too late for a crop of any sort, but much of the sown land will prove to be foul, or otherwise in a bad state for corn-growing. On the wet or poor soils destined for wheat, signs that mischief is going on are apparent. The time for planting mangel-wurzel may now be said to have passed away, and very little has been planted, while the time for preparing land for the turnip is rapidly going by, without any adequate preparation for this important crop having been accomplished . . . Oat-sowing has been much interfered with by the snow and rain. Few oats were sown early, and late sown oats seldom produce a large crop . . . In many districts losses among the breeding flocks have been considerable.[47]

The price of other farm-produce than corn is from 20 to 30, and even 50 per cent higher than last year. On the Continent, corn has risen comparatively more than in England. Rye has risen in

46. 21 May 1853.   47. 14 May 1853.

Belgium and Holland full 100 per cent. Wheat and other grains are following suit.

Under these circumstances, as the greater part of the regular commercial circle has already been run through by British trade, it may safely be augured that the Chinese revolution will throw the spark into the overloaded mine of the present industrial system and cause the explosion of the long-prepared general crisis, which, spreading abroad, will be closely followed by political revolutions on the Continent. It would be a curious spectacle, that of China sending disorder into the Western world while the Western powers, by English, French and American war-steamers, are conveying 'order' to Shanghai, Nanking, and the mouths of the Great Canal. Do these order-mongering powers, which would attempt to support the wavering Manchu dynasty, forget that the hatred against foreigners and their exclusion from the Empire, once the mere result of China's geographical and ethnographical situation, have become a political system only since the conquest of the country by the race of the Manchu Tartars?[48] There can be no doubt that the turbulent dissensions among the European nations who, at the latter end of the seventeenth century, rivalled each other in the trade with China, lent a mighty aid to the exclusive policy adopted by the Manchus. But more than this was done by the fear of the new dynasty, lest the foreigners might favour the discontent existing among a large proportion of the Chinese during the first half century or thereabouts of their subjection to the Tartars. From these considerations, foreigners were then prohibited from all communication with the Chinese except through Canton, a town at a great distance from Peking and the tea districts, and their commerce restricted to intercourse with the Hong[49] merchants, licensed by the government expressly for the foreign trade, in order to keep the rest of its subjects from all connection with the odious strangers. In any case an interference on the part of the Western governments at this time can only serve to render the revolution more violent and protract the stagnation of trade.

48. The Manchu dynasty was established in 1644, by which time the Manchus had conquered the greater part of the country.

49. Ko Hong was a Canton merchants' guild, responsible to the Chinese government for import and export control, and therefore for the attempts to curb the opium trade. By the Nanking treaty the Chinese government undertook to dissolve the Hong.

At the same time it is to be observed with regard to India that the British government of that country depends for full one seventh of its revenue on the sale of opium to the Chinese, while a considerable proportion of the Indian demand for British manufactures depends on the production of that opium in India. The Chinese, it is true, are no more likely to renounce the use of opium than are the Germans to forswear tobacco. But as the new emperor is understood to be favourable to the culture of the poppy and the preparation of opium in China itself, it is evident that a death-blow is very likely to be struck at once at the business of opium-raising in India, the Indian revenue, and the commercial resources of Hindustan. Though this blow would not immediately be felt by the interests concerned, it would operate effectually in due time, and would come in to intensify and prolong the universal financial crisis whose horoscope we have cast above.

Since the commencement of the eighteenth century there has been no serious revolution in Europe which had not been preceded by a commercial and financial crisis. This applies no less to the revolution of 1789 than to that of 1848. It is true, not only that we every day behold more threatening symptoms of conflict between the ruling powers and their subjects, between the state and society, between the various classes; but also the conflict of the existing powers among each other gradually reaching that height where the sword must be drawn, and the *ultima ratio* of princes be recurred to. In the European capitals, every day brings dispatches big with universal war, vanishing under the dispatches of the following day, bearing the assurance of peace for a week or so. We may be sure, nevertheless, that to whatever height the conflict between the European powers may rise, however threatening the aspect of the diplomatic horizon may appear, whatever movements may be attempted by some enthusiastic fraction in this or that country, the rage of princes and the fury of the people are alike enervated by the breath of prosperity. Neither wars nor revolutions are likely to pull Europe by the ears, unless in consequence of a general commercial and industrial crisis, the signal of which has, as usual, to be given by England, the representative of European industry in the market of the world.

It is unnecessary to dwell on the political consequences such a crisis must produce in these times, with the unprecedented extension of factories in England, with the utter dissolution of her official parties, with the whole state machinery of France transformed into one immense swindling and stock-jobbing concern, with Austria on the eve of bankruptcy, with wrongs everywhere accumulated to be revenged by the people, with the conflicting interests of the reactionary powers themselves, and with the Russian dream of conquest once more revealed to the world.

Articles on the North American Civil War[1]

THE NORTH AMERICAN CIVIL WAR

London, 20 October 1861

For months now the leading London papers, both weekly and daily, have been repeating the same litany on the American Civil War. While they insult the free states of the North, they anxiously defend themselves against the suspicion of sympathizing with the slave states of the South. In fact, they continually write two articles: one in which they attack the North, another in which they excuse their attacks on the North. *Qui s'excuse, s'accuse*.[2]

Their extenuating arguments are basically as follow. The war between North and South is a tariff war. Furthermore, the war is not being fought over any issue of principle; it is not concerned with the question of slavery but in fact centres on the North's lust for sovereignty. In the final analysis, even if justice is on the side of the North, does it not remain a futile endeavour to subjugate eight million Anglo-Saxons by force! Would not a separation from the South release the North from all connection with Negro slavery and assure to it, with its 20 million inhabitants and its vast territory, a higher level of development up to now scarcely dreamt of? Should the North not then welcome secession as a happy event, instead of wanting to crush it by means of a bloody and futile civil war?

Let us examine point by point the case made out by the English press.

The war between North and South – so runs the first excuse – is merely a tariff war, a war between a protectionist system and a

1. The following two articles began a series of thirty-seven that Marx and Engels wrote on events in North America for the liberal Vienna paper *Die Presse*. They are translated here from the texts printed in *MEW* 15. This article appeared in the paper's edition of 25 October 1861.

2. He who excuses himself, accuses himself.

free-trade system; and England, of course, is on the side of free trade. Is the slave-owner to enjoy the fruits of slave labour to the full, or is he to be cheated of part of these fruits by the Northern protectionists? This is the question at issue in the war. It was reserved for *The Times* to make this brilliant discovery; the *Economist*, *Examiner*, *Saturday Review* and the like have elaborated on the same theme. It is characteristic that this discovery was made, not in Charleston, but in London. In America everyone knew, of course, that between 1846 and 1861 a system of free trade prevailed and that Representative Morrill only carried his protectionist tariff through Congress after the rebellion had already broken out. Secession did not take place, therefore, because Congress had passed the Morrill tariff; at most, the Morrill tariff was passed by Congress because secession had taken place. To be sure, when South Carolina had its first attack of secessionism in 1832 the protectionist tariff of 1828 served as a pretext; but that a pretext is all it was is shown by a statement made by General Jackson. This time, however, the old pretext has in fact not been repeated. In the secession Congress at Montgomery[3] every mention of the tariff question was avoided because in Louisiana, one of the most influential Southern states, the cultivation of sugar is based entirely on protection.

But, the London press pleads further, the war in the United States is nothing but a war aimed at preserving the Union by force. The Yankees cannot make up their minds to strike off fifteen stars from their banner.[4] They want to cut a colossal figure on the world stage. Indeed, it would be quite a different matter if the war were being fought in order to abolish slavery. But the slavery question, as the *Saturday Review*, among others, categorically declares, has absolutely nothing to do with this war.

It must be remembered above all that the war was started not by the North but by the South. The North is on the defensive. For months it had quietly stood by and watched while the secessionists took possession of forts, arsenals, shipyards, customs houses, pay offices, ships and stores of arms belonging to the Union, insulted its flag, and took Northern troops prisoner. The

3. The Congress of Montgomery founded, on 4 February 1861, the Confederate States of America, with eleven member states, under the presidency of Jefferson Davis.

4. This total includes the contested border states which the South also claimed.

secessionists finally decided to force the Union government out of its passive stance by means of a blatant act of war; *for no other reason than this* they proceeded to bombard Fort Sumter near Charleston. On 11 April [1861] their General Beauregard had learnt in a meeting with Major Anderson, the commander of Fort Sumter, that the fort only had rations for three more days and that it would therefore have to be surrendered peacefully after this period. In order to forestall this peaceful surrender the secessionists opened the bombardment early the next morning (12 April), bringing about the fall of the place after a few hours. Hardly had this news been telegraphed to Montgomery, the seat of the secession Congress, when War Minister Walker declared publicly in the name of the new Confederacy: 'No man can say where *the war opened today* will end.' At the same time he prophesied that before the first of May the flag of the Southern Confederacy would wave from the dome of the old Capitol in Washington and within a short time perhaps also from the Faneuil Hall in Boston. Only then did Lincoln issue the proclamation summoning 75,000 men to protect the Union. The bombardment of Fort Sumter cut off the only possible constitutional way out: the summoning of a general convention of the American people, as Lincoln had proposed in his inaugural address. As it was, Lincoln was left with the choice of fleeing from Washington, evacuating Maryland and Delaware, surrendering Kentucky, Missouri and Virginia, or of answering war with war.

The question as to the principle underlying the American Civil War is answered by the battle slogan with which the South broke the peace. [Alexander H.] Stephens, the Vice-President of the Southern Confederacy, declared in the secession Congress that what fundamentally distinguished the constitution recently hatched in Montgomery from that of Washington and Jefferson was that slavery was now recognized for the first time as an institution good in itself and as the foundation of the whole political edifice, whereas the revolutionary fathers, men encumbered by the prejudices of the eighteenth century, had treated slavery as an evil imported from England and to be eradicated in the course of time. Another Southern matador, Mr Spratt, declared, 'For us it is a question of the foundation of a great slave republic.' Thus if the North drew its sword only in defence of the Union, had not the South already declared that the continuance of slavery was no longer compatible with the continuance of the Union?

Just as the bombardment of Fort Sumter gave the signal for the opening of the war, the electoral victory of the Northern Republican party, Lincoln's election to the presidency, had given the signal for secession. Lincoln was elected on 6 November 1860. On 8 November the message was telegraphed from South Carolina, 'Secession is regarded here as an accomplished fact'; on 10 November the Georgia legislature occupied itself with plans for secession, and on 13 November a special sitting of the Mississippi legislature was called to consider secession. But Lincoln's election was itself only the result of a split in the Democratic camp. During the election campaign the Northern Democrats concentrated their votes on Douglas, the Southern Democrats on [John C.] Breckinridge; the Republican party owed its victory to this split in the Democratic vote. How, on the one hand, did the Republican party achieve this dominant position in the North; how, on the other hand, did this division arise *within* the Democratic party, whose members, North and South, had operated in conjunction for more than half a century?

Buchanan's presidency[5] saw the control which the South had gradually usurped over the Union as a result of its alliance with the Northern Democrats, reach its peak. The last Continental Congress of 1787 and the first constitutional Congress of 1789–90 had legally excluded slavery from all territories of the republic north-west of Ohio. (Territories are the colonies lying within the United States which have not yet achieved the population level laid down in the Constitution for the formation of autonomous states.) The so-called Missouri Compromise (1820), as a result of which Missouri entered the ranks of the United States as a slave-owning state, excluded slavery from all other territories north of 36° 30′ latitude and west of the Missouri. As a result of this compromise the area of slavery was extended by several degrees of longitude while, on the other hand, quite definite geographical limits seemed to be placed on its future propagation. This geographical barrier was in turn torn down by the so-called Kansas-Nebraska Bill, whose author, Stephen A. Douglas, was at the time leader of the Northern Democrats. This bill, which passed both Houses of Congress, repealed the Missouri Compromise, placed slavery and freedom on an equal footing, enjoined the Union government to treat both with indifference, and left it to the

5. James Buchanan was U.S. President from 1857 to 1861.

sovereign people to decide whether slavery was to be introduced in a territory or not. Thus, for the first time in the history of the United States, every geographical and legal barrier in the way of an extension of slavery in the territories was removed. Under this new legislation the hitherto free territory of New Mexico, an area five times greater than New York state, was transformed into a slave territory, and the area of slavery was extended from the Mexican republic to latitude 38° north. In 1859 New Mexico was given a legal slave code which vies in barbarity with the statute-books of Texas and Alabama. However, as the 1860 census shows, New Mexico does not yet have fifty slaves in a population of about 100,000. The South therefore only had to send over the border a few adventurers with some slaves and, with the help of the central government in Washington, get its officials and contractors to drum up a sham representative body in New Mexico, in order to impose slavery and the rule of the slave-holders on the territory.

However, this convenient method proved inapplicable in the other territories. The South, therefore, went one step further and appealed from Congress to the Supreme Court of the United States. This Supreme Court, which numbers nine judges, five of whom are Southerners, had long been the most amenable instrument of the slave-holders. In 1857, in the notorious Dred Scott case, it decided that every American citizen had the right to take with him into any territory any property recognized by the Constitution. The Constitution recognizes slaves as property and commits the Union government to the protection of this property. Consequently, on the basis of the Constitution, slaves could be forced by their owners to work in the territories and thus every individual slave-holder was entitled to introduce slavery into territories hitherto free against the will of the majority of the settlers. The territorial legislatures were denied the right to exclude slavery, and Congress and the Union government were charged with the duty of protecting the pioneers of the slave system.

While the Missouri Compromise of 1820 had extended the geographical boundaries of slavery in the territories, and while the Kansas-Nebraska Bill of 1854 had eliminated all geographical boundaries and replaced them by a political barrier – the will of the majority of the settlers – the Supreme Court's decision of 1857 tore down even this political barrier and transformed all territories of the republic, present and future, from nurseries of free states into nurseries of slavery.

At the same time, under Buchanan's administration, the more severe law of 1850 on the extradition of fugitive slaves was ruthlessly carried out in the Northern states. It seemed to be the constitutional calling of the North to play slave-catcher for the Southern slave-holders. On the other hand, in order to hinder as far as possible the colonization of the territories by free settlers, the slave-holders' party frustrated all so-called free-soil measures, that is, measures intended to guarantee the settlers a fixed amount of uncultivated public land free of charge.

As in domestic policy, so also in the foreign policy of the United States the interests of the slave-holders served as the guiding star. Buchanan had in fact purchased the presidential office by issuing the Ostend Manifesto,[6] in which the acquisition of Cuba, whether by payment or by force of arms, is proclaimed as the great political task of the nation. Under his administration northern Mexico had already been divided up among American land speculators, who were impatiently awaiting the signal to fall upon Chihuahua, Coahuila and Sonora. The incessant piratical filibusters against the Central American states were no less carried out under the direction of the White House in Washington.[7] Closely connected with this foreign policy, which was manifestly aimed at conquering new territory for the expansion of slavery and the rule of the slave-holders, was the *resumption of the slave trade*, secretly supported by the Union government. Stephen A. Douglas himself declared in the American Senate on 20 August 1859 that during the previous year more Negroes had been requisitioned from Africa than ever before in any single year, even at the time when the slave trade was still legal. The number of slaves imported in the last year amounted to fifteen thousand.

Armed propaganda abroad on behalf of slavery was the avowed aim of national policy; the Union had in fact become the slave of the 300,000 slave-holders who rule the South. This state of affairs had been brought about by a series of compromises which the South owed to its alliance with the Northern Democrats. All the periodic attempts made since 1817 to resist the ever-increasing

6. The Ostend Manifesto was issued in 1854 by the United States ambassadors to Spain, France and England (the latter being Buchanan); it contained an offer to purchase Cuba from Spain and threatened to seize it by force if Spain refused.

7. Nicaragua was the particular object of these expeditions.

encroachments of the slave-holders had come to grief against this alliance. Finally there came a turning point.

Hardly had the Kansas-Nebraska Bill been passed, erasing the geographical boundary of slavery and making its introduction into new territories subject to the will of the majority of the settlers, when armed emissaries of the slave-holders, border rabble from Missouri and Arkansas, fell upon Kansas, a bowie-knife in one hand and a revolver in the other, and with the most atrocious barbarity tried to drive out its settlers from the territory which they had colonized. As these raids were supported by the central government in Washington, a tremendous reaction ensued. In the whole of the North, but particularly in the North-west, a relief organization was formed to provide support for Kansas in the shape of men, weapons and money. Out of this relief organization grew the Republican party, which thus has its origins in the struggle for Kansas. After the failure of the attempts to transform Kansas into a slave territory by force of arms the South tried to achieve the same result by way of political intrigue. Buchanan's administration, in particular, did its utmost to manoeuvre Kansas into the ranks of the United States as a slave state by the imposition of a slave constitution. Hence a new struggle took place this time conducted for the most part in the Washington Congress. Even Stephen A. Douglas, leader of the Northern Democrats, now (1857–8) entered the lists, against the administration and against his Southern allies, because the imposition of a slave constitution would contradict the principle of settlers' sovereignty passed in the Nebraska Bill of 1854. Douglas, Senator for Illinois, a north-western state, would naturally have forfeited all his influence if he had wanted to concede to the South the right to steal by force of arms or acts of Congress the territories colonized by the North. Thus while the struggle for Kansas gave birth to the Republican party, it simultaneously gave rise to the first split within the Democratic party itself.

The Republican party issued its first programme for the presidential election of 1856. Although its candidate, John Frémont, did not win, the huge number of votes cast for him demonstrated the rapid growth of the party, particularly in the North-west. In their second national convention for the presidential election (17 May 1860), the Republicans repeated their programme of 1856, enriched by only a few additional points. Its main contents were that not a foot of new territory would be conceded to slavery, and that the filibustering policy abroad must cease; the resumption of the slave trade was condemned, and lastly, free-soil laws would be enacted in order to further free colonization.

The point of decisive importance in this programme was that slavery was not to be conceded another foot of new ground; rather it was to remain confined once and for all within the limits of the states where it already legally existed. Slavery was thus to be interned for good. However, permanent territorial expansion and the continual extension of slavery beyond its old borders is a law of existence for the slave states of the Union.

The cultivation of the Southern export crops, i.e., cotton, tobacco, sugar, etc., by slaves is only profitable so long as it is conducted on a mass scale by large gangs of slaves and in wide areas of naturally fertile soil requiring only simple labour. Intensive cultivation, which depends less on the fertility of the soil and more on capital investment and on intelligent and energetic labour, runs contrary to the nature of slavery. Hence the rapid transformation of states such as Maryland and Virginia, which in earlier times employed slavery in the production of export commodities, into states which raise slaves in order to export them to states lying further south. Even in South Carolina, where slaves form four sevenths of the population, the cultivation of cotton has remained almost stationary for years due to the exhaustion of the soil. Indeed, South Carolina has become partly transformed into a slave-raising state by pressure of circumstances in so far as it already sells slaves to the states of the deep South and South-west to a value of four million dollars annually. As soon as this point is reached the acquisition of new territory becomes necessary, so that one section of the slave-holders can introduce slave labour into new fertile estates and thus create a new market for slave-raising and the sale of slaves by the section it has left behind. There is not the least doubt, for example, that without the acquisition of Louisiana, Missouri and Arkansas by the United States, slavery would long ago have disappeared in Virginia and Maryland. In the secession Congress at Montgomery one of the Southern spokesmen, Senator Toombs, strikingly formulated the economic law that necessitates the constant expansion of the slave territory. 'In fifteen years more,' he said, 'without a great increase in slave territory, either the slaves must be permitted to flee from the whites, or the whites must flee from the slaves.'

As is well known, individual states are represented in the

Congressional House of Representatives according to the size of their respective populations. Since the population of the free states is growing incomparably more quickly than that of the slave states, the number of Northern representatives has inevitably overtaken the number of Southerners. The actual seat of Southern political power, therefore, is being transferred more and more to the American Senate, where every state, whether its population is great or small, is represented by two senators. In order to assert its influence in the Senate and, through the Senate, its hegemony over the United States, the South thus needed a continual formation of new slave states. But this could only be brought about by conquering foreign countries, as in the case of Texas, or by transforming the United States territories first into slave territories, later into slave states, as in the case of Missouri, Arkansas, etc. John Calhoun, whom the slave-holders admire as their statesman *par excellence*, declared in the Senate as early as 19 February 1847 that only the Senate offered the South the means of restoring a balance of power between South and North, that the extension of the slave territory was necessary to restore this balance and that therefore the attempts of the South to create new slave states by force were justified.

When it comes down to it the number of actual slave-holders in the South of the Union is not more than 300,000; an exclusive oligarchy confronted by the many million so-called 'poor whites', whose number has constantly grown as a result of the concentration of landed property, and whose situation can only be compared with that of the Roman plebeians in the direst period of Rome's decline. Only with the acquisition of new territories, the prospect of such acquisition, and filibustering expeditions, is it possible to harmonize the interests of these 'poor whites' successfully with those of the slave-holders, to channel their restless thirst for action in a harmless direction and to tempt them with the prospect of becoming slave-holders themselves one day.

As a result of economic laws, then, to confine slavery to the limits of its old terrain would inevitably have led to its gradual extinction; politically it would have destroyed the hegemony exercised by the slave states by way of the Senate; and finally it would have exposed the slave-holding oligarchy to ominous dangers within their own states from the 'poor whites'. With the principle that every further extension of slave territories was to be prohibited by law the Republicans therefore mounted a radical attack on the rule of the slave-holders. Consequently, the Republican election victory could not help but lead to open struggle between North and South. However, as has already been mentioned, this election victory was itself conditioned by the split in the Democratic camp.

The Kansas struggle had already provoked a split between the slave party and its Democratic allies in the North. The same quarrel now broke out again in a more general form with the presidential election of 1860. The Northern Democrats, with Douglas as their candidate, made the introduction of slavery into the territories dependent upon the will of the majority of settlers. The slave-holders' party, with Breckinridge as its candidate, asserted that the Constitution of the United States, as the Supreme Court had also declared, made legal provision for slavery; slavery was in actual fact already legal in all territories and did not require special naturalization. Thus, while the Republicans prohibited any growth of slave territories, the Southern party laid claim to all territories as legally warranted domains. What they had tried, for instance, with Kansas – imposing slavery on a territory against the will of the settlers themselves, by way of the central government – they now held up as a law for all Union territories. Such a concession lay beyond the power of the Democratic leaders and would only have caused their army to desert to the Republican camp. On the other hand Douglas's 'settlers' sovereignty' could not satisfy the slave-holders' party. What the slave-holders wanted to achieve had to be brought about in the next four years under the new President; it could only be brought about by means of the central government and could not be delayed any longer. It did not escape the slave-holders' notice that a new power had arisen, the North-west, whose population, which had almost doubled between 1850 and 1860, was already more or less equal to the white population of the slave states – a power which neither by tradition, temperament nor way of life was inclined to let itself be dragged from compromise to compromise in the fashion of the old Northern states. The Union was only of value for the South in so far as it let it use federal power as a means of implementing its slave policy. If it did not, it was better to break now than to watch the development of the Republican party and the rapid growth of the North-west for another four years, and to begin the struggle under less favourable conditions. The slave-holders' party, therefore, now staked its all!

When the Northern Democrats refused to play the role of the Southern 'poor whites' any longer, the South brought about Lincoln's victory by splitting the votes and used this victory as an excuse for drawing the sword.

As is clear, the whole movement was and is based on the *slave question*. Not in the sense of whether the slaves within the existing slave states should be directly emancipated or not, but whether the twenty million free Americans of the North should subordinate themselves any longer to an oligarchy of 300,000 slave-holders; whether the vast territories of the Republic should become the nurseries of free states or of slavery; finally whether the foreign policy of the Union should take the armed propaganda of slavery as its device throughout Mexico, Central and South America.

In a foreign article we shall examine the assertion of the London press that the North should sanction secession as the most favourable and only possible solution of the conflict.

THE CIVIL WAR IN THE UNITED STATES[8]

'Let him go, he is not worth thine ire!'[9] This advice from Leporello to Don Juan's deserted love is now the repeated call of English statesmanship to the North of the United States – recently voiced anew by Lord John Russell. If the North lets the South go, it will free itself from any complicity in slavery – its historical original sin – and it will create the basis for a new and higher stage of development.

Indeed, if North and South formed two autonomous countries like England and Hanover, for instance, their separation would be no more difficult than was the separation of England and Hanover. 'The South', however, is neither geographically clearly separate from the North nor is it a moral entity. It is not a country at all, but a battle-cry.

The advice of an amicable separation presupposes that the Southern Confederacy, although it took the offensive in the Civil War, is at least conducting it for defensive purposes. It presupposes that the slave-holders' party is concerned only to unite the areas it has controlled up till now into an autonomous group of states, and to release them from the domination of the Union. Nothing could be more wrong. '*The South needs its entire territory*. It will

8. From *Die Presse* of 7 November 1861.
9. From Byron's *Don Juan*. Leporello's advice was mischievous in its intent.

and must have it.' This was the battle-cry with which the secessionists fell upon Kentucky. By their 'entire territory' they understand primarily all the so-called *border states*: Delaware, Maryland, Virginia, North Carolina, Kentucky, Tennessee, Missouri and Arkansas. Moreover, they claim the whole territory south of the line which runs from the north-west corner of Missouri to the Pacific Ocean. Thus what the slave-holders call 'the South' covers more than three quarters of the present area of the Union. A large part of the territory which they claim is still in the possession of the Union and would first have to be conquered from it. But none of the so-called border states, including those in Confederate possession, was ever *an actual slave state*. The border states form, rather, that area of the United States where the system of slavery and the system of free labour exist side by side and struggle for mastery: the actual battle-ground between South and North, between slavery and freedom. The war waged by the Southern Confederacy is, therefore, not a war of defence but a war of conquest, aimed at extending and perpetuating slavery.

The chain of mountains which begins in Alabama and stretches North to the Hudson River – in a manner of speaking the spinal column of the United States – cuts the so-called South into three parts. The mountainous country formed by the Allegheny Mountains with their two parallel ranges, the Cumberland Range to the west and the Blue Ridge Mountains to the east, forms a wedgelike division between the lowlands along the western coast of the Atlantic Ocean and the lowlands of the southern valleys of the Mississippi. The two lowland regions separated by this mountain country form, with their vast rice swamps and wide expanses of cotton-plantations, the actual area of slavery. The long wedge of mountain country which penetrates into the heart of slavery, with its correspondingly freer atmosphere, invigorating climate and soil rich in coal, salt, limestone, iron ore and gold – in short, every raw material necessary for diversified industrial development – is for the most part already a free country. As a result of its physical composition the soil here can only be successfully cultivated by free small farmers. The slave system vegetates here only as a sporadic growth and has never struck roots. In the largest part of the so-called border states it is the inhabitants of these highland regions who comprise the core of the free population, which out of self-interest, if nothing else, has sided with the Northern party.

Let us consider the contested area in detail.

Delaware, the north-easternmost of the border states, belongs to the Union both morally and in actual fact. Since the beginning of the war all attempts on the part of the secessionists to form even a faction favourable to them have come to grief against the unanimity of the population. The slave element in this state has long been dying out. Between 1850 and 1860 alone the number of slaves declined by a half, so that Delaware now has only 1,798 slaves out of a total population of 112,218. Nevertheless, the Southern Confederacy lays claim to Delaware, and it would in fact be militarily untenable as soon as the South took control of Maryland.

Maryland exhibits the above-mentioned conflict between highlands and lowlands. Out of a total population of 687,034 there are in Maryland 87,188 slaves. The recent general elections to the Washington Congress have again forcefully proved that the overwhelming majority of the people sides with the Union. The army of 30,000 Union troops at present occupying Maryland is not only to serve as a reserve for the army on the Potomac, but also to hold the rebellious slave-holders in the interior of the state in check. Here a phenomenon can be seen similar to those in other border states, i.e., that the great mass of the people sides with the North and a numerically insignificant slave-holders' party sides with the South. What the slave-holders' party lacks in numbers it makes up for in the instruments of power, secured by many years' possession of all state offices, an hereditary preoccupation with political intrigue, and the concentration of great wealth in a few hands.

Virginia at present forms the great cantonment where the main secessionist army and the main Unionist army confront each other. In the north-west highlands of Virginia the slaves number 15,000, while the free majority, which is twenty times as large, consists for the most part of independent farmers. The eastern lowlands of Virginia, on the other hand, have almost half a million slaves. The raising and selling of Negroes represents its main source of income. As soon as the lowland ringleaders had carried through the secession ordinance in the state legislature at Richmond, by means of intrigue, and had in all haste thrown open the gates of Virginia to the Southern army, north-western Virginia seceded from the secession and formed a new state; it took up arms under the banner of the Union and is now defending its territory against the Southern invaders.

Tennessee, with 1,109,847 inhabitants, of whom 275,784 are slaves, is in the hands of the Southern Confederacy, which has placed the whole state under martial law and imposed a system of proscription which recalls the days of the Roman triumvirate. In the winter of 1860–61, when the slave-holders suggested a general people's convention to vote on the question of secession, the majority of the people turned down a convention in order to forestall any pretext for the secessionist movement. Later, when Tennessee had been militarily overrun by the Southern Confederacy and had been subjected to a system of terror, a third of the voters in the elections still declared themselves in favour of the Union. As in most of the border states, the actual centre of resistance to the slave-holders' party here is to be found in the mountainous country, in east Tennessee. On 17 June 1861 a general convention of the people of east Tennessee assembled in Greenville, declared itself for the Union, delegated the former Governor of the state, Andrew Johnson, one of the most ardent Unionists, to the Senate in Washington and published a 'declaration of grievances', which exposes all the deception, intrigue and terror used to 'vote out' Tennessee from the Union. Since then the secessionists have held east Tennessee in check by force of arms.

Similar situations to those in West Virginia and east Tennessee are to be found in the north of Alabama, north-west Georgia and the north of North Carolina.

Farther west in the border state of Missouri, whose population of 1,173,317 includes 114,965 slaves – the latter mostly concentrated in the north-western area of the state – the people's convention of August 1861 decided in favour of the Union. Jackson, the Governor of the state and tool of the slave-holders' party, rebelled against the Missouri legislature and was outlawed; he then put himself at the head of the armed hordes which fell upon Missouri from Texas, Arkansas and Tennessee in order to bring it to its knees before the Confederacy and to sever its bond with the Union by the sword. Next to Virginia, Missouri represents the main theatre of the civil war at the moment.

New Mexico – not a state, but merely a territory, whose twenty-five slaves were imported under Buchanan's presidency so that a slave constitution could be sent after them from Washington – has felt no enthusiasm for the South, as even the South concedes. But the South's enthusiasm for New Mexico caused it to spew a band of armed adventurers over the border from Texas. New

Mexico has entreated the Union government for protection against these liberators.

As will have been noticed, we lay particular stress on the numerical proportion of slaves to free citizens in the individual border states. This proportion is in fact of decisive importance. It is the thermometer with which the vitality of the slave system must be measured. The very soul of the whole secessionist movement is to be found in South Carolina. It has 402,541 slaves to 301,127 free men. Second comes Mississippi, which gave the Southern Confederacy its dictator, Jefferson Davis. It has 436,696 slaves to 354,699 free men. Third comes Alabama, with 435,132 slaves to 529,164 free men.

The last of the contested border states which we still have to mention is Kentucky. Its recent history is particularly characteristic of the policy of the Southern Confederacy. Kentucky, with 1,135,713 inhabitants, has 225,490 slaves. In three successive general elections (in winter 1860–61, when delegates were elected for a congress of the border states; June 1861, when the elections for the Washington Congress were held; and finally in August 1861 in the elections for the Kentucky state legislature) an increasing majority decided in favour of the Union. On the other hand, Magoffin, the Governor of Kentucky, and all the state dignitaries are fanatical supporters of the slave-holders' party, as is Breckinridge, Kentucky's representative in the Senate at Washington, Vice-President of the United States under Buchanan and presidential candidate of the slave-holders' party in 1860. Although the influence of the slave-holders' party was too weak to win Kentucky for secession, it was powerful enough to tempt it into a declaration of neutrality at the outbreak of war. The Confederacy recognized its neutrality as long as it suited its purpose, as long as it was busy crushing the resistance in east Tennessee. No sooner had this been achieved when it hammered on the gates of Kentucky with the butt-end of a gun: '*The South needs its entire territory*. It will and must have it!'

At the same time a corps of Confederate freebooters invaded the 'neutral' state from the south-west and south-east. Kentucky awoke from its dream of neutrality; its legislature openly sided with the Union, surrounded the treacherous Governor with a committee of public safety, called the people to arms, outlawed Breckinridge and ordered the secessionists to withdraw immediately from the area which they had invaded. This was the signal for war. A Confederate army is moving in on Louisville while volunteers stream in from Illinois, Indiana and Ohio to save Kentucky from the armed missionaries of slavery.

The attempts made by the Confederacy to annex Missouri and Kentucky, for example, expose the hollowness of the pretext that it is fighting for the rights of the individual states against the encroachment of the Union. To be sure, it acknowledges the rights of the individual states which it counts as belonging to the 'South' to break away from the Union, but by no means their right to remain in the Union.

No matter how much slavery, the war without and military dictatorship within give the actual slave states a temporary semblance of harmony, even they are not without dissident elements. Texas, with 180,388 slaves out of 601,039 inhabitants is a striking example. The law of 1845, by virtue of which Texas entered the ranks of the United States as a slave state, entitled it to form not just one but five states out of its territory. As a result the South would have won ten instead of two new votes in the American Senate; and an increase in the number of its votes in the Senate was a major political objective at that time. From 1845 to 1860, however, the slave-holders found it impracticable to split up Texas – where the German population plays a great part[10] – into even two states without giving the party of free labour the upper hand over the party of slavery. This is the best proof of how strong the opposition to the slave-holders' oligarchy is in Texas itself.

Georgia is the biggest and most populous of the slave states. With a total of 1,057,327 inhabitants it has 462,230 slaves; that is, nearly half the population. Nevertheless, the slave-holders' party has not yet succeeded in having the constitution which it imposed on the South at Montgomery sanctioned in Georgia by a general vote of the people.

In the Louisiana state convention, which met on 21 March 1861 at New Orleans, Roselius, the state's political veteran, declared: 'The Montgomery constitution is not a constitution, but a conspiracy. It does not inaugurate a government by the people, but *a detestable and unrestricted oligarchy.* The people were not permitted to play any part in this matter. The Convention of

10. The German Texans, who formed in the 1850s about one fifth of the state's white population, included a large proportion of refugees from the 1848 revolution.

Montgomery has dug the grave of political liberty and now we are summoned to attend its funeral.'

The oligarchy of 300,000 slave-holders used the Montgomery Congress not only to proclaim the separation of the South from the North; it also exploited the Congress to overturn the internal system of government of the slave states, to completely subjugate that part of the white population which had still maintained some degree of independence under the protection of the democratic Constitution of the Union. Even between 1856 and 1860 the political spokesmen, lawyers, moralists and theologians of the slave-holders' party had tried to prove not so much that Negro slavery is justified but rather that colour is immaterial and that slavery is the lot of the working class everywhere.

It can be seen, then, that the war of the Southern Confederacy is, in the truest sense of the word, a war of conquest for the extension and perpetuation of slavery. The larger part of the border states and territories are still in the possession of the Union, whose side they have taken first by way of the ballot-box and then with arms. But for the Confederacy they count as 'the South', and it is trying to conquer them from the Union. In the border states which the Confederacy has for the time being occupied it holds the relatively free highland areas in check by means of martial law. Within the actual slave states themselves it is supplanting the democracy which existed hitherto by the unbridled oligarchy of 300,000 slave-holders.

By abandoning its plans for conquest the Southern Confederacy would abandon its own economic viability and the very purpose of secession. Indeed, secession only took place because it no longer seemed possible to bring about the transformation of the border states and territories within the Union. On the other hand, with a peaceful surrender of the contested area to the Southern Confederacy the North would relinquish more than three quarters of the entire territory of the United States to the slave republic. The North would lose the Gulf of Mexico completely, the Atlantic Ocean with the exception of the narrow stretch from the Penobscot estuary to Delaware Bay, and would even cut itself off from the Pacific Ocean. Missouri, Kansas, New Mexico, Arkansas and Texas would be followed by California. Unable to wrest the mouth of the Mississippi from the hands of the strong, hostile slave republic in the South, the great agricultural states in the basin between the Rocky Mountains and the Alleghenies, in the valleys of the Mississippi, Missouri and Ohio, would be forced by economic interests to secede from the North and to join the Southern Confederacy. These North-western states would in turn draw the other Northern states lying further east after them – with the possible exception of New England – into the same vortex of secession.

The Union would thus not in fact be dissolved, but rather *reorganized*, a *reorganization on the basis of slavery*, under the acknowledged control of the slave-holding oligarchy. The plan for such a reorganization was openly proclaimed by the leading Southern spokesmen at the Montgomery Congress and accounts for the article of the new constitution which leaves open the possibility of each state of the old Union joining the new Confederacy. The slave system would thus infect the whole Union. In the Northern states, where Negro slavery is, in practice, inoperable, the whole working class would be gradually reduced to the level of helotry. This would be in full accord with the loudly proclaimed principle that only certain races are capable of freedom, and as in the South actual labour is the lot of the Negroes, so in the North it is the lot of the Germans and Irish or their direct descendants.

The present struggle between South and North is thus nothing less than a struggle between two social systems: the system of slavery and the system of free labour. The struggle has broken out because the two systems can no longer peacefully co-exist on the North American continent. It can only be ended by the victory of one system or the other.

While the border states, the contested areas in which the two systems have so far fought for control, are a thorn in the flesh of the South, it cannot, on the other hand, be overlooked that they have formed the North's main weak point in the course of the war. Some of the slave-holders in these districts feigned loyalty to the North at the bidding of the Southern conspirators; others indeed found that it accorded with their real interests and traditional outlook to side with the Union. Both groups have equally crippled the North. Anxiety to keep the 'loyal' slave-holders of the border states in good humour and fear of driving them into the arms of the secession, in a word, a tender regard for the interests, prejudices and sensibilities of these ambiguous allies, have afflicted the Union government with incurable paralysis since the beginning of the war, driven it to take half-measures, forced it to hypocritically disavow the principle at issue in the war and to spare the enemy's most vulnerable spot – the root of the evil – *slavery itself.*

When Lincoln recently was faint-hearted enough to revoke Frémont's Missouri proclamation emancipating Negroes belonging to the rebels,[11] this was only in deference to the loud protest of the 'loyal' slave-holders of Kentucky. However, a turning point has already been reached. With Kentucky the last border state has been pressed into the series of battlefields between South and North. With the real war for the border states being conducted in the border states themselves, the question of winning or losing them has been withdrawn from the sphere of diplomatic and parliamentary negotiations. One section of the slave-holders will cast off its loyalist mask; the other will content itself with the prospect of compensation, such as Great Britain gave the West Indian planters.[12] Events themselves demand that the decisive pronouncement be made: *the emancipation of the slaves.*

Several recent declarations demonstrate that even the most obdurate Northern Democrats and diplomats feel themselves drawn to this point. In an open letter General Cass, War Minister under Buchanan and hitherto one of the South's most ardent allies, declares the emancipation of the slaves to be the *sine qua non* for the salvation of the Union. Dr Brownson, the spokesman of the Northern Catholic party, and according to his own admission the most energetic opponent of the emancipation movement between 1836 and 1860, published in his last *Review* for October an article *in favour of* abolition. Among other things he says, 'If we have opposed Abolition heretofore because we would preserve the Union, we must *a fortiori* now oppose slavery whenever, in our judgement, its continuance becomes incompatible with the maintenance of the Union, or of the nation as a free republican state.'[13]

Finally, the *World*, a New York organ of the Washington

11. General Frémont, the first Republican candidate for the presidency in 1856, issued this proclamation in August 1861 and began granting freedom to slaves on his military authority. Lincoln soon ordered Frémont to stop these measures.

12. In 1833 the British government paid West Indian planters £2 for every slave set free.

13. *Brownson's Quarterly Review*, 3rd New York Series, New York, 1861, vol. II, pp. 510–46.

Cabinet's diplomats, closes one of its latest tirades against the abolitionists with these words: 'On the day when it shall be decided that either slavery or the Union must go down, on that day sentence of death is passed on slavery. If the North cannot triumph *without* emancipation, it will triumph *with* emancipation.'

Proclamation on Poland by the German Workers Educational Association in London[1]

October 1863

In agreement with an agent of the Polish National Government,[2] the German Workers Educational Association in London has authorized the undersigned committee to organize a collection for Poland among the German workers in England, Germany, Switzerland and the United States. Even though the material support given to the Poles in this way will be but little, the moral support provided by the collection will be great.

The Polish question and the German question are identical. Without an independent Poland there can be no independent and united Germany, nor can Germany be emancipated from Russian domination, which began with the first partition of Poland.[3] The German aristocracy have long regarded the tsar as the secret master of their nation. Mute, inactive and indifferent, the German bourgeoisie stands by and watches the butchery of the heroic nation which alone continues to protect Germany from the Muscovite deluge. Another section of the bourgeoisie realizes the danger but

1. This proclamation was written by Marx at the request of the German Workers Educational Association and distributed as a leaflet among the German workers in England and elsewhere. It is translated here from the text reproduced in *MEW* 15. The German Workers Educational Association had been a front organization for the secret Communist League, but survived the latter's dissolution in 1852. When the League split in 1850, Marx and his followers withdrew from the Association, but in the late 1850s there was a rapprochement. Marx's position on the Polish question is discussed in the Introductions to *The Revolutions of 1848* and *The First International and After*.

2. The Polish National Committee, which directed the insurrection of January 1863, transformed itself in May into the Polish National Government. The insurrection had by this time been to all intents crushed by Prussian and Russian forces, although sporadic resistance continued until the end of 1864.

3. In 1772 Poland was first partitioned between Russia, Austria and Prussia. The third and final partition, which completely abolished Poland as an independent state, was in 1795.

readily sacrifices German interests to the interests of the particular German states, whose survival is conditional upon the fragmentation of Germany and the maintenance of Russian hegemony. Another section of the bourgeoisie regards the autocracy in the east in the same light as the rule of the coup d'état in the west[4] – a necessary buttress of *Order*. Finally, a third section is so utterly and completely subservient to the important business of making money that it has completely forfeited its ability to understand and recognize situations of great historical importance. With its noisy demonstrations on behalf of Poland the German citizens of 1831 and 1832 at least forced the Federal Diet to take forceful measures.[5] Today Poland finds its most zealous opponents and Russia its most useful tools among the liberal celebrities of the so-called National Association.[6] Each can decide for himself how far this liberal pro-Russian sentiment is connected with the *Prussian élite*.

In this fateful hour the German working class owes it to the Polish people, to countries abroad and to its own honour, to utter the loudest possible protest against the German betrayal of Poland, which is also a betrayal of Germany and Europe. It must inscribe the *reunification of Poland* in flaming letters upon its banner now that bourgeois liberalism has erased this glorious device from its own. The English working class has reaped everlasting historic honour by its enthusiastic mass meetings held to crush the repeated attempts of the ruling classes to intervene on the side of the American slave-holders, although the continuation of the American Civil War has inflicted the most terrible suffering and privation on a million English workers.[7]

Even though the activities of the police prevent the working class in Germany from holding such large demonstrations for

4. I.e., the French Second Empire.

5. The national and democratic agitation of 1830–33 in Germany was sparked off by the French revolution of July 1830, and solidarity with the Polish insurrection of 1831–2 was only one aspect of it. The 'forcible measures' referred to were the 'Six Acts' which the German Federal Diet passed in 1832 under Prussian and Austrian pressure, and which re-established repressive measures throughout the German Confederation.

6. The National Association was formed by the pro-Prussian wing of the German liberal bourgeoisie in September 1850 to campaign for a 'little Germany' under Prussian hegemony.

7. This suffering was caused by the Northern blockade of Southern ports preventing the export of cotton. See Marx's article 'A London Workers' Meeting', *MECW* 19, pp. 153–6.

Poland, this by no means forces them to remain mutely inactive, to be branded in the eyes of the world as accessories to treason.

The undersigned committee requests contributions of money to be sent to Herr Bolleter, the owner of the Association Tavern, 2, Nassau Street, Soho, London. The money will be used under the supervision of the [German Workers Educational] Association, and as soon as the purpose for which this collection is intended allows, public account will be rendered.

BOLLETER	BERGER
ECCARIUS	KRÜGER
LINDEN	MATZRATH
TATSCHKY	TOUPS
WOLFF	

Index